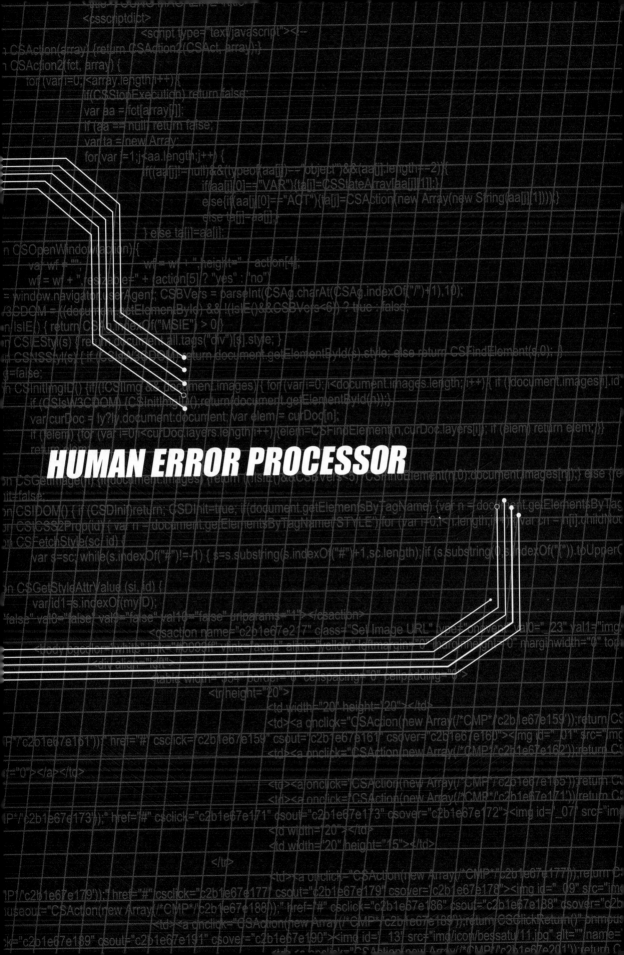

HUMAN ERROR PROCESSOR

攻殻機動隊1.5

Programmed by *SHIROW MASAMUNE*

border-width: 3px 3px 1px 6px; border-color: #ff8100 #ff8100 #ff8100 silver; outline-width 0; outline-color: orange }
h: 0 1px; border-color: #ff6000 black #ff6000 #000}

1px 6px border-color: orange orange #ff8100 silver; outline-width: 0; outline-color: orange }
6}

<tr>
border="0"></a> <a href="http://www.shonenmagazine.com/" target="_blank"><img src="img/banner/magazine.gif" alt="
30" height="30" border="0"></a> <a href="http://shop.kodansha.jp/bc" target="_blank"><img src="img/banner/book.gif" alt
rder="0"></a> <a href="http://www.missmaga.com" target="_blank"><img src="img/banner/missmaga_k.gif" alt=" width="

l"></a> <a href="http://www.vap.co.jp/" target="_blank"><img src="img/banner/bnr86_33.gif" alt=" width="88" height="33
<a href="http://sega.jp" target="_blank"><img src="http://sega.jp/images/segamini.gif" alt="" border="0"></a> <a
a href="http://www.chakuchaku.com/" target="_blank"><img src="img/banner/un_chakuchaku2.gif" alt="" height="30
vcastv.jp/ssm/"target="_blank"><img src="img/banner/ssm.gif" alt="" border="0"></a>

READ ME FIRST

The various situations, explanations, and concepts that appear in this book are a product of my wild imagination, a form of entertainment with no connection to reality. Take according to directions, and enjoy. Be advised that the author assumes no responsibility for any collateral damage resulting from improper use of the various constructs, fabrications, and gimmicks in the story.

ng=new Array(25);
j]="img/top/final07/gp.jpg"

Math.floor(simg.length*Math.random());
on Gazou2(){
ent.images["rimg"].src=simg[n%simg.length];

eout("Gazou2()",3000);

ent.write("<Vcenter><Vcenter>")
eout("Gazou2()",3000);

t>
rip>
src="img/top/final07/01.jpg" alt="random_img">
<td><marquee height="20" loop="infinite" vspace="0" width="628" bgcolor="#c6e7f"><font

#0044ff">

</marquee>

</table>

<tr height="58">
<head>
http-equiv="content-type" content="text/html;charset=Shift_JIS">
YOUNG MAGAZINE</title>
<link href="ym.css" rel="styleshee
<cssscriptdlct>
<script type="text/javascript"><!-
pExecution=false;
 CSAction(array){ return CSAction2(
h CSAction2(fct, array){
ult;
=0;i<array.length;i++){
opExecution) return false;
= fct[array[i]];
 null) return false;
 new Array;
j=1;j<aa.length;j++)
 if(aa[j][0]=="VAR"){aa[j]=CSS
 else ta[j]=aa[j];

result=aa[0](ta);

esult;

 new Object;

n CSOpenWindow(action) {
var wf="";
wf = wf + "width=" + action[3]
wf = wf + ",height=" + action[4];   ne="rimg" alt="random_img"><Vcenter>")

CSClickReturn () {
var bAgent = window.navigator.userAgent;
var bAppName = window.navigator.appName;

CONTENTS
HUMAN-ERROR PROCESSOR

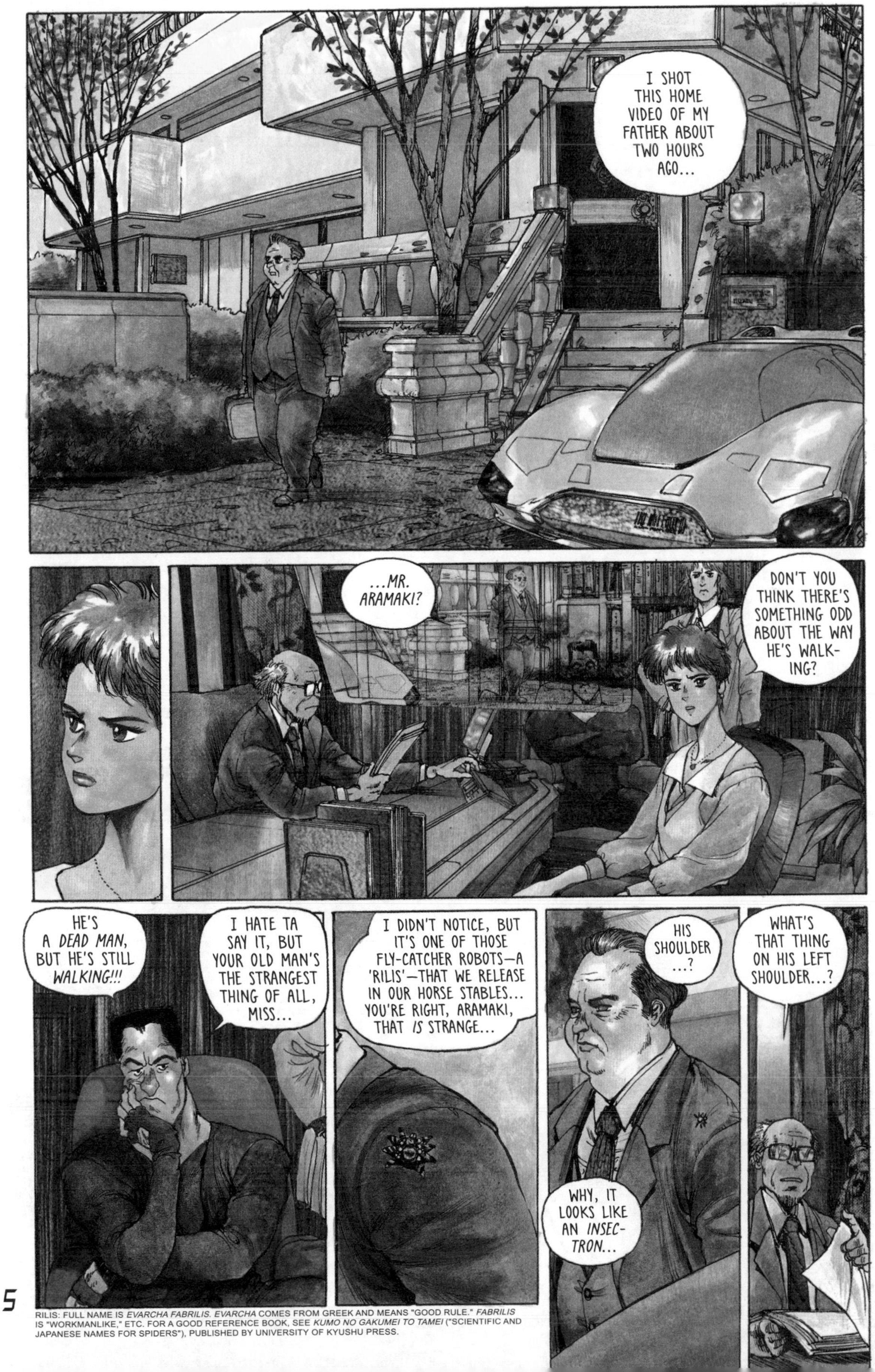
I SHOT THIS HOME VIDEO OF MY FATHER ABOUT TWO HOURS AGO...
DON'T YOU THINK THERE'S SOMETHING ODD ABOUT THE WAY HE'S WALK-ING?
...MR. ARAMAKI?
WHAT'S THAT THING ON HIS LEFT SHOULDER...?
HIS SHOULDER...?
WHY, IT LOOKS LIKE AN *INSEC-TRON*...
I DIDN'T NOTICE, BUT IT'S ONE OF THOSE FLY-CATCHER ROBOTS—A 'RILIS'—THAT WE RELEASE IN OUR HORSE STABLES... YOU'RE RIGHT, ARAMAKI, THAT *IS* STRANGE...
I HATE TA SAY IT, BUT YOUR OLD MAN'S THE STRANGEST THING OF ALL, MISS...
HE'S A *DEAD MAN*, BUT HE'S STILL *WALKING!!!*

RILIS: FULL NAME IS *EVARCHA FABRILIS. EVARCHA* COMES FROM GREEK AND MEANS "GOOD RULE." *FABRILIS* IS "WORKMANLIKE," ETC. FOR A GOOD REFERENCE BOOK, SEE *KUMO NO GAKUMEI TO TAMEI* ("SCIENTIFIC AND JAPANESE NAMES FOR SPIDERS"), PUBLISHED BY UNIVERSITY OF KYUSHU PRESS.

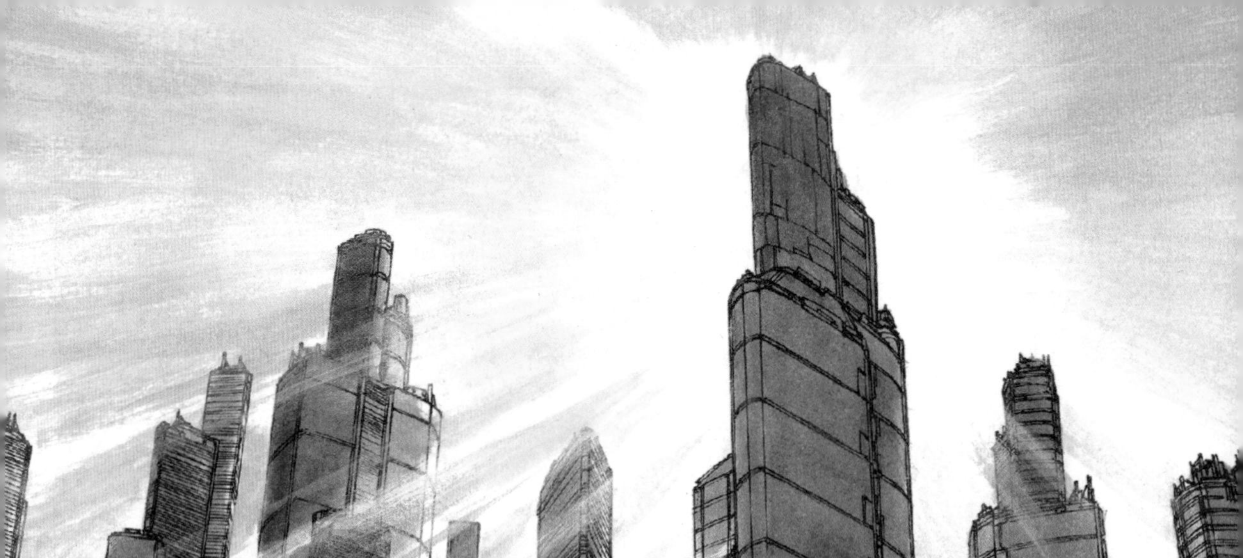

01

FAT CAT Part. 1

1991

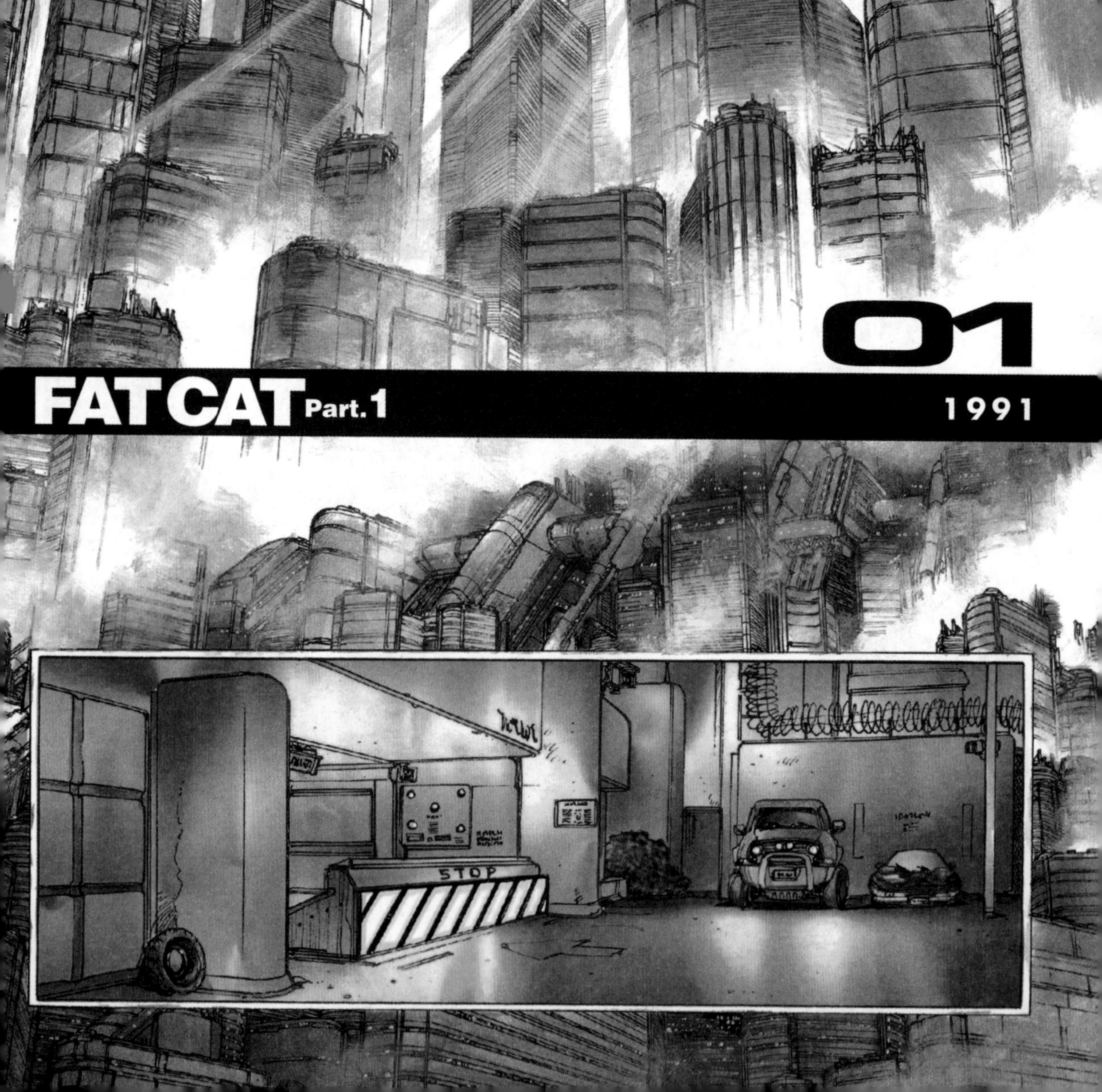
STOP

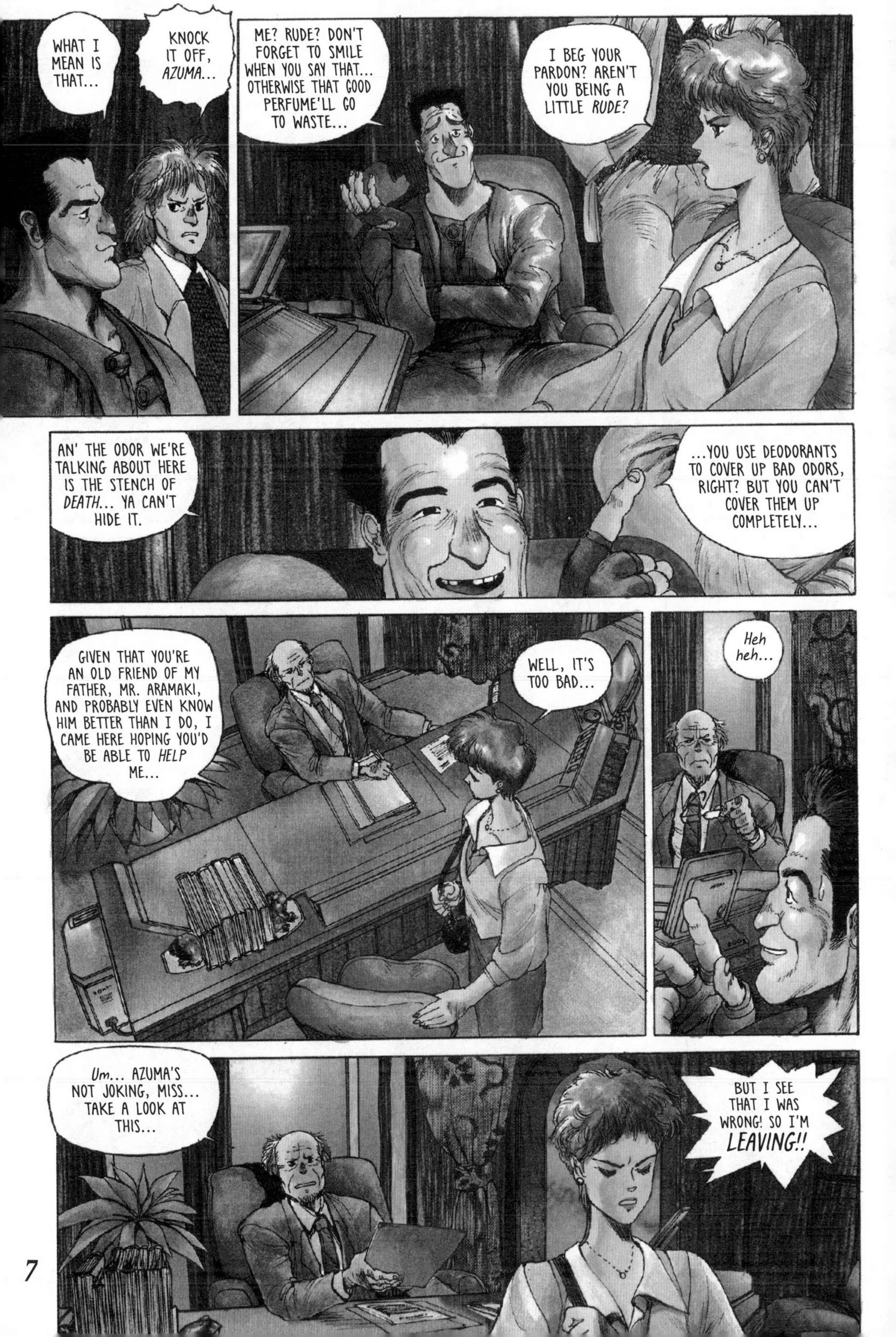
I BEG YOUR PARDON? AREN'T YOU BEING A LITTLE *RUDE?*
ME? RUDE? DON'T FORGET TO SMILE WHEN YOU SAY THAT... OTHERWISE THAT GOOD PERFUME'LL GO TO WASTE...
KNOCK IT OFF, *AZUMA*...
WHAT I MEAN IS THAT...
...YOU USE DEODORANTS TO COVER UP BAD ODORS, RIGHT? BUT YOU CAN'T COVER THEM UP COMPLETELY...
AN' THE ODOR WE'RE TALKING ABOUT HERE IS THE STENCH OF *DEATH*... YA CAN'T HIDE IT.
Heh heh...
WELL, IT'S TOO BAD...
GIVEN THAT YOU'RE AN OLD FRIEND OF MY FATHER, MR. ARAMAKI, AND PROBABLY EVEN KNOW HIM BETTER THAN I DO, I CAME HERE HOPING YOU'D BE ABLE TO *HELP* ME...
BUT I SEE THAT I WAS WRONG! SO I'M *LEAVING!!*
Um... AZUMA'S NOT JOKING, MISS... TAKE A LOOK AT THIS...

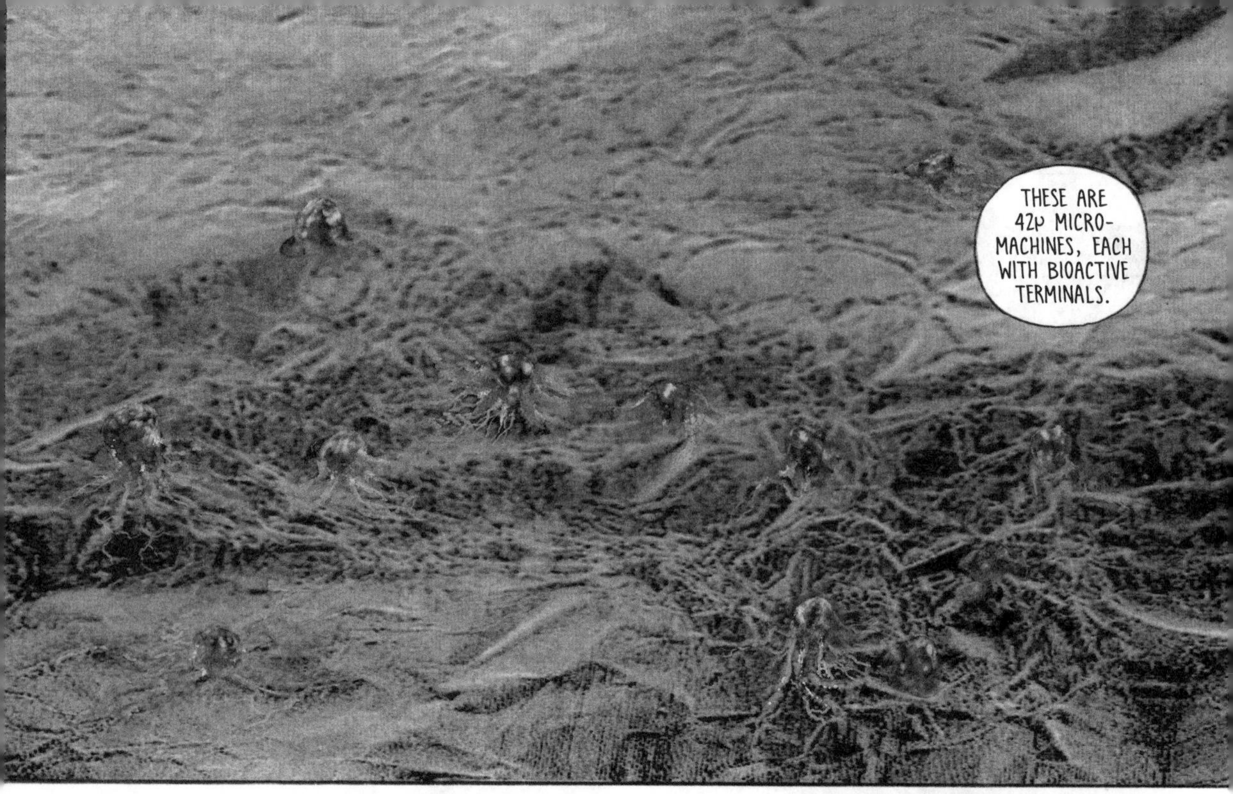
THESE ARE 42μ MICRO-MACHINES, EACH WITH BIOACTIVE TERMINALS.

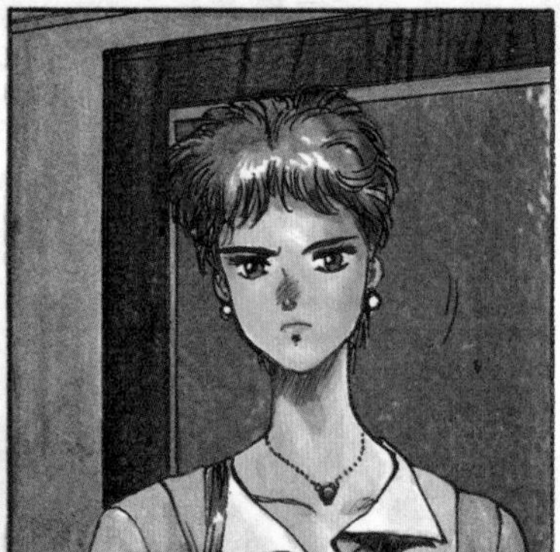

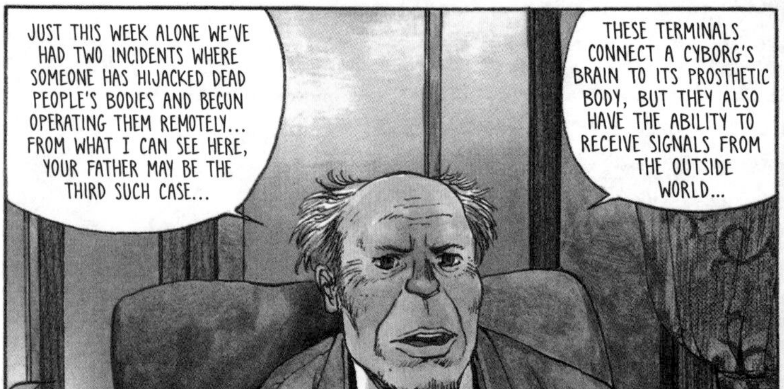
THESE TERMINALS CONNECT A CYBORG'S BRAIN TO ITS PROSTHETIC BODY, BUT THEY ALSO HAVE THE ABILITY TO RECEIVE SIGNALS FROM THE OUTSIDE WORLD...
JUST THIS WEEK ALONE WE'VE HAD TWO INCIDENTS WHERE SOMEONE HAS HIJACKED DEAD PEOPLE'S BODIES AND BEGUN OPERATING THEM REMOTELY... FROM WHAT I CAN SEE HERE, YOUR FATHER MAY BE THE THIRD SUCH CASE...

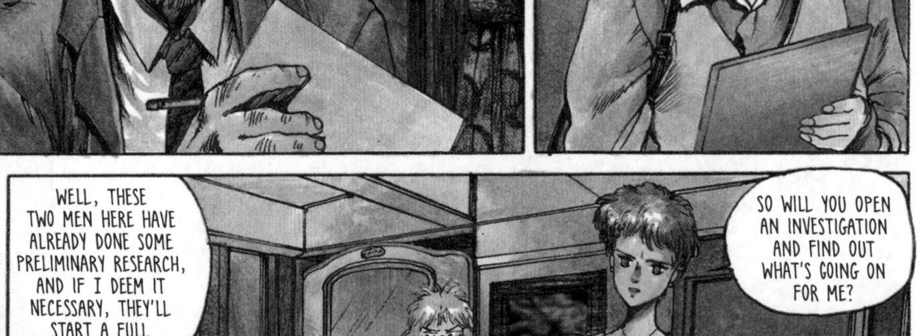
SO WILL YOU OPEN AN INVESTIGATION AND FIND OUT WHAT'S GOING ON FOR ME?
WELL, THESE TWO MEN HERE HAVE ALREADY DONE SOME PRELIMINARY RESEARCH, AND IF I DEEM IT NECESSARY, THEY'LL START A FULL INVESTIGATION...

BIOACTIVE: IN THIS CASE, THE MICROMACHINES ENTER AN ORGANISM AND INTERACT WITH IT NATURALLY, ACTUALLY FUSING AND FUNCTIONING WITH IT. INACTIVE MATERIALS, SUCH AS TITANIUM OR CERAMICS, DO NOT FUSE WITH BIOLOGICAL MATERIAL AND ARE ESSENTIALLY TREATED BY THE BODY AS FOREIGN MATTER.

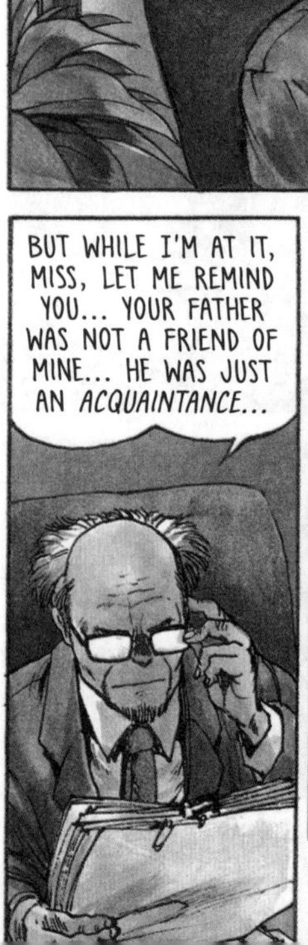
BUT WHILE I'M AT IT, MISS, LET ME REMIND YOU... YOUR FATHER WAS NOT A FRIEND OF MINE... HE WAS JUST AN *ACQUAINTANCE*...

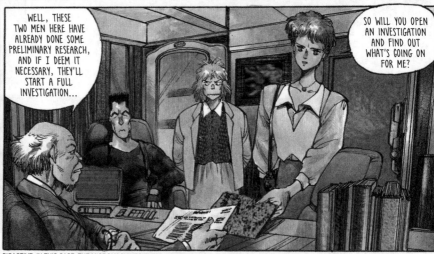

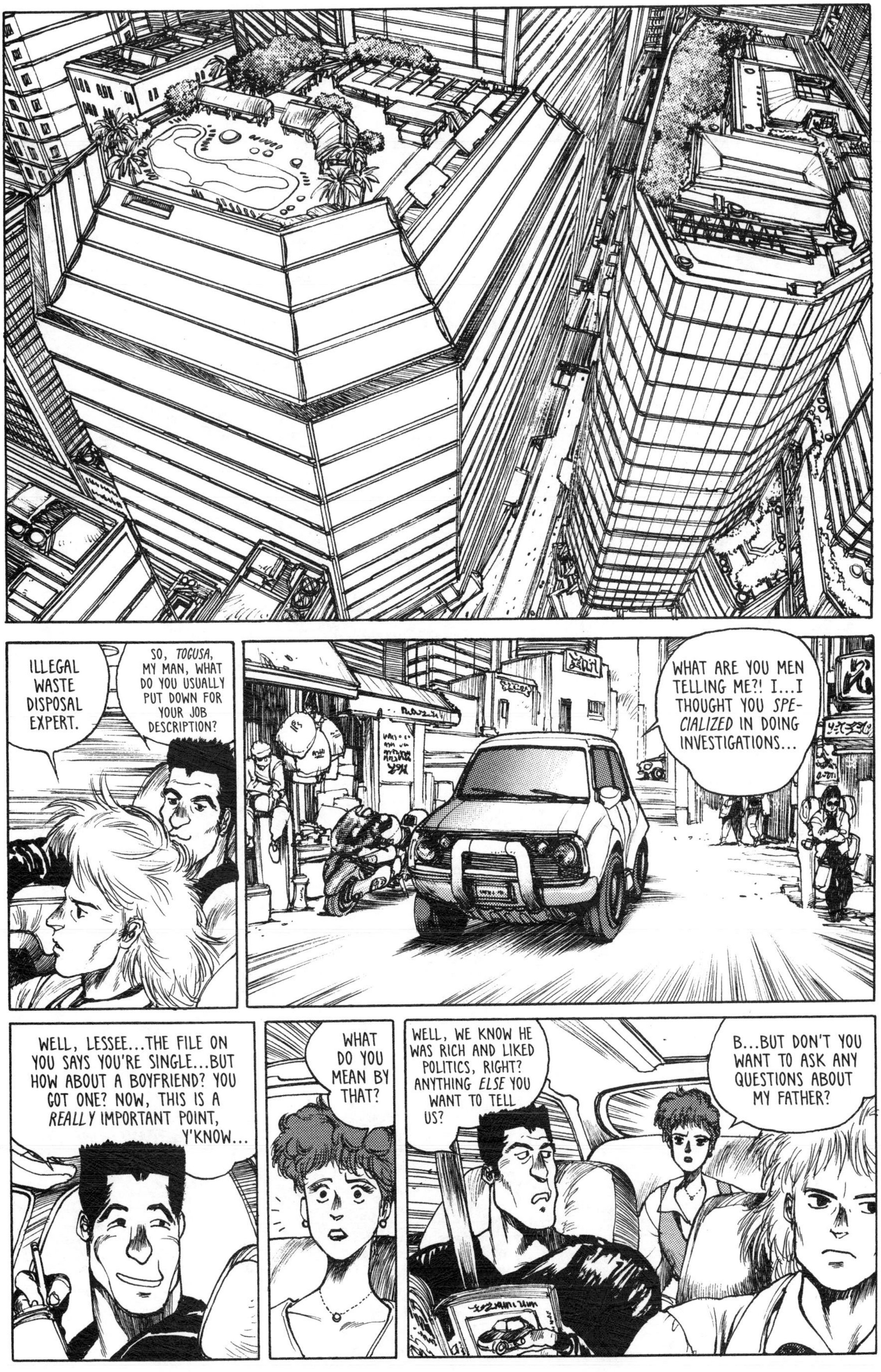
WHAT ARE YOU MEN TELLING ME?! I...I THOUGHT YOU *SPECIALIZED* IN DOING INVESTIGATIONS...
SO, *TOGUSA*, MY MAN, WHAT DO YOU USUALLY PUT DOWN FOR YOUR JOB DESCRIPTION?
ILLEGAL WASTE DISPOSAL EXPERT.
B...BUT DON'T YOU WANT TO ASK ANY QUESTIONS ABOUT MY FATHER?
WELL, WE KNOW HE WAS RICH AND LIKED POLITICS, RIGHT? ANYTHING *ELSE* YOU WANT TO TELL US?
WHAT DO YOU MEAN BY THAT?
WELL, LESSEE...THE FILE ON YOU SAYS YOU'RE SINGLE...BUT HOW ABOUT A BOYFRIEND? YOU GOT ONE? NOW, THIS IS A *REALLY* IMPORTANT POINT, Y'KNOW...

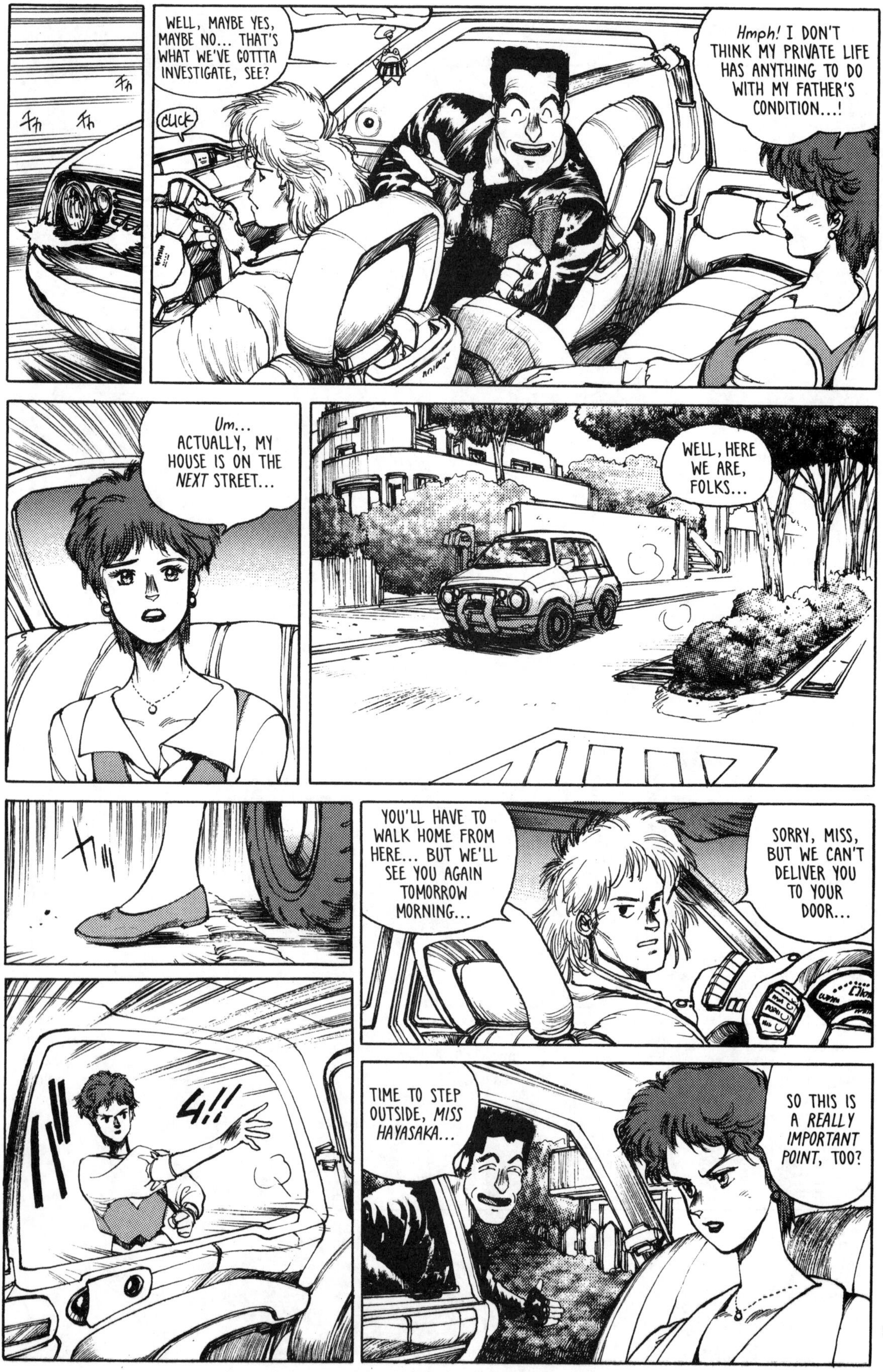
Hmph! I DON'T THINK MY PRIVATE LIFE HAS ANYTHING TO DO WITH MY FATHER'S CONDITION...!
WELL, MAYBE YES, MAYBE NO... THAT'S WHAT WE'VE GOTTTA INVESTIGATE, SEE?
CLICK
WELL, HERE WE ARE, FOLKS...
Um... ACTUALLY, MY HOUSE IS ON THE *NEXT* STREET...
SORRY, MISS, BUT WE CAN'T DELIVER YOU TO YOUR DOOR...
YOU'LL HAVE TO WALK HOME FROM HERE... BUT WE'LL SEE YOU AGAIN TOMORROW MORNING...
SO THIS IS A *REALLY IMPORTANT POINT*, TOO?
TIME TO STEP OUTSIDE, MISS HAYASAKA...

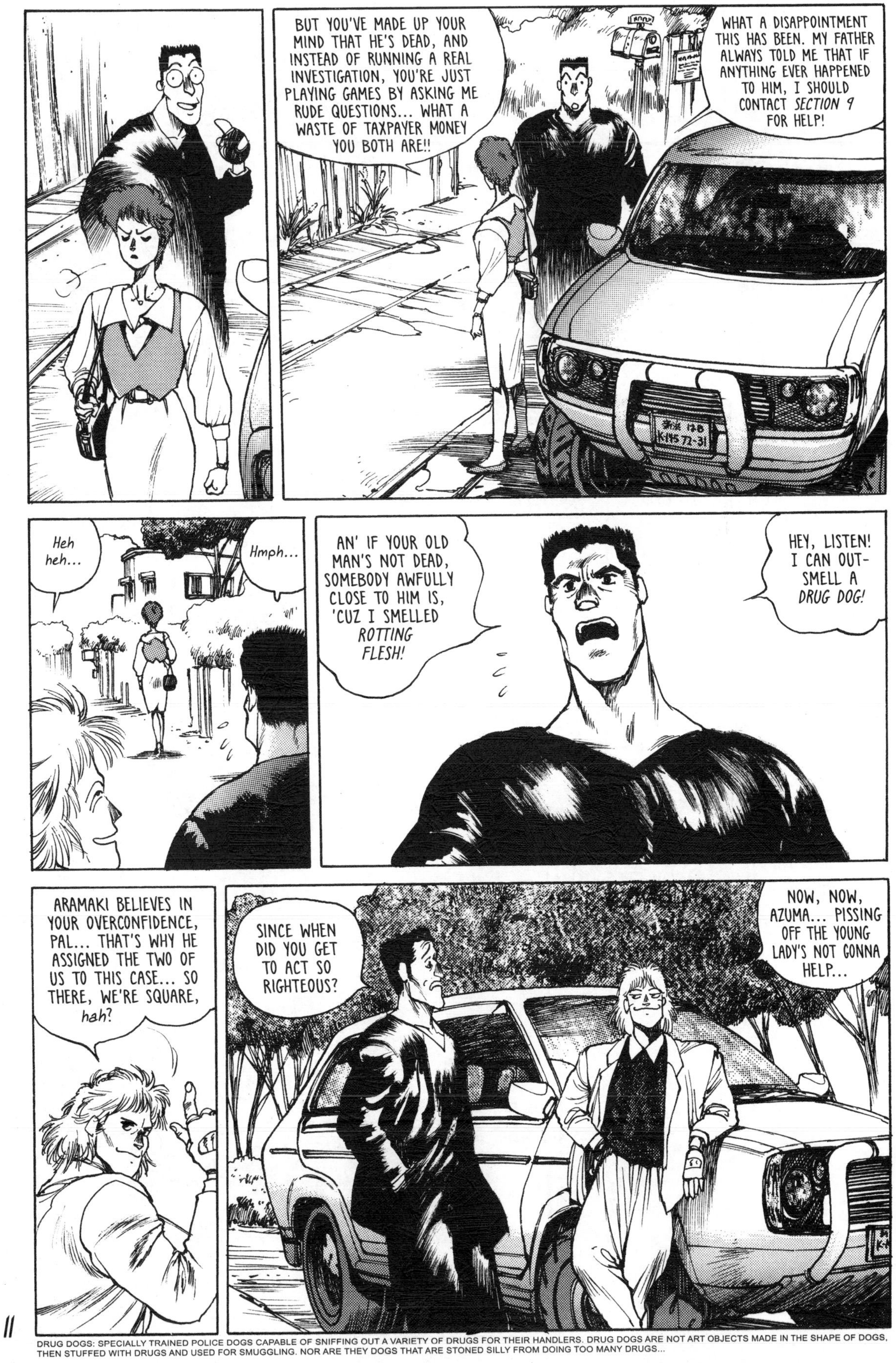
WHAT A DISAPPOINTMENT THIS HAS BEEN. MY FATHER ALWAYS TOLD ME THAT IF ANYTHING EVER HAPPENED TO HIM, I SHOULD CONTACT SECTION 9 FOR HELP!
BUT YOU'VE MADE UP YOUR MIND THAT HE'S DEAD, AND INSTEAD OF RUNNING A REAL INVESTIGATION, YOU'RE JUST PLAYING GAMES BY ASKING ME RUDE QUESTIONS... WHAT A WASTE OF TAXPAYER MONEY YOU BOTH ARE!!
HEY, LISTEN! I CAN OUT-SMELL A DRUG DOG!
AN' IF YOUR OLD MAN'S NOT DEAD, SOMEBODY AWFULLY CLOSE TO HIM IS, 'CUZ I SMELLED ROTTING FLESH!
Hmph...
Heh heh...
NOW, NOW, AZUMA... PISSING OFF THE YOUNG LADY'S NOT GONNA HELP...
SINCE WHEN DID YOU GET TO ACT SO RIGHTEOUS?
ARAMAKI BELIEVES IN YOUR OVERCONFIDENCE, PAL... THAT'S WHY HE ASSIGNED THE TWO OF US TO THIS CASE... SO THERE, WE'RE SQUARE, hah?

DRUG DOGS: SPECIALLY TRAINED POLICE DOGS CAPABLE OF SNIFFING OUT A VARIETY OF DRUGS FOR THEIR HANDLERS. DRUG DOGS ARE NOT ART OBJECTS MADE IN THE SHAPE OF DOGS, THEN STUFFED WITH DRUGS AND USED FOR SMUGGLING. NOR ARE THEY DOGS THAT ARE STONED SILLY FROM DOING TOO MANY DRUGS...

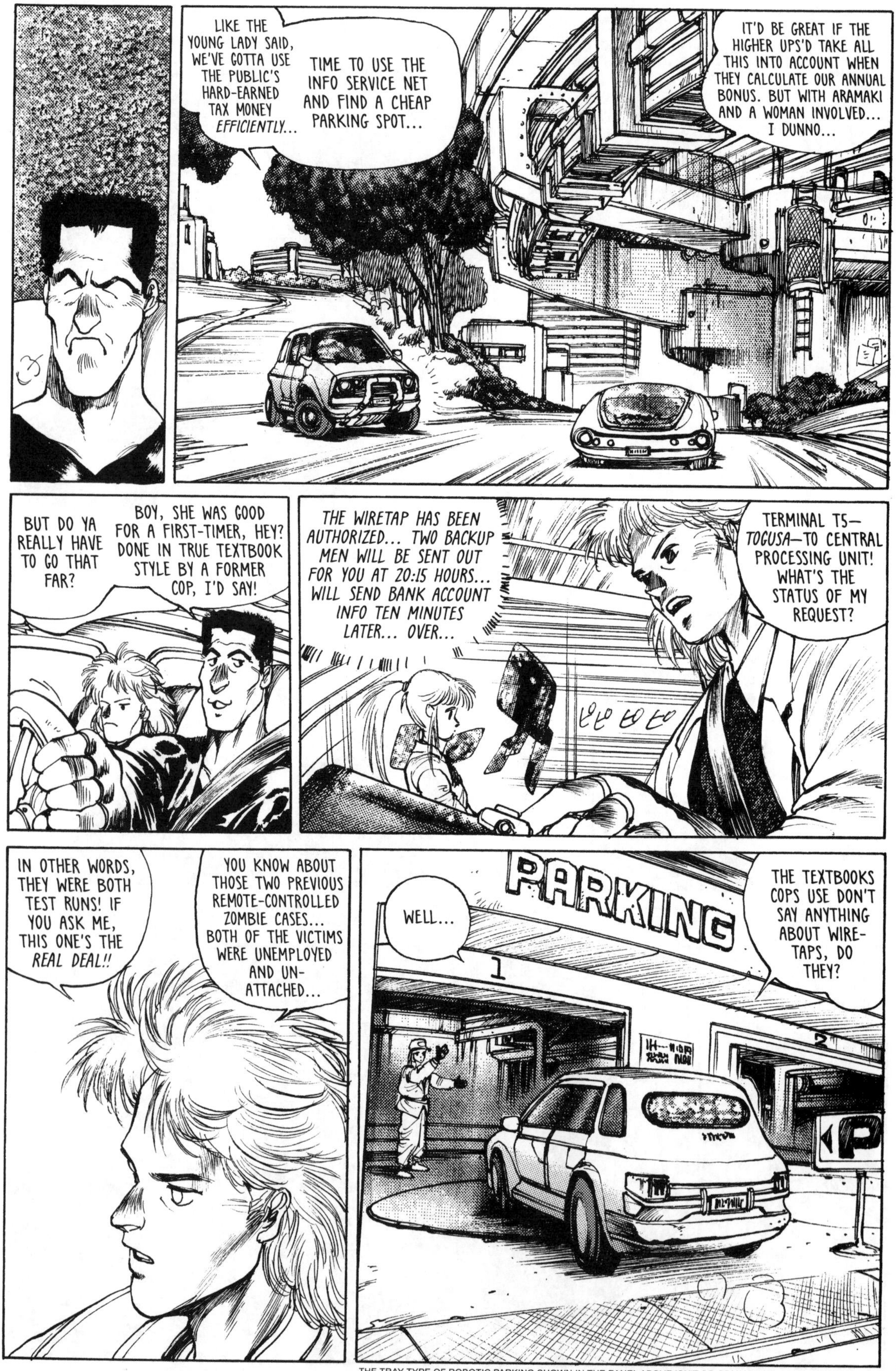
IT'D BE GREAT IF THE HIGHER UPS'D TAKE ALL THIS INTO ACCOUNT WHEN THEY CALCULATE OUR ANNUAL BONUS. BUT WITH ARAMAKI AND A WOMAN INVOLVED... I DUNNO...
TIME TO USE THE INFO SERVICE NET AND FIND A CHEAP PARKING SPOT...
LIKE THE YOUNG LADY SAID, WE'VE GOTTA USE THE PUBLIC'S HARD-EARNED TAX MONEY *EFFICIENTLY*...
TERMINAL TS—*TOGUSA*—TO CENTRAL PROCESSING UNIT! WHAT'S THE STATUS OF MY REQUEST?
THE WIRETAP HAS BEEN AUTHORIZED... TWO BACKUP MEN WILL BE SENT OUT FOR YOU AT 20:15 HOURS... WILL SEND BANK ACCOUNT INFO TEN MINUTES LATER... OVER...
ピピピピ
BOY, SHE WAS GOOD FOR A FIRST-TIMER, HEY? DONE IN TRUE TEXTBOOK STYLE BY A FORMER COP, I'D SAY!
BUT DO YA REALLY HAVE TO GO THAT FAR?
THE TEXTBOOKS COPS USE DON'T SAY ANYTHING ABOUT WIRE-TAPS, DO THEY?
PARKING
WELL...
YOU KNOW ABOUT THOSE TWO PREVIOUS REMOTE-CONTROLLED ZOMBIE CASES... BOTH OF THE VICTIMS WERE UNEMPLOYED AND UN-ATTACHED...
IN OTHER WORDS, THEY WERE BOTH TEST RUNS! IF YOU ASK ME, THIS ONE'S THE *REAL DEAL!!*

THE TRAY-TYPE OF ROBOTIC PARKING SHOWN IN THE PANEL ABOVE ISN'T SO COMMON IN JAPAN ANYMORE. INSTEAD, AUTO-PARKING SYSTEMS TEND TO ROTATE THE CARGO HORIZONTALLY. THIS SAVES TIME AND TROUBLE, SINCE IT'S NO LONGER NECESSARY TO BACK OUT OF THE FACILITY.

SIGN: SANDWICHES

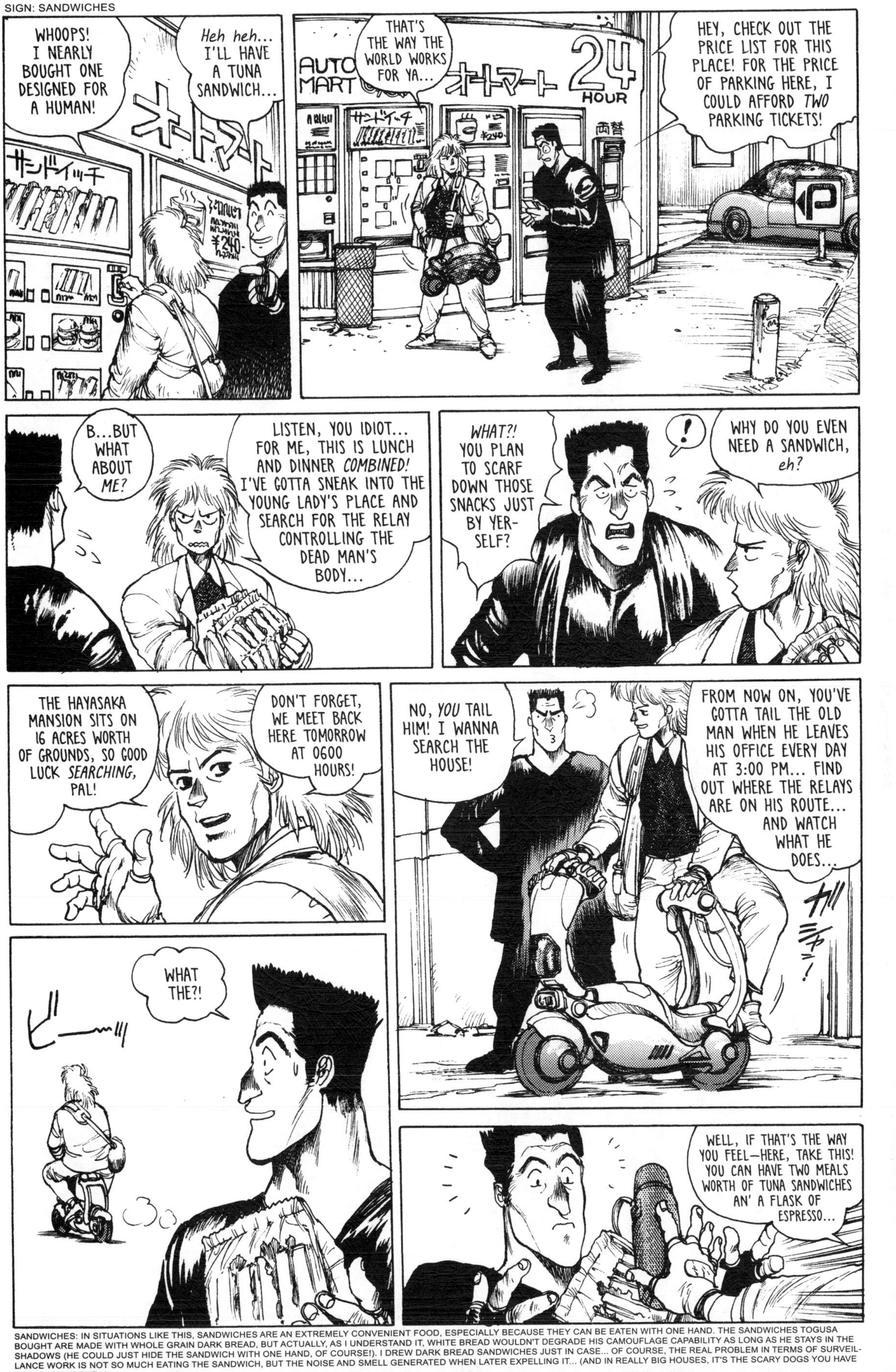
HEY, CHECK OUT THE PRICE LIST FOR THIS PLACE! FOR THE PRICE OF PARKING HERE, I COULD AFFORD *TWO* PARKING TICKETS!
AUTO MART
オートマート
24 HOUR
THAT'S THE WAY THE WORLD WORKS FOR YA...
Heh heh... I'LL HAVE A TUNA SANDWICH...
WHOOPS! I NEARLY BOUGHT ONE DESIGNED FOR A HUMAN!
WHY DO YOU EVEN NEED A SANDWICH, *eh?*
!
WHAT?! YOU PLAN TO SCARF DOWN THOSE SNACKS JUST BY YER-SELF?
LISTEN, YOU IDIOT... FOR ME, THIS IS LUNCH AND DINNER *COMBINED!* I'VE GOTTA SNEAK INTO THE YOUNG LADY'S PLACE AND SEARCH FOR THE RELAY CONTROLLING THE DEAD MAN'S BODY...
B...BUT WHAT ABOUT *ME?*
FROM NOW ON, YOU'VE GOTTA TAIL THE OLD MAN WHEN HE LEAVES HIS OFFICE EVERY DAY AT 3:00 PM... FIND OUT WHERE THE RELAYS ARE ON HIS ROUTE... AND WATCH WHAT HE DOES...
NO, *YOU* TAIL HIM! I WANNA SEARCH THE HOUSE!
WELL, IF THAT'S THE WAY YOU FEEL—HERE, TAKE THIS! YOU CAN HAVE TWO MEALS WORTH OF TUNA SANDWICHES AN' A FLASK OF ESPRESSO...
DON'T FORGET, WE MEET BACK HERE TOMORROW AT 0600 HOURS!
THE HAYASAKA MANSION SITS ON 16 ACRES WORTH OF GROUNDS, SO GOOD LUCK *SEARCHING,* PAL!
WHAT THE?!

SANDWICHES: IN SITUATIONS LIKE THIS, SANDWICHES ARE AN EXTREMELY CONVENIENT FOOD, ESPECIALLY BECAUSE THEY CAN BE EATEN WITH ONE HAND. THE SANDWICHES TOGUSA BOUGHT ARE MADE WITH WHOLE GRAIN DARK BREAD, BUT ACTUALLY, AS I UNDERSTAND IT, WHITE BREAD WOULDN'T DEGRADE HIS CAMOUFLAGE CAPABILITY AS LONG AS HE STAYS IN THE SHADOWS (HE COULD JUST HIDE THE SANDWICH WITH ONE HAND, OF COURSE!). I DREW DARK BREAD SANDWICHES JUST IN CASE... OF COURSE, THE REAL PROBLEM IN TERMS OF SURVEILLANCE WORK IS NOT SO MUCH EATING THE SANDWICH, BUT THE NOISE AND SMELL GENERATED WHEN LATER EXPELLING IT... (AND IN REALLY BIG HOUSES, IT'S THE SCARY DOGS YOU HAVE

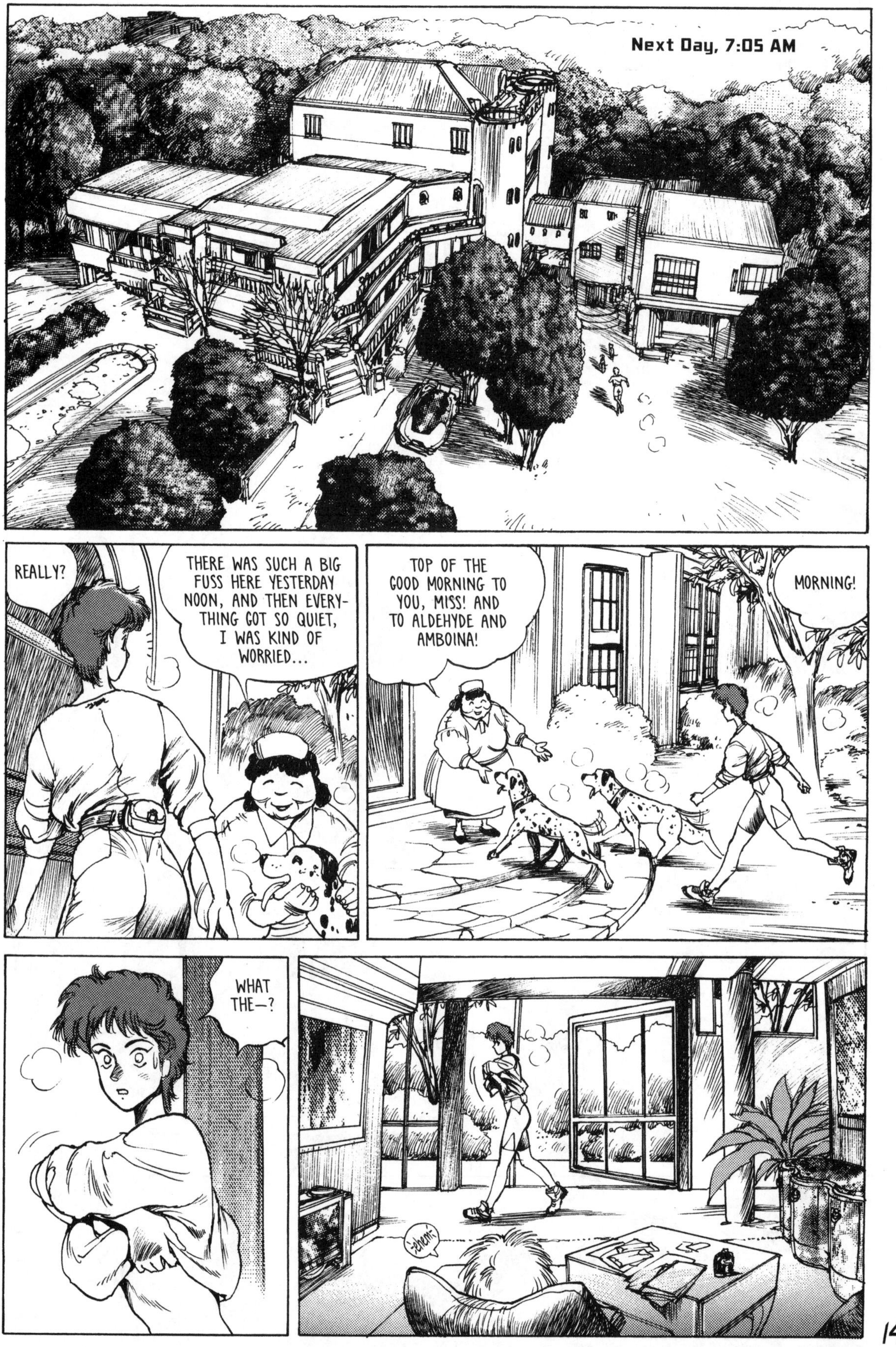
Next Day, 7:05 AM
MORNING!
TOP OF THE GOOD MORNING TO YOU, MISS! AND TO ALDEHYDE AND AMBOINA!
THERE WAS SUCH A BIG FUSS HERE YESTERDAY NOON, AND THEN EVERY-THING GOT SO QUIET, I WAS KIND OF WORRIED...
REALLY?
-ahem-
WHAT THE—?

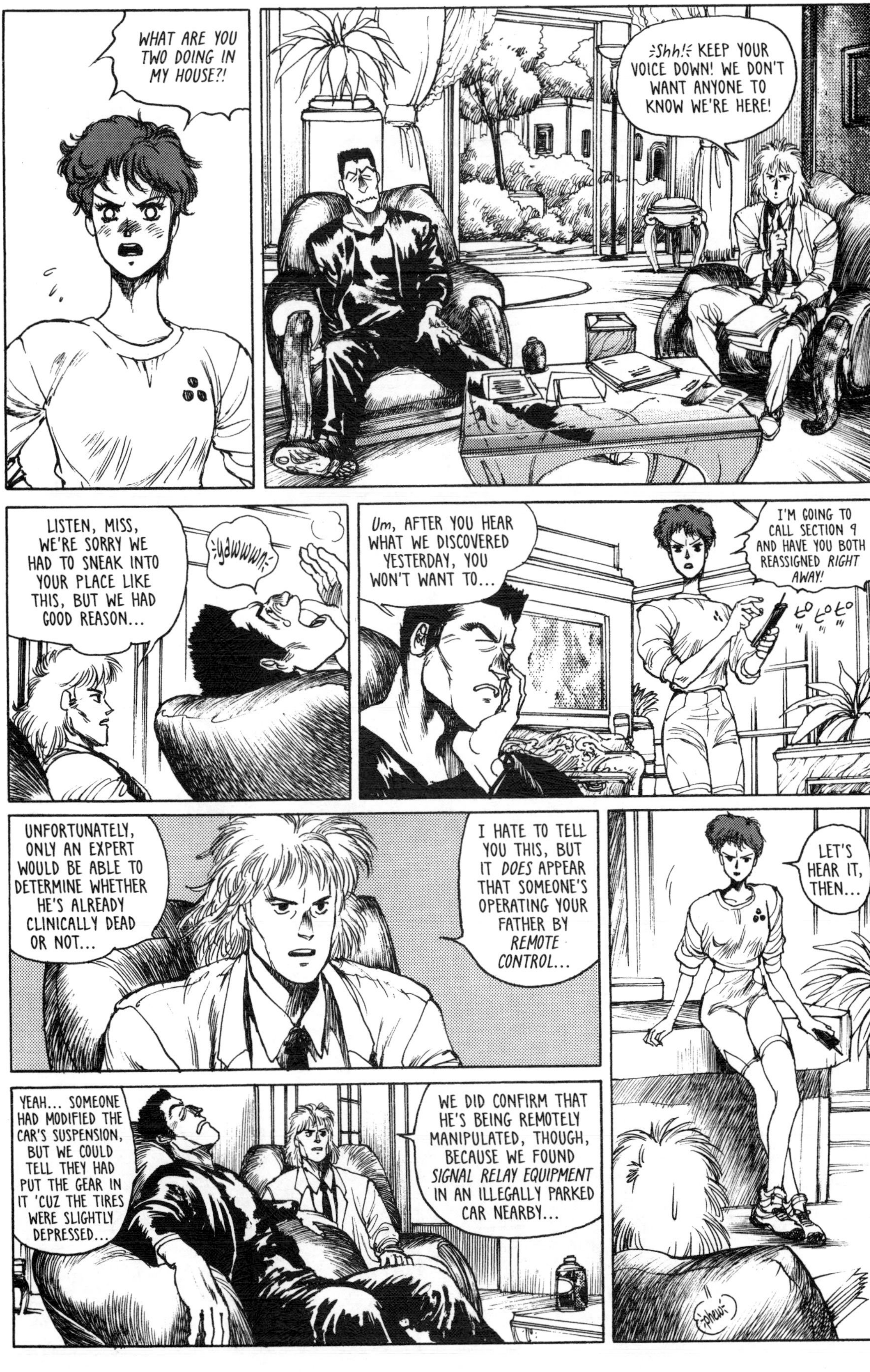
Shh! KEEP YOUR VOICE DOWN! WE DON'T WANT ANYONE TO KNOW WE'RE HERE!
WHAT ARE YOU TWO DOING IN MY HOUSE?!
I'M GOING TO CALL SECTION 9 AND HAVE YOU BOTH REASSIGNED *RIGHT AWAY!*
ピピピ
Um, AFTER YOU HEAR WHAT WE DISCOVERED YESTERDAY, YOU WON'T WANT TO...
yawwwn
LISTEN, MISS, WE'RE SORRY WE HAD TO SNEAK INTO YOUR PLACE LIKE THIS, BUT WE HAD GOOD REASON...
LET'S HEAR IT, THEN...
phew
I HATE TO TELL YOU THIS, BUT IT *DOES* APPEAR THAT SOMEONE'S OPERATING YOUR FATHER BY *REMOTE CONTROL*...
UNFORTUNATELY, ONLY AN EXPERT WOULD BE ABLE TO DETERMINE WHETHER HE'S ALREADY CLINICALLY DEAD OR NOT...
WE DID CONFIRM THAT HE'S BEING REMOTELY MANIPULATED, THOUGH, BECAUSE WE FOUND *SIGNAL RELAY EQUIPMENT* IN AN ILLEGALLY PARKED CAR NEARBY...
YEAH... SOMEONE HAD MODIFIED THE CAR'S SUSPENSION, BUT WE COULD TELL THEY HAD PUT THE GEAR IN IT 'CUZ THE TIRES WERE SLIGHTLY DEPRESSED...

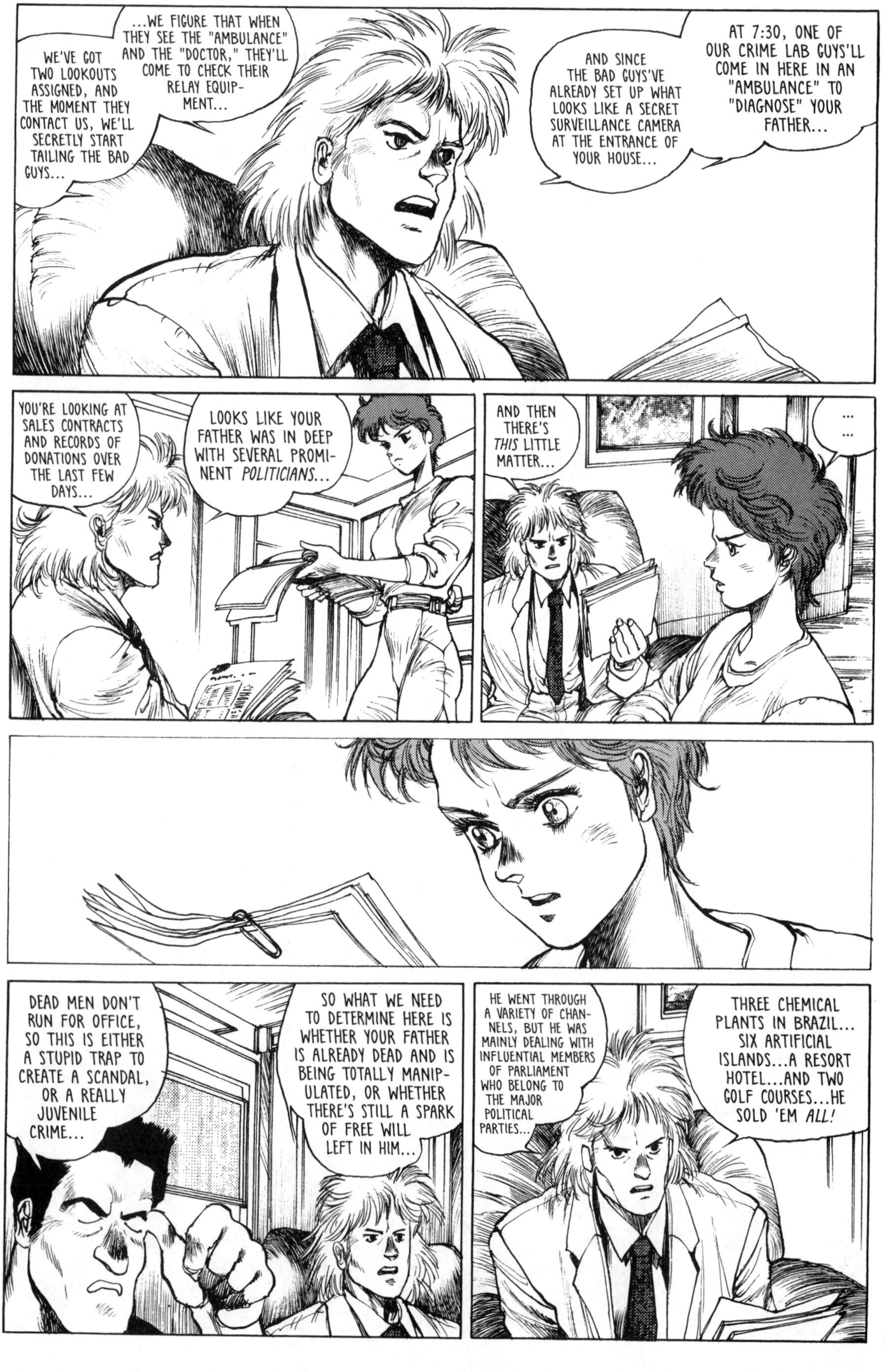
AT 7:30, ONE OF OUR CRIME LAB GUYS'LL COME IN HERE IN AN "AMBULANCE" TO "DIAGNOSE" YOUR FATHER...
AND SINCE THE BAD GUYS'VE ALREADY SET UP WHAT LOOKS LIKE A SECRET SURVEILLANCE CAMERA AT THE ENTRANCE OF YOUR HOUSE...
...WE FIGURE THAT WHEN THEY SEE THE "AMBULANCE" AND THE "DOCTOR," THEY'LL COME TO CHECK THEIR RELAY EQUIPMENT...
WE'VE GOT TWO LOOKOUTS ASSIGNED, AND THE MOMENT THEY CONTACT US, WE'LL SECRETLY START TAILING THE BAD GUYS...
... ...
AND THEN THERE'S *THIS* LITTLE MATTER...
LOOKS LIKE YOUR FATHER WAS IN DEEP WITH SEVERAL PROMINENT *POLITICIANS*...
YOU'RE LOOKING AT SALES CONTRACTS AND RECORDS OF DONATIONS OVER THE LAST FEW DAYS...
THREE CHEMICAL PLANTS IN BRAZIL... SIX ARTIFICIAL ISLANDS...A RESORT HOTEL...AND TWO GOLF COURSES...HE SOLD 'EM *ALL!*
HE WENT THROUGH A VARIETY OF CHANNELS, BUT HE WAS MAINLY DEALING WITH INFLUENTIAL MEMBERS OF PARLIAMENT WHO BELONG TO THE MAJOR POLITICAL PARTIES...
SO WHAT WE NEED TO DETERMINE HERE IS WHETHER YOUR FATHER IS ALREADY DEAD AND IS BEING TOTALLY MANIPULATED, OR WHETHER THERE'S STILL A SPARK OF FREE WILL LEFT IN HIM...
DEAD MEN DON'T RUN FOR OFFICE, SO THIS IS EITHER A STUPID TRAP TO CREATE A SCANDAL, OR A REALLY JUVENILE CRIME...

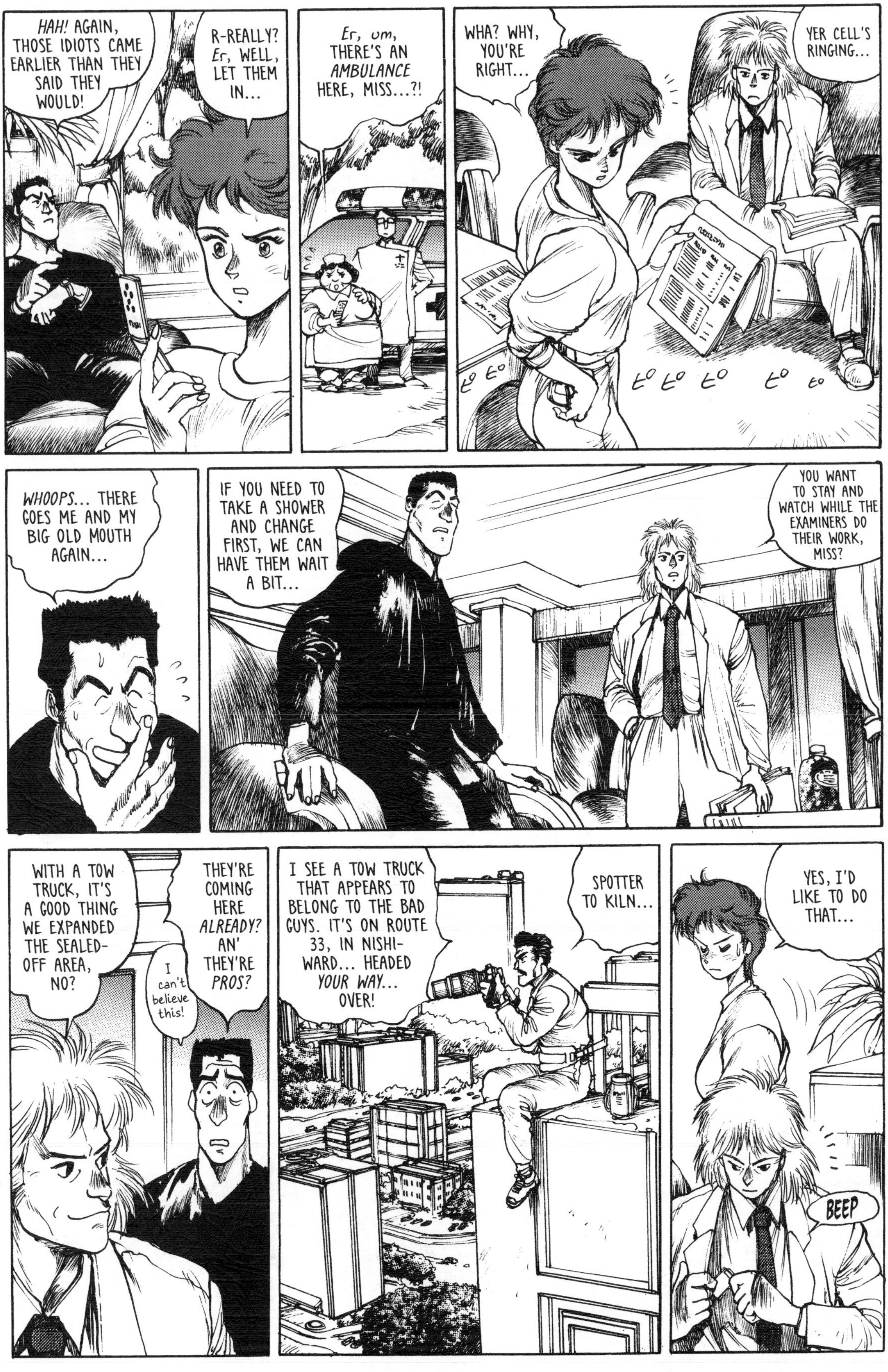
YER CELL'S RINGING...
WHA? WHY, YOU'RE RIGHT...
Er, um, THERE'S AN AMBULANCE HERE, MISS...?!
R-REALLY? Er, WELL, LET THEM IN...
HAH! AGAIN, THOSE IDIOTS CAME EARLIER THAN THEY SAID THEY WOULD!
YOU WANT TO STAY AND WATCH WHILE THE EXAMINERS DO THEIR WORK, MISS?
IF YOU NEED TO TAKE A SHOWER AND CHANGE FIRST, WE CAN HAVE THEM WAIT A BIT...
WHOOPS... THERE GOES ME AND MY BIG OLD MOUTH AGAIN...
YES, I'D LIKE TO DO THAT...
BEEP
SPOTTER TO KILN...
I SEE A TOW TRUCK THAT APPEARS TO BELONG TO THE BAD GUYS. IT'S ON ROUTE 33, IN NISHI-WARD... HEADED YOUR WAY... OVER!
THEY'RE COMING HERE ALREADY? AN' THEY'RE PROS?
I can't believe this!
WITH A TOW TRUCK, IT'S A GOOD THING WE EXPANDED THE SEALED-OFF AREA, NO?

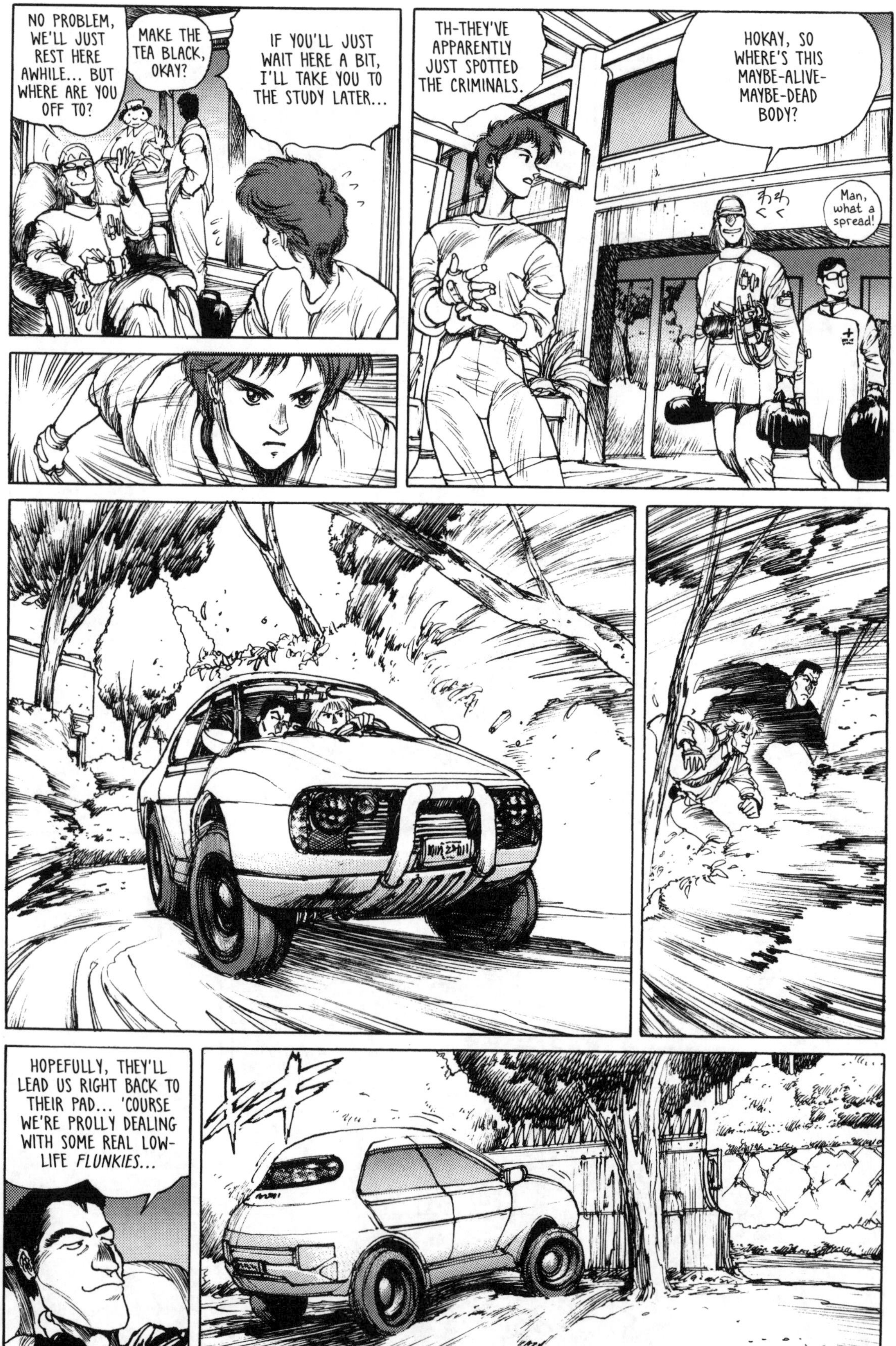
HOKAY, SO WHERE'S THIS MAYBE-ALIVE-MAYBE-DEAD BODY?
TH-THEY'VE APPARENTLY JUST SPOTTED THE CRIMINALS.
Man, what a spread!
IF YOU'LL JUST WAIT HERE A BIT, I'LL TAKE YOU TO THE STUDY LATER...
MAKE THE TEA BLACK, OKAY?
NO PROBLEM, WE'LL JUST REST HERE AWHILE... BUT WHERE ARE YOU OFF TO?
HOPEFULLY, THEY'LL LEAD US RIGHT BACK TO THEIR PAD... 'COURSE WE'RE PROLLY DEALING WITH SOME REAL LOW-LIFE *FLUNKIES*...

TOGUSA AND AZUMA ARE USING A FAIRLY TALL CAR HERE BECAUSE IT'S BETTER SUITED FOR TAILING AND SURVEILLANCE AND ALSO HARDER TO SEE INTO. CHOICE OF VEHICLE DOES NOT NECESSARILY REFLECT THE PERSONAL PREFERENCE OF THE CHARACTERS OR THE ARTIST...

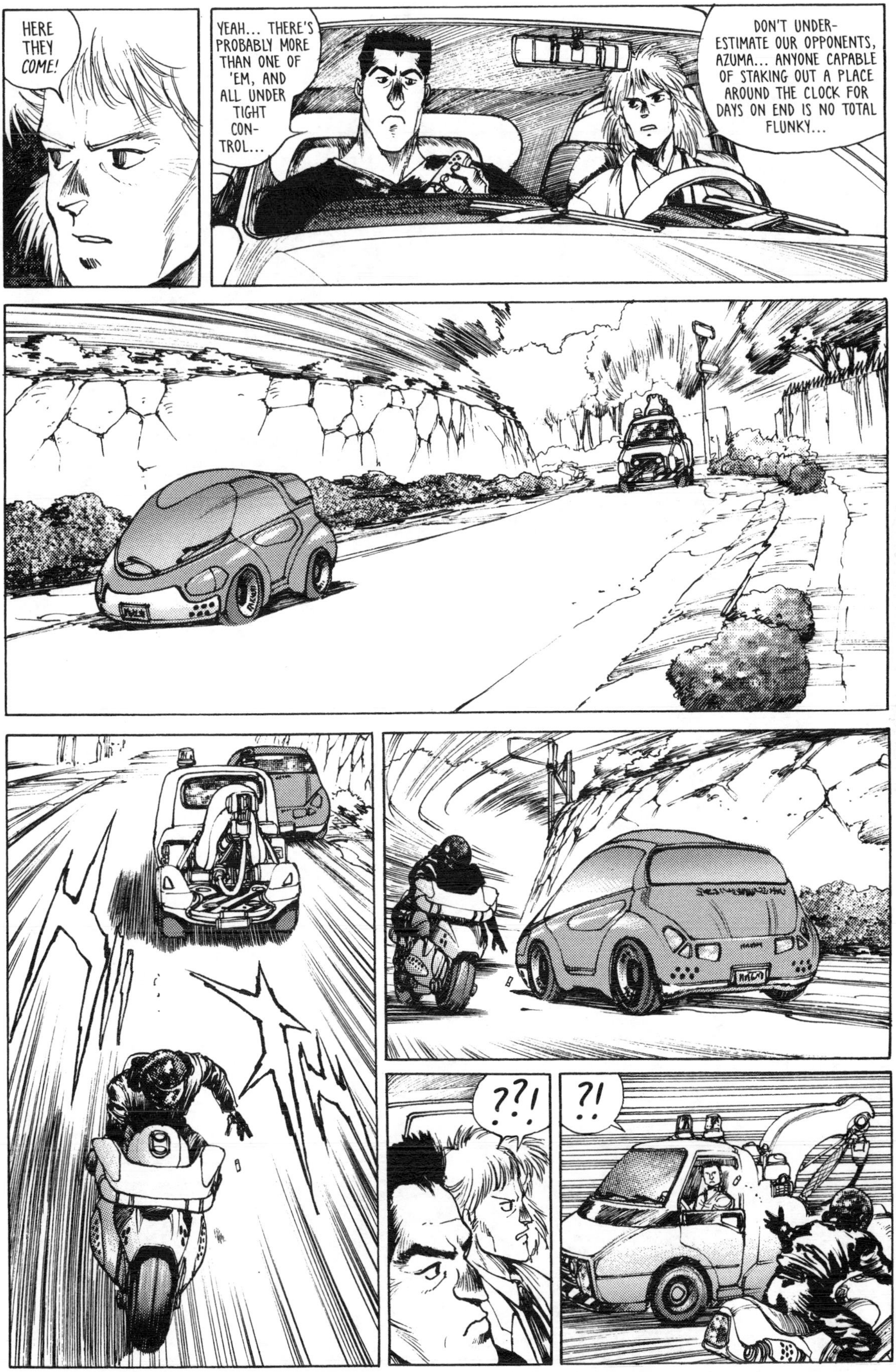
DON'T UNDER-ESTIMATE OUR OPPONENTS, AZUMA... ANYONE CAPABLE OF STAKING OUT A PLACE AROUND THE CLOCK FOR DAYS ON END IS NO TOTAL FLUNKY...
YEAH... THERE'S PROBABLY MORE THAN ONE OF 'EM, AND ALL UNDER TIGHT CON-TROL...
HERE THEY *COME!*
?!
??!

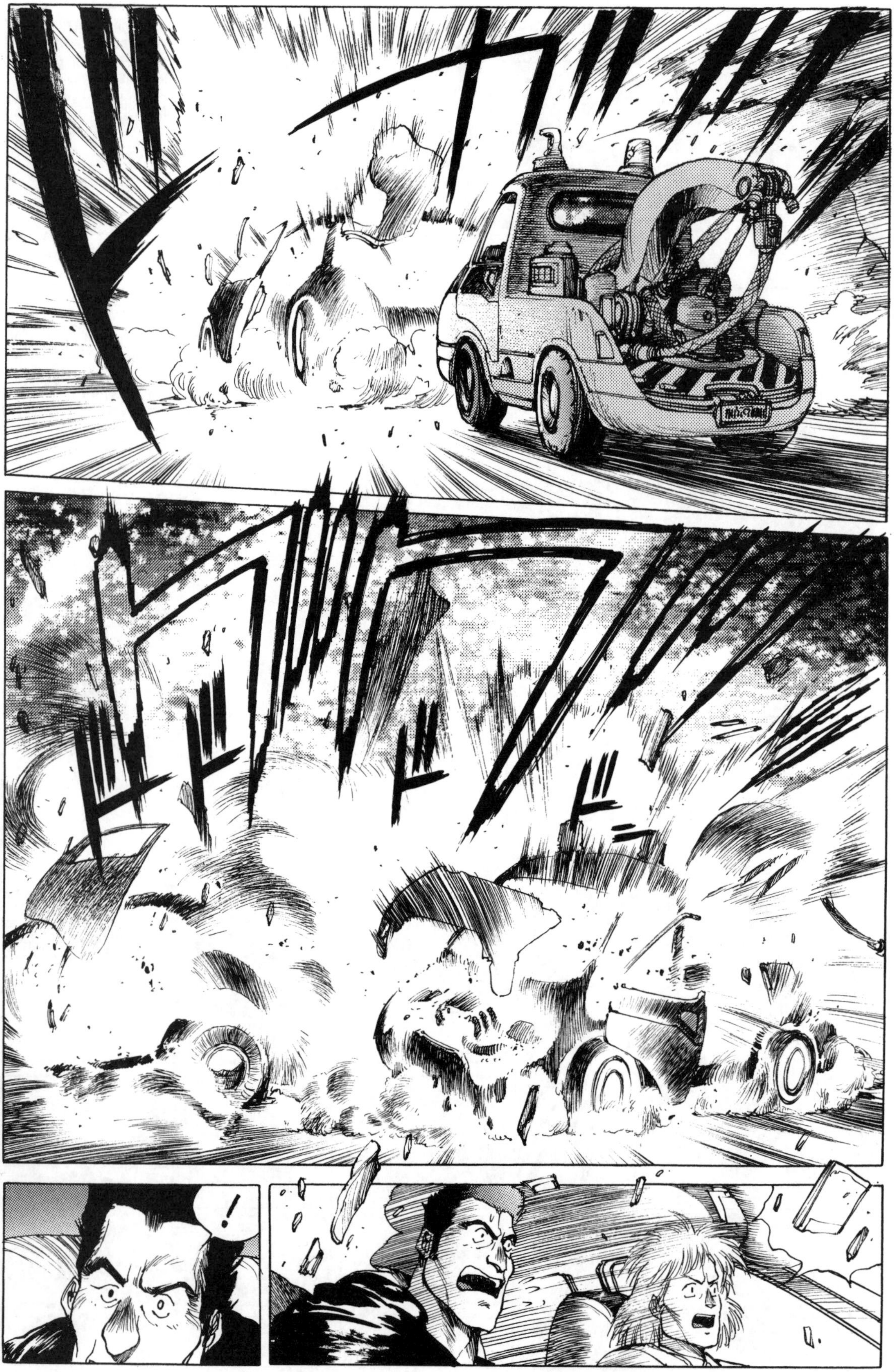
!

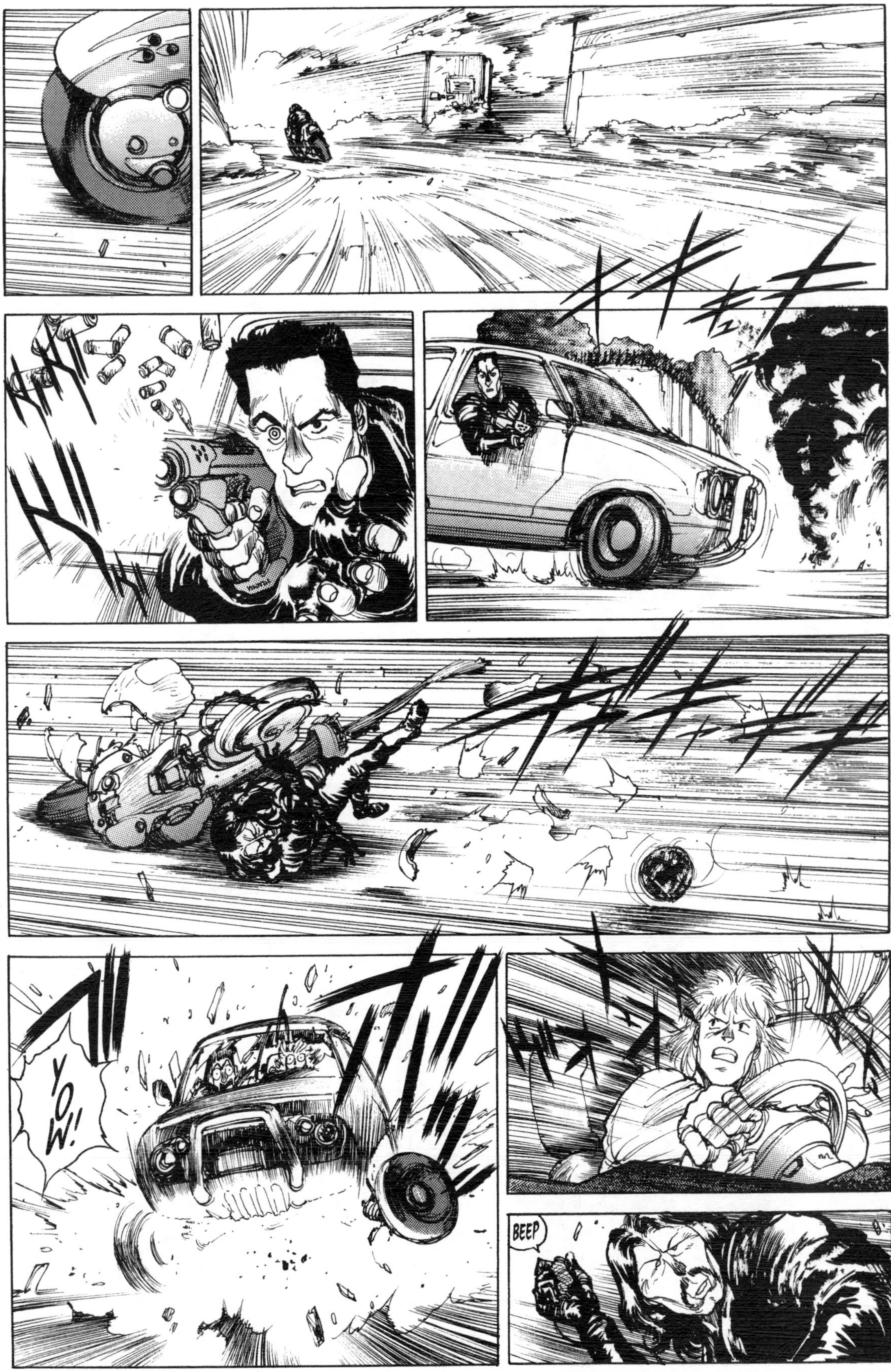
BEEP
YOW!

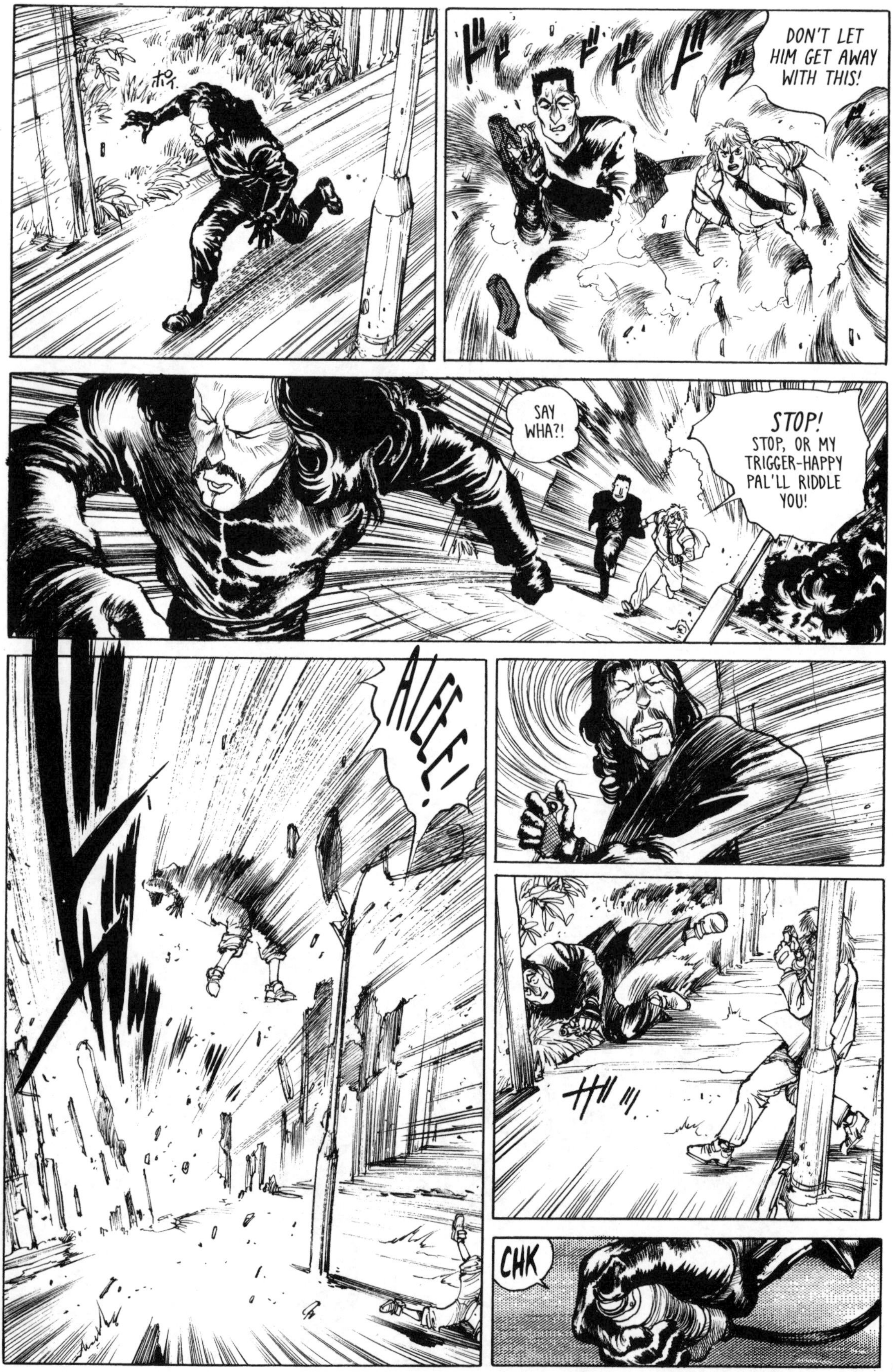
DON'T LET HIM GET AWAY WITH THIS!
ポイ
STOP! STOP, OR MY TRIGGER-HAPPY PAL'LL RIDDLE YOU!
SAY WHA?!
CHK
AIEEE!

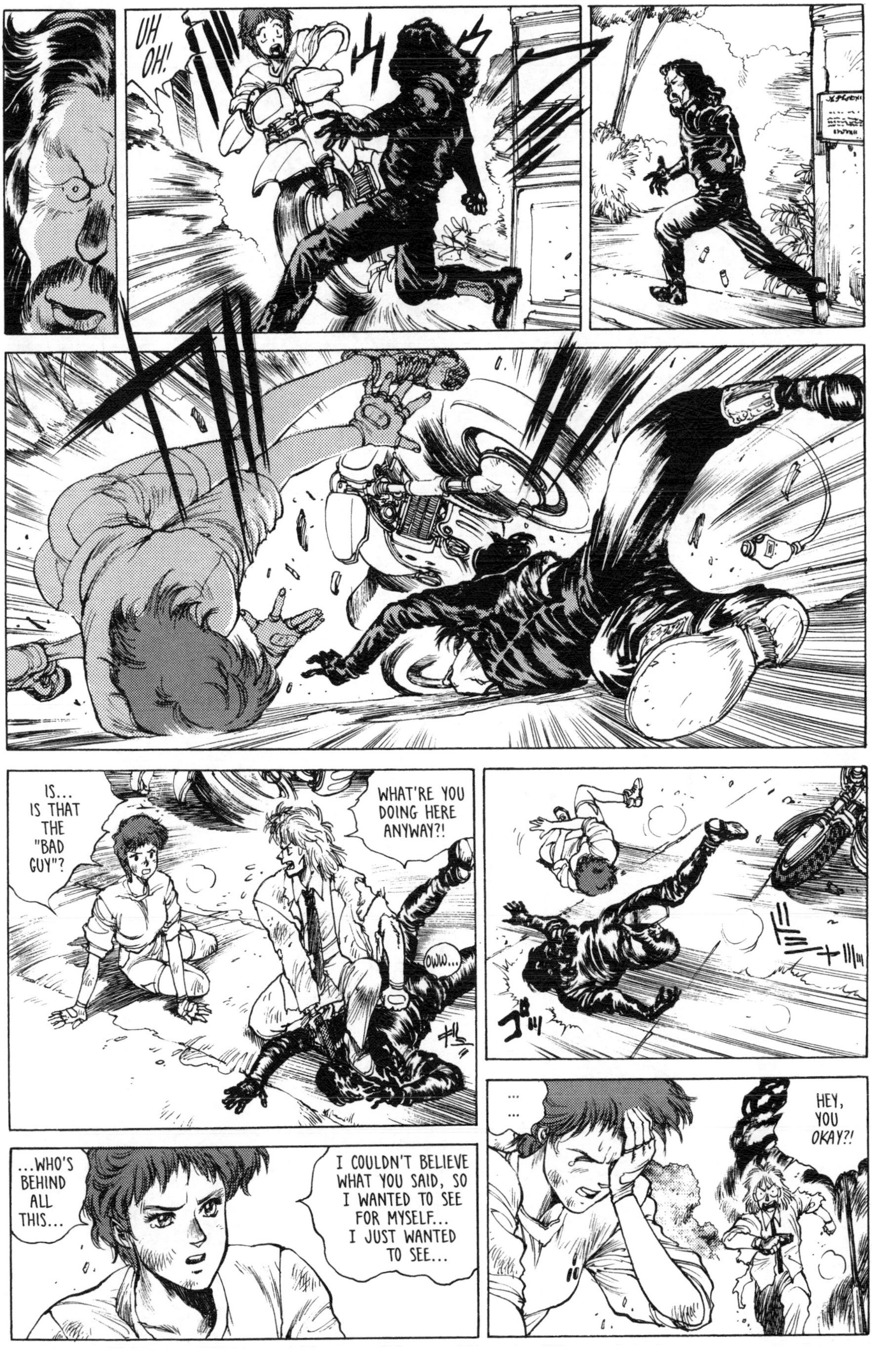
UH OH!
WHAT'RE YOU DOING HERE ANYWAY?!
OWW...
IS... IS THAT THE "BAD GUY"?
HEY, YOU OKAY?!
... ...
I COULDN'T BELIEVE WHAT YOU SAID, SO I WANTED TO SEE FOR MYSELF... I JUST WANTED TO SEE...
...WHO'S BEHIND ALL THIS...

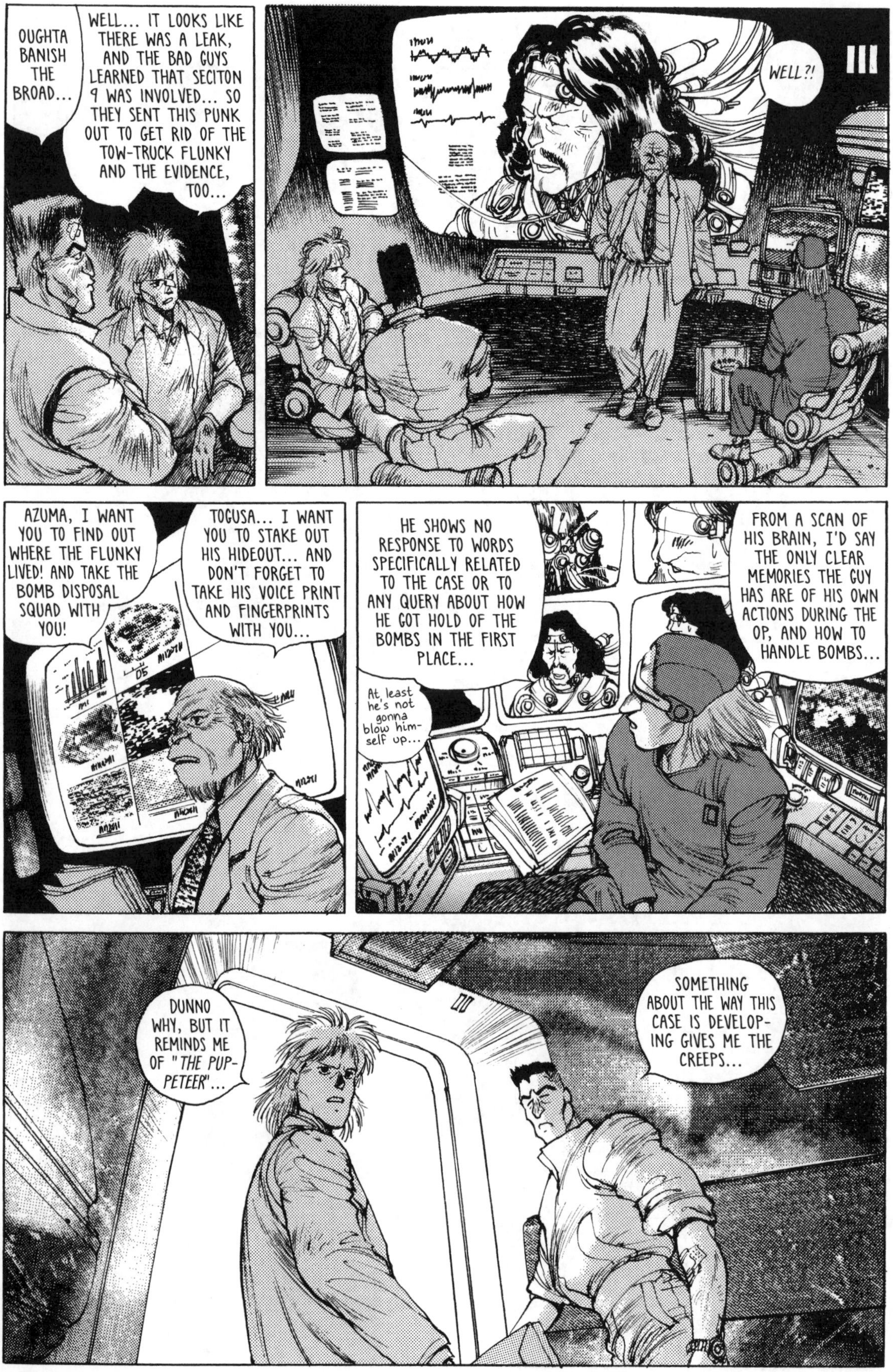
WELL?!
WELL... IT LOOKS LIKE THERE WAS A LEAK, AND THE BAD GUYS LEARNED THAT SECITON 9 WAS INVOLVED... SO THEY SENT THIS PUNK OUT TO GET RID OF THE TOW-TRUCK FLUNKY AND THE EVIDENCE, TOO...
OUGHTA BANISH THE BROAD...
FROM A SCAN OF HIS BRAIN, I'D SAY THE ONLY CLEAR MEMORIES THE GUY HAS ARE OF HIS OWN ACTIONS DURING THE OP, AND HOW TO HANDLE BOMBS...
HE SHOWS NO RESPONSE TO WORDS SPECIFICALLY RELATED TO THE CASE OR TO ANY QUERY ABOUT HOW HE GOT HOLD OF THE BOMBS IN THE FIRST PLACE...
At least he's not gonna blow himself up...
TOGUSA... I WANT YOU TO STAKE OUT HIS HIDEOUT... AND DON'T FORGET TO TAKE HIS VOICE PRINT AND FINGERPRINTS WITH YOU...
AZUMA, I WANT YOU TO FIND OUT WHERE THE FLUNKY LIVED! AND TAKE THE BOMB DISPOSAL SQUAD WITH YOU!
SOMETHING ABOUT THE WAY THIS CASE IS DEVELOPING GIVES ME THE CREEPS...
DUNNO WHY, BUT IT REMINDS ME OF "*THE PUPPETEER*"...

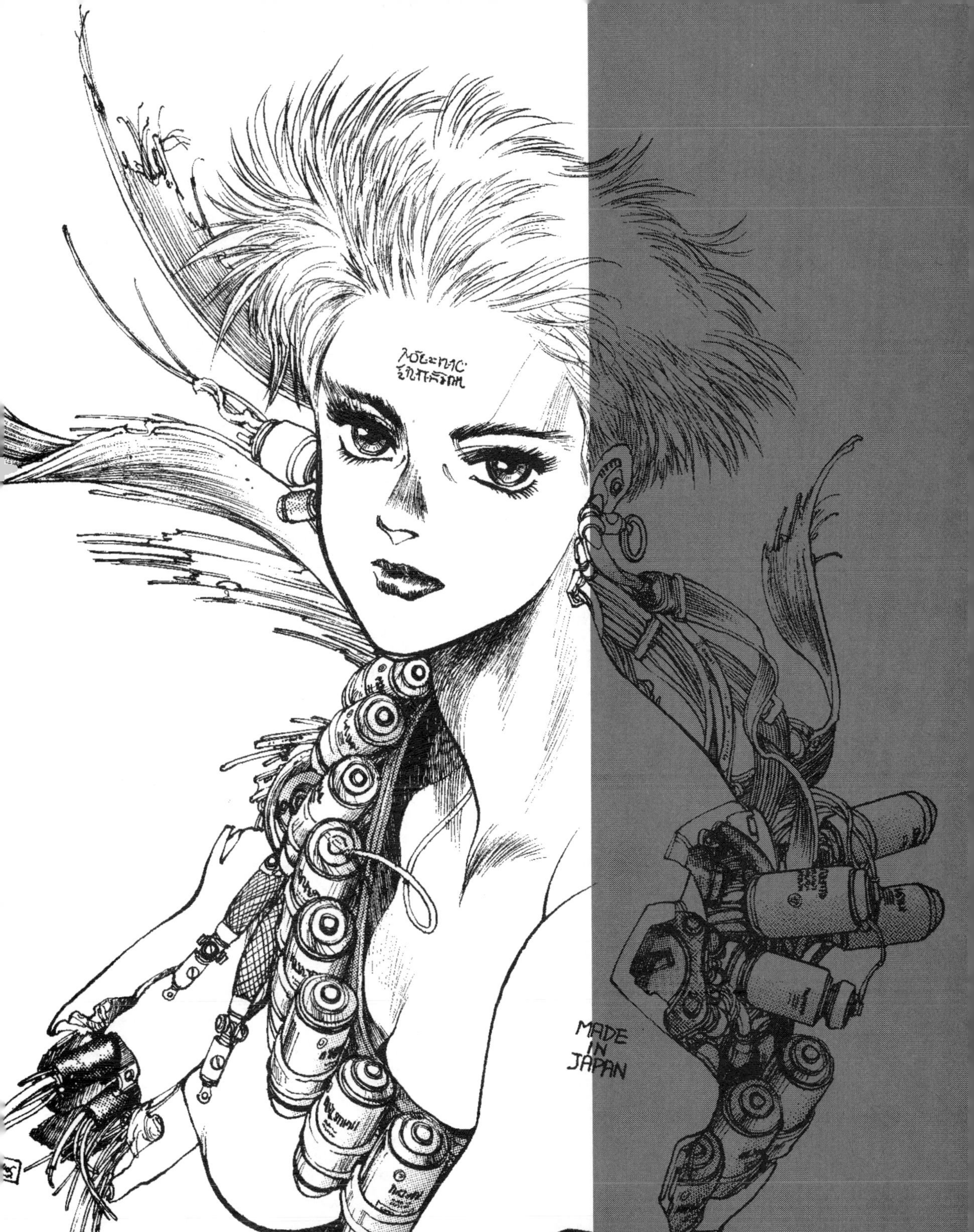
MADE IN JAPAN

02

FAT CAT Part.2

1991

THE STORY THUS FAR...

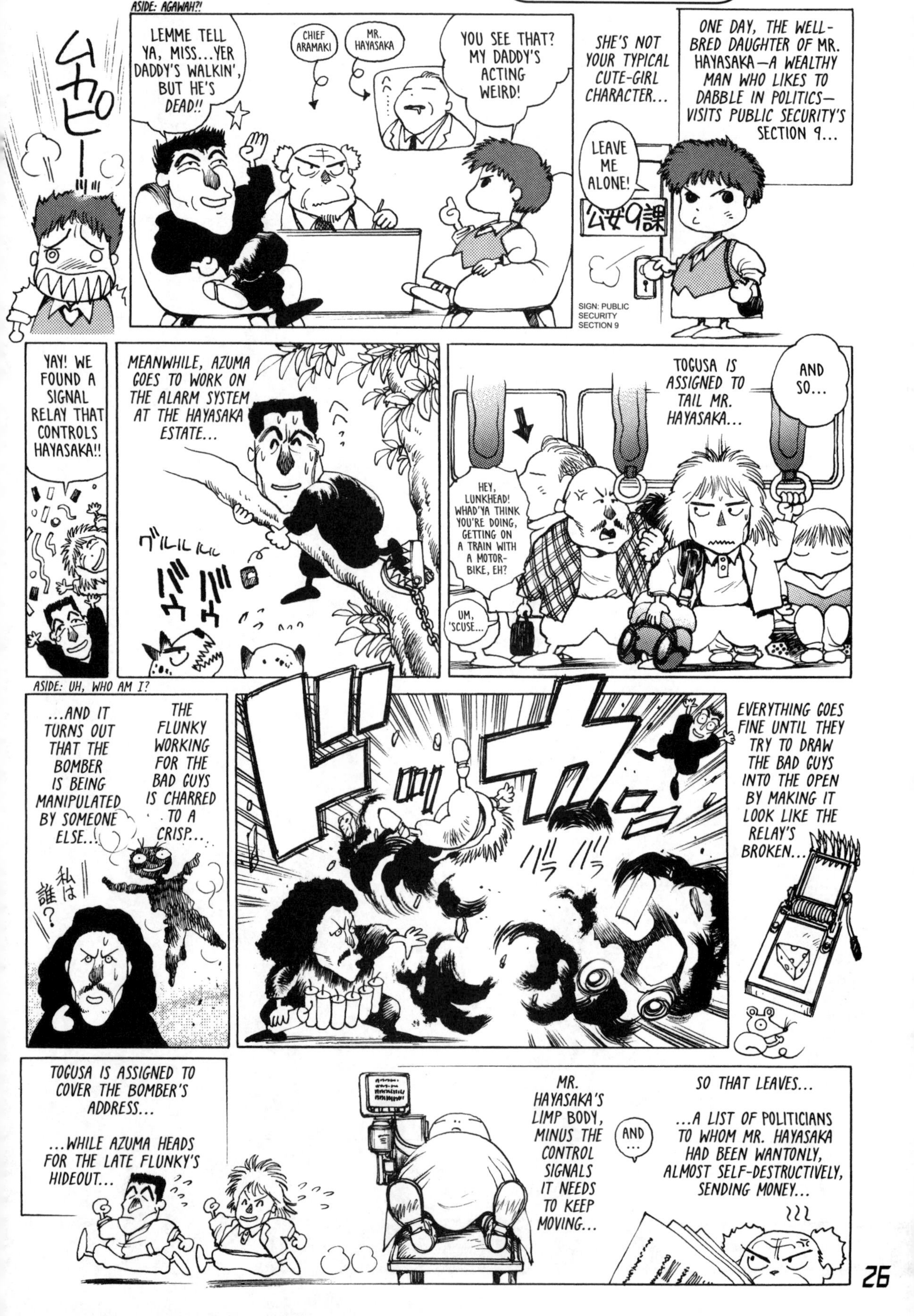

ONE DAY, THE WELL-BRED DAUGHTER OF MR. HAYASAKA—A WEALTHY MAN WHO LIKES TO DABBLE IN POLITICS—VISITS PUBLIC SECURITY'S SECTION 9...
SHE'S NOT YOUR TYPICAL CUTE-GIRL CHARACTER...
LEAVE ME ALONE!
公安9課
SIGN: PUBLIC SECURITY SECTION 9
YOU SEE THAT? MY DADDY'S ACTING WEIRD!
MR. HAYASAKA
CHIEF ARAMAKI
LEMME TELL YA, MISS...YER DADDY'S WALKIN', BUT HE'S DEAD!!
ASIDE: AGAWAH?!
ムカピー
AND SO...
TOGUSA IS ASSIGNED TO TAIL MR. HAYASAKA...
HEY, LUNKHEAD! WHAD'YA THINK YOU'RE DOING, GETTING ON A TRAIN WITH A MOTOR-BIKE, EH?
UM, 'SCUSE...
MEANWHILE, AZUMA GOES TO WORK ON THE ALARM SYSTEM AT THE HAYASAKA ESTATE...
グルルルル
ヴヴ
YAY! WE FOUND A SIGNAL RELAY THAT CONTROLS HAYASAKA!!
EVERYTHING GOES FINE UNTIL THEY TRY TO DRAW THE BAD GUYS INTO THE OPEN BY MAKING IT LOOK LIKE THE RELAY'S BROKEN...
ドウン
バラバラ
THE FLUNKY WORKING FOR THE BAD GUYS IS CHARRED TO A CRISP...
...AND IT TURNS OUT THAT THE BOMBER IS BEING MANIPULATED BY SOMEONE ELSE...
私は誰?
ASIDE: UH, WHO AM I?
SO THAT LEAVES...
...A LIST OF POLITICIANS TO WHOM MR. HAYASAKA HAD BEEN WANTONLY, ALMOST SELF-DESTRUCTIVELY, SENDING MONEY...
AND...
MR. HAYASAKA'S LIMP BODY, MINUS THE CONTROL SIGNALS IT NEEDS TO KEEP MOVING...
TOGUSA IS ASSIGNED TO COVER THE BOMBER'S ADDRESS...
...WHILE AZUMA HEADS FOR THE LATE FLUNKY'S HIDEOUT...

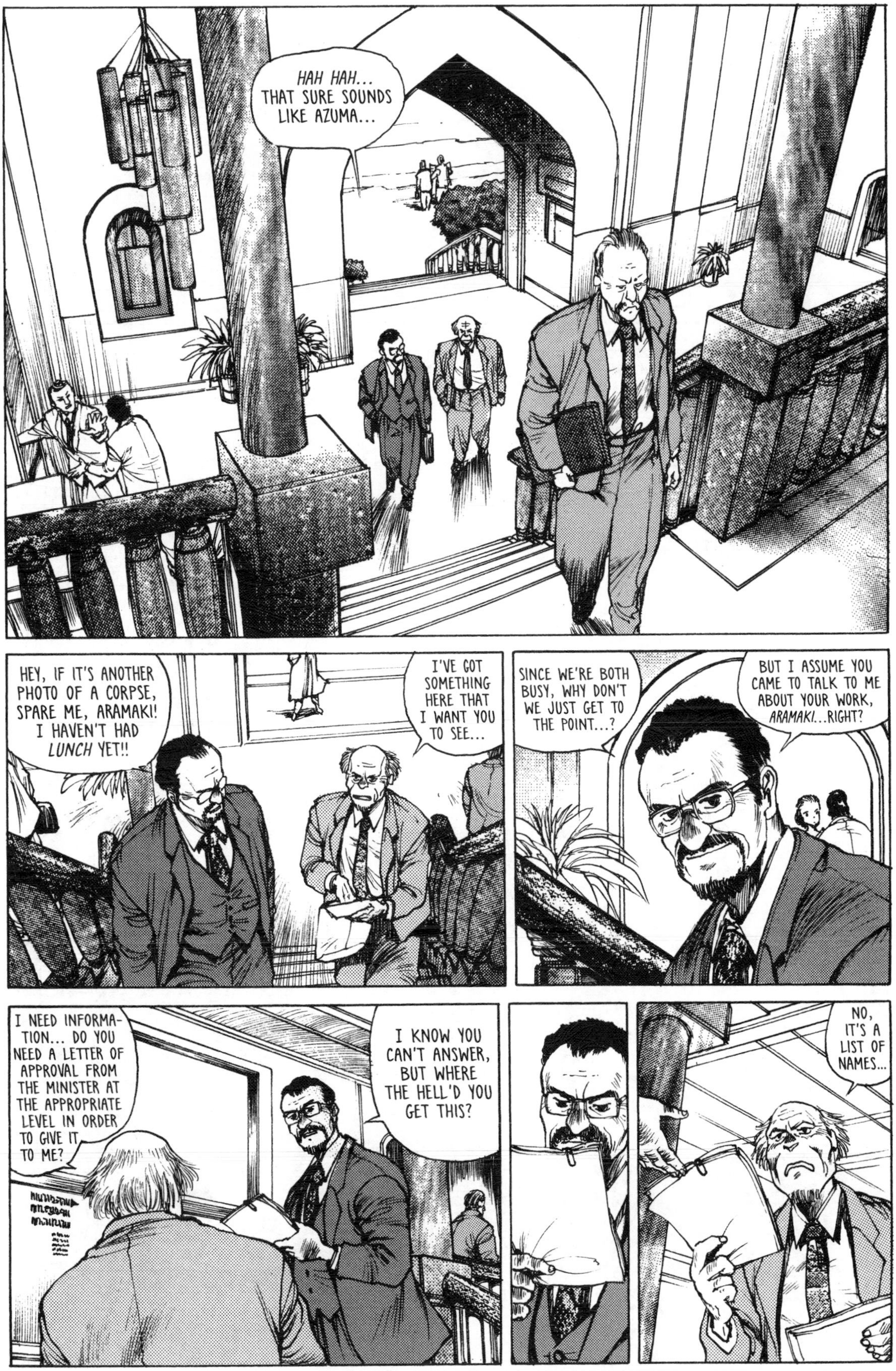
HAH HAH... THAT SURE SOUNDS LIKE AZUMA...
BUT I ASSUME YOU CAME TO TALK TO ME ABOUT YOUR WORK, ARAMAKI...RIGHT?
SINCE WE'RE BOTH BUSY, WHY DON'T WE JUST GET TO THE POINT...?
I'VE GOT SOMETHING HERE THAT I WANT YOU TO SEE...
HEY, IF IT'S ANOTHER PHOTO OF A CORPSE, SPARE ME, ARAMAKI! I HAVEN'T HAD LUNCH YET!!
NO, IT'S A LIST OF NAMES...
I KNOW YOU CAN'T ANSWER, BUT WHERE THE HELL'D YOU GET THIS?
I NEED INFORMATION... DO YOU NEED A LETTER OF APPROVAL FROM THE MINISTER AT THE APPROPRIATE LEVEL IN ORDER TO GIVE IT TO ME?

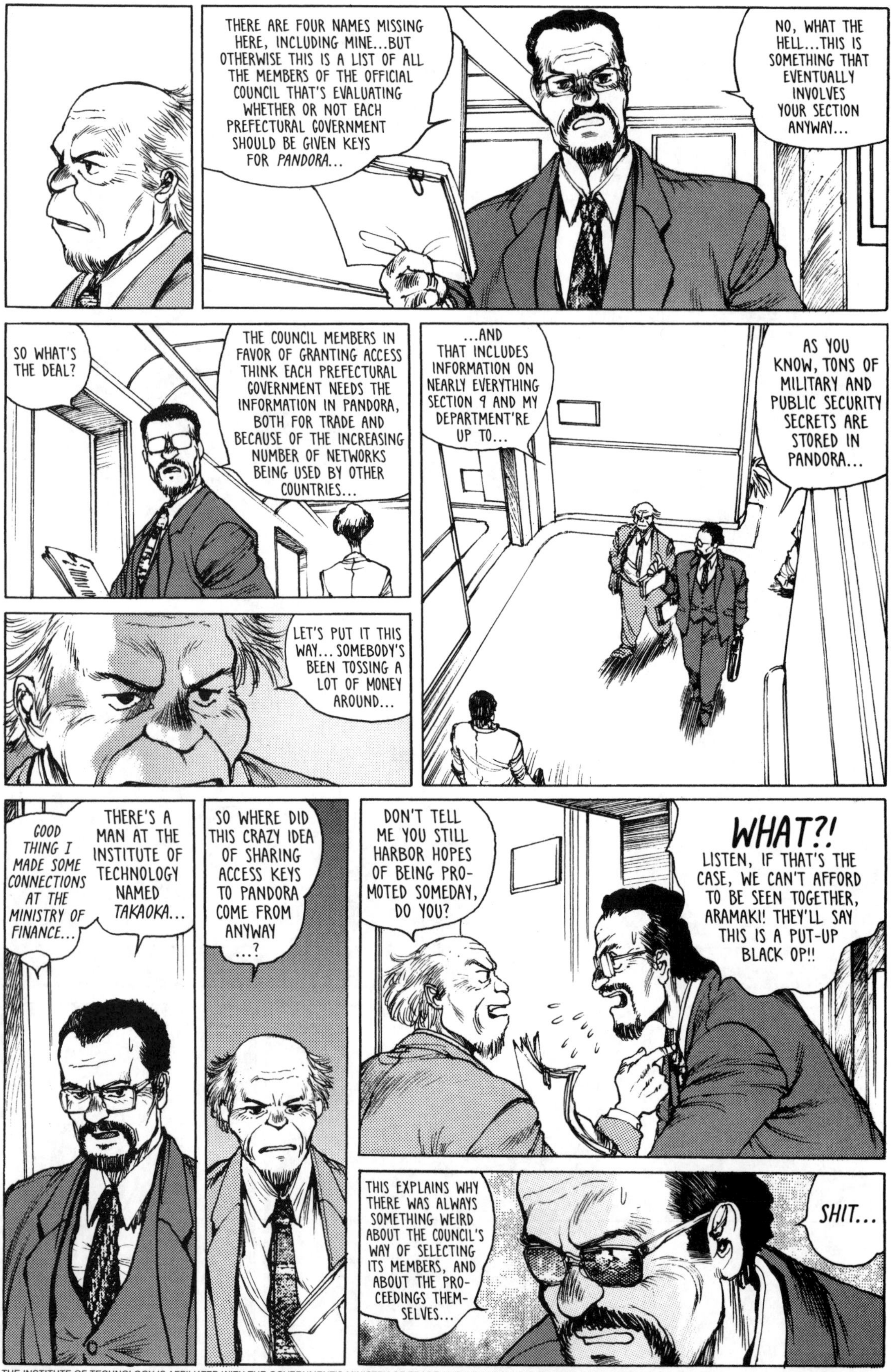
NO, WHAT THE HELL...THIS IS SOMETHING THAT EVENTUALLY INVOLVES YOUR SECTION ANYWAY...
THERE ARE FOUR NAMES MISSING HERE, INCLUDING MINE...BUT OTHERWISE THIS IS A LIST OF ALL THE MEMBERS OF THE OFFICIAL COUNCIL THAT'S EVALUATING WHETHER OR NOT EACH PREFECTURAL GOVERNMENT SHOULD BE GIVEN KEYS FOR *PANDORA*...
AS YOU KNOW, TONS OF MILITARY AND PUBLIC SECURITY SECRETS ARE STORED IN PANDORA...
...AND THAT INCLUDES INFORMATION ON NEARLY EVERYTHING SECTION 9 AND MY DEPARTMENT'RE UP TO...
THE COUNCIL MEMBERS IN FAVOR OF GRANTING ACCESS THINK EACH PREFECTURAL GOVERNMENT NEEDS THE INFORMATION IN PANDORA, BOTH FOR TRADE AND BECAUSE OF THE INCREASING NUMBER OF NETWORKS BEING USED BY OTHER COUNTRIES...
SO WHAT'S THE DEAL?
LET'S PUT IT THIS WAY... SOMEBODY'S BEEN TOSSING A LOT OF MONEY AROUND...
WHAT?!
LISTEN, IF THAT'S THE CASE, WE CAN'T AFFORD TO BE SEEN TOGETHER, ARAMAKI! THEY'LL SAY THIS IS A PUT-UP BLACK OP!!
DON'T TELL ME YOU STILL HARBOR HOPES OF BEING PROMOTED SOMEDAY, DO YOU?
SHIT...
THIS EXPLAINS WHY THERE WAS ALWAYS SOMETHING WEIRD ABOUT THE COUNCIL'S WAY OF SELECTING ITS MEMBERS, AND ABOUT THE PROCEEDINGS THEMSELVES...
SO WHERE DID THIS CRAZY IDEA OF SHARING ACCESS KEYS TO PANDORA COME FROM ANYWAY...?
THERE'S A MAN AT THE INSTITUTE OF TECHNOLOGY NAMED *TAKAOKA*...
GOOD THING I MADE SOME CONNECTIONS AT THE MINISTRY OF FINANCE...

THE INSTITUTE OF TECHNOLOGY IS AFFILIATED WITH THE GOVERNMENT'S MINISTRY OF TRADE AND INDUSTRY. THE COUNCIL IN QUESTION IS COMPRISED OF ALL THE RELATED GOVERNMENT AGENCIES, AND ITS MEMBERS ARE SUPPOSED TO RESOLVE THEIR DIFFERENCES THROUGH DISCUSSION AND COMPROMISE. WHAT THE OFFICIAL IS REFERRING TO AS "WEIRD" IS THAT FACT THAT CERTAIN OPINIONS IN THE GROUP SEEM TO PASS WITHOUT DEBATE. THE MINUTES OF THE COUNCIL MEETINGS ARE NEVER MADE PUBLIC, OF COURSE.

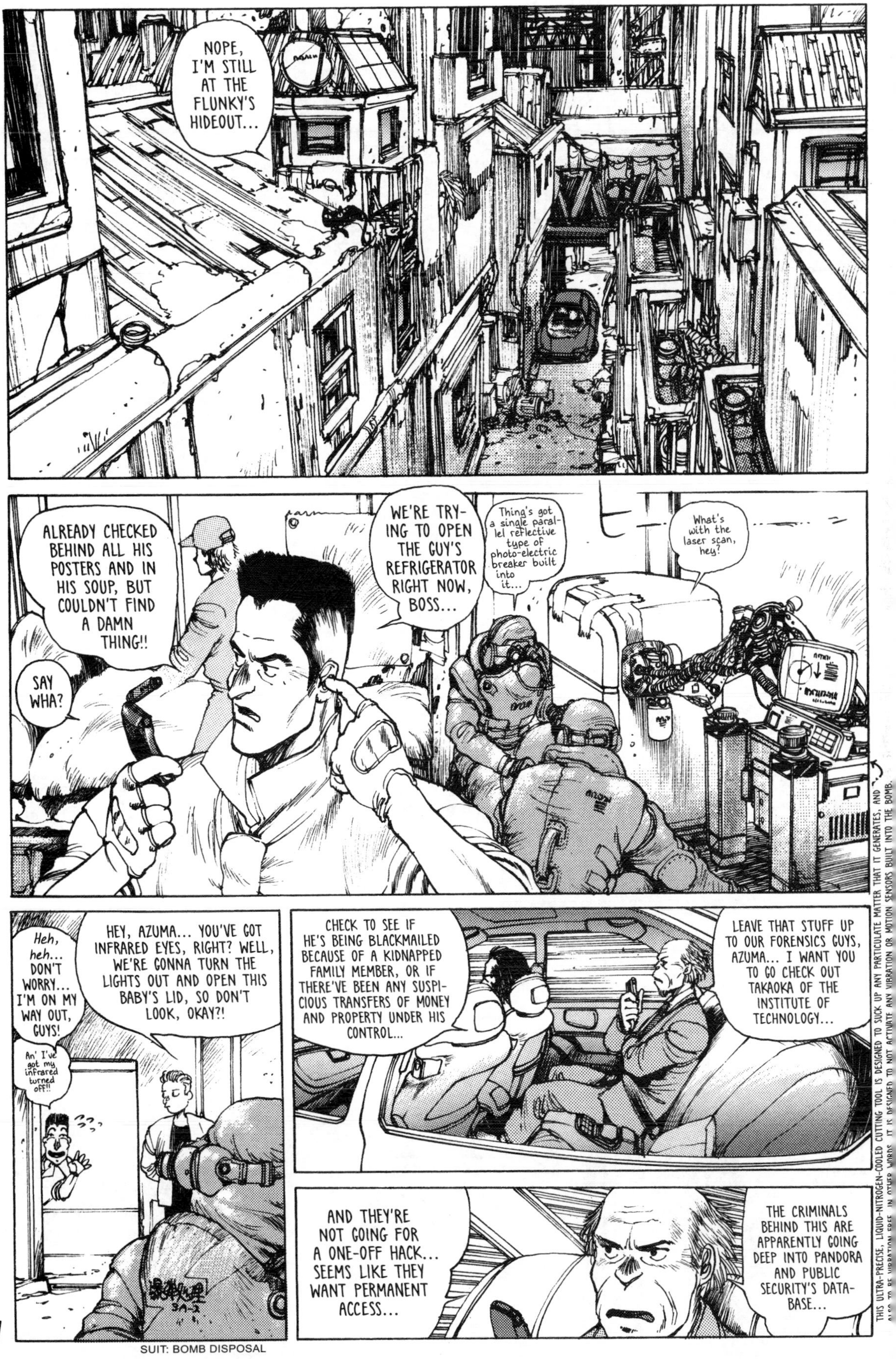
NOPE, I'M STILL AT THE FLUNKY'S HIDEOUT...
What's with the laser scan, hey?
Thing's got a single parallel reflective type of photo-electric breaker built into it...
WE'RE TRYING TO OPEN THE GUY'S REFRIGERATOR RIGHT NOW, BOSS...
ALREADY CHECKED BEHIND ALL HIS POSTERS AND IN HIS SOUP, BUT COULDN'T FIND A DAMN THING!!
SAY WHA?
THIS ULTRA-PRECISE, LIQUID-NITROGEN-COOLED CUTTING TOOL IS DESIGNED TO SUCK UP ANY PARTICULATE MATTER THAT IT GENERATES, AND ALSO TO BE VIBRATION-FREE. IN OTHER WORDS, IT IS DESIGNED TO NOT ACTIVATE ANY VIBRATION OR MOTION SENSORS BUILT INTO THE BOMB.
LEAVE THAT STUFF UP TO OUR FORENSICS GUYS, AZUMA... I WANT YOU TO GO CHECK OUT TAKAOKA OF THE INSTITUTE OF TECHNOLOGY...
CHECK TO SEE IF HE'S BEING BLACKMAILED BECAUSE OF A KIDNAPPED FAMILY MEMBER, OR IF THERE'VE BEEN ANY SUSPICIOUS TRANSFERS OF MONEY AND PROPERTY UNDER HIS CONTROL...
THE CRIMINALS BEHIND THIS ARE APPARENTLY GOING DEEP INTO PANDORA AND PUBLIC SECURITY'S DATABASE...
AND THEY'RE NOT GOING FOR A ONE-OFF HACK... SEEMS LIKE THEY WANT PERMANENT ACCESS...
HEY, AZUMA... YOU'VE GOT INFRARED EYES, RIGHT? WELL, WE'RE GONNA TURN THE LIGHTS OUT AND OPEN THIS BABY'S LID, SO DON'T LOOK, OKAY?!
Heh, heh... DON'T WORRY... I'M ON MY WAY OUT, GUYS!
An' I've got my infrared turned off!!
SUIT: BOMB DISPOSAL

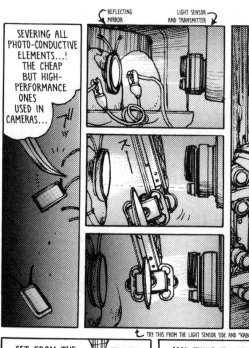

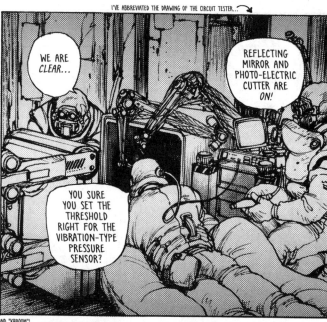

I'VE ABBREVIATED THE DRAWING OF THE CIRCUIT TESTER...
REFLECTING MIRROR AND PHOTO-ELECTRIC CUTTER ARE ON!
WE ARE CLEAR...
YOU SURE YOU SET THE THRESHOLD RIGHT FOR THE VIBRATION-TYPE PRESSURE SENSOR?
LIGHT SENSOR AND TRANSMITTER
REFLECTING MIRROR
SEVERING ALL PHOTO-CONDUCTIVE ELEMENTS...! THE CHEAP BUT HIGH-PERFORMANCE ONES USED IN CAMERAS...
TRY THIS FROM THE LIGHT SENSOR SIDE AND "KABOOM"!
WHOEVER MADE THIS WAS EITHER TRYING TO SHOW OFF OR WARN US... OR MAYBE THIS WAS THE ONLY BOMB DESIGN HE COULD COME UP WITH...
GOOD THING IT WASN'T JUST A TRICK TO PREVENT US FROM DOING OUR JOB... TAKE A LOOK AT THE BOLTS ON THE REAR DOOR OF THIS THING...
FEW MORE TURNS AN' WE'D 'A BEEN BLOWN TO SHREDS...
SET FROM THE DOOR SIDE, AND ACTIVATED WITH A TIMER... WHOEVER DID THIS WAS OVER THE TOP...
THE SCREWS HERE ARE MADE OF EPOXY RESIN INSULATING MATERIAL. THE TOP ONE'S JUST TO TEST THE BOMB SQUAD'S LUCK. IT'S NOT A DUMMY, AND STILL HAS TO BE CLEARED TO GET THE REAR DOOR OPEN...
LOOKS LIKE GERTEX IS THE MAIN THING THEY GOT HOLD OF THAT'D REALLY WORK...
CANVAS TACK
CANVAS TACK
REMEMBER THE OLD DAYS, WHEN ALL THE BOMBERS LIKED TO USE SUPER ARAMID FIBER, ALUMINUM FOIL, AND **** ****** ***?
THOSE BOMBS HAD SWITCHES SUSPENDED INSIDE PIPES, SO WHEN SOMEBODY TRIED TO DO A CAT SCAN OF 'EM, THE MAGNETIC RESONANCE'D CAUSE 'EM TO BLOW SKY HIGH...
Jeez, the fog inside my goggles is causing a halation effect... I can't see inside this thing.
WHOEVER DID THIS IS BEHIND THE CURVE... REALLY OUT OF DATE FOR A PRO...
ふー
MAKE SURE YOU TELL AZUMA...
あーしんど

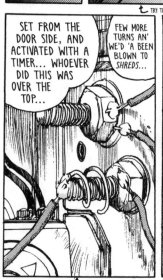

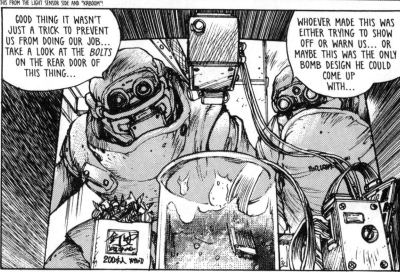

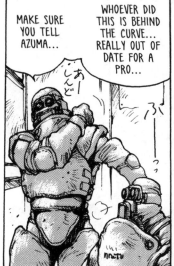

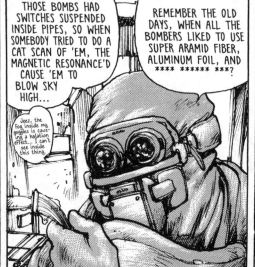

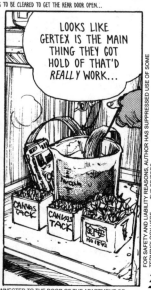

FOR SAFETY AND LIABILITY REASONS, AUTHOR HAS SUPPRESSED USE OF SOME TERMINOLOGY HERE... — THE EDITORS

RE: THE WARNING REFERRED TO IN PANEL SIX. IF THE GOAL HAD BEEN TO KILL THE FLUNKY, ALL IT WOULD TAKE IS FOR SOMETHING FAR MORE PRIMITIVE TO BE CONNECTED TO THE DOOR OF THE APARTMENT OR TO ONE OF THE MANY CONSUMER APPLIANCES IN THE ROOM. IF THE GOAL WERE TO BLOW UP THE POLICE ALONG WITH THE WHOLE ROOM, ALL IT WOULD TAKE IS A LOOKOUT NEARBY TO SPOT THEM ENTERING. THE LOOKOUT COULD THEN HIGHTAIL IT TO SAFETY A KLIK OR TWO AWAY BY CAR AND SEND A PASSWORD OR SIMPLE EXECUTION STRING BACK TO THE ROOM BY RADIO, OR SET THE SYSTEM TO BLOW WHEN THE PHONE RINGS (THEN PLACE A CALL AND WAIT FOR SOMEONE TO ANSWER, ETC.). IN OTHER WORDS, THERE WOULD HAVE BEEN LOTS OF EASIER WAYS TO GET THE JOB DONE...

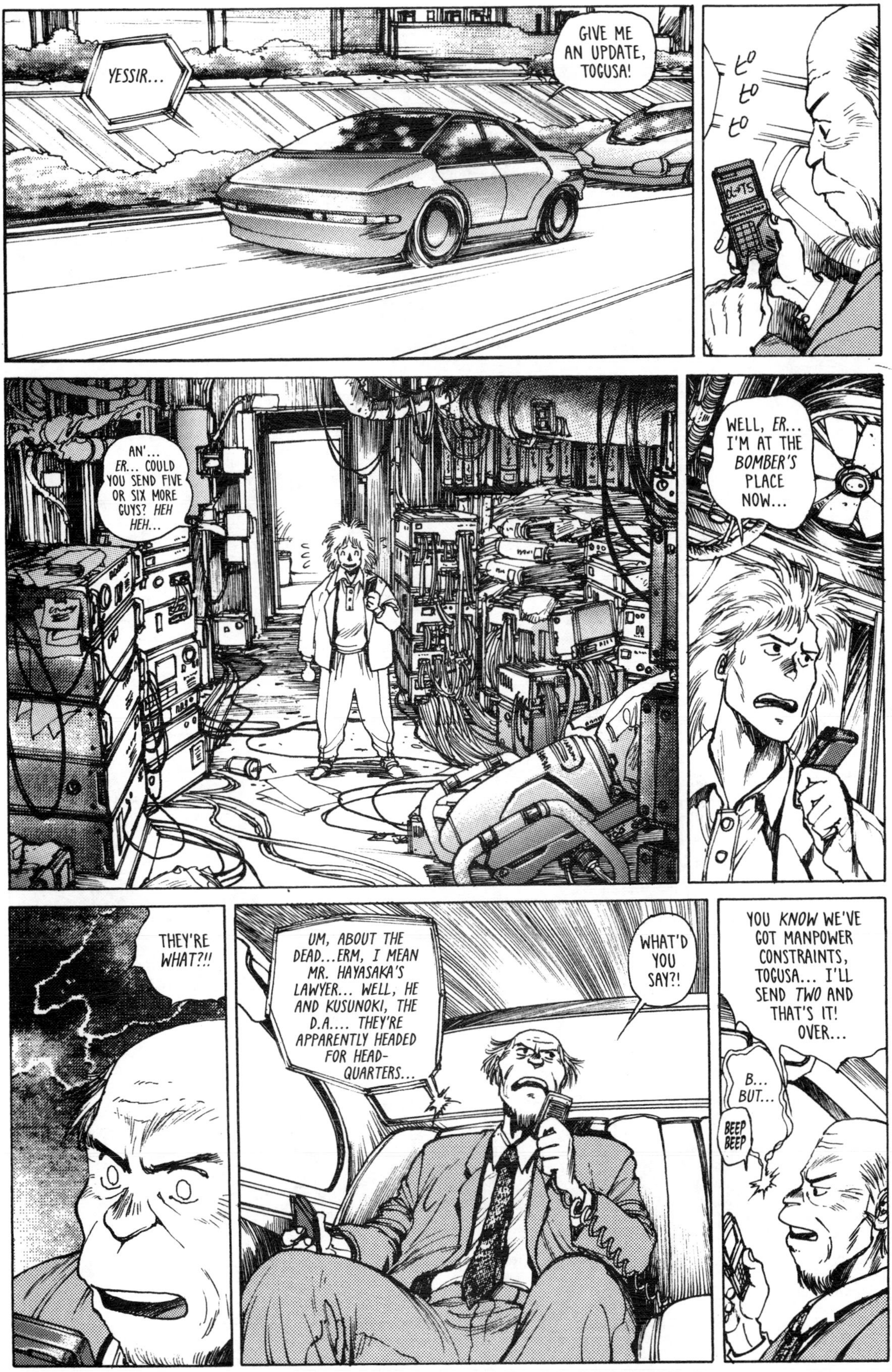
ピピピピ
GIVE ME AN UPDATE, TOGUSA!
YESSIR...
WELL, ER... I'M AT THE BOMBER'S PLACE NOW...
AN'... ER... COULD YOU SEND FIVE OR SIX MORE GUYS? HEH HEH...
YOU KNOW WE'VE GOT MANPOWER CONSTRAINTS, TOGUSA... I'LL SEND TWO AND THAT'S IT! OVER...
B... BUT...
BEEP BEEP
WHAT'D YOU SAY?!
UM, ABOUT THE DEAD...ERM, I MEAN MR. HAYASAKA'S LAWYER... WELL, HE AND KUSUNOKI, THE D.A.... THEY'RE APPARENTLY HEADED FOR HEAD-QUARTERS...
THEY'RE WHAT?!!

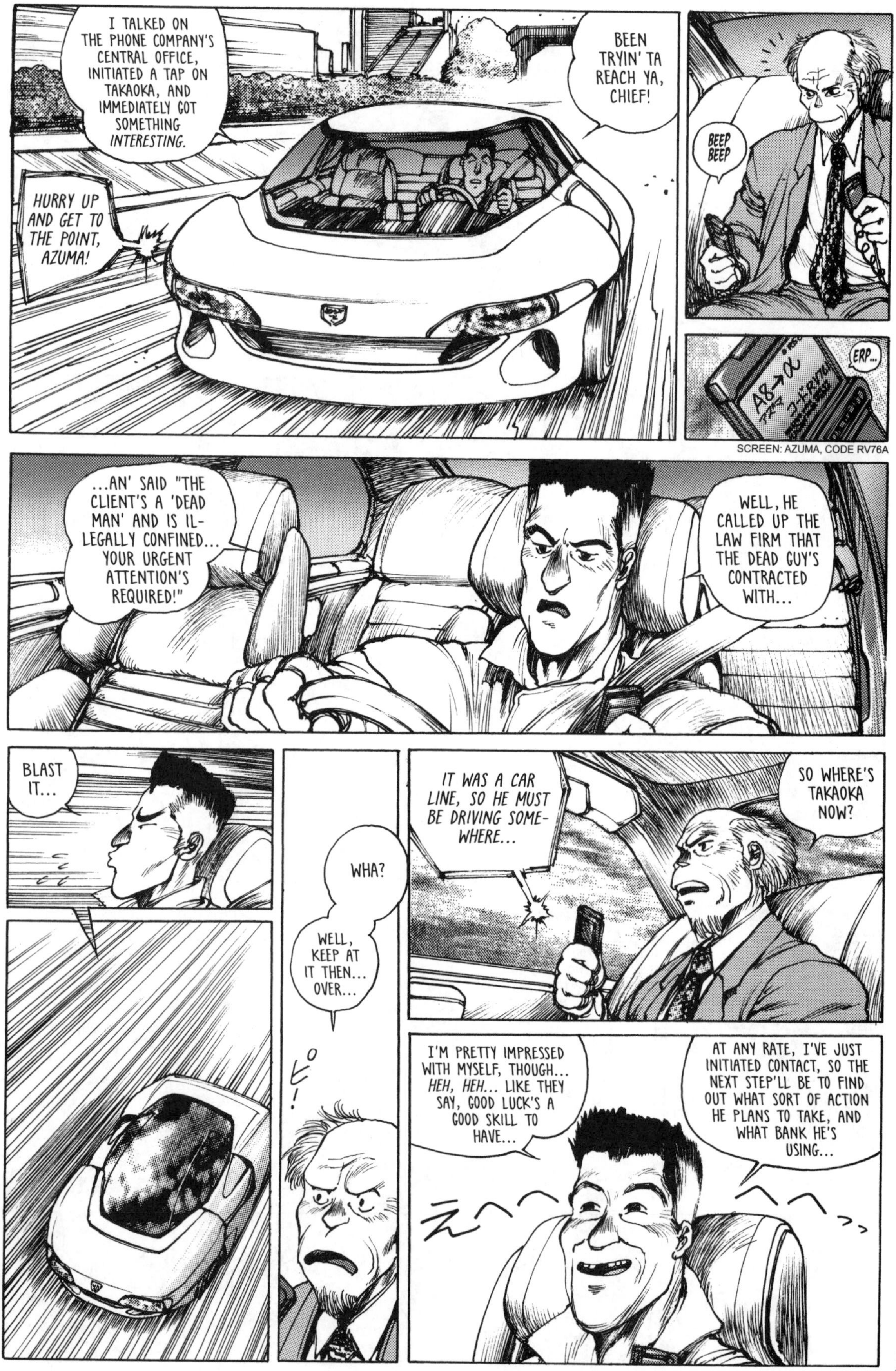
BEEP BEEP
ERP...
BEEN TRYIN' TA REACH YA, CHIEF!
I TALKED ON THE PHONE COMPANY'S CENTRAL OFFICE, INITIATED A TAP ON TAKAOKA, AND IMMEDIATELY GOT SOMETHING *INTERESTING*.
HURRY UP AND GET TO THE POINT, AZUMA!
WELL, HE CALLED UP THE LAW FIRM THAT THE DEAD GUY'S CONTRACTED WITH...
...AN' SAID "THE CLIENT'S A 'DEAD MAN' AND IS ILLEGALLY CONFINED... YOUR URGENT ATTENTION'S REQUIRED!"
SO WHERE'S TAKAOKA NOW?
IT WAS A CAR LINE, SO HE MUST BE DRIVING SOMEWHERE...
AT ANY RATE, I'VE JUST INITIATED CONTACT, SO THE NEXT STEP'LL BE TO FIND OUT WHAT SORT OF ACTION HE PLANS TO TAKE, AND WHAT BANK HE'S USING...
I'M PRETTY IMPRESSED WITH MYSELF, THOUGH... *HEH, HEH...* LIKE THEY SAY, GOOD LUCK'S A GOOD SKILL TO HAVE...
WHA?
WELL, KEEP AT IT THEN... OVER...
BLAST IT...
SCREEN: AZUMA, CODE RV76A

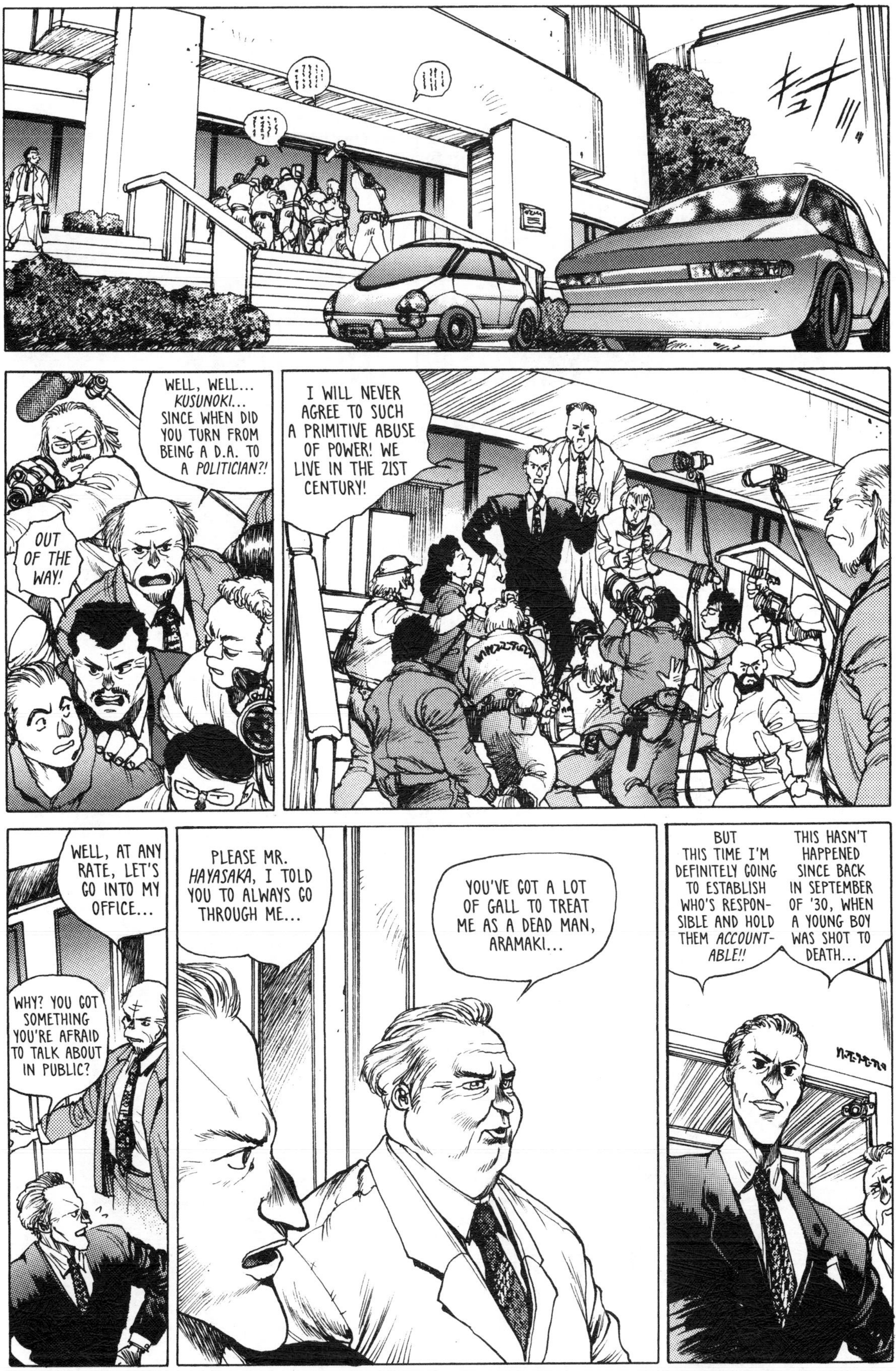
I WILL NEVER AGREE TO SUCH A PRIMITIVE ABUSE OF POWER! WE LIVE IN THE 21ST CENTURY!
WELL, WELL... *KUSUNOKI*... SINCE WHEN DID YOU TURN FROM BEING A D.A. TO A *POLITICIAN?!*
OUT OF THE WAY!
THIS HASN'T HAPPENED SINCE BACK IN SEPTEMBER OF '30, WHEN A YOUNG BOY WAS SHOT TO DEATH...
BUT THIS TIME I'M DEFINITELY GOING TO ESTABLISH WHO'S RESPON-SIBLE AND HOLD THEM *ACCOUNT-ABLE!!*
YOU'VE GOT A LOT OF GALL TO TREAT ME AS A DEAD MAN, ARAMAKI...
PLEASE MR. *HAYASAKA*, I TOLD YOU TO ALWAYS GO THROUGH ME...
WELL, AT ANY RATE, LET'S GO INTO MY OFFICE...
WHY? YOU GOT SOMETHING YOU'RE AFRAID TO TALK ABOUT IN PUBLIC?

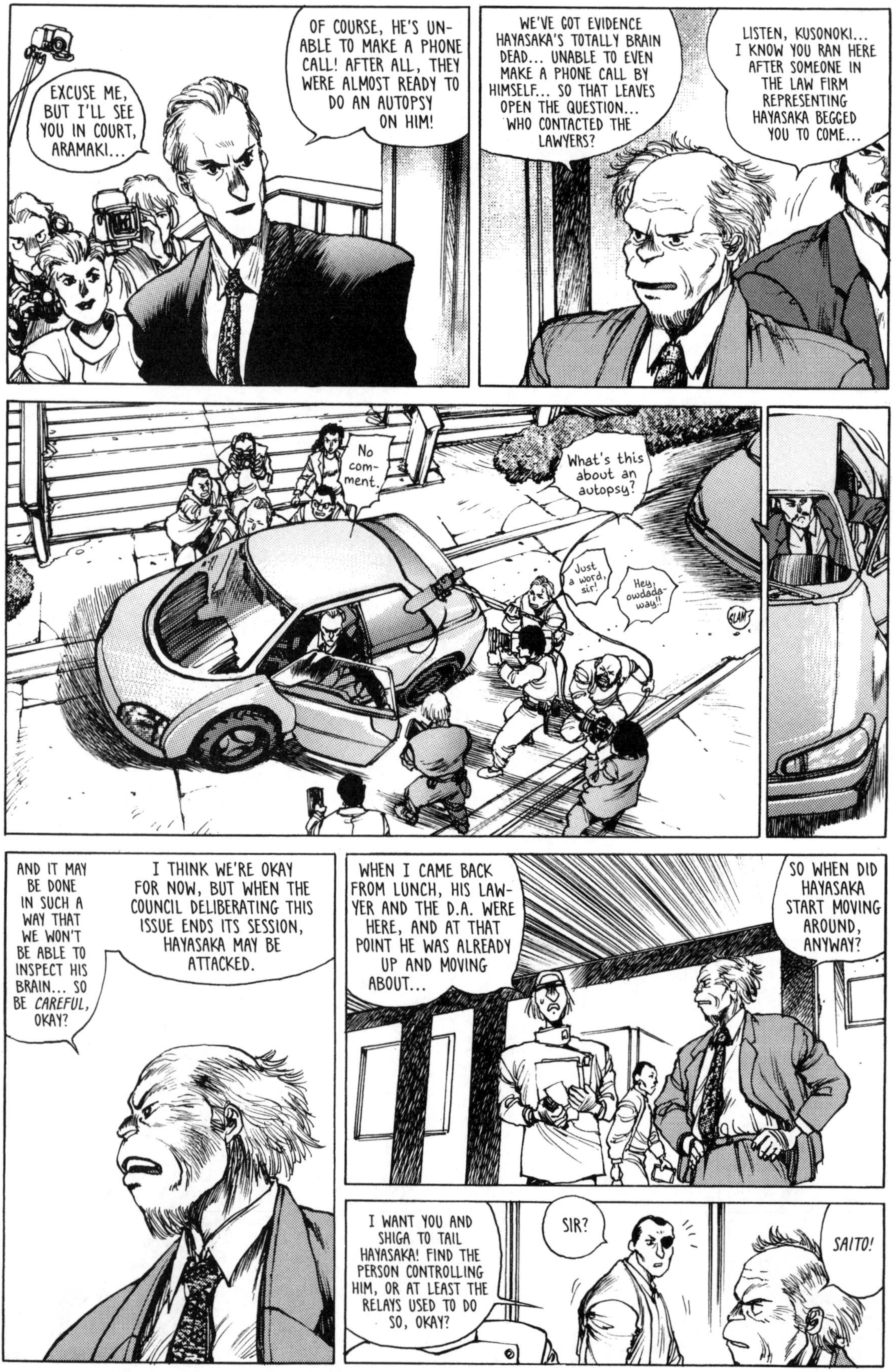
LISTEN, KUSONOKI... I KNOW YOU RAN HERE AFTER SOMEONE IN THE LAW FIRM REPRESENTING HAYASAKA BEGGED YOU TO COME...
WE'VE GOT EVIDENCE HAYASAKA'S TOTALLY BRAIN DEAD... UNABLE TO EVEN MAKE A PHONE CALL BY HIMSELF... SO THAT LEAVES OPEN THE QUESTION... WHO CONTACTED THE LAWYERS?
OF COURSE, HE'S UNABLE TO MAKE A PHONE CALL! AFTER ALL, THEY WERE ALMOST READY TO DO AN AUTOPSY ON HIM!
EXCUSE ME, BUT I'LL SEE YOU IN COURT, ARAMAKI...
What's this about an autopsy?
No comment.
Just a word, sir!
Hey, owdada-way!!
SLAM
SO WHEN DID HAYASAKA START MOVING AROUND, ANYWAY?
WHEN I CAME BACK FROM LUNCH, HIS LAWYER AND THE D.A. WERE HERE, AND AT THAT POINT HE WAS ALREADY UP AND MOVING ABOUT...
SAITO!
SIR?
I WANT YOU AND SHIGA TO TAIL HAYASAKA! FIND THE PERSON CONTROLLING HIM, OR AT LEAST THE RELAYS USED TO DO SO, OKAY?
I THINK WE'RE OKAY FOR NOW, BUT WHEN THE COUNCIL DELIBERATING THIS ISSUE ENDS ITS SESSION, HAYASAKA MAY BE ATTACKED.
AND IT MAY BE DONE IN SUCH A WAY THAT WE WON'T BE ABLE TO INSPECT HIS BRAIN... SO BE *CAREFUL*, OKAY?

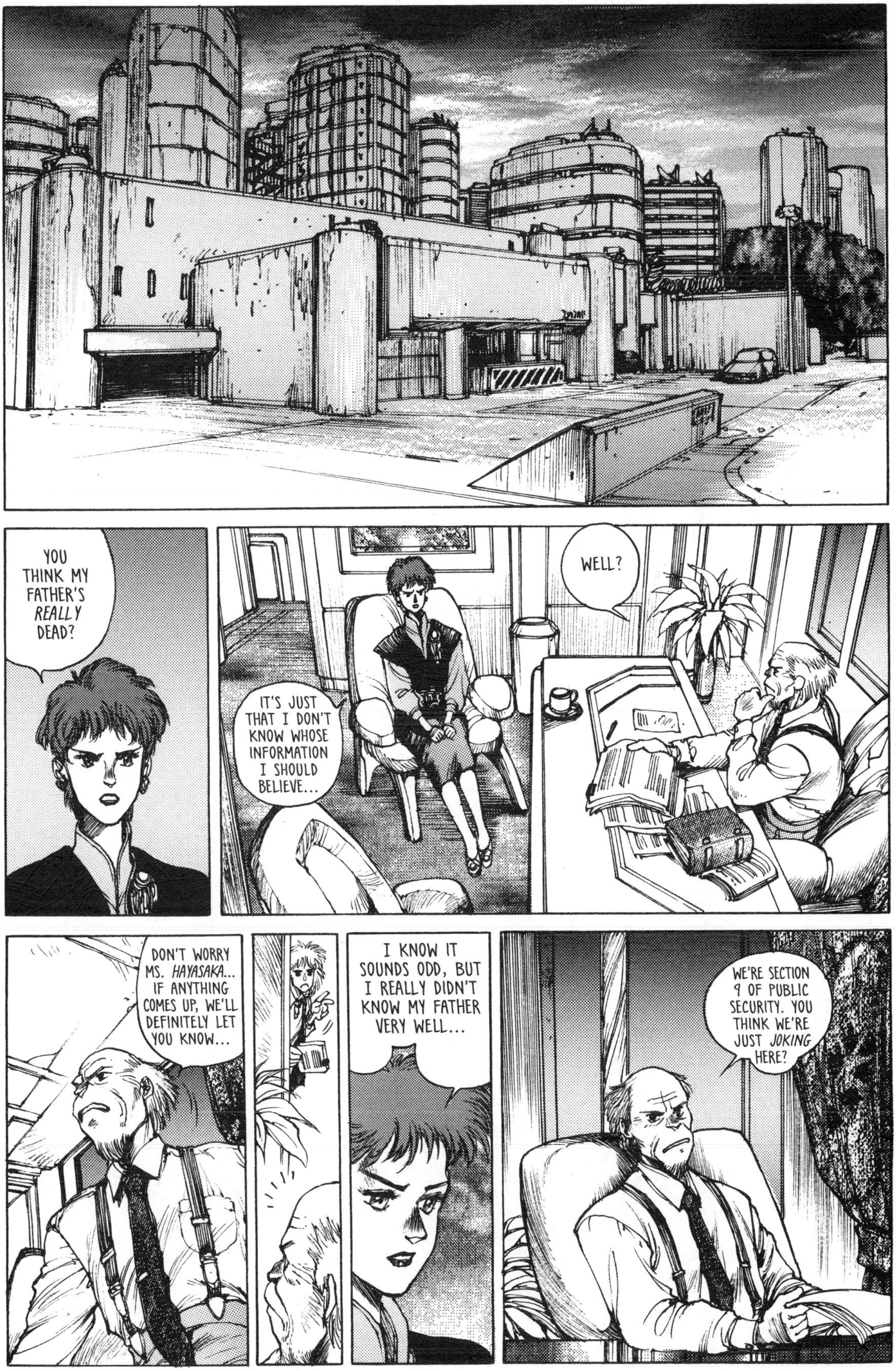
WELL?
IT'S JUST THAT I DON'T KNOW WHOSE INFORMATION I SHOULD BELIEVE...
YOU THINK MY FATHER'S *REALLY* DEAD?
WE'RE SECTION 9 OF PUBLIC SECURITY. YOU THINK WE'RE JUST *JOKING* HERE?
I KNOW IT SOUNDS ODD, BUT I REALLY DIDN'T KNOW MY FATHER VERY WELL...
DON'T WORRY MS. *HAYASAKA*... IF ANYTHING COMES UP, WE'LL DEFINITELY LET YOU KNOW...

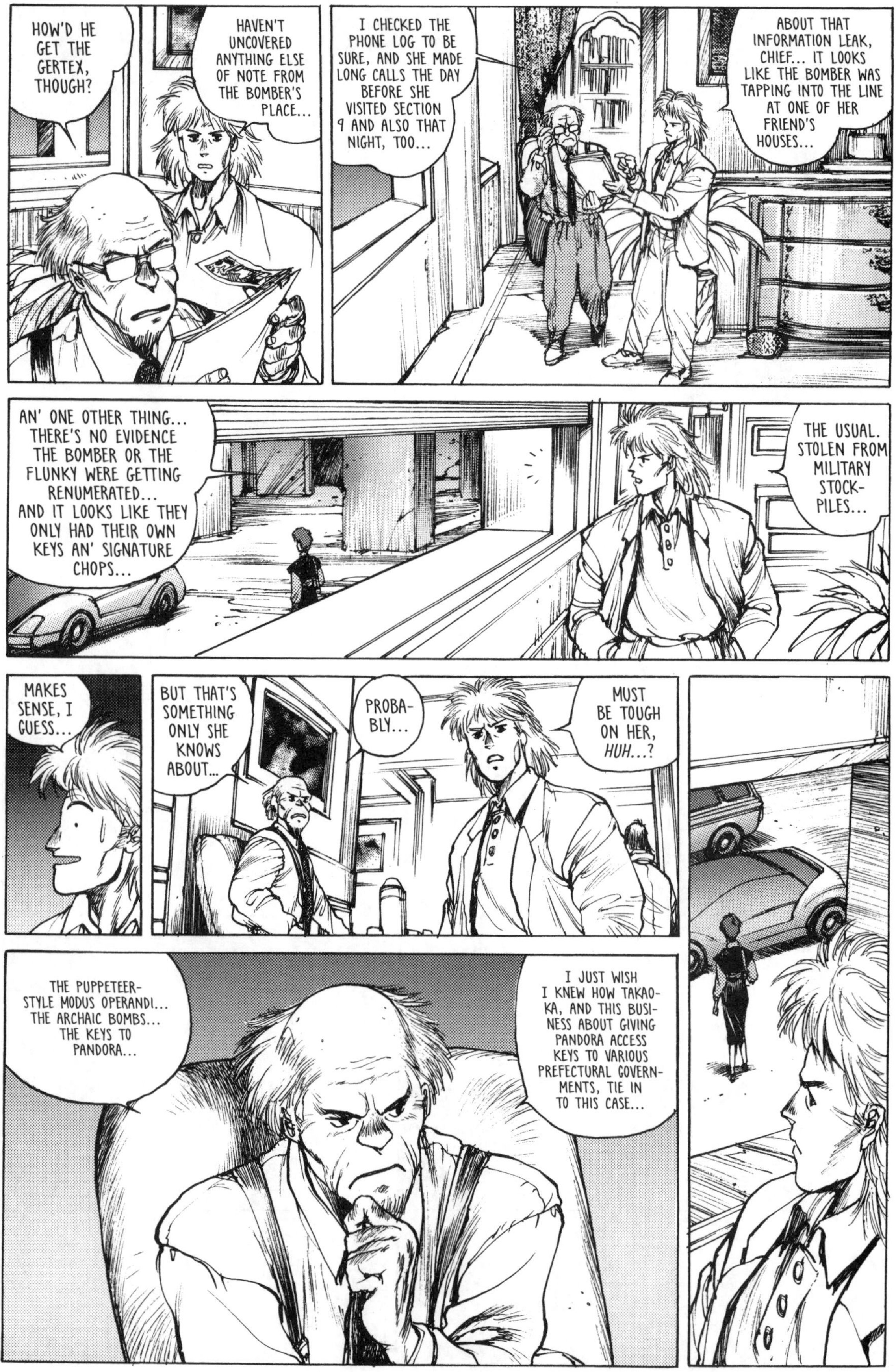
ABOUT THAT INFORMATION LEAK, CHIEF... IT LOOKS LIKE THE BOMBER WAS TAPPING INTO THE LINE AT ONE OF HER FRIEND'S HOUSES...
I CHECKED THE PHONE LOG TO BE SURE, AND SHE MADE LONG CALLS THE DAY BEFORE SHE VISITED SECTION 9 AND ALSO THAT NIGHT, TOO...
HAVEN'T UNCOVERED ANYTHING ELSE OF NOTE FROM THE BOMBER'S PLACE...
HOW'D HE GET THE GERTEX, THOUGH?
THE USUAL. STOLEN FROM MILITARY STOCK-PILES...
AN' ONE OTHER THING... THERE'S NO EVIDENCE THE BOMBER OR THE FLUNKY WERE GETTING RENUMERATED... AND IT LOOKS LIKE THEY ONLY HAD THEIR OWN KEYS AN' SIGNATURE CHOPS...
MUST BE TOUGH ON HER, *HUH*...?
PROBA-BLY...
BUT THAT'S SOMETHING ONLY SHE KNOWS ABOUT...
MAKES SENSE, I GUESS...
I JUST WISH I KNEW HOW TAKAO-KA, AND THIS BUSI-NESS ABOUT GIVING PANDORA ACCESS KEYS TO VARIOUS PREFECTURAL GOVERN-MENTS, TIE IN TO THIS CASE...
THE PUPPETEER-STYLE MODUS OPERANDI... THE ARCHAIC BOMBS... THE KEYS TO PANDORA...

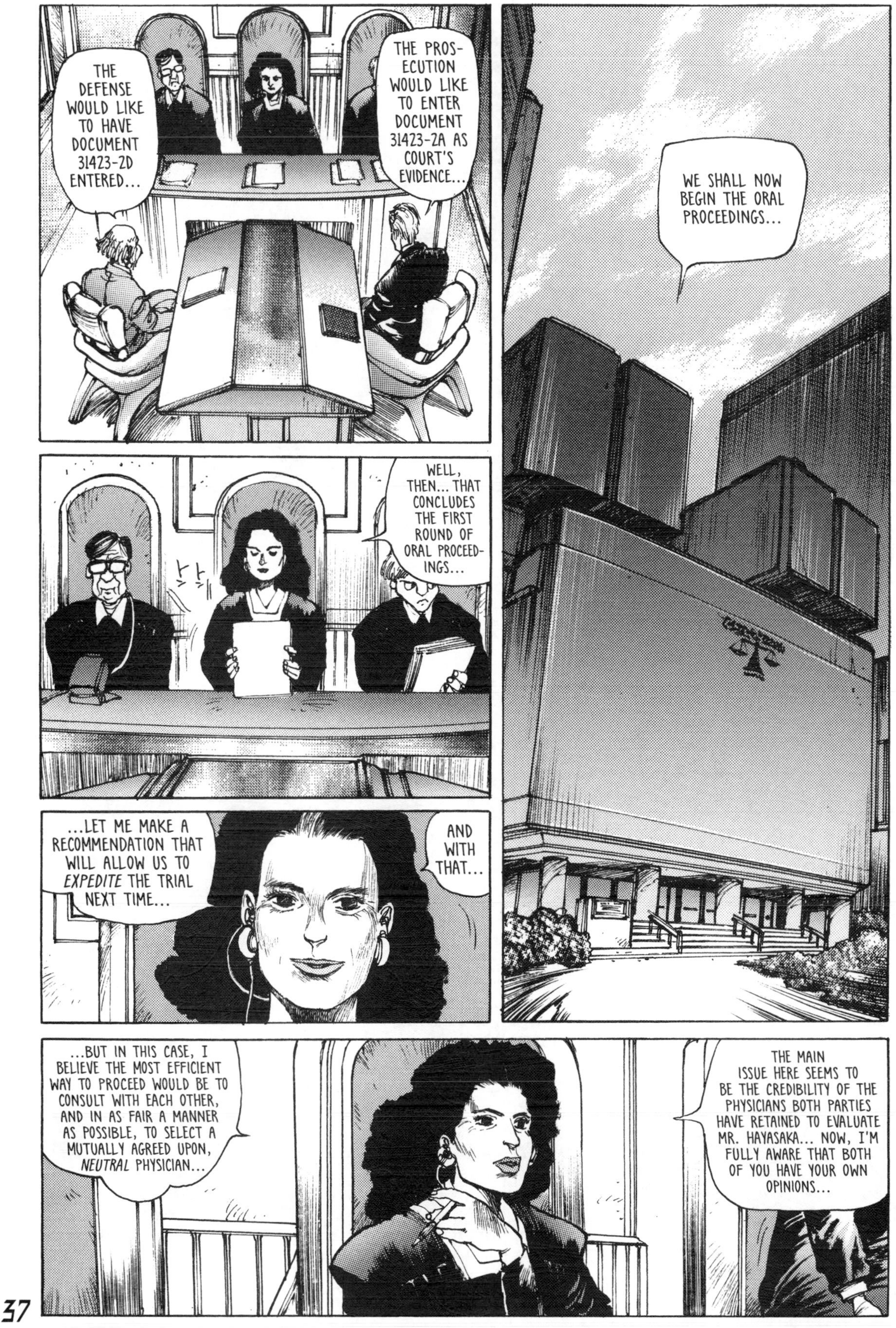
WE SHALL NOW BEGIN THE ORAL PROCEEDINGS...
THE PROSECUTION WOULD LIKE TO ENTER DOCUMENT 31423-2A AS COURT'S EVIDENCE...
THE DEFENSE WOULD LIKE TO HAVE DOCUMENT 31423-2D ENTERED...
WELL, THEN... THAT CONCLUDES THE FIRST ROUND OF ORAL PROCEEDINGS...
AND WITH THAT...
...LET ME MAKE A RECOMMENDATION THAT WILL ALLOW US TO *EXPEDITE* THE TRIAL NEXT TIME...
THE MAIN ISSUE HERE SEEMS TO BE THE CREDIBILITY OF THE PHYSICIANS BOTH PARTIES HAVE RETAINED TO EVALUATE MR. HAYASAKA... NOW, I'M FULLY AWARE THAT BOTH OF YOU HAVE YOUR OWN OPINIONS...
...BUT IN THIS CASE, I BELIEVE THE MOST EFFICIENT WAY TO PROCEED WOULD BE TO CONSULT WITH EACH OTHER, AND IN AS FAIR A MANNER AS POSSIBLE, TO SELECT A MUTUALLY AGREED UPON, *NEUTRAL* PHYSICIAN...

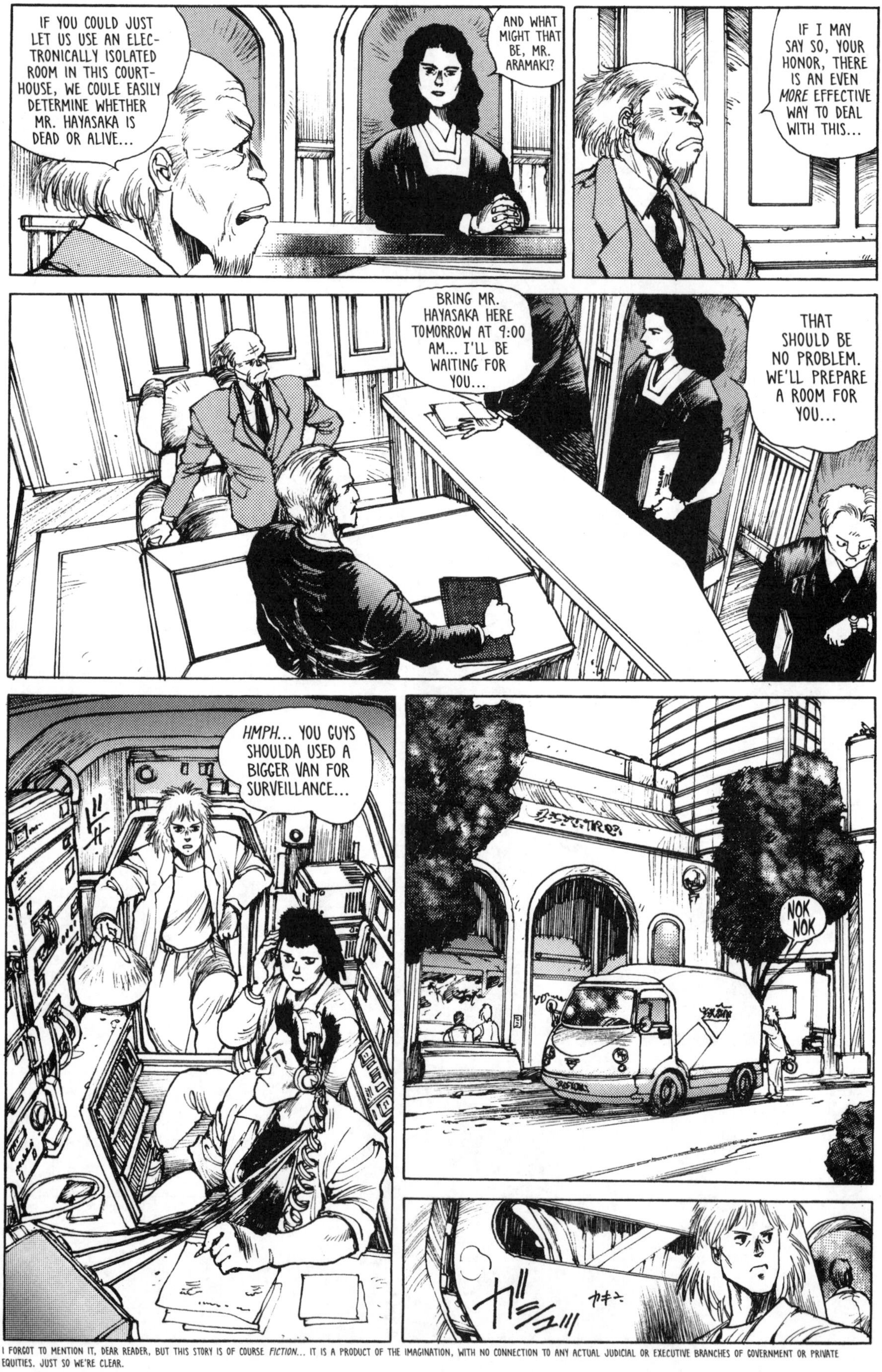
IF I MAY SAY SO, YOUR HONOR, THERE IS AN EVEN *MORE* EFFECTIVE WAY TO DEAL WITH THIS...
AND WHAT MIGHT THAT BE, MR. ARAMAKI?
IF YOU COULD JUST LET US USE AN ELECTRONICALLY ISOLATED ROOM IN THIS COURTHOUSE, WE COULE EASILY DETERMINE WHETHER MR. HAYASAKA IS DEAD OR ALIVE...
THAT SHOULD BE NO PROBLEM. WE'LL PREPARE A ROOM FOR YOU...
BRING MR. HAYASAKA HERE TOMORROW AT 9:00 AM... I'LL BE WAITING FOR YOU...
NOK NOK
ガシュ
カキュ
HMPH... YOU GUYS SHOULDA USED A BIGGER VAN FOR SURVEILLANCE...

I FORGOT TO MENTION IT, DEAR READER, BUT THIS STORY IS OF COURSE *FICTION*... IT IS A PRODUCT OF THE IMAGINATION, WITH NO CONNECTION TO ANY ACTUAL JUDICIAL OR EXECUTIVE BRANCHES OF GOVERNMENT OR PRIVATE EQUITIES. JUST SO WE'RE CLEAR.

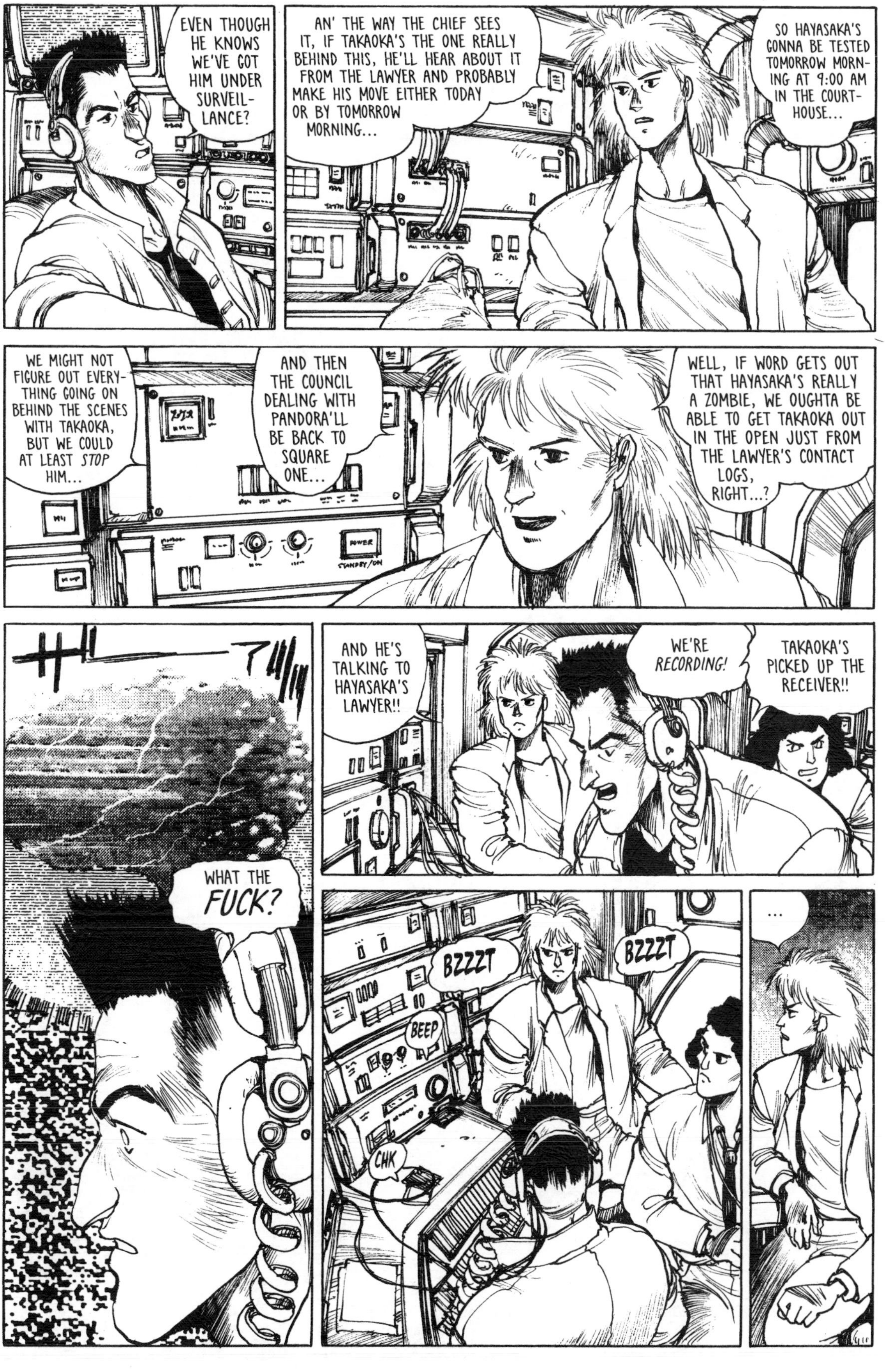

SO HAYASAKA'S GONNA BE TESTED TOMORROW MORNING AT 9:00 AM IN THE COURTHOUSE...
AN' THE WAY THE CHIEF SEES IT, IF TAKAOKA'S THE ONE REALLY BEHIND THIS, HE'LL HEAR ABOUT IT FROM THE LAWYER AND PROBABLY MAKE HIS MOVE EITHER TODAY OR BY TOMORROW MORNING...
EVEN THOUGH HE KNOWS WE'VE GOT HIM UNDER SURVEILLANCE?
WELL, IF WORD GETS OUT THAT HAYASAKA'S REALLY A ZOMBIE, WE OUGHTA BE ABLE TO GET TAKAOKA OUT IN THE OPEN JUST FROM THE LAWYER'S CONTACT LOGS, RIGHT...?
AND THEN THE COUNCIL DEALING WITH PANDORA'LL BE BACK TO SQUARE ONE...
WE MIGHT NOT FIGURE OUT EVERYTHING GOING ON BEHIND THE SCENES WITH TAKAOKA, BUT WE COULD AT LEAST *STOP* HIM...
TAKAOKA'S PICKED UP THE RECEIVER!!
WE'RE *RECORDING!*
AND HE'S TALKING TO HAYASAKA'S LAWYER!!
...
BZZZT
BZZZT
BEEP
CHK
WHAT THE *FUCK?*

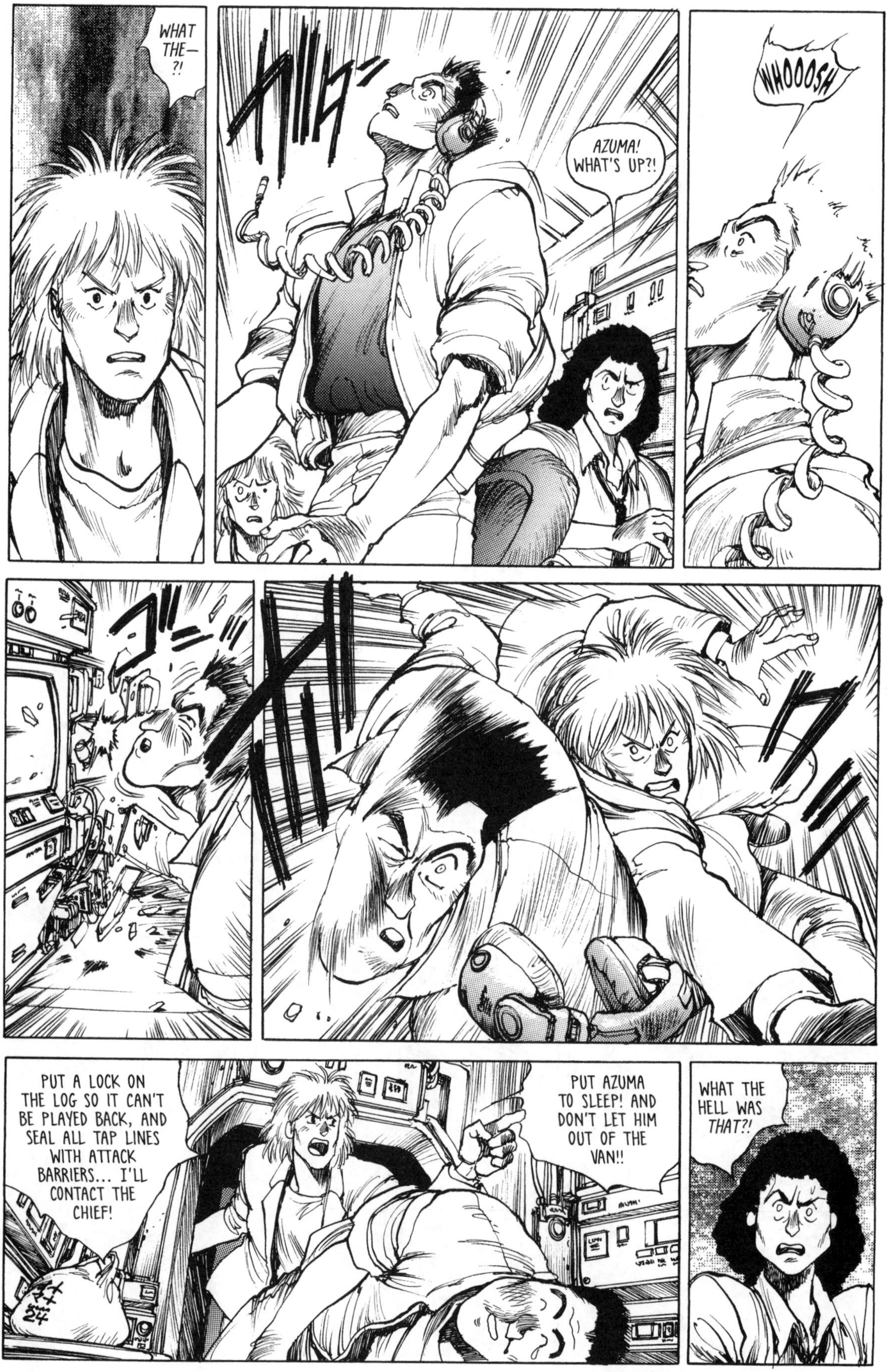
WHOOOSH
AZUMA! WHAT'S UP?!
WHAT THE— ?!
WHAT THE HELL WAS THAT?!
PUT AZUMA TO SLEEP! AND DON'T LET HIM OUT OF THE VAN!!
PUT A LOCK ON THE LOG SO IT CAN'T BE PLAYED BACK, AND SEAL ALL TAP LINES WITH ATTACK BARRIERS... I'LL CONTACT THE CHIEF!

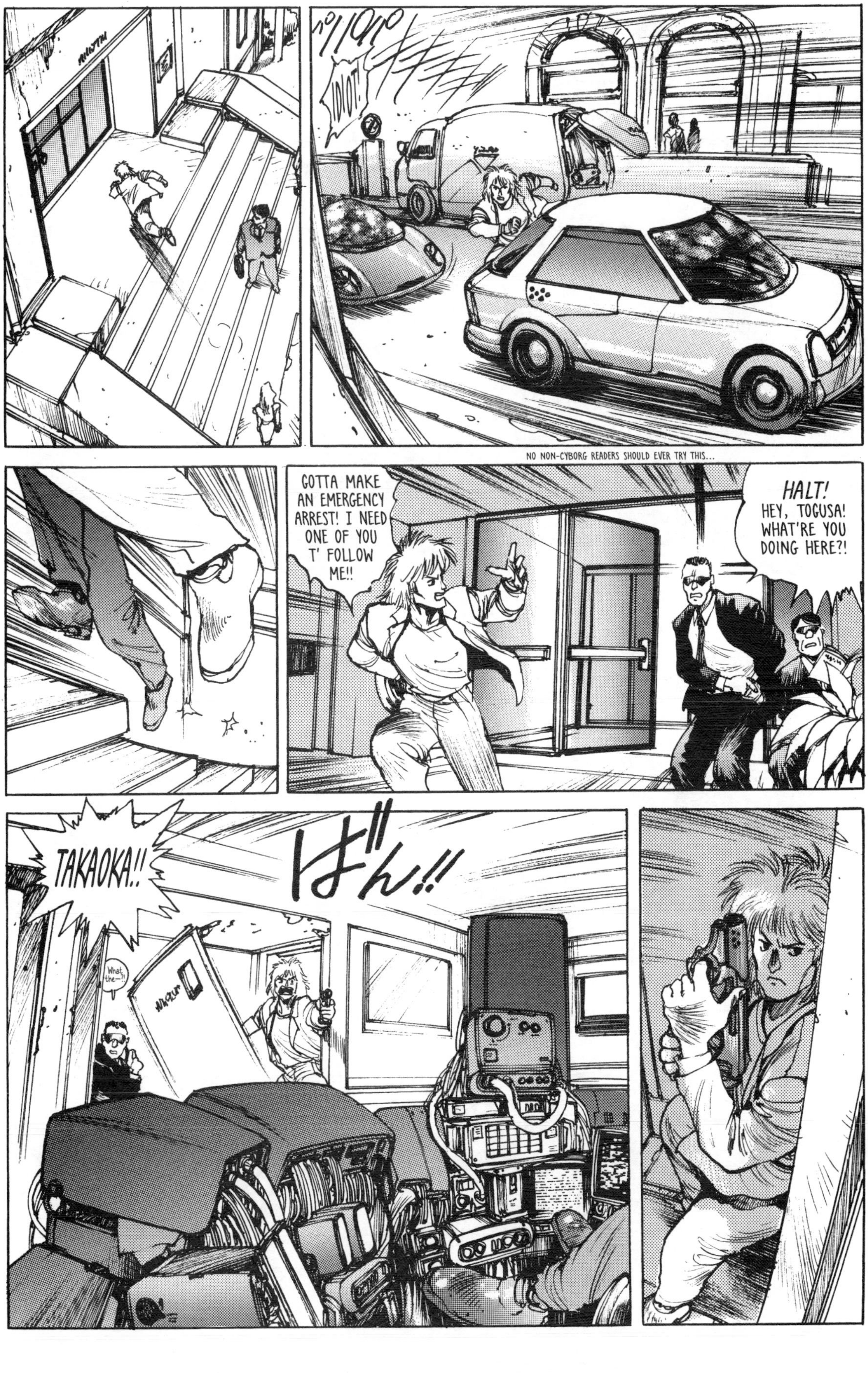
IDIOT!
NO NON-CYBORG READERS SHOULD EVER TRY THIS...
HALT!
HEY, TOGUSA! WHAT'RE YOU DOING HERE?!
GOTTA MAKE AN EMERGENCY ARREST! I NEED ONE OF YOU T' FOLLOW ME!!
ばん!!
TAKAOKA!!
What the—?!

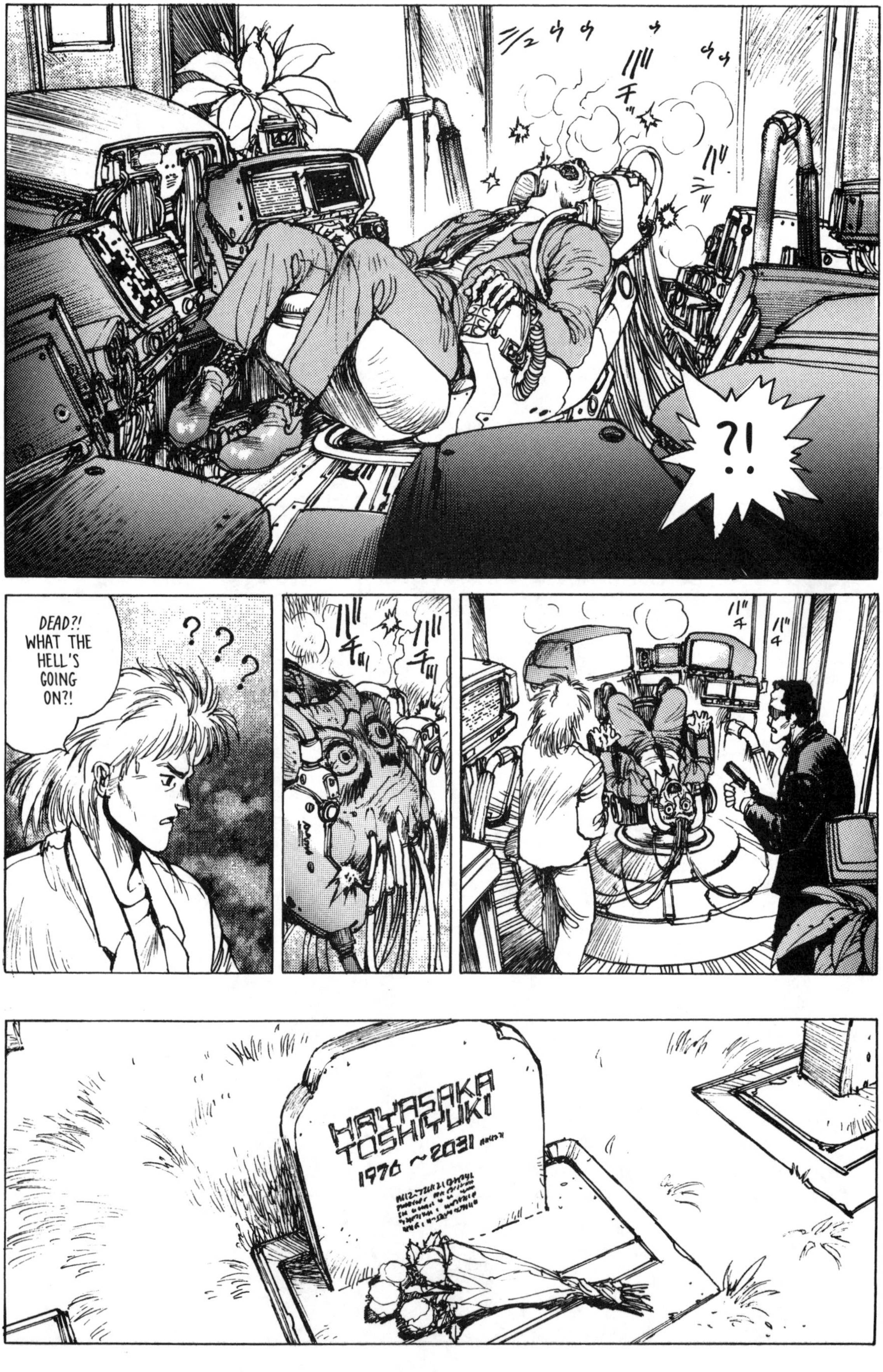
?!
DEAD?! WHAT THE HELL'S GOING ON?!
? ? ?
HAYASAKA TOSHIYUKI
1976 ~ 2031

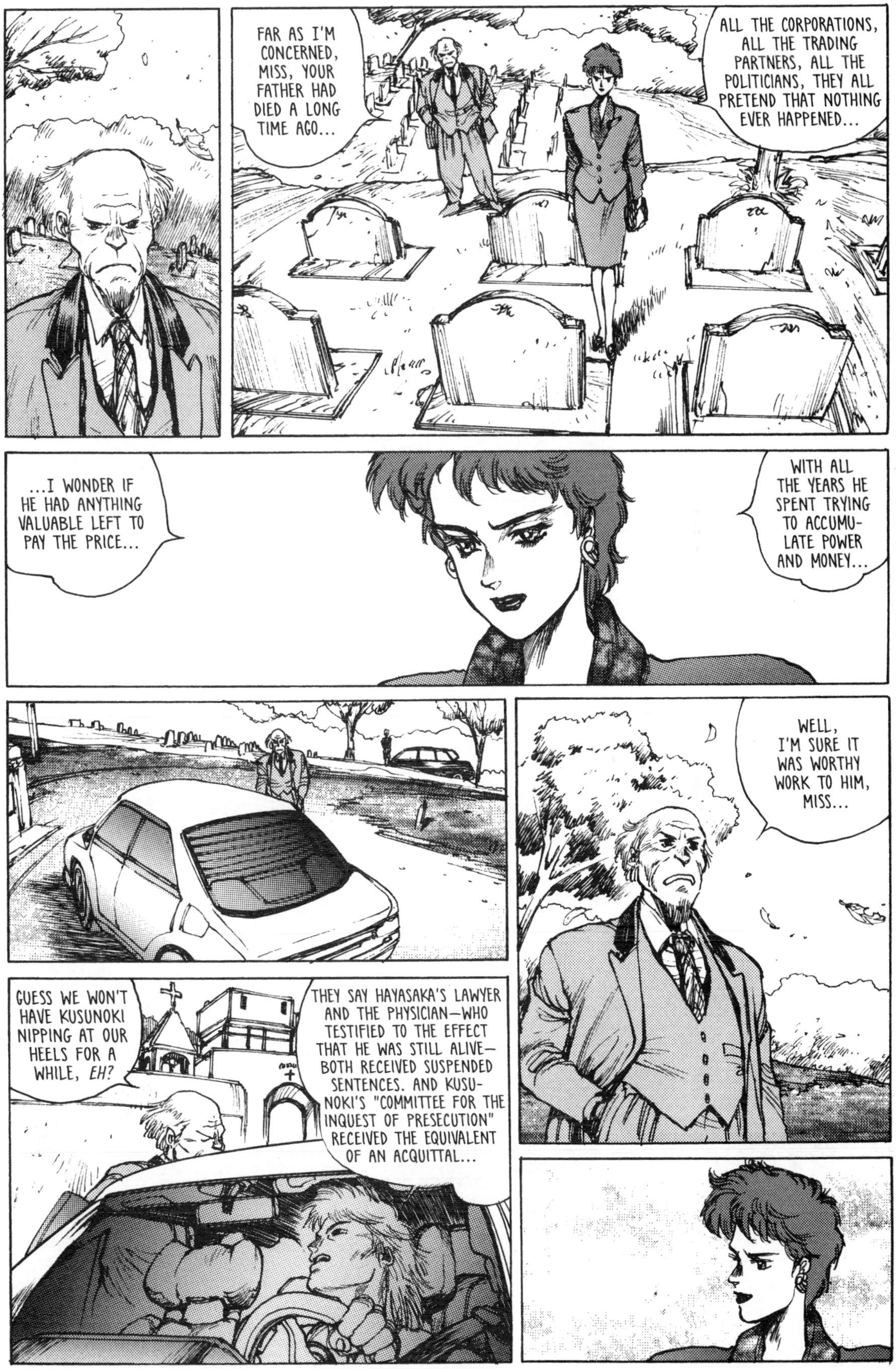
ALL THE CORPORATIONS, ALL THE TRADING PARTNERS, ALL THE POLITICIANS, THEY ALL PRETEND THAT NOTHING EVER HAPPENED...
FAR AS I'M CONCERNED, MISS, YOUR FATHER HAD DIED A LONG TIME AGO...
WITH ALL THE YEARS HE SPENT TRYING TO ACCUMU-LATE POWER AND MONEY...
...I WONDER IF HE HAD ANYTHING VALUABLE LEFT TO PAY THE PRICE...
WELL, I'M SURE IT WAS WORTHY WORK TO HIM, MISS...
THEY SAY HAYASAKA'S LAWYER AND THE PHYSICIAN—WHO TESTIFIED TO THE EFFECT THAT HE WAS STILL ALIVE—BOTH RECEIVED SUSPENDED SENTENCES. AND KUSU-NOKI'S "COMMITTEE FOR THE INQUEST OF PRESECUTION" RECEIVED THE EQUIVALENT OF AN ACQUITTAL...
GUESS WE WON'T HAVE KUSUNOKI NIPPING AT OUR HEELS FOR A WHILE, *EH?*

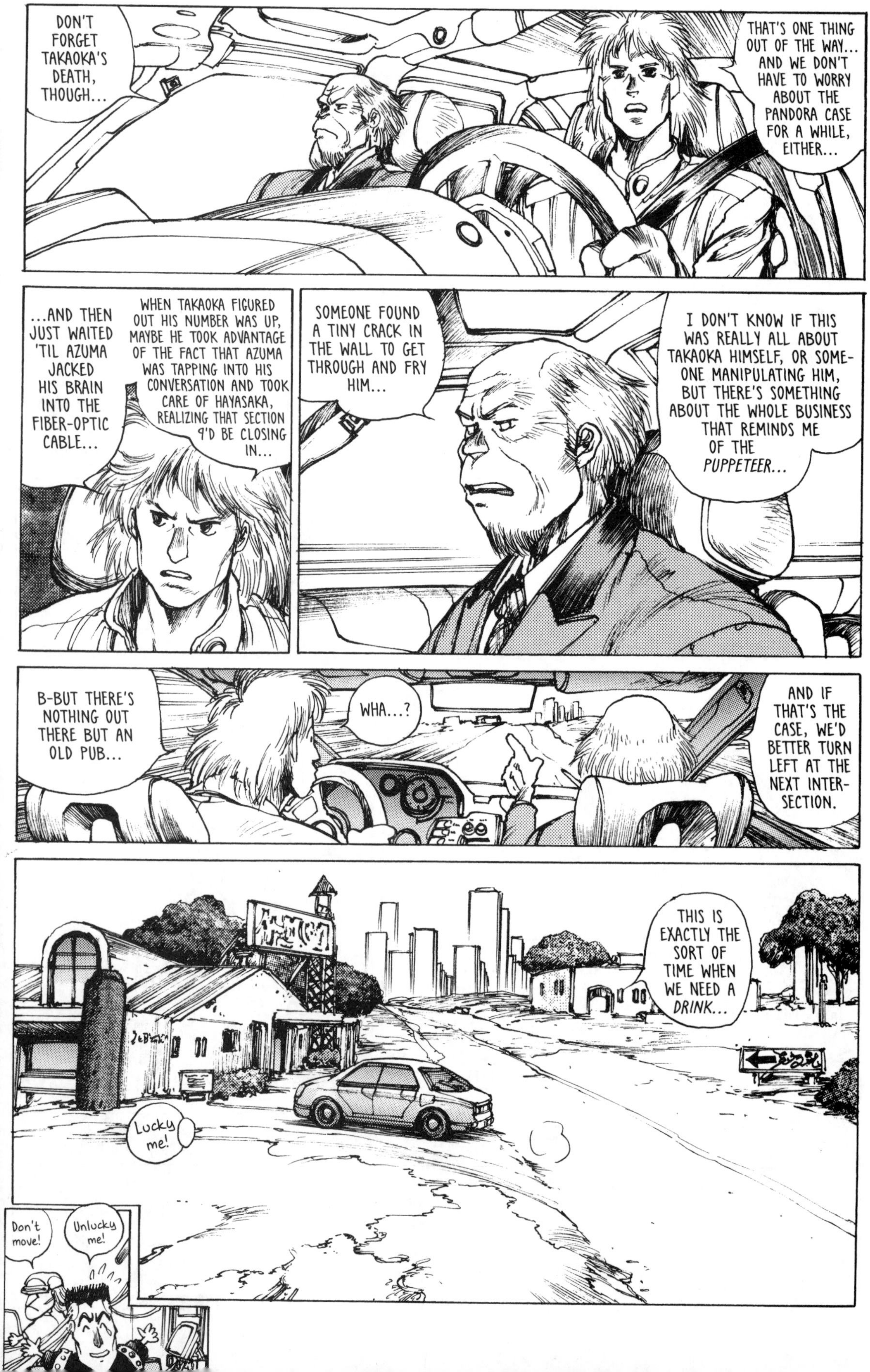
THAT'S ONE THING OUT OF THE WAY... AND WE DON'T HAVE TO WORRY ABOUT THE PANDORA CASE FOR A WHILE, EITHER...
DON'T FORGET TAKAOKA'S DEATH, THOUGH...
I DON'T KNOW IF THIS WAS REALLY ALL ABOUT TAKAOKA HIMSELF, OR SOMEONE MANIPULATING HIM, BUT THERE'S SOMETHING ABOUT THE WHOLE BUSINESS THAT REMINDS ME OF THE *PUPPETEER*...
SOMEONE FOUND A TINY CRACK IN THE WALL TO GET THROUGH AND FRY HIM...
WHEN TAKAOKA FIGURED OUT HIS NUMBER WAS UP, MAYBE HE TOOK ADVANTAGE OF THE FACT THAT AZUMA WAS TAPPING INTO HIS CONVERSATION AND TOOK CARE OF HAYASAKA, REALIZING THAT SECTION 9'D BE CLOSING IN...
...AND THEN JUST WAITED 'TIL AZUMA JACKED HIS BRAIN INTO THE FIBER-OPTIC CABLE...
AND IF THAT'S THE CASE, WE'D BETTER TURN LEFT AT THE NEXT INTERSECTION.
WHA...?
B-BUT THERE'S NOTHING OUT THERE BUT AN OLD PUB...
THIS IS EXACTLY THE SORT OF TIME WHEN WE NEED A *DRINK*...
Lucky me!
Unlucky me!
Don't move!

03

DRIVE SLAVE Part. 1

1992

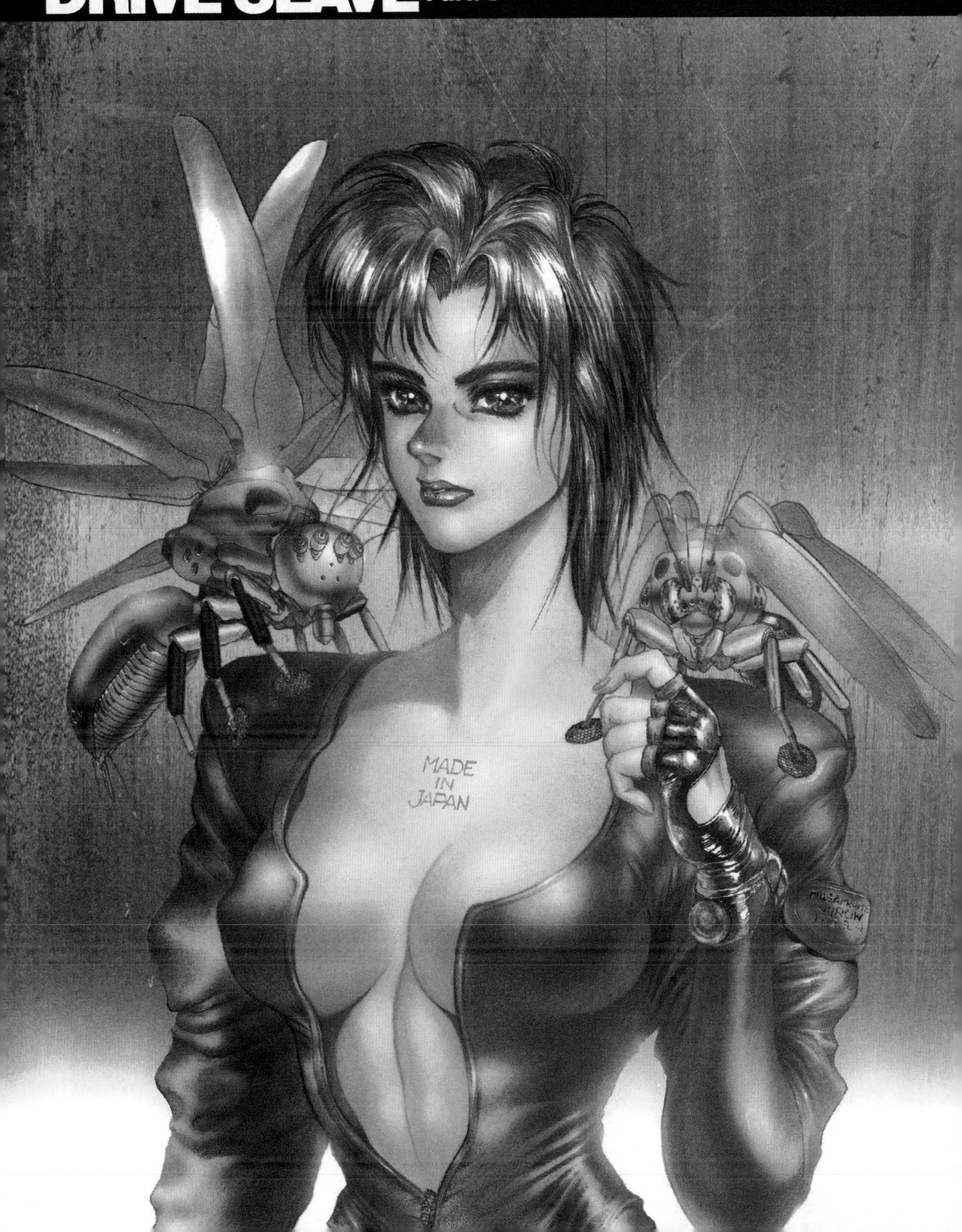
MADE
IN
JAPAN

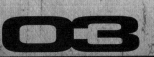

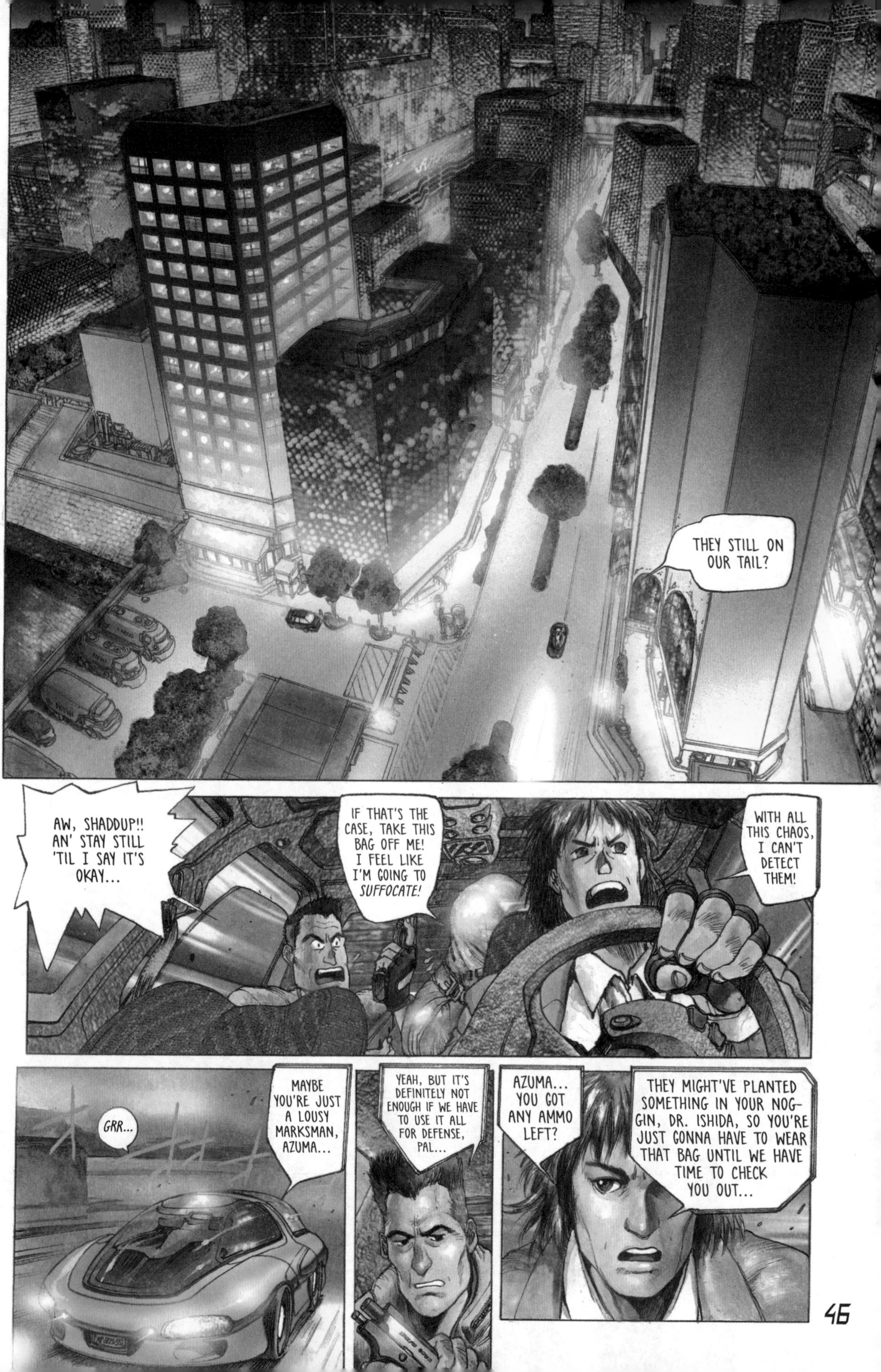
THEY STILL ON OUR TAIL?
WITH ALL THIS CHAOS, I CAN'T DETECT THEM!
IF THAT'S THE CASE, TAKE THIS BAG OFF ME! I FEEL LIKE I'M GOING TO *SUFFOCATE!*
AW, SHADDUP!! AN' STAY STILL 'TIL I SAY IT'S OKAY...
THEY MIGHT'VE PLANTED SOMETHING IN YOUR NOG-GIN, DR. ISHIDA, SO YOU'RE JUST GONNA HAVE TO WEAR THAT BAG UNTIL WE HAVE TIME TO CHECK YOU OUT...
AZUMA... YOU GOT ANY AMMO LEFT?
YEAH, BUT IT'S DEFINITELY NOT ENOUGH IF WE HAVE TO USE IT ALL FOR DEFENSE, PAL...
MAYBE YOU'RE JUST A LOUSY MARKSMAN, AZUMA...
GRR...

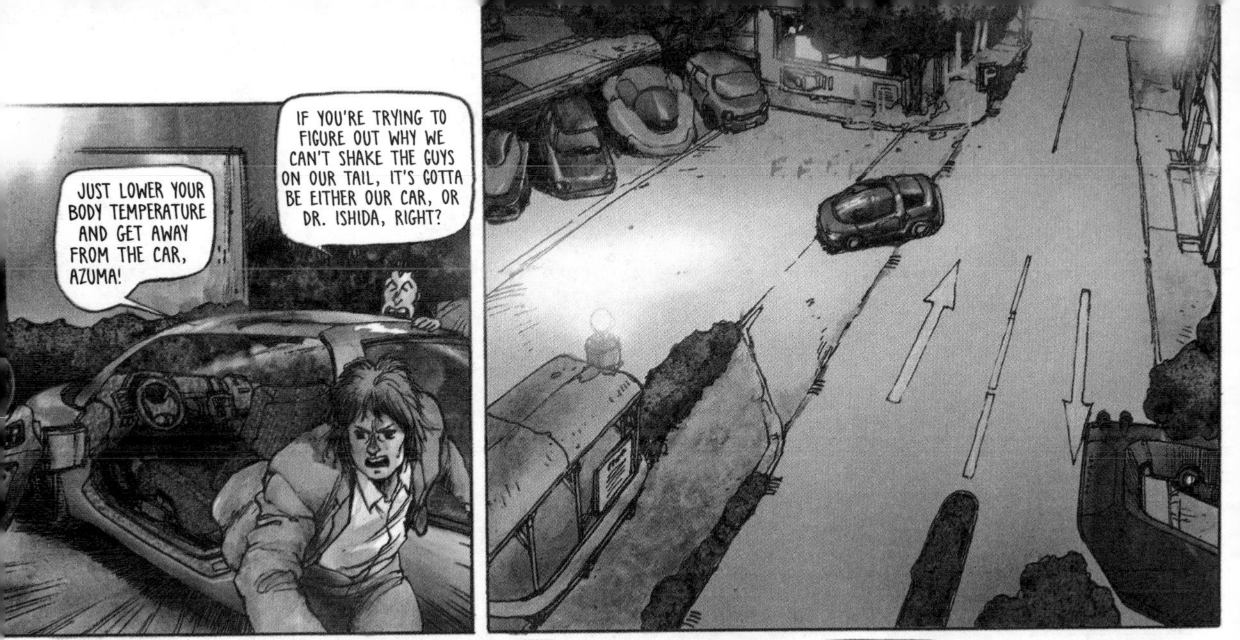
IF YOU'RE TRYING TO FIGURE OUT WHY WE CAN'T SHAKE THE GUYS ON OUR TAIL, IT'S GOTTA BE EITHER OUR CAR, OR DR. ISHIDA, RIGHT?
JUST LOWER YOUR BODY TEMPERATURE AND GET AWAY FROM THE CAR, AZUMA!

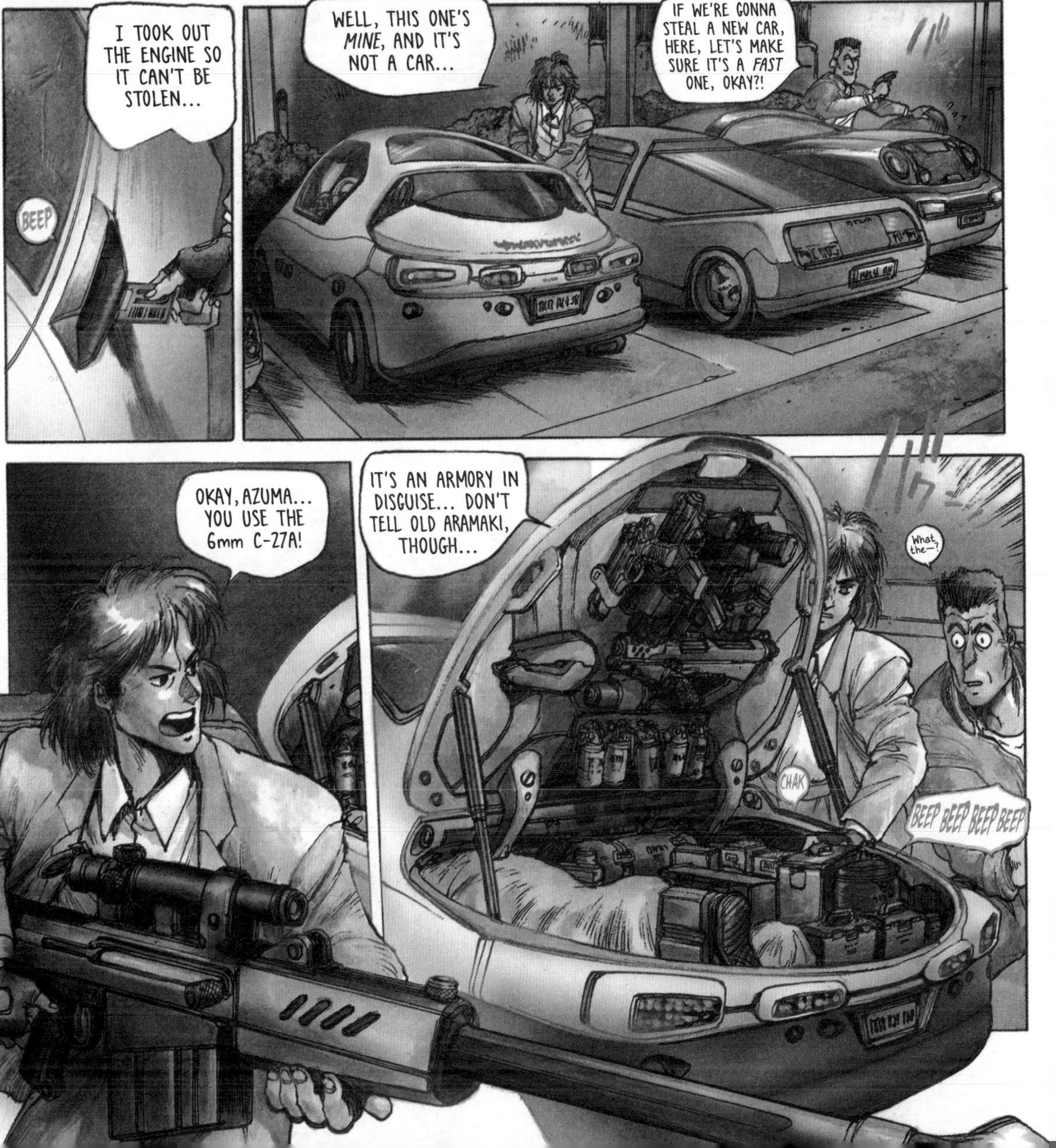
IF WE'RE GONNA STEAL A NEW CAR, HERE, LET'S MAKE SURE IT'S A *FAST* ONE, OKAY?!
WELL, THIS ONE'S *MINE*, AND IT'S NOT A CAR...
I TOOK OUT THE ENGINE SO IT CAN'T BE STOLEN...
BEEP
IT'S AN ARMORY IN DISGUISE... DON'T TELL OLD ARAMAKI, THOUGH...
What the—?
CHAK
BEEP BEEP BEEP BEEP
OKAY, AZUMA... YOU USE THE 6mm C-27A!

THE RIDICULOUSLY ENORMOUS WEAPON TOGUSA'S HOLDING IS A .50 CALIBER RIFLE. IT'S A TYPE OF ANTI-TANK RIFLE, BUT IT'S SOMETIMES USED FOR SNIPING, TOO. I MADE UP THE DETAILS ON THIS GUN, BUT THERE ARE SOME VERY SIMILAR-LOOKING ONES IN THE REAL WORLD. C-27A IS THE NAME FOR A '27 MODEL SEBURO COMPACT 50M SUPPRESSION FIREARM. THE MAGAZINE HOLDS SIX 25MM HESH SHELLS.

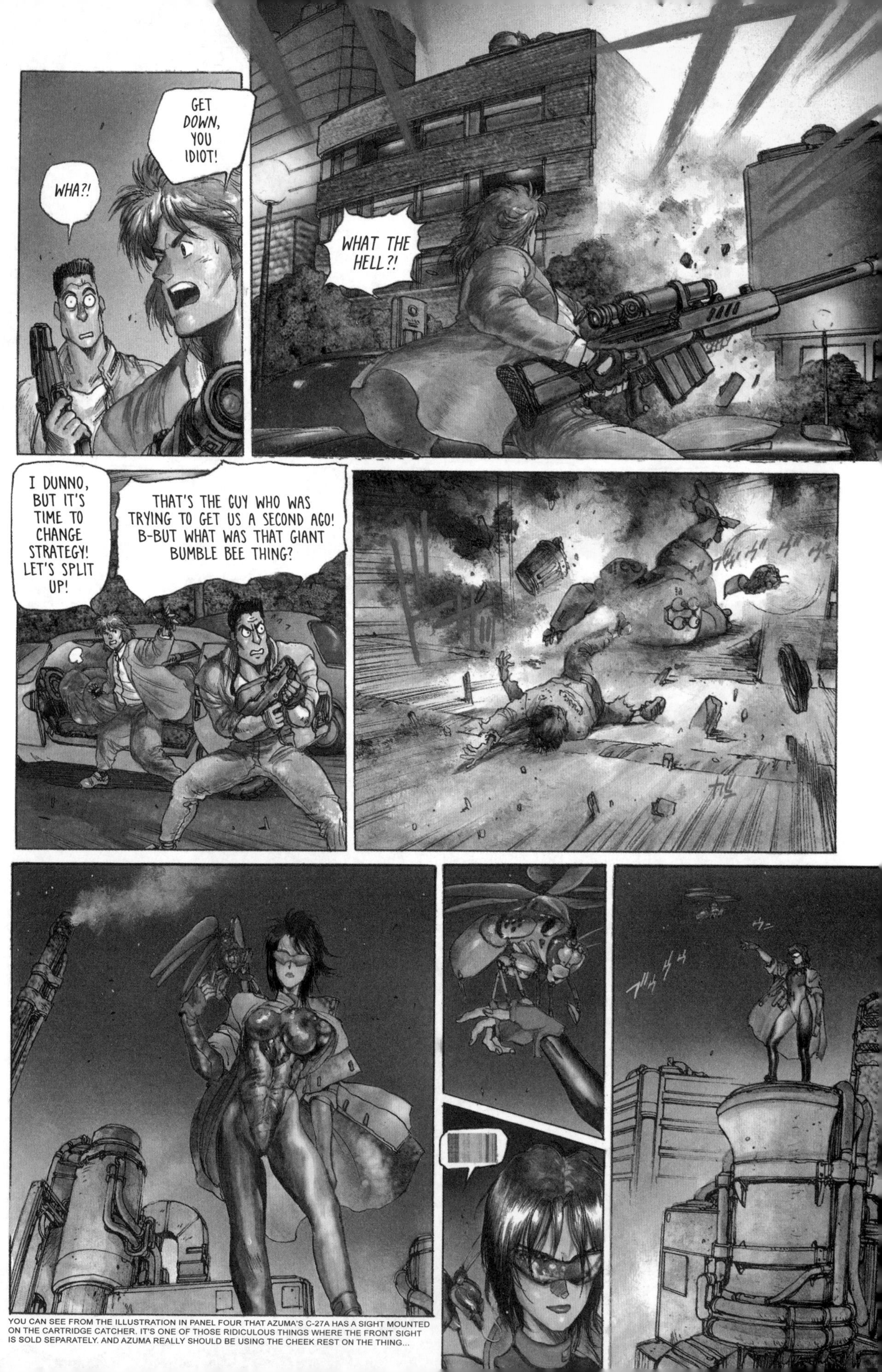
WHAT THE HELL?!
GET DOWN, YOU IDIOT!
WHA?!
THAT'S THE GUY WHO WAS TRYING TO GET US A SECOND AGO! B-BUT WHAT WAS THAT GIANT BUMBLE BEE THING?
I DUNNO, BUT IT'S TIME TO CHANGE STRATEGY! LET'S SPLIT UP!

YOU CAN SEE FROM THE ILLUSTRATION IN PANEL FOUR THAT AZUMA'S C-27A HAS A SIGHT MOUNTED ON THE CARTRIDGE CATCHER. IT'S ONE OF THOSE RIDICULOUS THINGS WHERE THE FRONT SIGHT IS SOLD SEPARATELY. AND AZUMA REALLY SHOULD BE USING THE CHEEK REST ON THE THING...

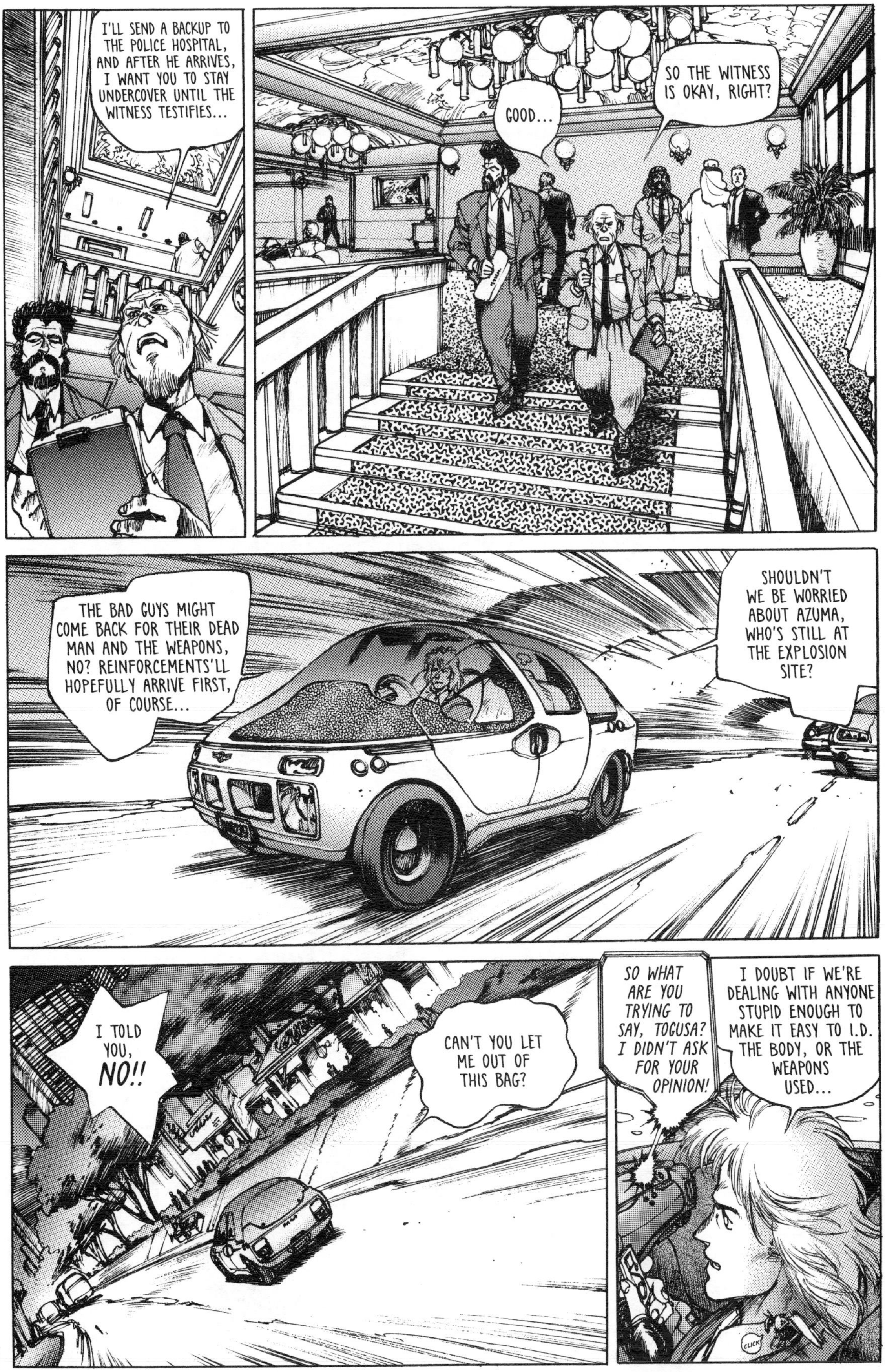
SO THE WITNESS IS OKAY, RIGHT?
GOOD...
I'LL SEND A BACKUP TO THE POLICE HOSPITAL, AND AFTER HE ARRIVES, I WANT YOU TO STAY UNDERCOVER UNTIL THE WITNESS TESTIFIES...
SHOULDN'T WE BE WORRIED ABOUT AZUMA, WHO'S STILL AT THE EXPLOSION SITE?
THE BAD GUYS MIGHT COME BACK FOR THEIR DEAD MAN AND THE WEAPONS, NO? REINFORCEMENTS'LL HOPEFULLY ARRIVE FIRST, OF COURSE...
I DOUBT IF WE'RE DEALING WITH ANYONE STUPID ENOUGH TO MAKE IT EASY TO I.D. THE BODY, OR THE WEAPONS USED...
SO WHAT ARE YOU TRYING TO SAY, TOGUSA? I DIDN'T ASK FOR YOUR OPINION!
CLICK
CAN'T YOU LET ME OUT OF THIS BAG?
I TOLD YOU, NO!!

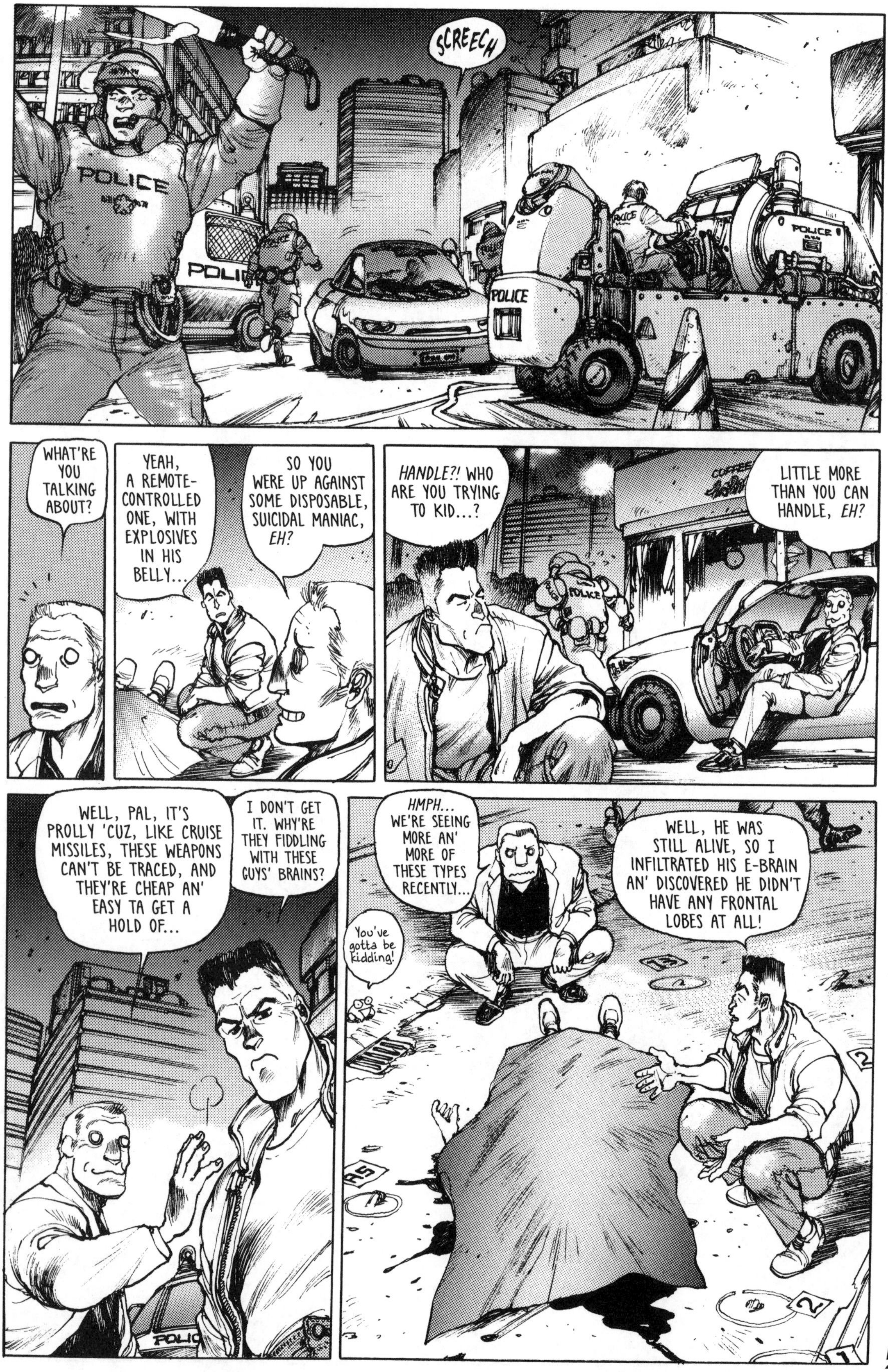
SCREECH
LITTLE MORE THAN YOU CAN HANDLE, *EH?*
HANDLE?! WHO ARE YOU TRYING TO KID...?
SO YOU WERE UP AGAINST SOME DISPOSABLE, SUICIDAL MANIAC, *EH?*
YEAH, A REMOTE-CONTROLLED ONE, WITH EXPLOSIVES IN HIS BELLY...
WHAT'RE YOU TALKING ABOUT?
WELL, HE WAS STILL ALIVE, SO I INFILTRATED HIS E-BRAIN AN' DISCOVERED HE DIDN'T HAVE ANY FRONTAL LOBES AT ALL!
HMPH... WE'RE SEEING MORE AN' MORE OF THESE TYPES RECENTLY...
You've gotta be kidding!
I DON'T GET IT. WHY'RE THEY FIDDLING WITH THESE GUYS' BRAINS?
WELL, PAL, IT'S PROLLY 'CUZ, LIKE CRUISE MISSILES, THESE WEAPONS CAN'T BE TRACED, AND THEY'RE CHEAP AN' EASY TA GET A HOLD OF...

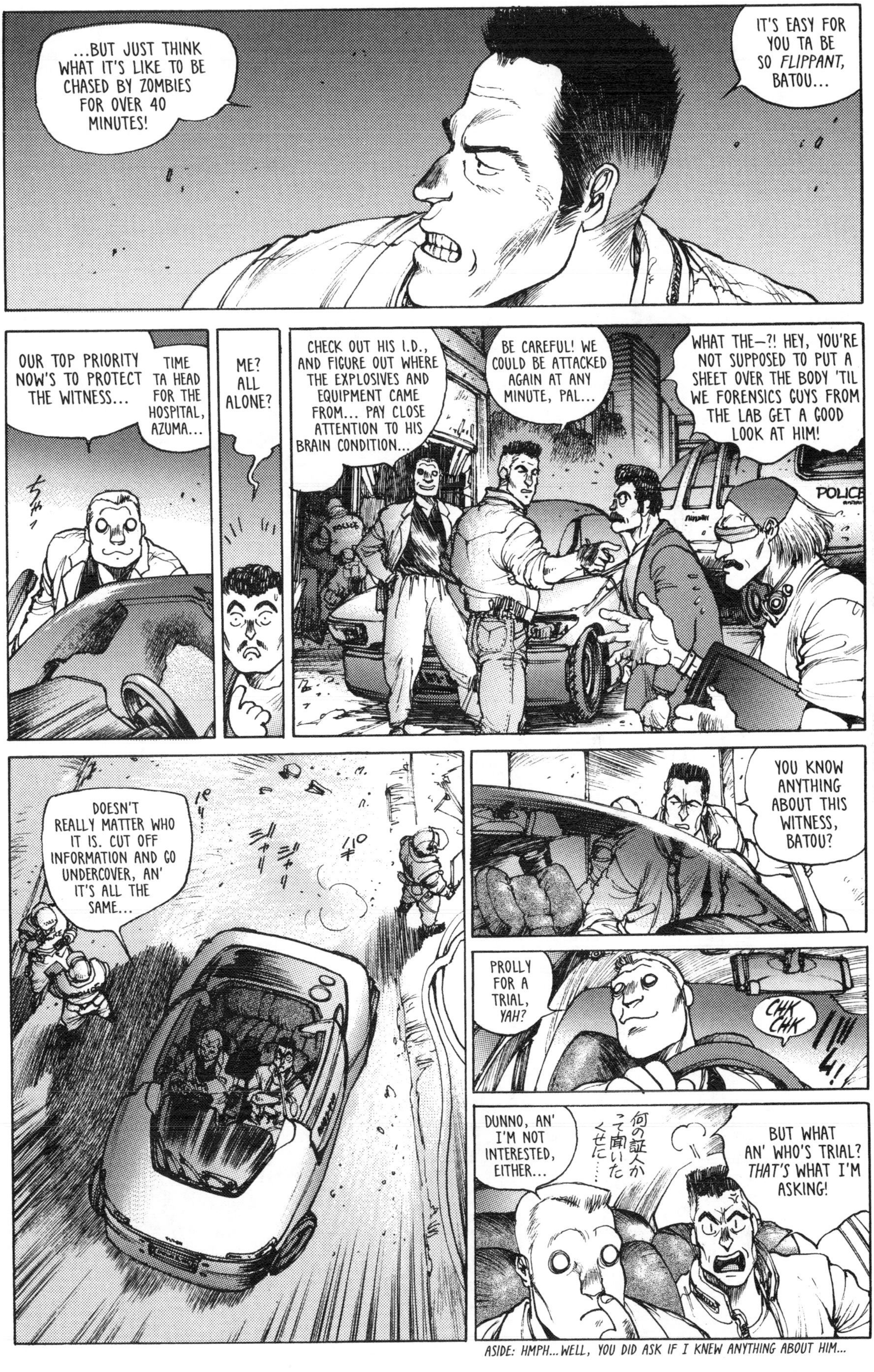
IT'S EASY FOR YOU TA BE SO *FLIPPANT*, BATOU...
...BUT JUST THINK WHAT IT'S LIKE TO BE CHASED BY ZOMBIES FOR OVER 40 MINUTES!
WHAT THE—?! HEY, YOU'RE NOT SUPPOSED TO PUT A SHEET OVER THE BODY 'TIL WE FORENSICS GUYS FROM THE LAB GET A GOOD LOOK AT HIM!
BE CAREFUL! WE COULD BE ATTACKED AGAIN AT ANY MINUTE, PAL...
CHECK OUT HIS I.D., AND FIGURE OUT WHERE THE EXPLOSIVES AND EQUIPMENT CAME FROM... PAY CLOSE ATTENTION TO HIS BRAIN CONDITION...
POLICE
ME? ALL ALONE?
OUR TOP PRIORITY NOW'S TO PROTECT THE WITNESS...
TIME TA HEAD FOR THE HOSPITAL, AZUMA...
YOU KNOW ANYTHING ABOUT THIS WITNESS, BATOU?
PROLLY FOR A TRIAL, *YAH?*
CHK CHK
BUT WHAT AN' WHO'S TRIAL? *THAT'S* WHAT I'M ASKING!
何の証人かって聞いたくせに……
DUNNO, AN' I'M NOT INTERESTED, EITHER...
DOESN'T REALLY MATTER WHO IT IS. CUT OFF INFORMATION AND GO UNDERCOVER, AN' IT'S ALL THE SAME...

ASIDE: HMPH... WELL, YOU DID ASK IF I KNEW ANYTHING ABOUT HIM...

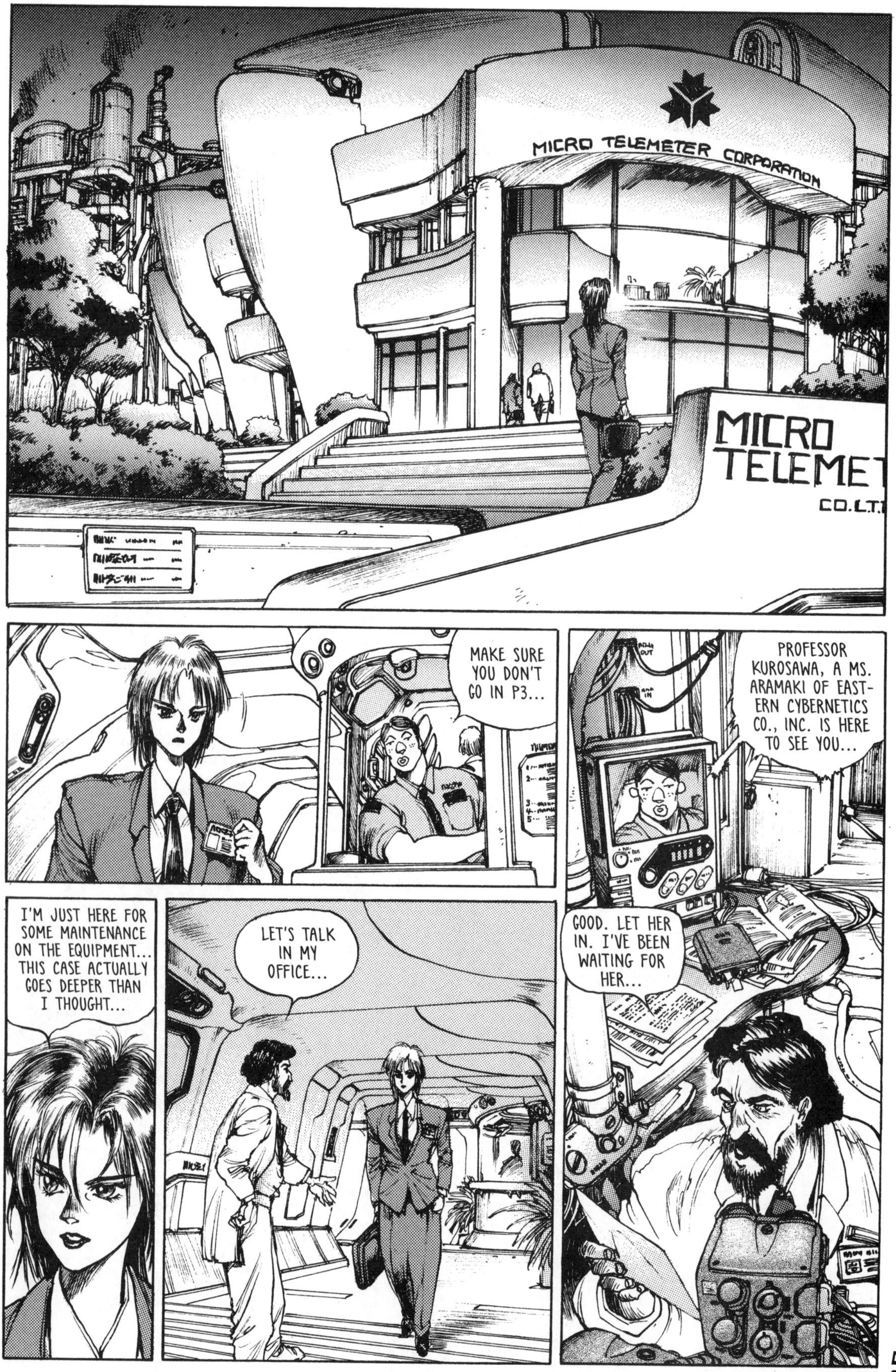
MICRO TELEMETER CORPORATION
MICRO TELEMET
CO.L.T.
PROFESSOR KUROSAWA, A MS. ARAMAKI OF EASTERN CYBERNETICS CO., INC. IS HERE TO SEE YOU...
GOOD. LET HER IN. I'VE BEEN WAITING FOR HER...
MAKE SURE YOU DON'T GO IN P3...
LET'S TALK IN MY OFFICE...
I'M JUST HERE FOR SOME MAINTENANCE ON THE EQUIPMENT... THIS CASE ACTUALLY GOES DEEPER THAN I THOUGHT...

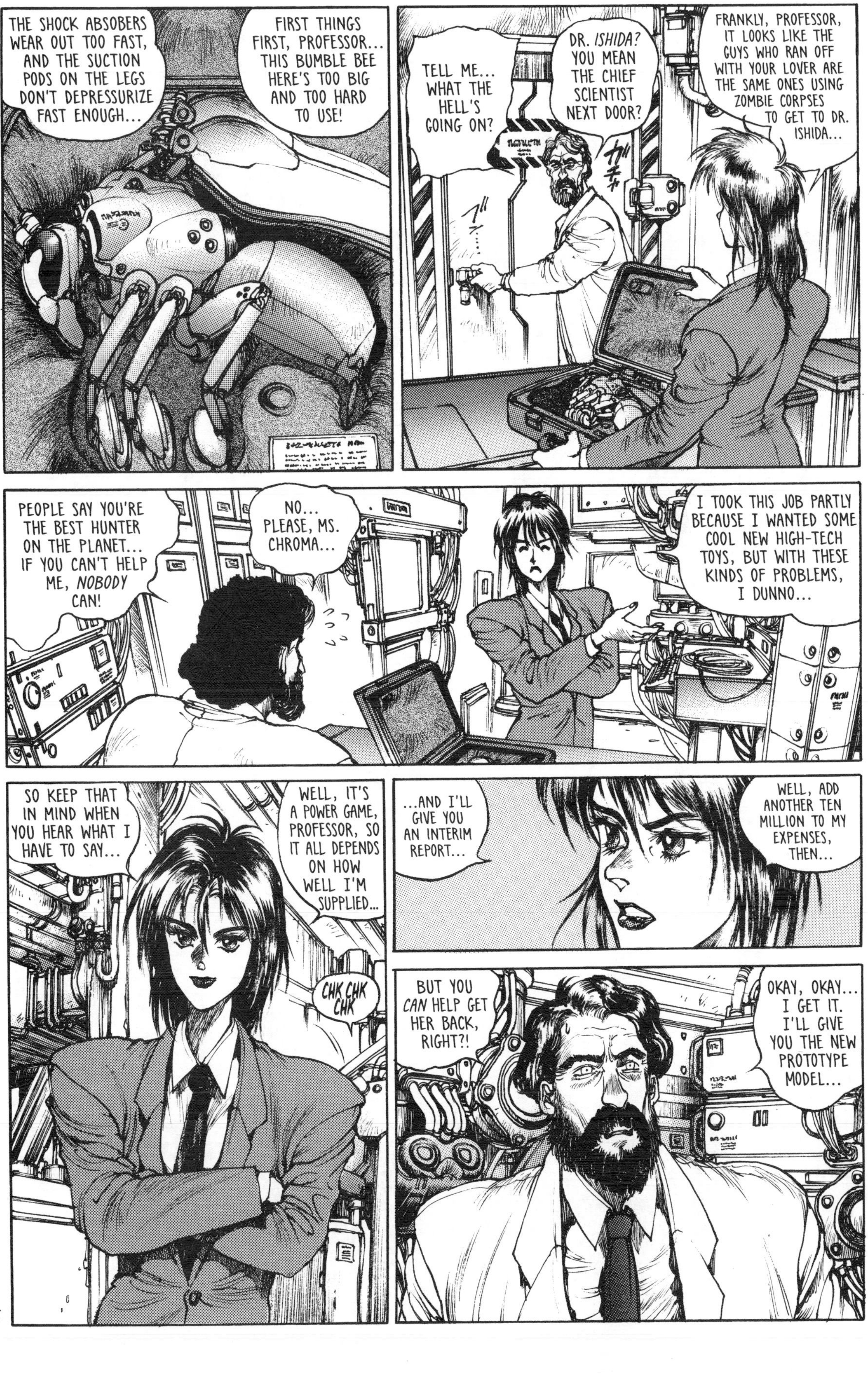
FRANKLY, PROFESSOR, IT LOOKS LIKE THE GUYS WHO RAN OFF WITH YOUR LOVER ARE THE SAME ONES USING ZOMBIE CORPSES TO GET TO DR. ISHIDA...
DR. *ISHIDA?* YOU MEAN THE CHIEF SCIENTIST NEXT DOOR?
TELL ME... WHAT THE HELL'S GOING ON?
FIRST THINGS FIRST, PROFESSOR... THIS BUMBLE BEE HERE'S TOO BIG AND TOO HARD TO USE!
THE SHOCK ABSOBERS WEAR OUT TOO FAST, AND THE SUCTION PODS ON THE LEGS DON'T DEPRESSURIZE FAST ENOUGH...
I TOOK THIS JOB PARTLY BECAUSE I WANTED SOME COOL NEW HIGH-TECH TOYS, BUT WITH THESE KINDS OF PROBLEMS, I DUNNO...
NO... PLEASE, MS. CHROMA...
PEOPLE SAY YOU'RE THE BEST HUNTER ON THE PLANET... IF YOU CAN'T HELP ME, *NOBODY* CAN!
WELL, ADD ANOTHER TEN MILLION TO MY EXPENSES, THEN...
...AND I'LL GIVE YOU AN INTERIM REPORT...
OKAY, OKAY... I GET IT. I'LL GIVE YOU THE NEW PROTOTYPE MODEL...
BUT YOU *CAN* HELP GET HER BACK, RIGHT?!
WELL, IT'S A POWER GAME, PROFESSOR, SO IT ALL DEPENDS ON HOW WELL I'M SUPPLIED...
SO KEEP THAT IN MIND WHEN YOU HEAR WHAT I HAVE TO SAY...
CHK CHK CHK

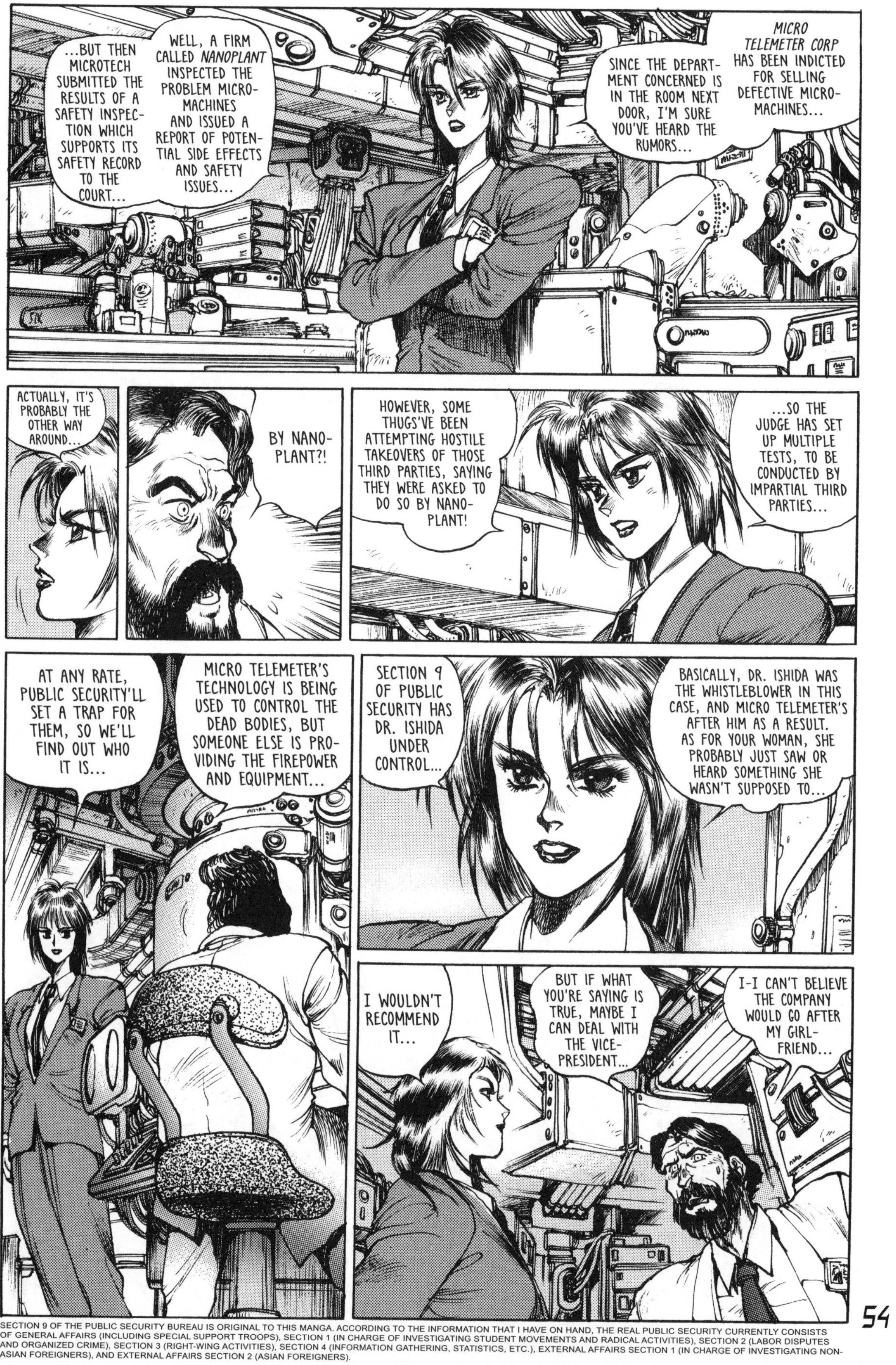
MICRO TELEMETER CORP HAS BEEN INDICTED FOR SELLING DEFECTIVE MICRO-MACHINES...
SINCE THE DEPARTMENT CONCERNED IS IN THE ROOM NEXT DOOR, I'M SURE YOU'VE HEARD THE RUMORS...
WELL, A FIRM CALLED NANOPLANT INSPECTED THE PROBLEM MICRO-MACHINES AND ISSUED A REPORT OF POTENTIAL SIDE EFFECTS AND SAFETY ISSUES...
...BUT THEN MICROTECH SUBMITTED THE RESULTS OF A SAFETY INSPECTION WHICH SUPPORTS ITS SAFETY RECORD TO THE COURT...
...SO THE JUDGE HAS SET UP MULTIPLE TESTS, TO BE CONDUCTED BY IMPARTIAL THIRD PARTIES...
HOWEVER, SOME THUGS'VE BEEN ATTEMPTING HOSTILE TAKEOVERS OF THOSE THIRD PARTIES, SAYING THEY WERE ASKED TO DO SO BY NANO-PLANT!
BY NANO-PLANT?!
ACTUALLY, IT'S PROBABLY THE OTHER WAY AROUND...
BASICALLY, DR. ISHIDA WAS THE WHISTLEBLOWER IN THIS CASE, AND MICRO TELEMETER'S AFTER HIM AS A RESULT. AS FOR YOUR WOMAN, SHE PROBABLY JUST SAW OR HEARD SOMETHING SHE WASN'T SUPPOSED TO...
SECTION 9 OF PUBLIC SECURITY HAS DR. ISHIDA UNDER CONTROL...
I-I CAN'T BELIEVE THE COMPANY WOULD GO AFTER MY GIRL-FRIEND...
BUT IF WHAT YOU'RE SAYING IS TRUE, MAYBE I CAN DEAL WITH THE VICE-PRESIDENT...
I WOULDN'T RECOMMEND IT...
MICRO TELEMETER'S TECHNOLOGY IS BEING USED TO CONTROL THE DEAD BODIES, BUT SOMEONE ELSE IS PROVIDING THE FIREPOWER AND EQUIPMENT...
AT ANY RATE, PUBLIC SECURITY'LL SET A TRAP FOR THEM, SO WE'LL FIND OUT WHO IT IS...

SECTION 9 OF THE PUBLIC SECURITY BUREAU IS ORIGINAL TO THIS MANGA. ACCORDING TO THE INFORMATION THAT I HAVE ON HAND, THE REAL PUBLIC SECURITY CURRENTLY CONSISTS OF GENERAL AFFAIRS (INCLUDING SPECIAL SUPPORT TROOPS), SECTION 1 (IN CHARGE OF INVESTIGATING STUDENT MOVEMENTS AND RADICAL ACTIVITIES), SECTION 2 (LABOR DISPUTES AND ORGANIZED CRIME), SECTION 3 (RIGHT-WING ACTIVITIES), SECTION 4 (INFORMATION GATHERING, STATISTICS, ETC.), EXTERNAL AFFAIRS SECTION 1 (IN CHARGE OF INVESTIGATING NON-ASIAN FOREIGNERS), AND EXTERNAL AFFAIRS SECTION 2 (ASIAN FOREIGNERS).

MACHINE: M.R. TEST UNIT

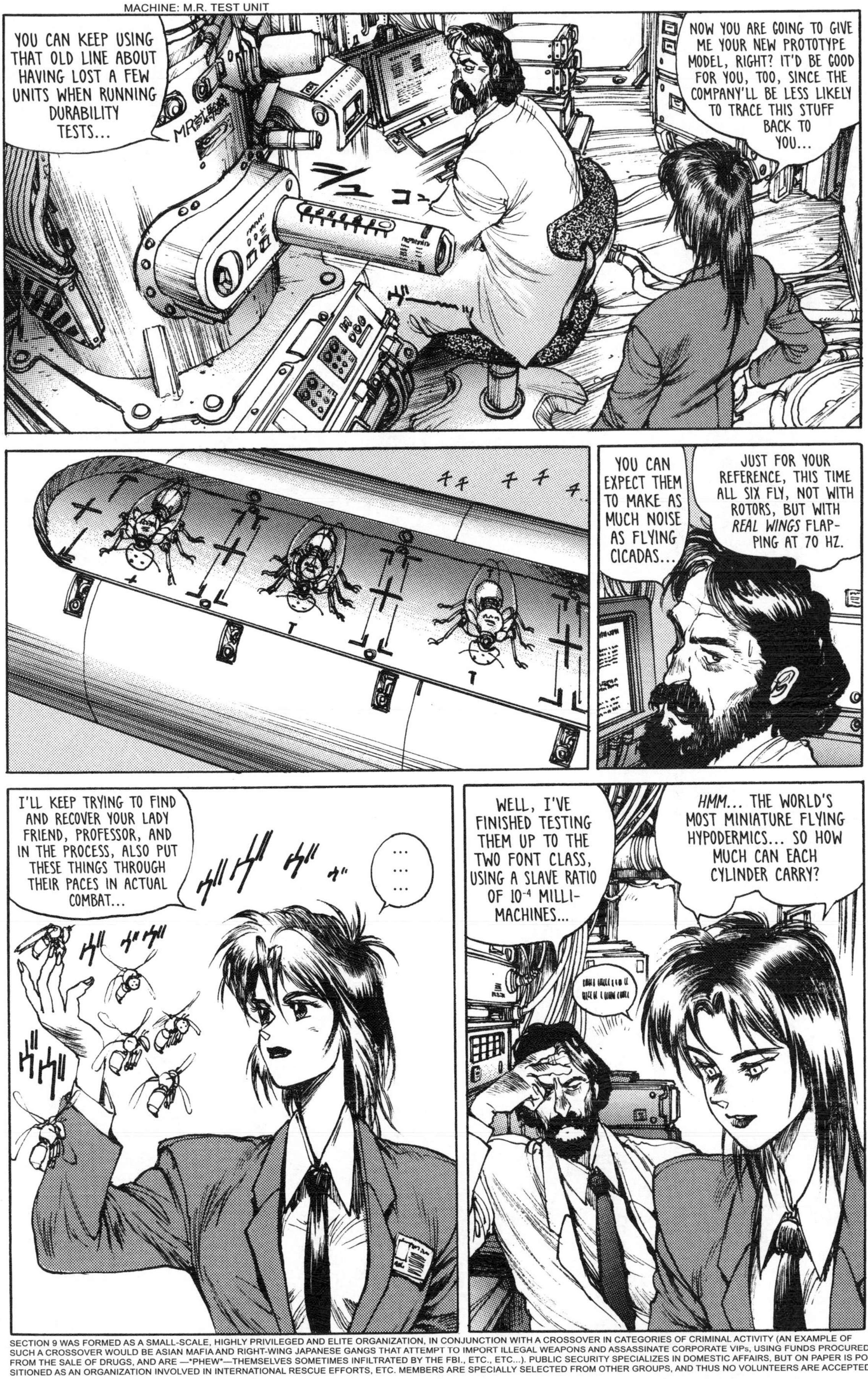

NOW YOU ARE GOING TO GIVE ME YOUR NEW PROTOTYPE MODEL, RIGHT? IT'D BE GOOD FOR YOU, TOO, SINCE THE COMPANY'LL BE LESS LIKELY TO TRACE THIS STUFF BACK TO YOU...
YOU CAN KEEP USING THAT OLD LINE ABOUT HAVING LOST A FEW UNITS WHEN RUNNING DURABILITY TESTS...
JUST FOR YOUR REFERENCE, THIS TIME ALL SIX FLY, NOT WITH ROTORS, BUT WITH *REAL WINGS* FLAPPING AT 70 HZ.
YOU CAN EXPECT THEM TO MAKE AS MUCH NOISE AS FLYING CICADAS...
HMM... THE WORLD'S MOST MINIATURE FLYING HYPODERMICS... SO HOW MUCH CAN EACH CYLINDER CARRY?
WELL, I'VE FINISHED TESTING THEM UP TO THE TWO FONT CLASS, USING A SLAVE RATIO OF 10^{-4} MILLI-MACHINES...
...
...
...
I'LL KEEP TRYING TO FIND AND RECOVER YOUR LADY FRIEND, PROFESSOR, AND IN THE PROCESS, ALSO PUT THESE THINGS THROUGH THEIR PACES IN ACTUAL COMBAT...

SECTION 9 WAS FORMED AS A SMALL-SCALE, HIGHLY PRIVILEGED AND ELITE ORGANIZATION, IN CONJUNCTION WITH A CROSSOVER IN CATEGORIES OF CRIMINAL ACTIVITY (AN EXAMPLE OF SUCH A CROSSOVER WOULD BE ASIAN MAFIA AND RIGHT-WING JAPANESE GANGS THAT ATTEMPT TO IMPORT ILLEGAL WEAPONS AND ASSASSINATE CORPORATE VIPs, USING FUNDS PROCURED FROM THE SALE OF DRUGS, AND ARE —*PHEW*—THEMSELVES SOMETIMES INFILTRATED BY THE FBI., ETC., ETC...). PUBLIC SECURITY SPECIALIZES IN DOMESTIC AFFAIRS, BUT ON PAPER IS POSITIONED AS AN ORGANIZATION INVOLVED IN INTERNATIONAL RESCUE EFFORTS, ETC. MEMBERS ARE SPECIALLY SELECTED FROM OTHER GROUPS, AND THUS NO VOLUNTEERS ARE ACCEPTED.

SIGN: SHINHAMA CENTRAL POLICE HOSPITAL

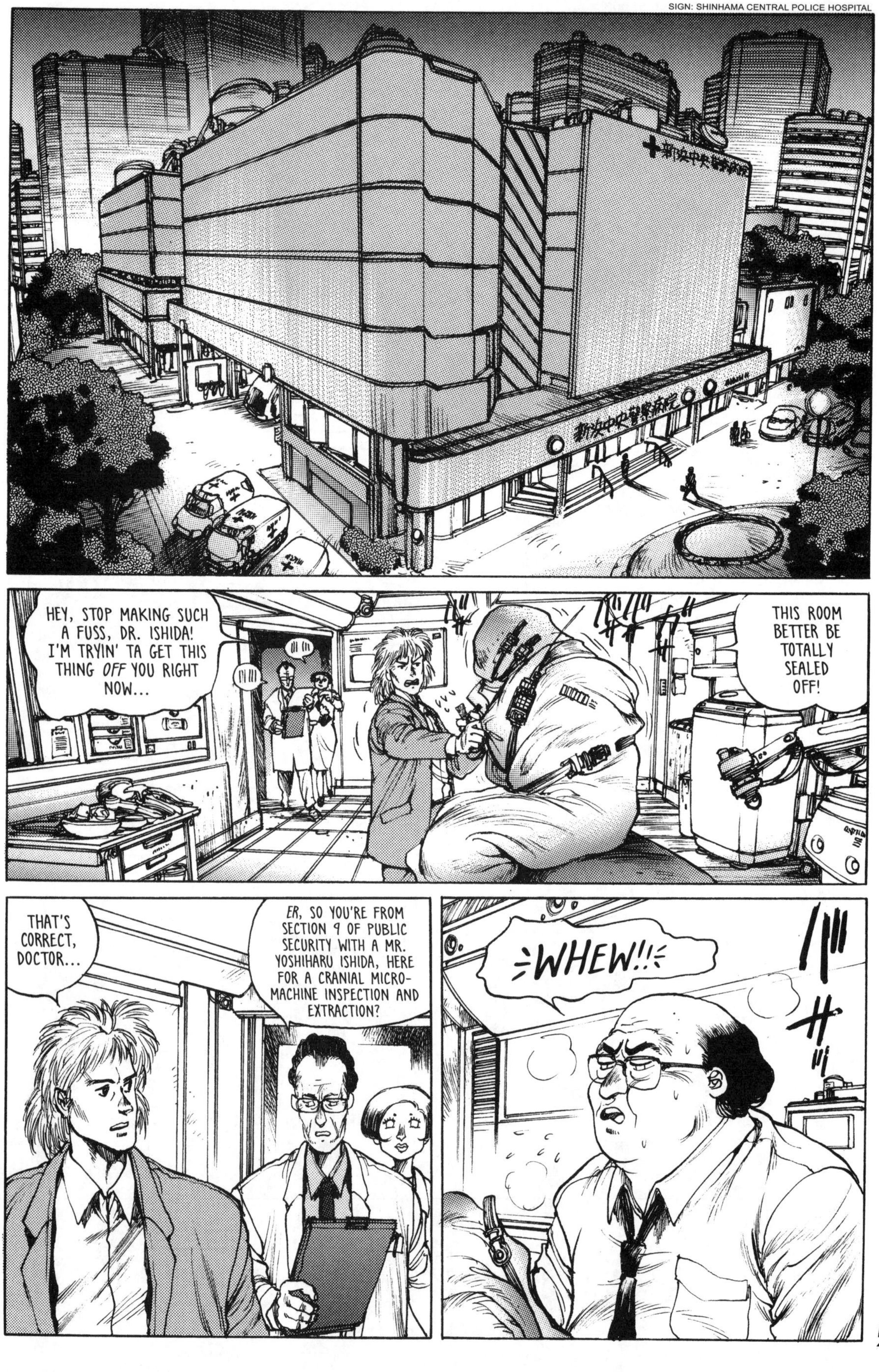
THIS ROOM BETTER BE TOTALLY SEALED OFF!
HEY, STOP MAKING SUCH A FUSS, DR. ISHIDA! I'M TRYIN' TA GET THIS THING *OFF* YOU RIGHT NOW...
WHEW!!
ER, SO YOU'RE FROM SECTION 9 OF PUBLIC SECURITY WITH A MR. YOSHIHARU ISHIDA, HERE FOR A CRANIAL MICRO-MACHINE INSPECTION AND EXTRACTION?
THAT'S CORRECT, DOCTOR...

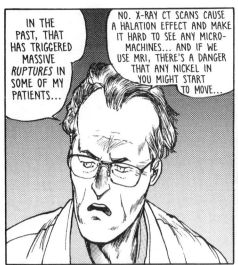

ANY ROOMS AVAILABLE FOR SONOGRAPHY? YOU SAY NUMBER FOUR'S OPEN? GOOD... RESERVE IT THEN...
WHA? YOU'RE NOT GOING TO DO A CT SCAN?
NO. X-RAY CT SCANS CAUSE A HALATION EFFECT AND MAKE IT HARD TO SEE ANY MICRO-MACHINES... AND IF WE USE MRI, THERE'S A DANGER THAT ANY NICKEL IN YOU MIGHT START TO MOVE...
IN THE PAST, THAT HAS TRIGGERED MASSIVE *RUPTURES* IN SOME OF MY PATIENTS...
PUT HIM UNDER AND TAKE HIM INTO THE ROOM, NURSE...
Y-YOU'RE GONNA *ANESTHETIZE* ME? B-BUT...
PSHH
YEAH... HOW COME YOU'RE USING ANESTHESIA?
DUNNO WHO YOU ARE, PAL, BUT I HATE PATIENTS WHO MAKE COMMENTS LIKE THAT...
BEEP

I DON'T MEAN TO IMPLY THAT NICKEL IS THE ONLY THING THAT WOULD MOVE IN THE HUMAN BODY WHEN DOING AN MRI... OTHER ELEMENTS WITH STRONG MAGNETIC SUSCEPTIBILITY, FROM SCANDIUM TO LEAD, WOULD ALSO BE A PROBLEM. THE AUTHOR OF THIS STORY (ME) CHOSE NICKEL HERE BECAUSE IT WOULD LIKELY BE USED NEAR E-BRAIN MICROMACHINES AND TRANSFORMERS. NICKEL-TITANIUM ALLOYS AND GRADE 316 STAINLESS STEEL WOULD ALSO PRESENT THE MOST PROBLEMS WITH BIOCOMPATIBILITY... I'VE NEVER DONE ANY EXPERIMENTS IN THIS REGARD, OF COURSE, OR EVEN DESIGNED ANY MICROMACHINES. AND WHAT THE DOCTOR REFERS TO AS "NICKEL" HERE IS IN REALITY PROBABLY THE FERROMAGNETIC MATERIAL NiO-Fe203 (FERRITES ARE, OF COURSE, USED IN STUFF LIKE HIGH-FREQUENCY TRANSFORMERS AND MAGNETIC RECORDING DEVICES...).

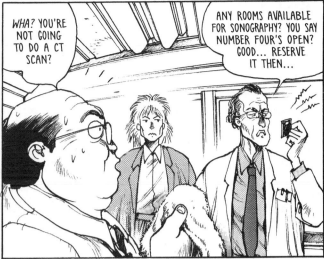

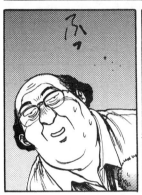

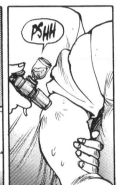

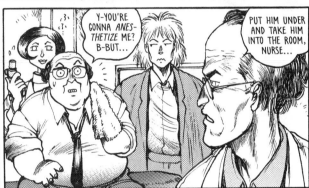

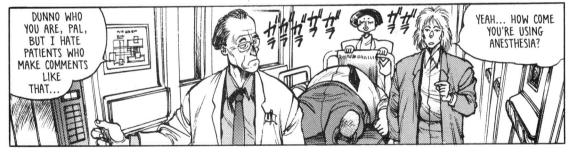

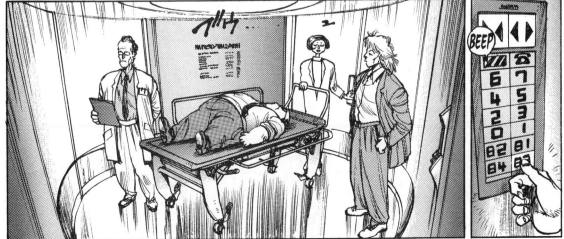

SIGN: SHINHAMA CENTRAL POLICE HOSPITAL

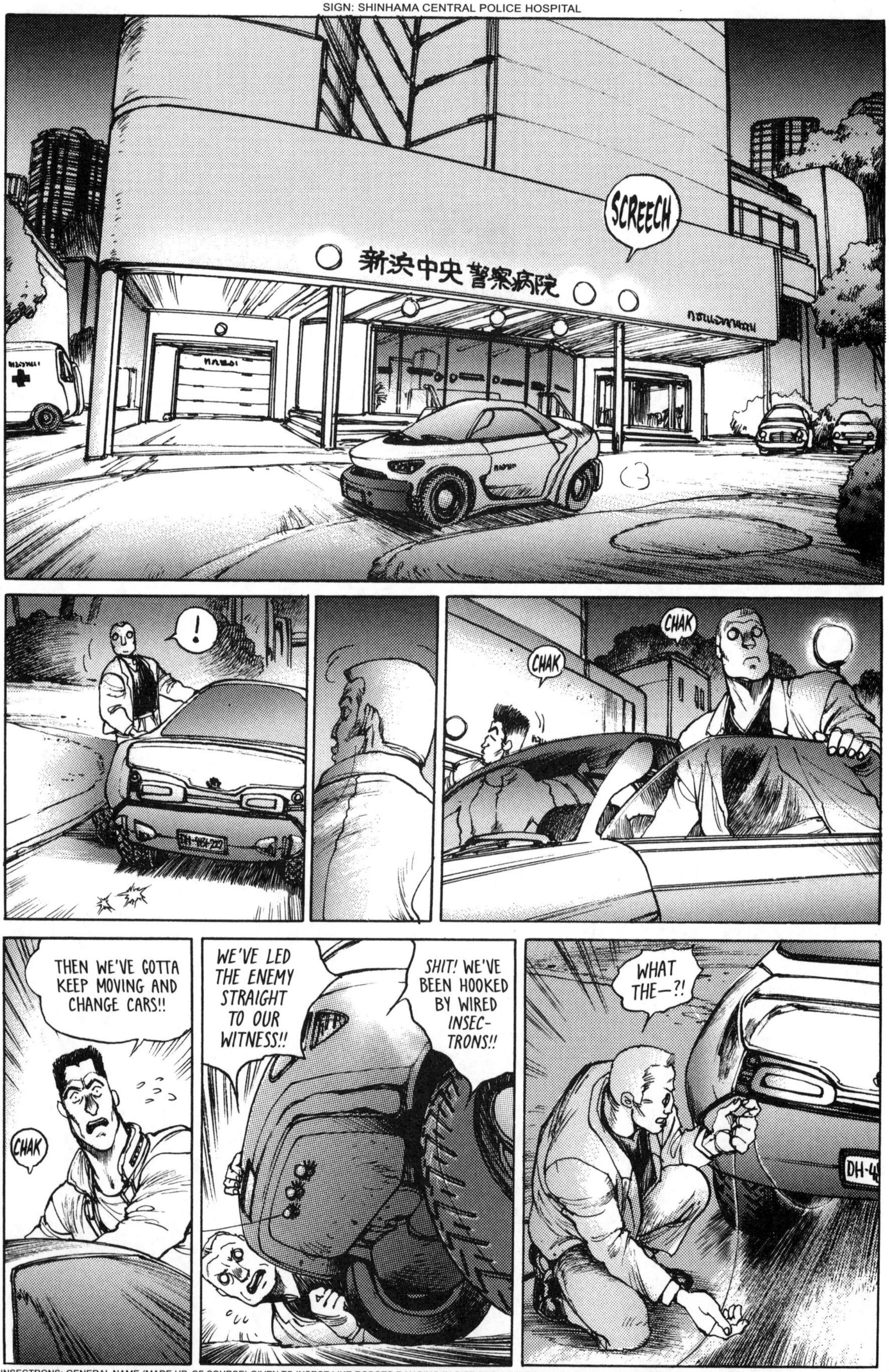

SCREECH
新浜中央警察病院
CHAK
CHAK
!
WHAT THE—?!
SHIT! WE'VE BEEN HOOKED BY WIRED INSEC-TRONS!!
WE'VE LED THE ENEMY STRAIGHT TO OUR WITNESS!!
THEN WE'VE GOTTA KEEP MOVING AND CHANGE CARS!!
CHAK

INSECTRONS: GENERAL NAME (MADE UP, OF COURSE) GIVEN TO INSECT-LIKE ROBOTS RANGING IN SIZE FROM SEVERAL MILLIMETERS TO SEVERAL CENTIMETERS. MICROMACHINING IS CURRENTLY A HOT FIELD OF RESEARCH, AND THERE IS A GREAT DEAL OF ANTICIPATION THAT FUTURE APPLICATIONS OF THE TECHNOLOGY COULD INCLUDE INSECT PEST ERADICATION OR PERFORMANCE OF MAINTENANCE PROCEDURES (INCLUDING INTERIOR PHOTOGRAPHY) ON TINY CAPILLARIES AND VESSELS. LARGER-SCALE APPLICATIONS ARE REPORTEDLY ALREADY IN USE. IN ADDITION TO SUCH MECHANICAL ENGINEERING APPROACHES, SOME SCIENTISTS ARE ALSO ATTEMPTING TO USE GENETICALLY ENGINEERED BIO-ORGANISMS TO ACCOMPLISH SIMILAR TASKS. RATHER THAN REFER TO "ROBOTS" IN THIS CASE, I PROBABLY SHOULD JUST SAY "DEVICES"...

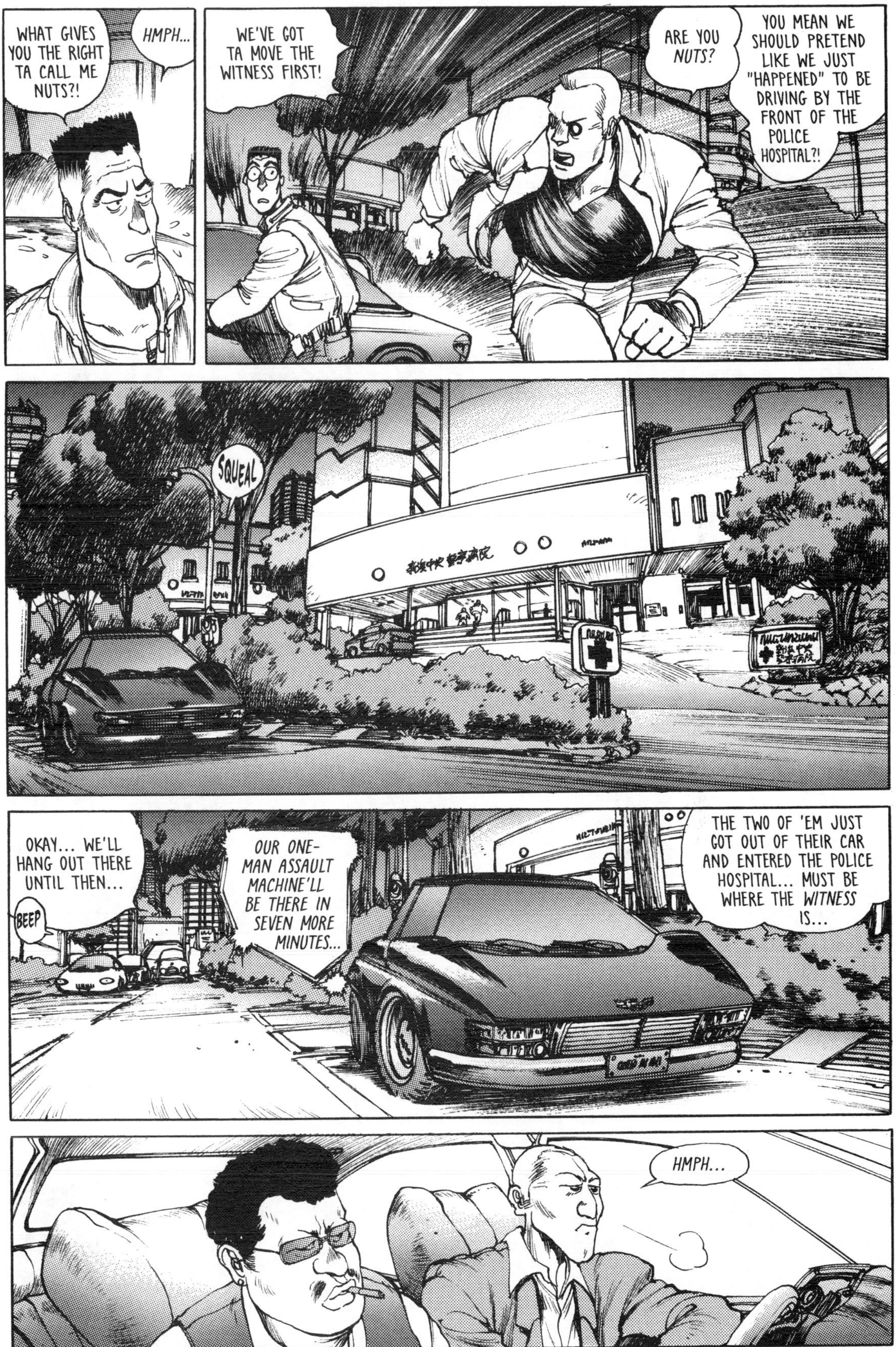
YOU MEAN WE SHOULD PRETEND LIKE WE JUST "HAPPENED" TO BE DRIVING BY THE FRONT OF THE POLICE HOSPITAL?!
ARE YOU *NUTS?*
WE'VE GOT TA MOVE THE WITNESS FIRST!
HMPH...
WHAT GIVES YOU THE RIGHT TA CALL ME NUTS?!
SQUEAL
THE TWO OF 'EM JUST GOT OUT OF THEIR CAR AND ENTERED THE POLICE HOSPITAL... MUST BE WHERE THE *WITNESS* IS...
OUR ONE-MAN ASSAULT MACHINE'LL BE THERE IN SEVEN MORE MINUTES...
OKAY... WE'LL HANG OUT THERE UNTIL THEN...
BEEP
HMPH...

REGARDING THE SPIDER THREADS SHOWN ON THE PREVIOUS PAGE, LIKE REAL SPIDER THREADS, THESE ARE "EXTRACTED" FROM A TANK IN THE BELLY OF A TINY ROBOT. BUT THAT DOESN'T MEAN THAT THE THREADS ARE ACTUALLY WOUND AND STORED ON AN INTERNAL REEL STRUCTURE (I USED TO THINK THAT SPIDER THREADS WERE CREATED THROUGH SOME SORT OF PHYSICAL INTERACTION OF LIQUID WITH THE AIR...). IN ADDITION TO SIMPLY MANEUVERING ABOUT, SPIDERS USED THEIR THREADS AS "BOOKMARKS" OR "SIGNPOSTS" WHEN EVACUATING AN AREA IN AN EMERGENCY OR WHEN ATTACKING. IN THE CASE OF INSECTRONS, ONE ALSO HAS TO TAKE INTO ACCOUNT THE EXTREME VISCOUS RESISTANCE AND TENSION OF THE THREADS THEY DEPLOY. SO EVEN IF THE INSECTRONS HAVE SUCCESSFULLY ATTACHED THEMSELVES TO A SURFACE WITH THEIR SUCTION CUPS, THEY PROBABLY HAVE TO SEVER THEIR THREADS IN A RELATIVE HURRY. ACTUAL SPIDER THREADS, BY THE WAY, ARE CREATED FROM A PROTEIN MATTER CALLED FIBROIN, AND ARE SAID TO HAVE GREATER ELASTICITY AND TENSILE STRENGTH THAN NYLON...

PHOTO: TELL US WHAT YOU KNOW ABOUT THIS WOMAN

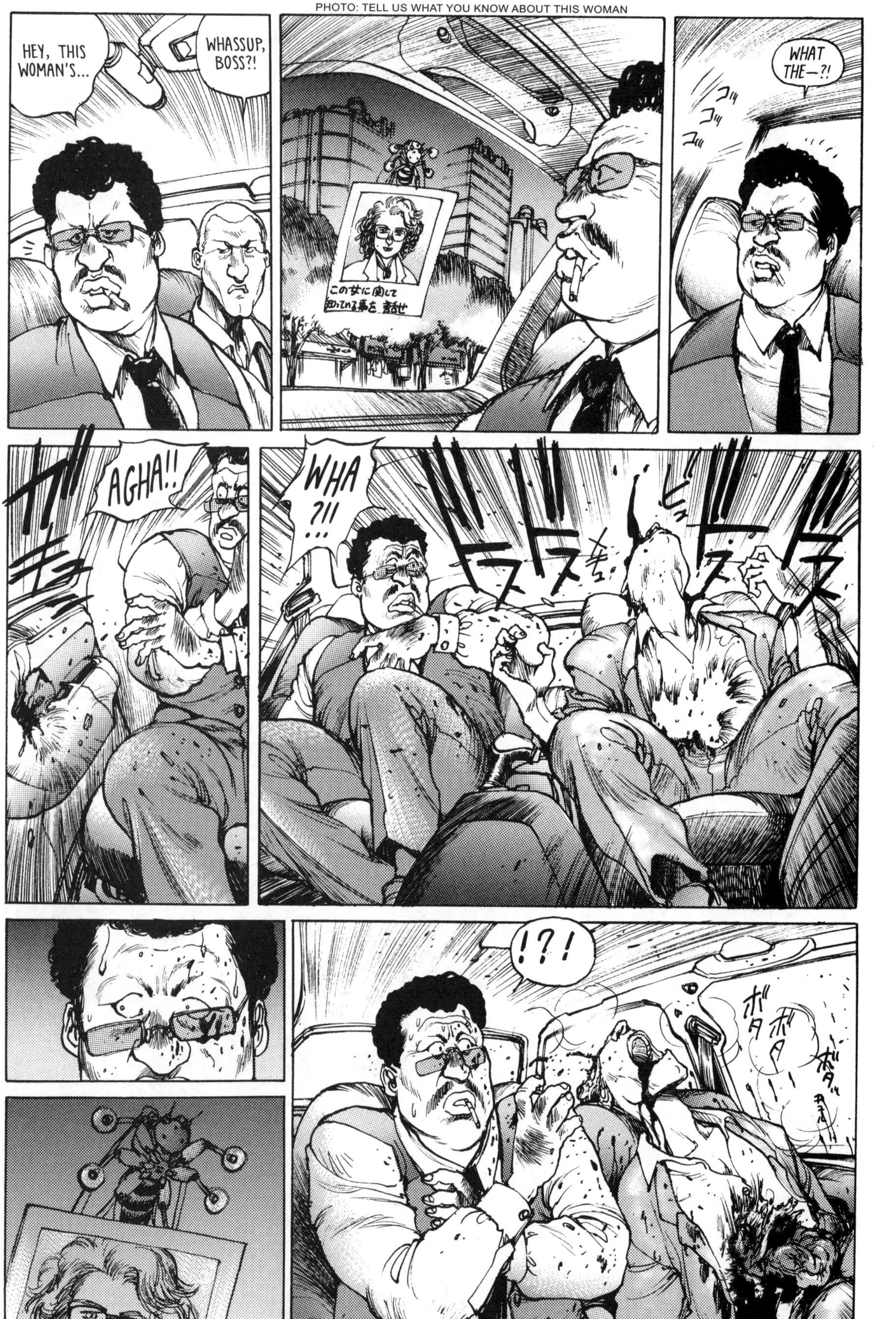
WHAT THE—?!
WHASSUP, BOSS?!
HEY, THIS WOMAN'S...
WHA ?!! ...
AGHA!!
!?!
ボタ
ボタ

FORGIVE ME, DEAR READERS, FOR CONTINUING WITH MY DISCUSSION OF SPIDER-STYLE INSECTRONS, BUT THERE IS ONE OTHER FACTOID THAT I SHOULD NOTE HERE. IF THE INSECTRON DEPOSITS MICRO DROPS OF ITS STICKY THREAD LIQUID AT ONE TO TWO METER INTERVALS AND THEN LETS THE THREADS PLAY OUT FROM THE CENTER OF THE CAR, THEY'D BE LESS LIKELY TO BE DISCONNECTED OR SEVERED EXCEPT DURING LANE CHANGES OR IN PEDESTRIAN CROSSINGS (OF COURSE THE THREAD LIQUID WOULD BE USED UP FASTER...). FOR TRAILING ANOTHER VEHICLE AT A DISTANCE OF ONE KILOMETER OR SO, THIS MIGHT DO THE TRICK (OF COURSE, THE INSECTRON'S TANK CAPACITY WOULD BE AN ISSUE, BUT THE *NEPHILA CLAVATA* SPIDER CAN REPORTEDLY SPIN OVER 700 METERS OF THREAD...).

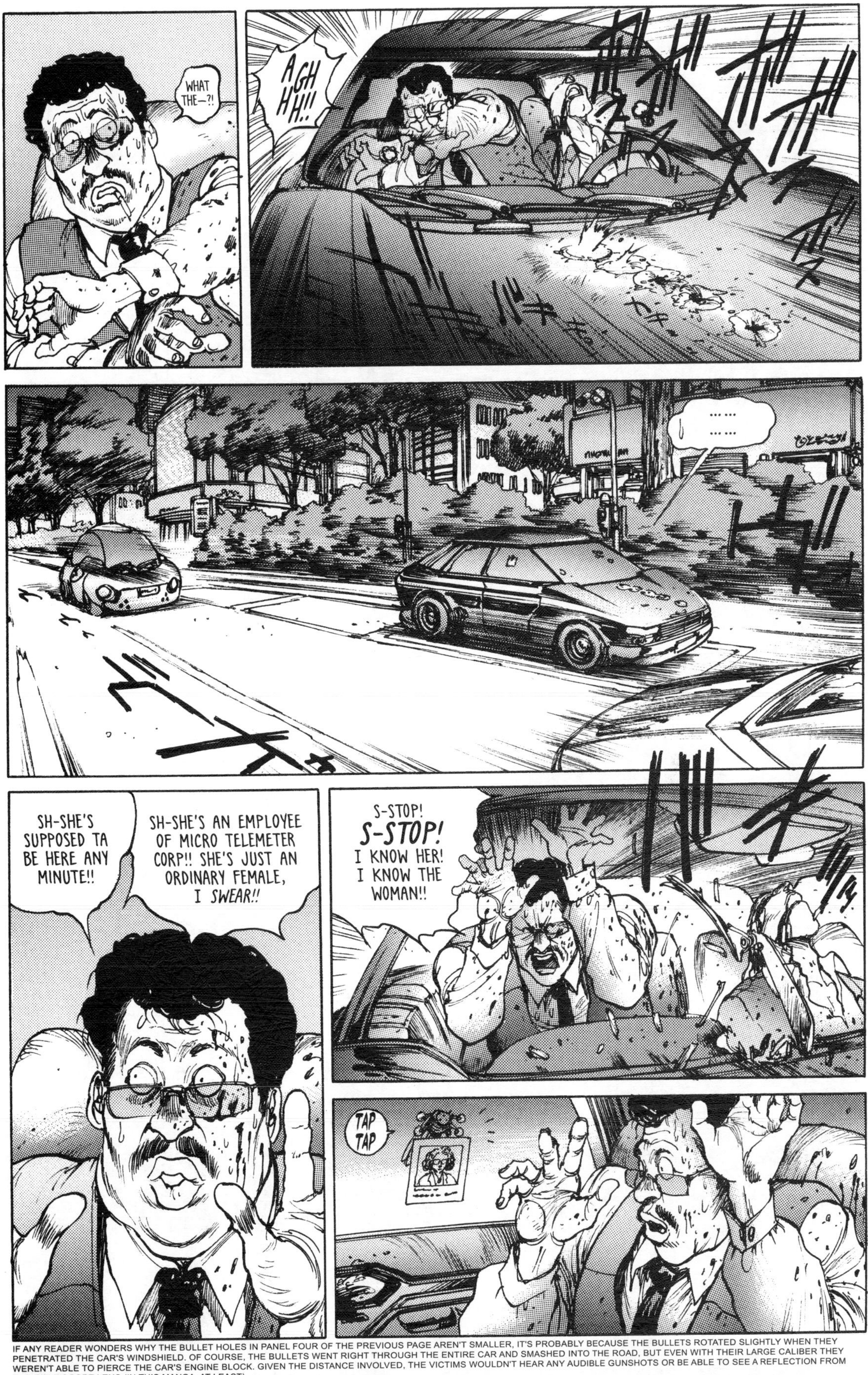
AGHHH!!
WHAT THE—?!
... ...
... ...
S-STOP! S-STOP! I KNOW HER! I KNOW THE WOMAN!!
TAP TAP
SH-SHE'S AN EMPLOYEE OF MICRO TELEMETER CORP!! SHE'S JUST AN ORDINARY FEMALE, I SWEAR!!
SH-SHE'S SUPPOSED TA BE HERE ANY MINUTE!!

IF ANY READER WONDERS WHY THE BULLET HOLES IN PANEL FOUR OF THE PREVIOUS PAGE AREN'T SMALLER, IT'S PROBABLY BECAUSE THE BULLETS ROTATED SLIGHTLY WHEN THEY PENETRATED THE CAR'S WINDSHIELD. OF COURSE, THE BULLETS WENT RIGHT THROUGH THE ENTIRE CAR AND SMASHED INTO THE ROAD, BUT EVEN WITH THEIR LARGE CALIBER THEY WEREN'T ABLE TO PIERCE THE CAR'S ENGINE BLOCK. GIVEN THE DISTANCE INVOLVED, THE VICTIMS WOULDN'T HEAR ANY AUDIBLE GUNSHOTS OR BE ABLE TO SEE A REFLECTION FROM THE RIFLE SCOPE LENS (IN THIS MANGA, AT LEAST)...

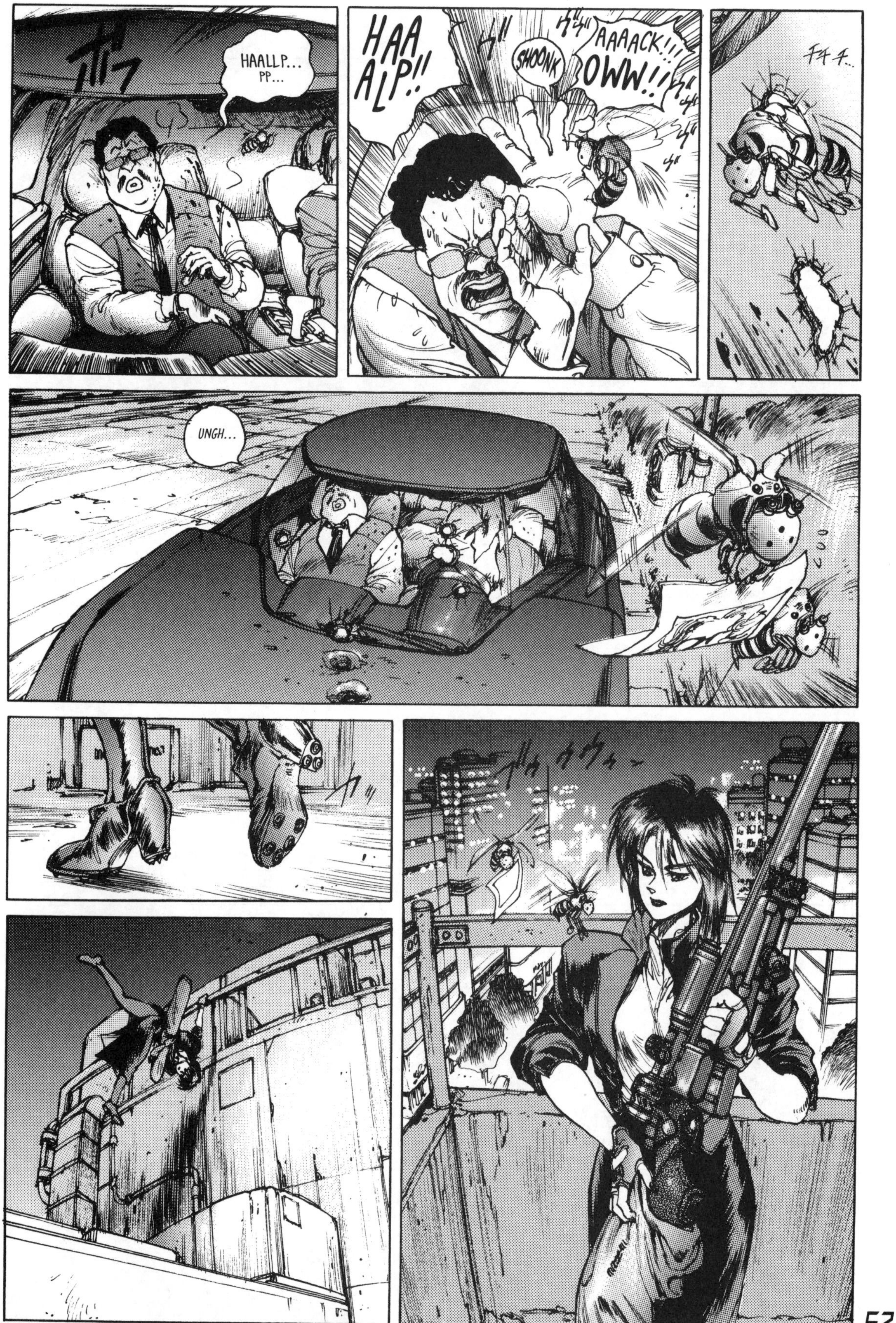

チキチ...
AAAACK!!! OWW!!!
SHOONK
HAA ALP!!
HAALLP... PP...
UNGH...

THE MAN IN THE DRIVER'S SEAT WAS SHOT TO DEATH AS A "WARNING," AND ALSO TO PHYSICALLY PREVENT ANYONE ELSE FROM EASILY TAKING OVER THE WHEEL AND CONTINUING TO DRIVE THE CAR. OF COURSE, WE'RE ASSUMING THAT IN THIS CASE THE FLUNKY DRIVING THE CAR IS LOWER DOWN THE ORGANIZATIONAL TOTEM POLE, AND WOULDN'T BE CARRYING ANY INFORMATION OF PARTICULAR IMPORTANCE IN HIS HEAD. ONE DOESN'T HEAR MUCH ABOUT IT ANY MORE (PERHAPS BECAUSE OF THE SEEMING CRUELTY INVOLVED), BUT WHEN SECURITY PERSONNEL ARE ESCORTING A VIP UNDER HEAVY GUARD AND THE CAR'S DRIVER IS SHOT, THE OTHER SECURITY PERSONNEL ARE SOMETIMES TAUGHT TO TOSS THE DRIVER'S BODY OUT OF THE CAR, TAKE OVER THE WHEEL, AND KEEP ON DRIVING. ALSO, IN THE FIRST PANEL ON THIS PAGE, PLEASE OVERLOOK THE FACT THAT I DREW THE BULLET HOLE IN THE WINDSHIELD IN

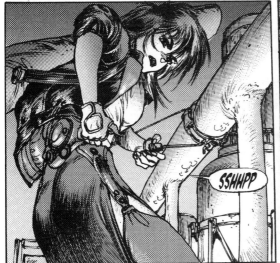

SSHHPP

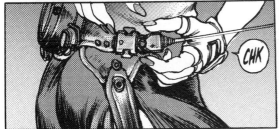

CHK

REGARDING SNIPING, IN THIS CASE, FOR CHROMA/MAJOR TO BE OUT OF NORMAL VISUAL RANGE, A DISTANCE OF ABOUT 400 METERS FROM THE VICTIM WOULD USUALLY SUFFICE. ONE OF THE MAIN THINGS THAT SHE HAS TO WORRY ABOUT IS THAT—SINCE SHE'S NOT USING A LINEAR RIFLE—THE SOUND OF THE GUNSHOT IS PRETTY LOUD. I MADE HER RIFLE A HEAVY BARREL, BOLT-ACTION DESIGN BECAUSE I'VE HEARD THAT M-16s, ETC., WOULDN'T BE EFFECTIVE, PRESUMABLY BECAUSE OF THEIR SMALL CALIBER. IN THIS STORY, HER RIFLE USES 9MM BULLETS. THE PROTRUSION ON THE SIDE OF THE MAGAZINE IS A CARTRIDGE CATCHER. ASSUME THAT SHE DOESN'T LEAVE ANY FOOTPRINTS BECAUSE HER SHOES HAVE SPIKES.

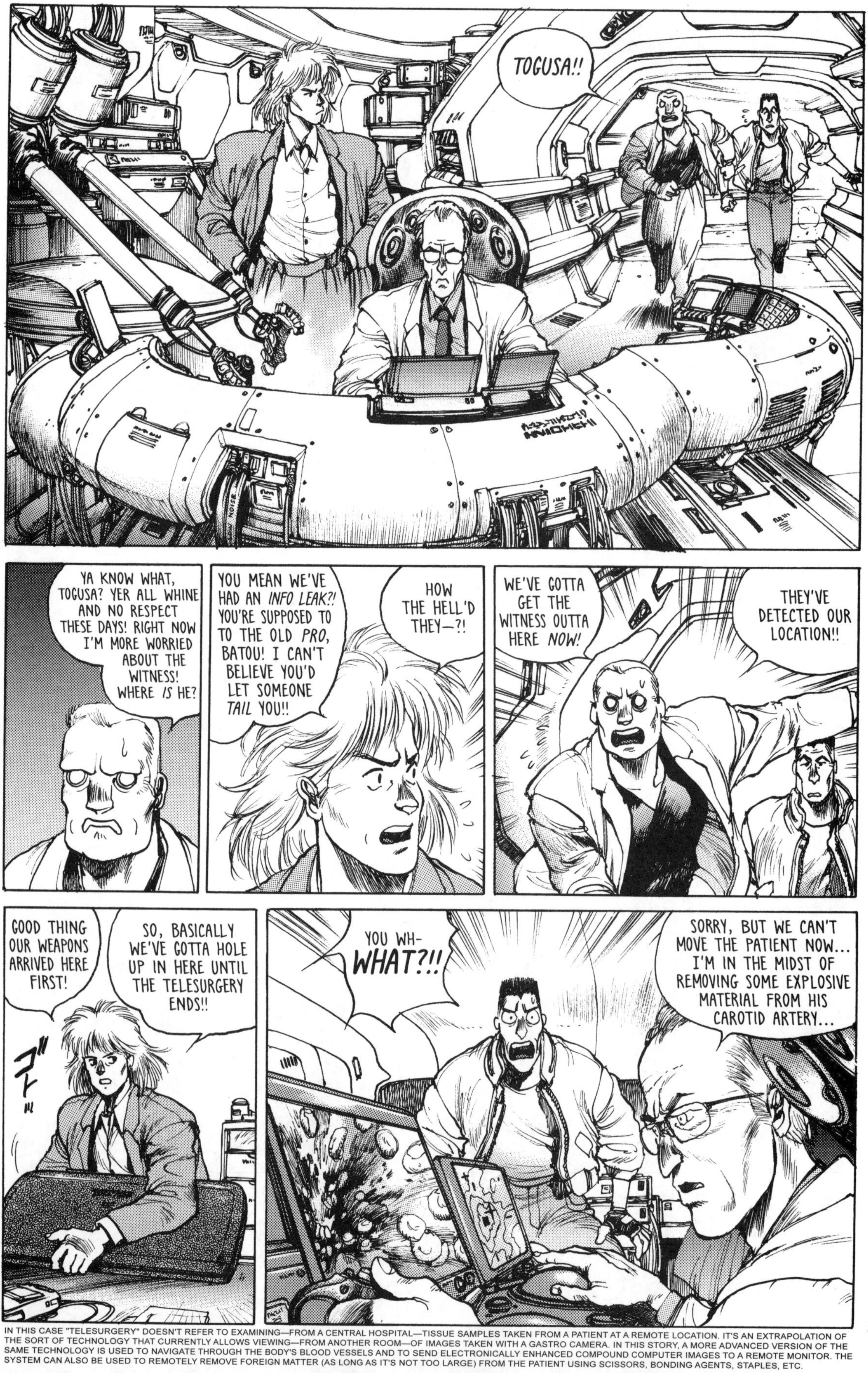

TOGUSA!!
THEY'VE DETECTED OUR LOCATION!!
WE'VE GOTTA GET THE WITNESS OUTTA HERE *NOW!*
HOW THE HELL'D THEY—?!
YOU MEAN WE'VE HAD AN *INFO LEAK?!* YOU'RE SUPPOSED TO TO THE OLD *PRO*, BATOU! I CAN'T BELIEVE YOU'D LET SOMEONE *TAIL* YOU!!
YA KNOW WHAT, TOGUSA? YER ALL WHINE AND NO RESPECT THESE DAYS! RIGHT NOW I'M MORE WORRIED ABOUT THE WITNESS! WHERE *IS* HE?
SORRY, BUT WE CAN'T MOVE THE PATIENT NOW... I'M IN THE MIDST OF REMOVING SOME EXPLOSIVE MATERIAL FROM HIS CAROTID ARTERY...
YOU WH- WHAT?!!
SO, BASICALLY WE'VE GOTTA HOLE UP IN HERE UNTIL THE TELESURGERY ENDS!!
GOOD THING OUR WEAPONS ARRIVED HERE FIRST!
ゴト

IN THIS CASE "TELESURGERY" DOESN'T REFER TO EXAMINING—FROM A CENTRAL HOSPITAL—TISSUE SAMPLES TAKEN FROM A PATIENT AT A REMOTE LOCATION. IT'S AN EXTRAPOLATION OF THE SORT OF TECHNOLOGY THAT CURRENTLY ALLOWS VIEWING—FROM ANOTHER ROOM—OF IMAGES TAKEN WITH A GASTRO CAMERA. IN THIS STORY, A MORE ADVANCED VERSION OF THE SAME TECHNOLOGY IS USED TO NAVIGATE THROUGH THE BODY'S BLOOD VESSELS AND TO SEND ELECTRONICALLY ENHANCED COMPOUND COMPUTER IMAGES TO A REMOTE MONITOR. THE SYSTEM CAN ALSO BE USED TO REMOTELY REMOVE FOREIGN MATTER (AS LONG AS IT'S NOT TOO LARGE) FROM THE PATIENT USING SCISSORS, BONDING AGENTS, STAPLES, ETC.

WOW... 9mm C-27A'S WITH *MINI-GRENADES!* WHO WOULD'VE THOUGHT OLD ARAMAKI'D ACTUALLY SUPPLY US WITH THIS SORT OF STUFF!
WELL, WE'RE UP AGAINST SOMEONE USING STATE-OF-THE-ART WEAPONRY... AND THERE'S THE BIG PUBLIC SECURITY MANAGER'S MEETING COMING UP... SO MAYBE THE OLD MAN'S EMPATHIZING WITH US MORE THAN USUAL...
GOOD THING WE'RE IN A POLICE HOSPITAL... AT LEAST WE'VE GOT GOOD SECURITY HERE, AND REINFORCED WALLS, TOO!
UP UNTIL NOW, THE ENEMY'S BEEN USING A FRONTAL ASSAULT APPROACH WITHOUT GIVING MUCH THOUGHT TO TACTICS... SO I FEEL PRETTY OPTIMISTIC ABOUT OUR CHANCES...
GOD, THESE GUYS MAKE A LOT OF NOISE... I WISH THEY'D GO ONLINE TO TALK, OR AT LEAST LEAVE THE ROOM...
Grumble, grumble...
ピ.
ピ.
ピ.
ピ.

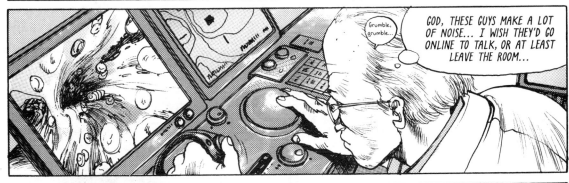

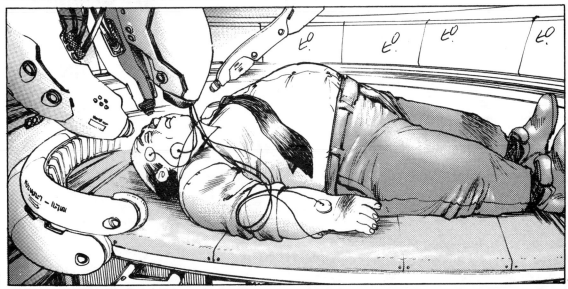

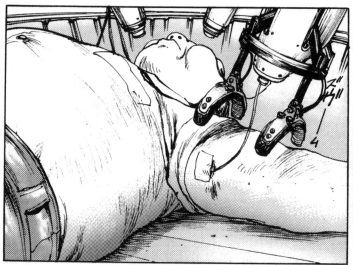

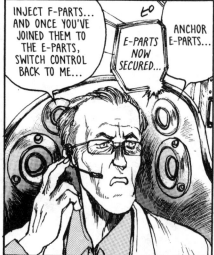

ANCHOR E-PARTS...
E-PARTS NOW SECURED...
INJECT F-PARTS... AND ONCE YOU'VE JOINED THEM TO THE E-PARTS, SWITCH CONTROL BACK TO ME...
WELL, I FOUND TWO SINGLE 15mm EXPLOSIVES IN HIM... AND THEY'VE COMPLETELY ADHERED TO HIS TISSUES, SO IT'LL TAKE A LITTLE WHILE TO REMOVE THEM...
IF THAT'S THE CASE, CAN'T YOU JUST EXCISE THE FUSES, OR THE RECEIVER PORTIONS?
EITHER WAY''LL TAKE THE SAME AMOUNT OF TIME, MY FRIEND... IT WON'T SPEED THINGS UP...

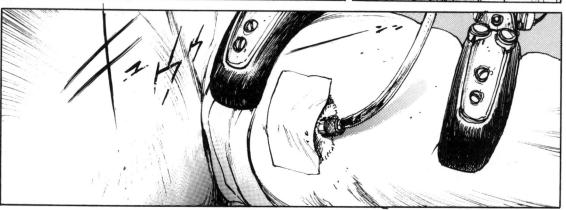

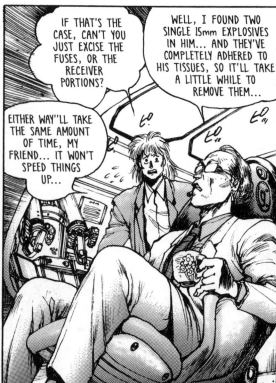

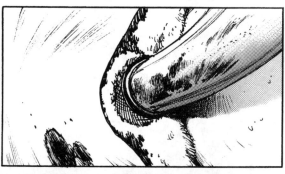

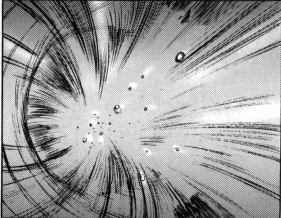

REGARDING THE "TWO" EXPLOSIVES—I ARBITRARILY CAME UP WITH THIS NUMBER. FIRST OF ALL, ONLY A LIMITED NUMBER OF BLOOD VESSELS ARE SEARCHED, BECAUSE THEY HAVE TO BE ONES WIDE ENOUGH TO ACCOMMODATE THE INSERTED EXPLOSIVES. THE DOCTOR THEN INJECTS THOUSANDS OF MICROMACHINES INTO THESE BLOOD VESSELS. THE MICROMACHINES PROCEED TO DETECT RELATIVELY LARGE FOREIGN PARTICLES (ESPECIALLY THE METALLIC PORTION OF ANY SIGNAL RECEIVERS ATTACHED TO THE EXPLOSIVE MATERIAL IN THE BODY), TO ADHERE TO THEM AND THEN TO EMIT AN AUDIO ALERT (OF COURSE, INAUDIBLE TO HUMANS UNDER NORMAL CIRCUMSTANCES).

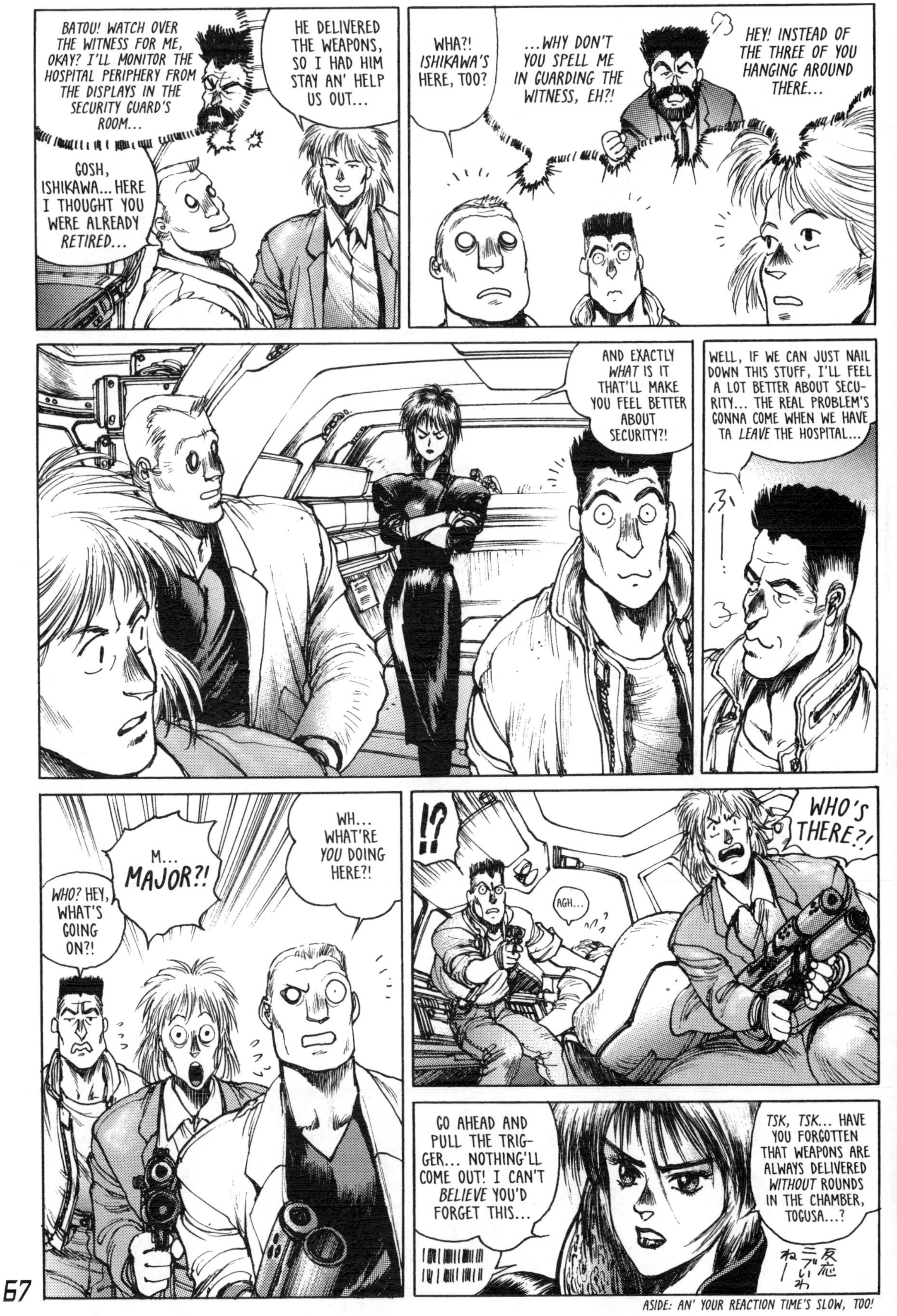
HEY! INSTEAD OF THE THREE OF YOU HANGING AROUND THERE...
...WHY DON'T YOU SPELL ME IN GUARDING THE WITNESS, EH?!
WHA?! ISHIKAWA'S HERE, TOO?
HE DELIVERED THE WEAPONS, SO I HAD HIM STAY AN' HELP US OUT...
BATOU! WATCH OVER THE WITNESS FOR ME, OKAY? I'LL MONITOR THE HOSPITAL PERIPHERY FROM THE DISPLAYS IN THE SECURITY GUARD'S ROOM...
GOSH, ISHIKAWA... HERE I THOUGHT YOU WERE ALREADY RETIRED...
WELL, IF WE CAN JUST NAIL DOWN THIS STUFF, I'LL FEEL A LOT BETTER ABOUT SECURITY... THE REAL PROBLEM'S GONNA COME WHEN WE HAVE TA LEAVE THE HOSPITAL...
AND EXACTLY WHAT IS IT THAT'LL MAKE YOU FEEL BETTER ABOUT SECURITY?!
WHO'S THERE?!
!?
AGH...
TSK, TSK... HAVE YOU FORGOTTEN THAT WEAPONS ARE ALWAYS DELIVERED WITHOUT ROUNDS IN THE CHAMBER, TOGUSA...?
GO AHEAD AND PULL THE TRIGGER... NOTHING'LL COME OUT! I CAN'T BELIEVE YOU'D FORGET THIS...
WH... WHAT'RE YOU DOING HERE?!
M... MAJOR?!
WHO? HEY, WHAT'S GOING ON?!

ASIDE: AN' YOUR REACTION TIME'S SLOW, TOO!

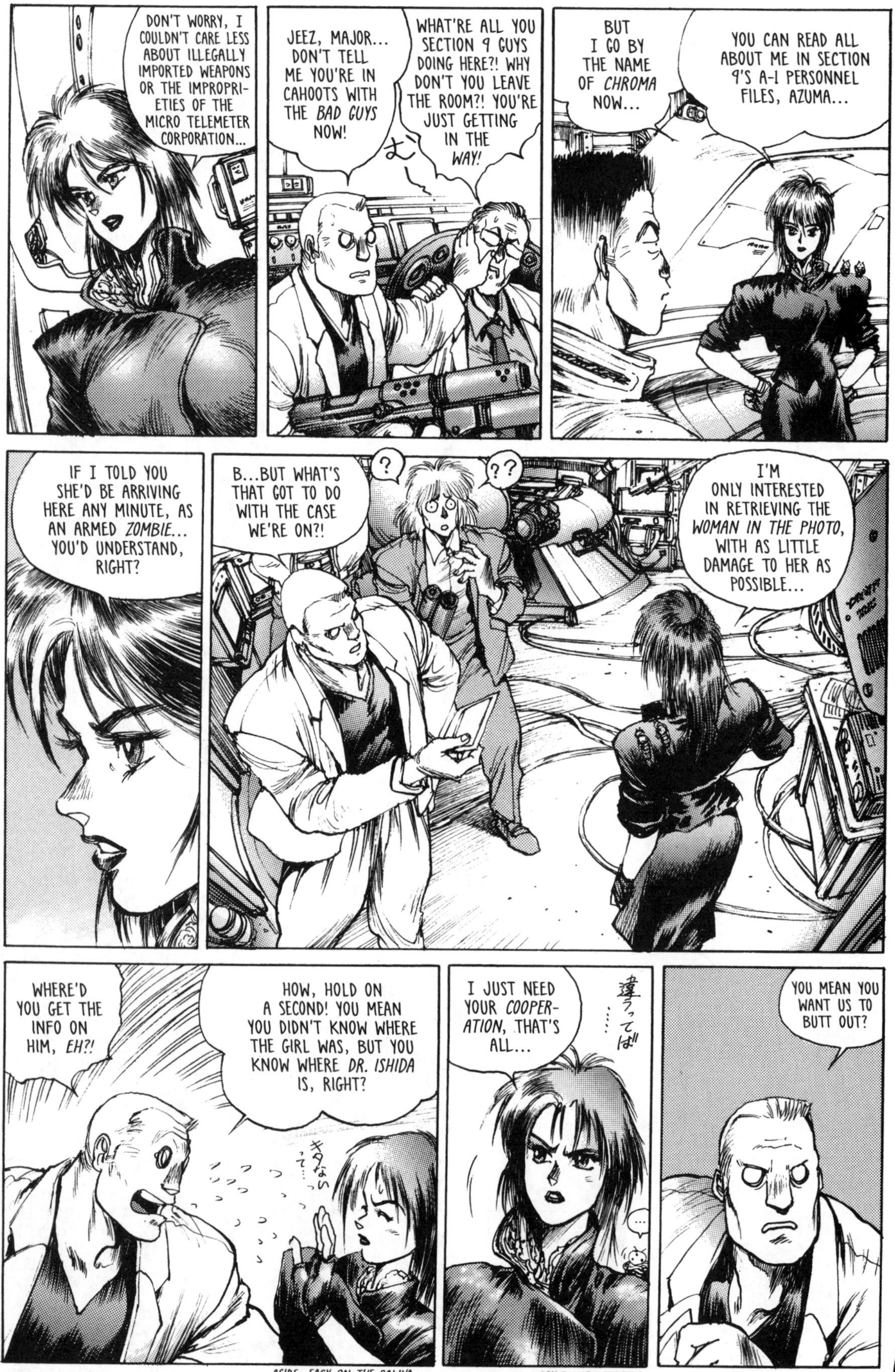

DON'T WORRY, I COULDN'T CARE LESS ABOUT ILLEGALLY IMPORTED WEAPONS OR THE IMPROPRIETIES OF THE MICRO TELEMETER CORPORATION...
JEEZ, MAJOR... DON'T TELL ME YOU'RE IN CAHOOTS WITH THE *BAD GUYS* NOW!
WHAT'RE ALL YOU SECTION 9 GUYS DOING HERE?! WHY DON'T YOU LEAVE THE ROOM?! YOU'RE JUST GETTING IN THE *WAY!*
BUT I GO BY THE NAME OF *CHROMA* NOW...
YOU CAN READ ALL ABOUT ME IN SECTION 9'S A-I PERSONNEL FILES, AZUMA...
IF I TOLD YOU SHE'D BE ARRIVING HERE ANY MINUTE, AS AN ARMED *ZOMBIE*... YOU'D UNDERSTAND, RIGHT?
B...BUT WHAT'S THAT GOT TO DO WITH THE CASE WE'RE ON?!
I'M ONLY INTERESTED IN RETRIEVING THE *WOMAN IN THE PHOTO*, WITH AS LITTLE DAMAGE TO HER AS POSSIBLE...
WHERE'D YOU GET THE INFO ON HIM, *EH?!*
HOW, HOLD ON A SECOND! YOU MEAN YOU DIDN'T KNOW WHERE THE GIRL WAS, BUT YOU KNOW WHERE *DR. ISHIDA* IS, RIGHT?
I JUST NEED YOUR *COOPERATION*, THAT'S ALL...
YOU MEAN YOU WANT US TO BUTT OUT?

ASIDE: EASY ON THE SALIVA...

ASIDE: NO, STUPID!

ASIDE: GOOD WORK.

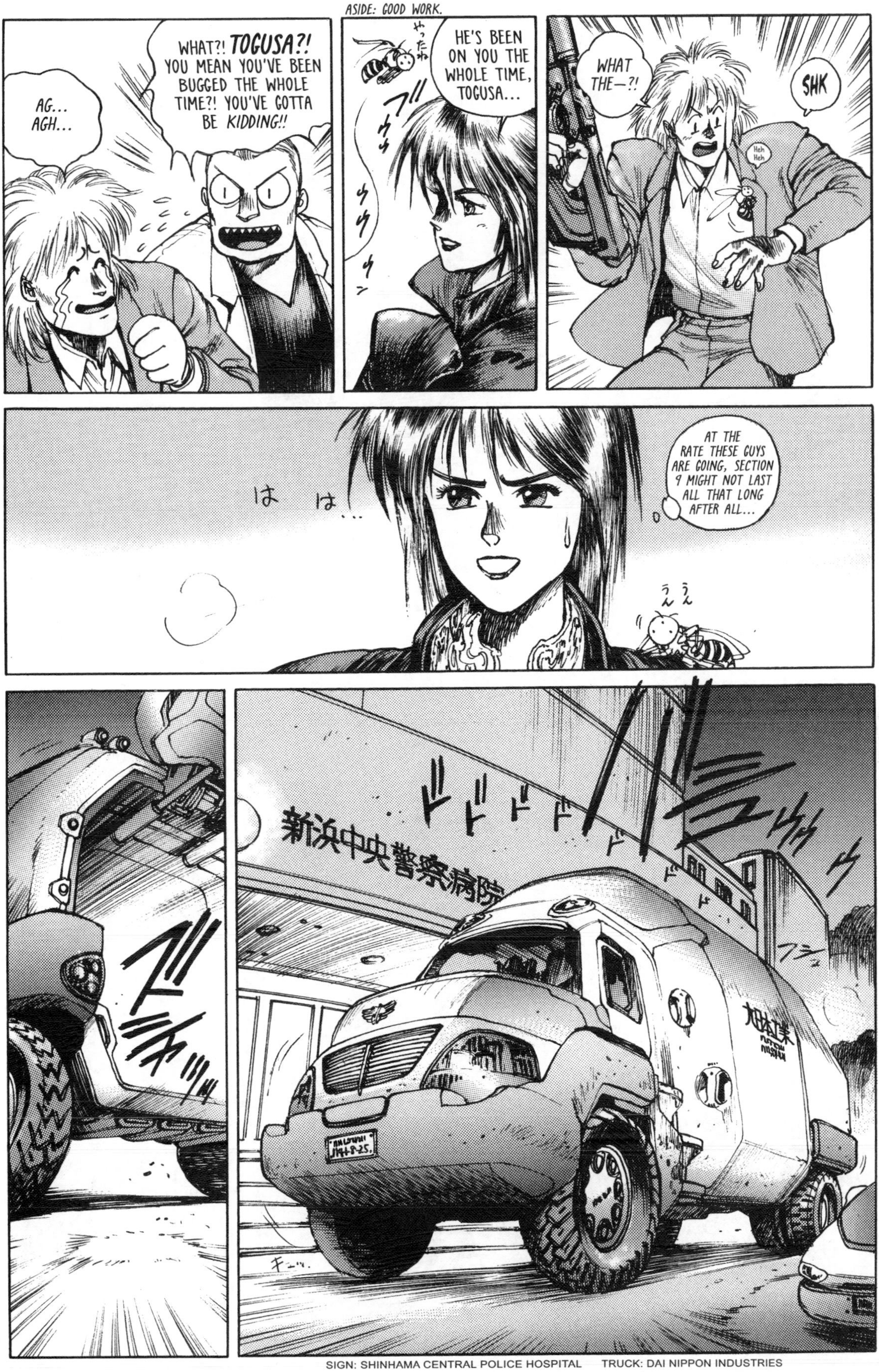
SHK
WHAT THE—?!
Heh Heh
やったね
HE'S BEEN ON YOU THE WHOLE TIME, TOGUSA...
WHAT?! TOGUSA?! YOU MEAN YOU'VE BEEN BUGGED THE WHOLE TIME?! YOU'VE GOTTA BE KIDDING!!
AG... AGH...
AT THE RATE THESE GUYS ARE GOING, SECTION 9 MIGHT NOT LAST ALL THAT LONG AFTER ALL...
はは…
うんうん
新浜中央警察病院

SIGN: SHINHAMA CENTRAL POLICE HOSPITAL TRUCK: DAI NIPPON INDUSTRIES

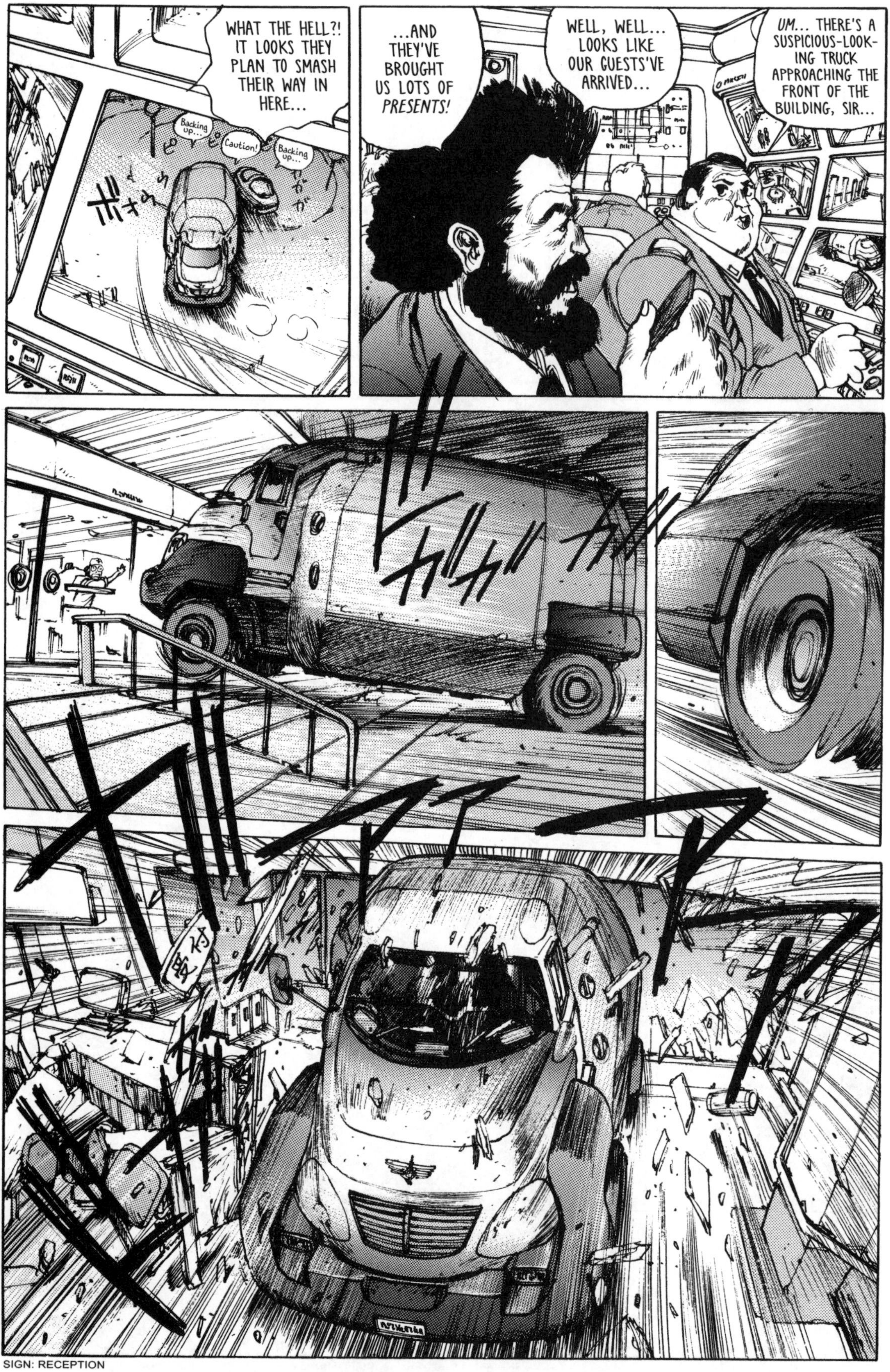
UM... THERE'S A SUSPICIOUS-LOOKING TRUCK APPROACHING THE FRONT OF THE BUILDING, SIR...
WELL, WELL... LOOKS LIKE OUR GUESTS'VE ARRIVED...
...AND THEY'VE BROUGHT US LOTS OF *PRESENTS!*
WHAT THE HELL?! IT LOOKS THEY PLAN TO SMASH THEIR WAY IN HERE...
Backing up...
Caution!
Backing up...

SIGN: RECEPTION

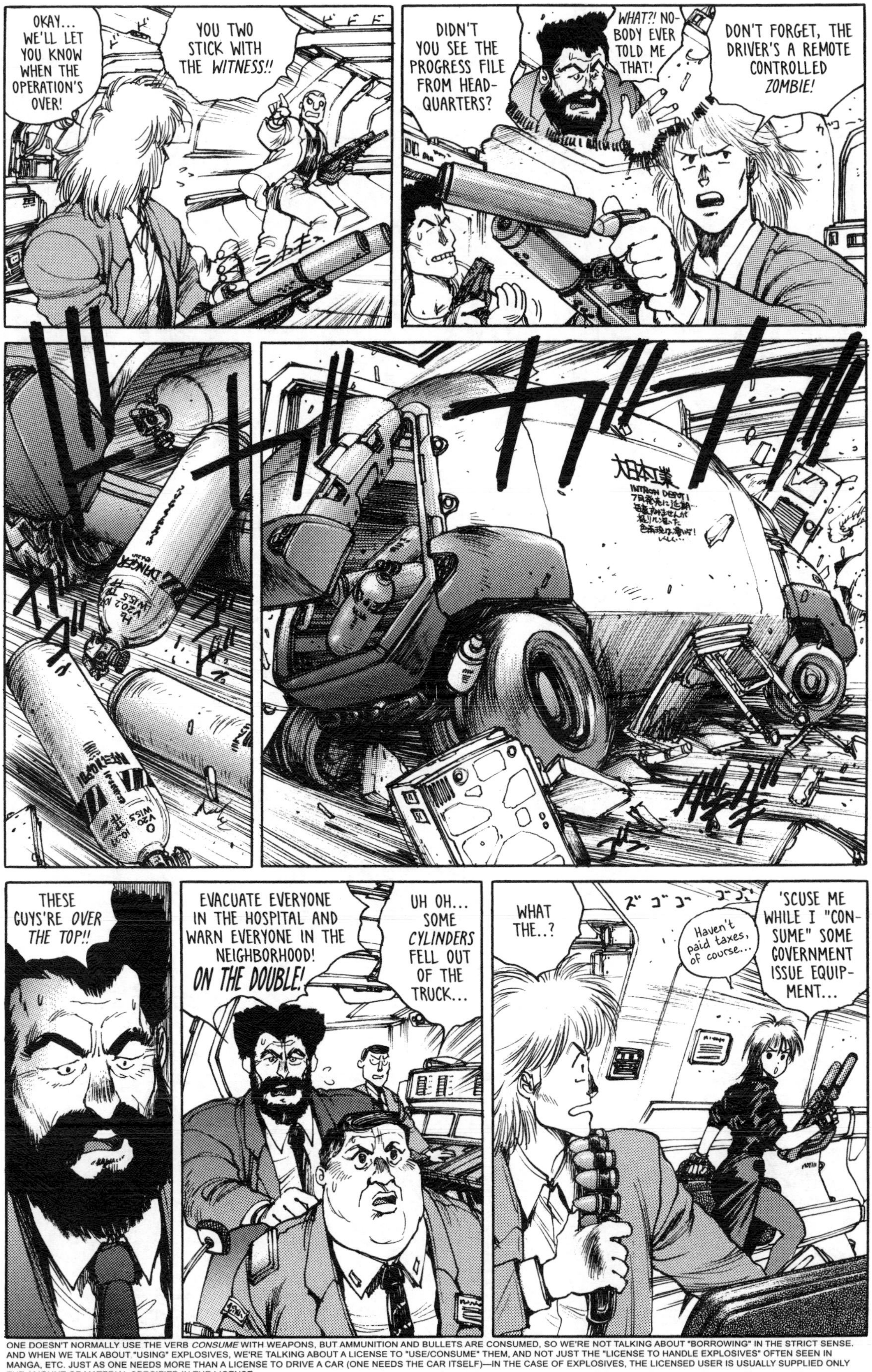
DON'T FORGET, THE DRIVER'S A REMOTE CONTROLLED ZOMBIE!
WHAT?! NOBODY EVER TOLD ME THAT!
DIDN'T YOU SEE THE PROGRESS FILE FROM HEADQUARTERS?
YOU TWO STICK WITH THE WITNESS!!
OKAY... WE'LL LET YOU KNOW WHEN THE OPERATION'S OVER!
'SCUSE ME WHILE I "CONSUME" SOME GOVERNMENT ISSUE EQUIPMENT...
Haven't paid taxes, of course...
WHAT THE..?
UH OH... SOME CYLINDERS FELL OUT OF THE TRUCK...
EVACUATE EVERYONE IN THE HOSPITAL AND WARN EVERYONE IN THE NEIGHBORHOOD! ON THE DOUBLE!
THESE GUYS'RE OVER THE TOP!!

ONE DOESN'T NORMALLY USE THE VERB *CONSUME* WITH WEAPONS, BUT AMMUNITION AND BULLETS ARE CONSUMED, SO WE'RE NOT TALKING ABOUT "BORROWING" IN THE STRICT SENSE. AND WHEN WE TALK ABOUT "USING" EXPLOSIVES, WE'RE TALKING ABOUT A LICENSE TO "USE/CONSUME" THEM, AND NOT JUST THE "LICENSE TO HANDLE EXPLOSIVES" OFTEN SEEN IN MANGA, ETC. JUST AS ONE NEEDS MORE THAN A LICENSE TO DRIVE A CAR (ONE NEEDS THE CAR ITSELF)—IN THE CASE OF EXPLOSIVES, THE LICENSED USER IS USUALLY SUPPLIED ONLY THE AMOUNT OF MATERIAL SPECIFIED IN THE LICENSE...

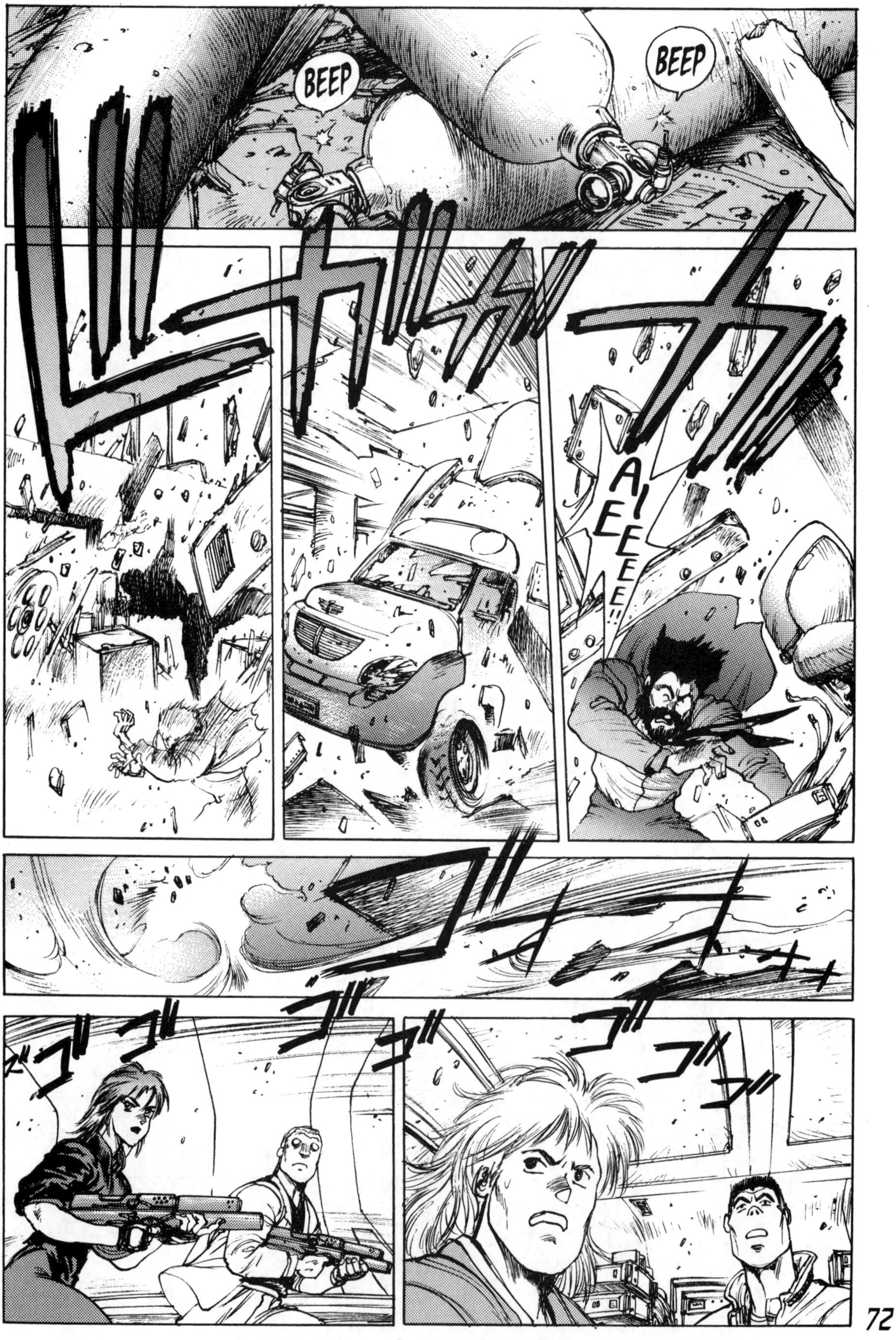
BEEP
BEEP
AIEEEEEE!!

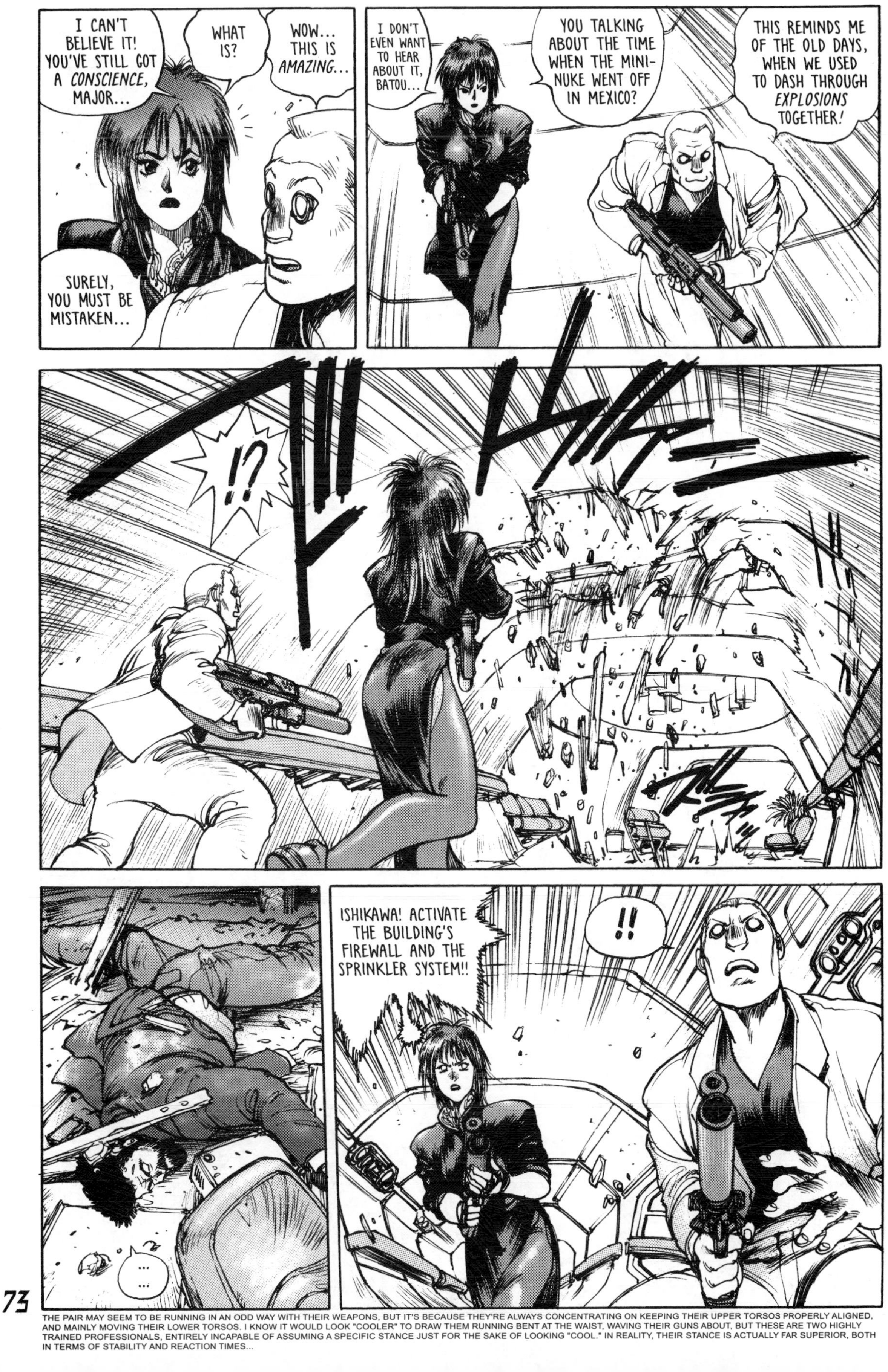
THIS REMINDS ME OF THE OLD DAYS, WHEN WE USED TO DASH THROUGH *EXPLOSIONS* TOGETHER!
YOU TALKING ABOUT THE TIME WHEN THE MINI-NUKE WENT OFF IN MEXICO?
I DON'T EVEN WANT TO HEAR ABOUT IT, BATOU...
WOW... THIS IS *AMAZING*...
WHAT IS?
I CAN'T BELIEVE IT! YOU'VE STILL GOT A *CONSCIENCE*, MAJOR...
SURELY, YOU MUST BE MISTAKEN...
!?
!!
ISHIKAWA! ACTIVATE THE BUILDING'S FIREWALL AND THE SPRINKLER SYSTEM!!
... ...

THE PAIR MAY SEEM TO BE RUNNING IN AN ODD WAY WITH THEIR WEAPONS, BUT IT'S BECAUSE THEY'RE ALWAYS CONCENTRATING ON KEEPING THEIR UPPER TORSOS PROPERLY ALIGNED, AND MAINLY MOVING THEIR LOWER TORSOS. I KNOW IT WOULD LOOK "COOLER" TO DRAW THEM RUNNING BENT AT THE WAIST, WAVING THEIR GUNS ABOUT, BUT THESE ARE TWO HIGHLY TRAINED PROFESSIONALS, ENTIRELY INCAPABLE OF ASSUMING A SPECIFIC STANCE JUST FOR THE SAKE OF LOOKING "COOL." IN REALITY, THEIR STANCE IS ACTUALLY FAR SUPERIOR, BOTH IN TERMS OF STABILITY AND REACTION TIMES...

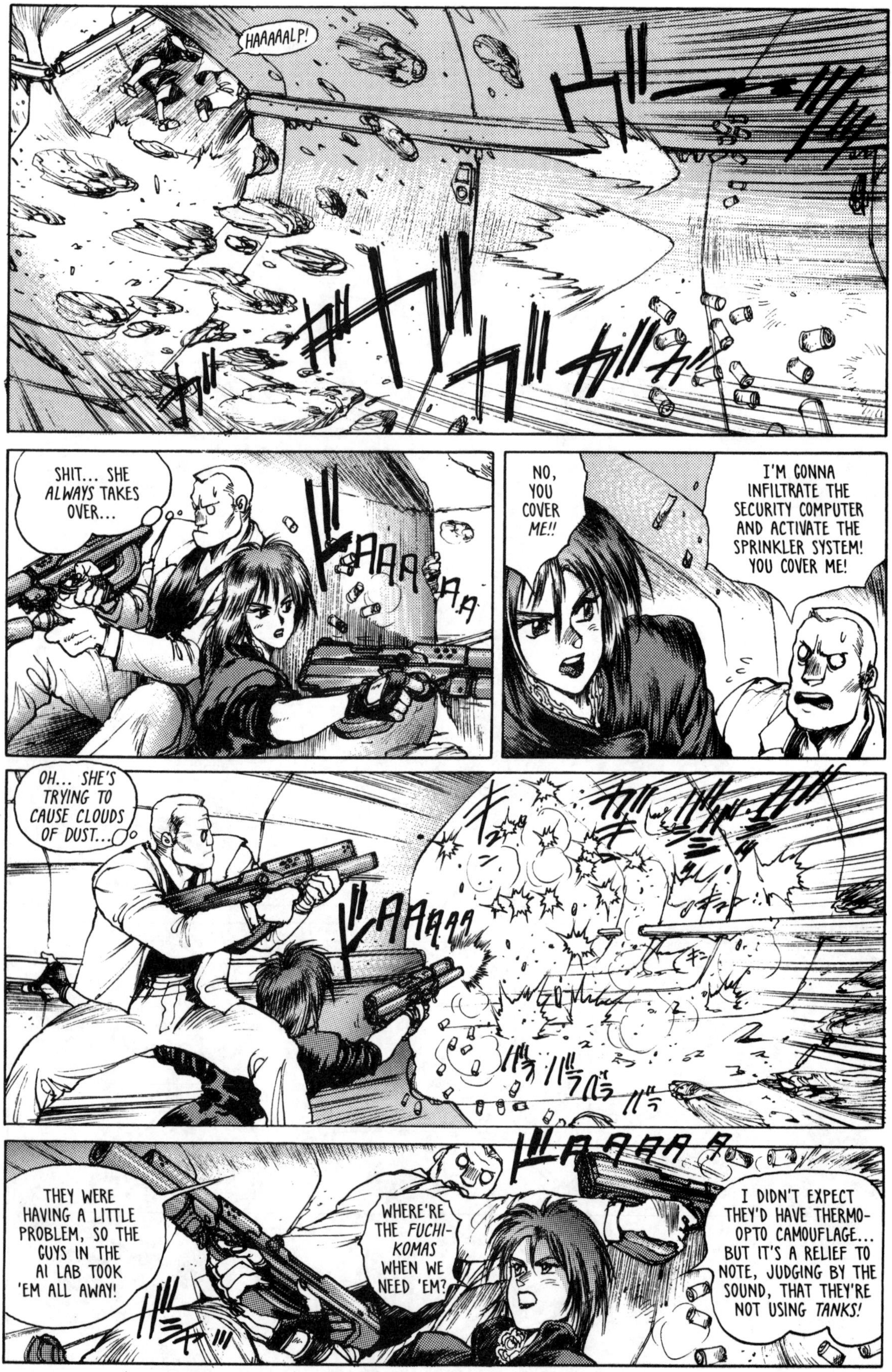
HAAAAALP!
I'M GONNA INFILTRATE THE SECURITY COMPUTER AND ACTIVATE THE SPRINKLER SYSTEM! YOU COVER ME!
NO, YOU COVER *ME!!*
SHIT... SHE *ALWAYS* TAKES OVER...
OH... SHE'S TRYING TO CAUSE CLOUDS OF DUST...
I DIDN'T EXPECT THEY'D HAVE THERMO-OPTO CAMOUFLAGE... BUT IT'S A RELIEF TO NOTE, JUDGING BY THE SOUND, THAT THEY'RE NOT USING *TANKS!*
WHERE'RE THE *FUCHI-KOMAS* WHEN WE NEED 'EM?
THEY WERE HAVING A LITTLE PROBLEM, SO THE GUYS IN THE AI LAB TOOK 'EM ALL AWAY!

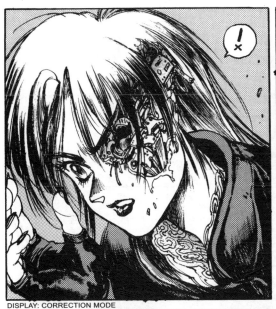

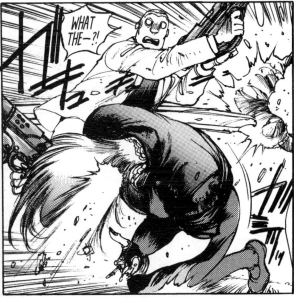

WHAT THE–?!
!
HEY, WHAT'S WITH THE TITANIUM SKULL?
WHERE'D YOUR *BRAINS* GO?
I'VE GOT THE INFO WE NEED. LET'S GET OUT OF HERE...
REPLAY
REPLAY
補正モード
DISPLAY: CORRECTION MODE
THEY'RE USING A *DEEP SEA CONSTRUCTION ROBOT*, BATOU! WE DON'T STAND A CHANCE WITH THESE WEAPONS!
YA MEAN THEY WON'T EVEN BUY US *TIME*?
DON'T FORGET, I'M ONLY AFTER THE WOMAN IN THE PHOTOGRAPH...

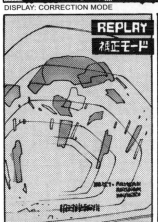

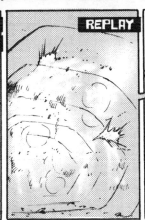

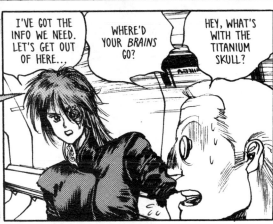

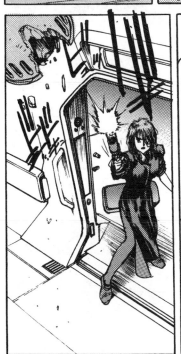

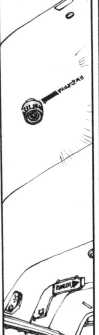

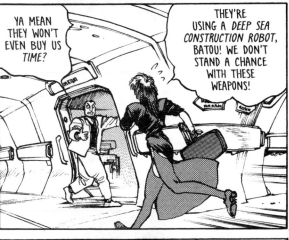

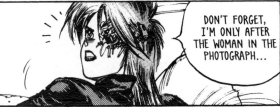

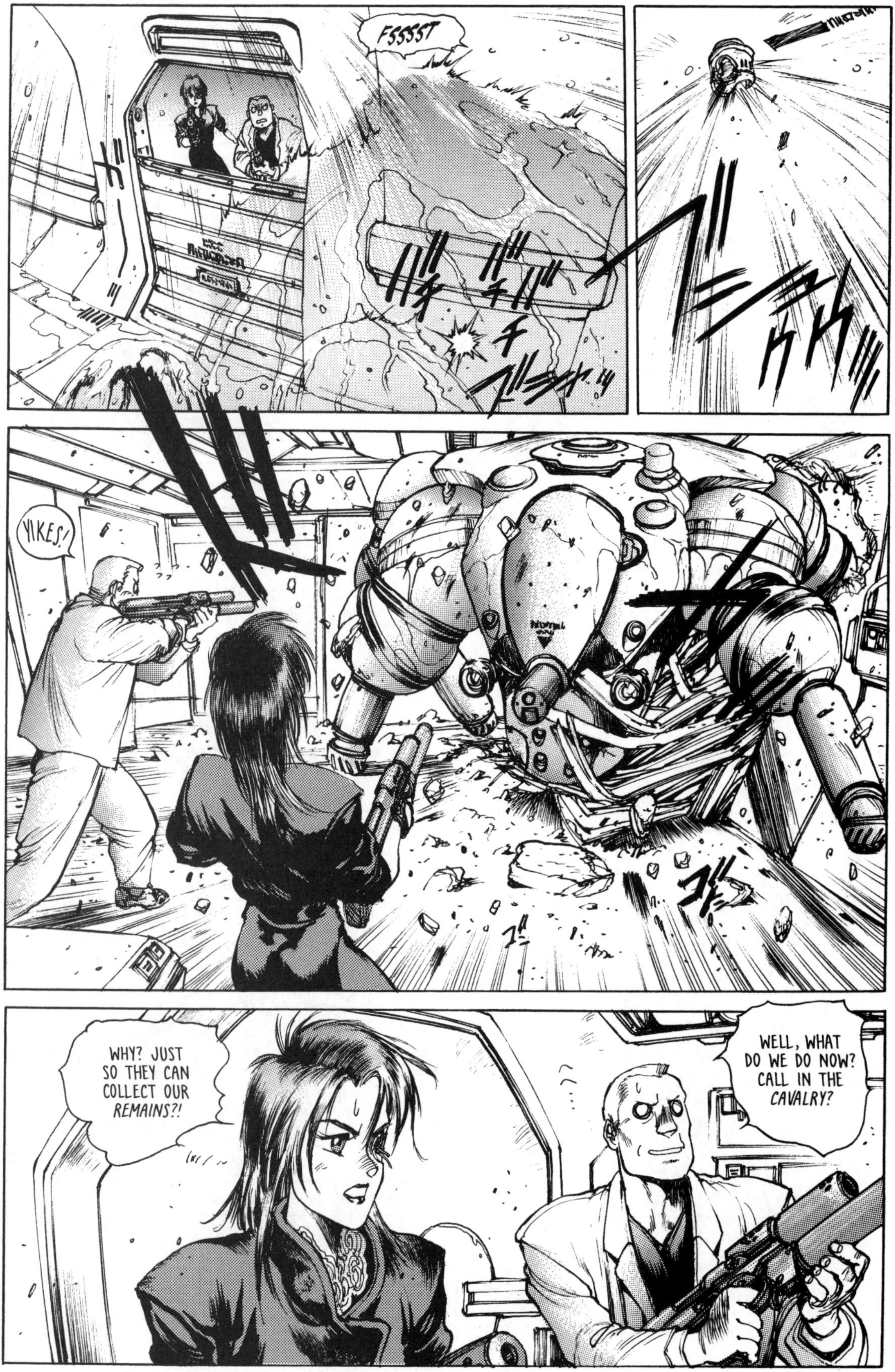
FSSSST
YIKES!
WELL, WHAT DO WE DO NOW? CALL IN THE *CAVALRY?*
WHY? JUST SO THEY CAN COLLECT OUR *REMAINS?!*

DRIVE SLAVE Part.2

1992

04

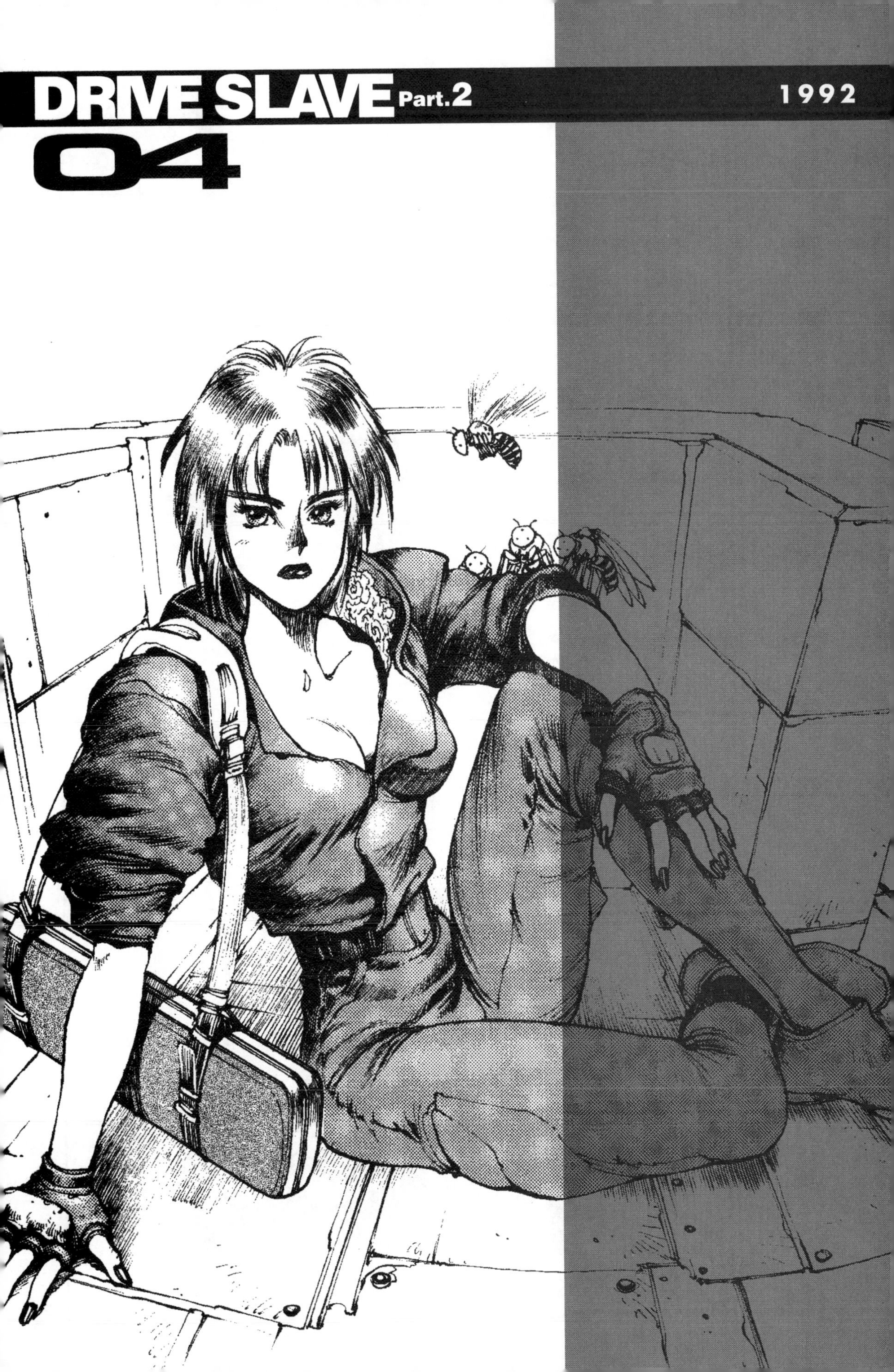

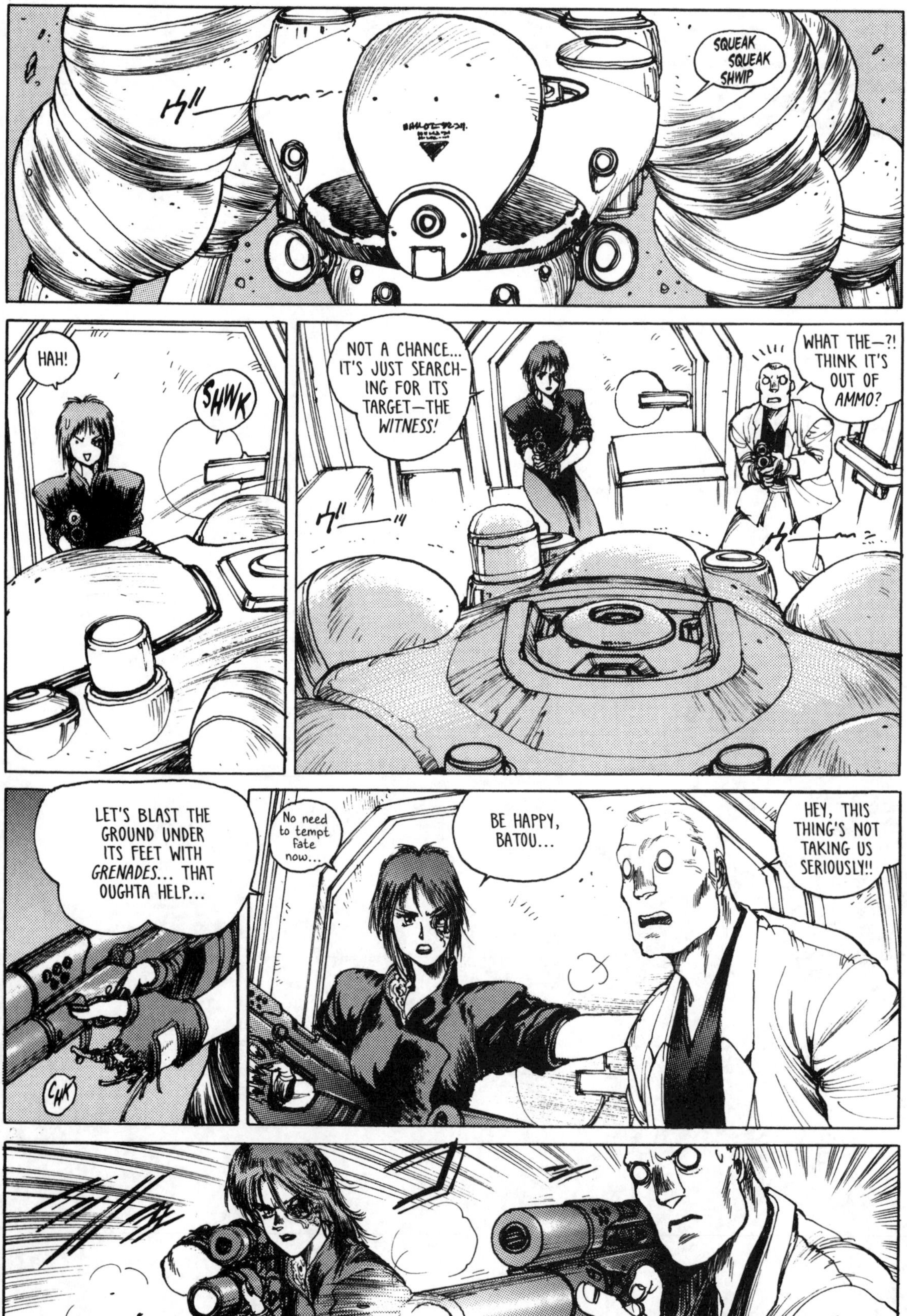
SQUEAK SQUEAK SHWIP
WHAT THE—?! THINK IT'S OUT OF AMMO?
NOT A CHANCE... IT'S JUST SEARCHING FOR ITS TARGET—THE WITNESS!
HAH!
SHWK
HEY, THIS THING'S NOT TAKING US SERIOUSLY!!
BE HAPPY, BATOU...
No need to tempt fate now...
LET'S BLAST THE GROUND UNDER ITS FEET WITH GRENADES... THAT OUGHTA HELP...
CHK

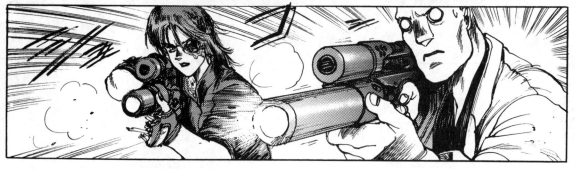

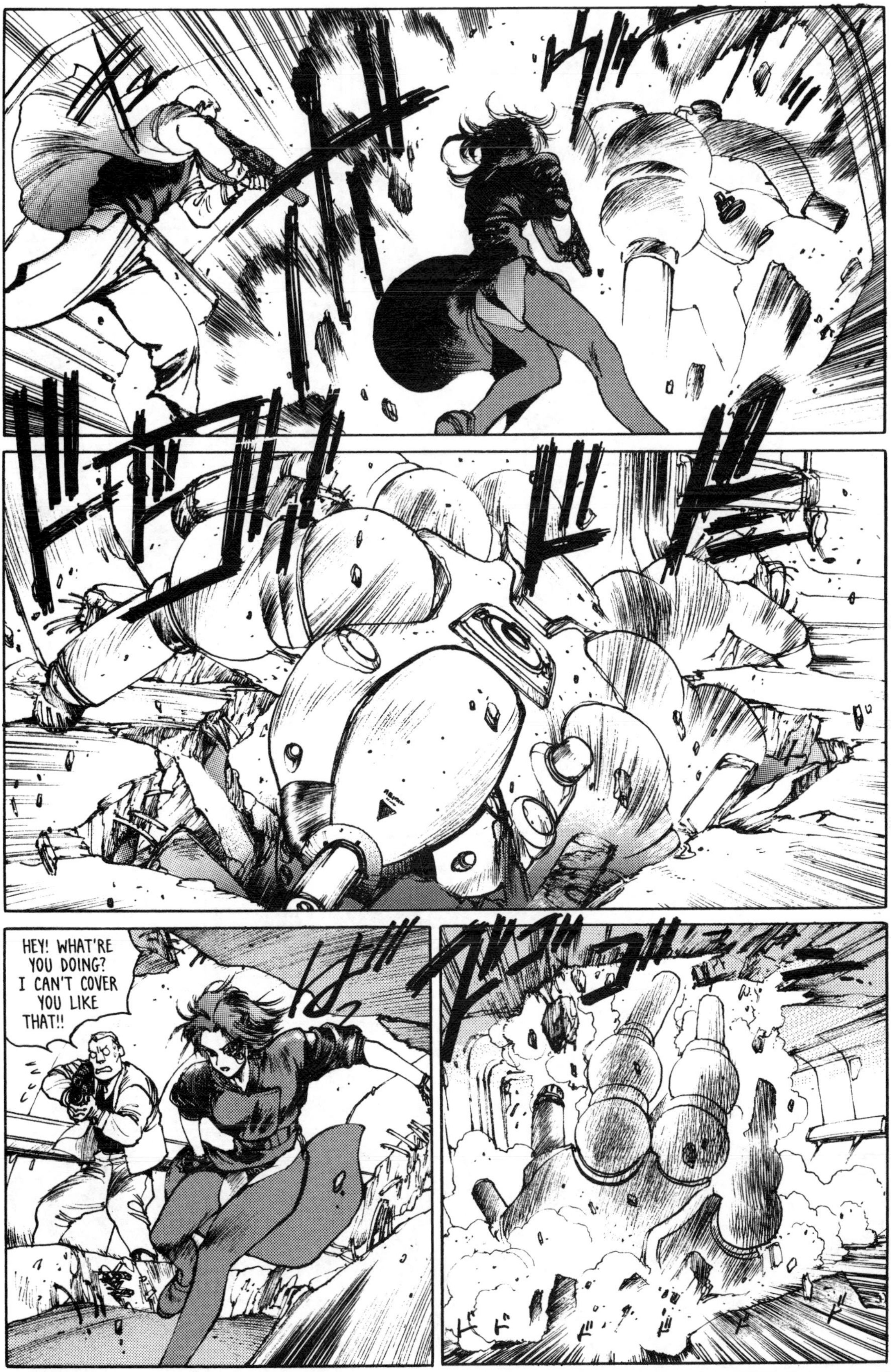
HEY! WHAT'RE YOU DOING? I CAN'T COVER YOU LIKE THAT!!

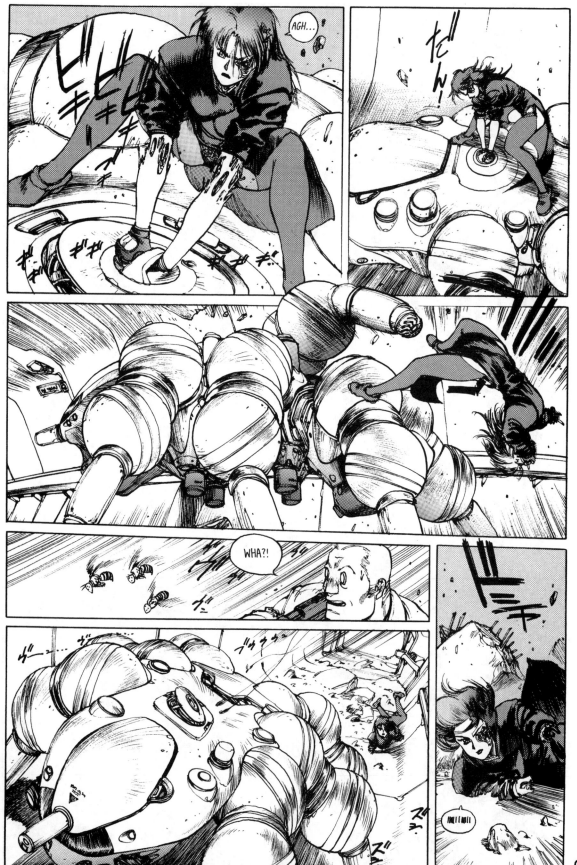

I MUST MAKE A COMMENT FOR THE SAKE OF FANS WHO MIGHT SNICKER WHEN THEY SEE THIS SORT OF MECHA... REAL ROBOTS HAVE DIFFERENT EXTERIOR COVERINGS, AND THEY ARE AL-
READY AT WORK IN A WIDE VARIETY OF INDUSTRIES. SO IT'S A LITTLE BEHIND THE TIMES TO SAY THIS ONE IS "SOMETHING OUT OF SCI-FI." THE REAL-LIFE ROBOTS THAT MOST RESEMBLE MY
DRAWING HERE ARE SURELY THOSE DEVELOPED TO WORK IN EXTREMELY HAZARDOUS ENVIRONMENTS—SUCH AS THE SIX-LEGGED MODEL DESIGNED TO WORK IN UNDERSEA OIL FIELDS,
OR "KEN-CHAN," WHICH WAS DEVELOPED FOR WORK IN NUCLEAR REACTORS. OF COURSE THE "ROBOTS" IN THIS CASE ARE ACTUALLY REMOTE-CONTROLLED, SO WHETHER THEY SHOULD
REALLY BE CALLED "ROBOTS" IS PROBABLY OPEN TO DEBATE. JUST FOR REFERENCE, ALTHOUGH THE WORD "ROBOT" APPEARS MANY TIMES IN THE OFFICIALLY RECOGNIZED LIST OF J.I.S.
(JAPAN INDUSTRIAL STANDARDS) TERMS, THERE APPARENTLY IS, STRICTLY SPEAKING, NO SINGLE, UNIVERSALLY AGREED-UPON DEFINITION IN EXISTENCE

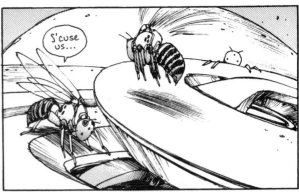

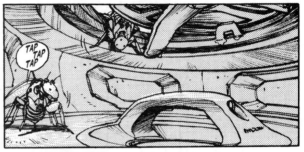

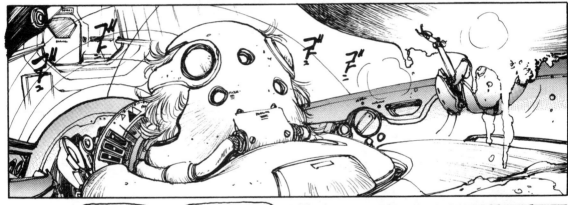

S'cuse us...
TAP TAP TAP
Heh Heh
CHK CHK CHK
Bingo...
I'VE *FOUND* HER!! I'LL JACK INTO HER BRAIN, BATOU...
WHY DON'T YOU GO AFTER THE PERSON WHO'S REMOTELY MANIPULATING HER...?
HEY, YOU *KNOW* I'M NO GOOD AT TRACKING PEOPLE...
せっかく降りてきたのに……
ASIDE: BESIDES, I JUST CLIMBED DOWN HERE...

THIS SIX-LEGGED DIVER MECHA IS NOT DESIGNED FOR TRULY DEEP-SEA WORK, AND THEREFORE IS MADE OF ALUMINUM RATHER THAN TITANIUM. THE BEE-PROBE ROBOTS ARE PROBABLY IMMUNE TO THE ACID BEING USED BECAUSE THEY ARE MADE OF SPECIAL PLASTIC RESIN AND GLASS ELEMENTS. WHEN THIS MECHA FIRST APPEARED, MOTOKO/CHROMA REFERRED TO IT AS A "CONSTRUCTION ROBOT," BUT THIS IS TECHNICALLY INCORRECT. IT CAN BE USED AS A ROBOT, OF COURSE, BUT WHEN THERE IS A HUMAN OPERATOR INSIDE IT MAY BE BETTER TO CONSIDER IT TO BE SOME SORT OF AN UNDERSEA "VESSEL." I KNOW IT PROBABLY SHOULD BE REMOTE-CONTROLLED... FOR READERS WHO WANT TO KNOW MORE ABOUT ROBOT WEAPONRY, ALLOW ME TO RECOMMEND THE JAPAN MILITARY REVIEW CO.'S APRIL 1992 ISSUE OF *GUNJI KENKYU* ("MILITARY RESEARCH").

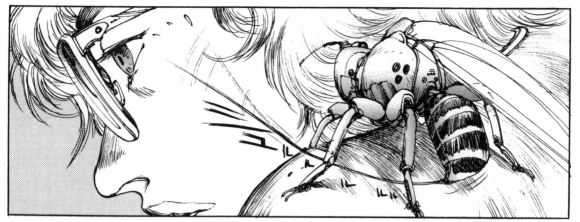

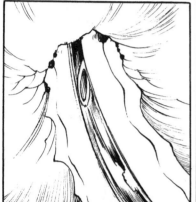

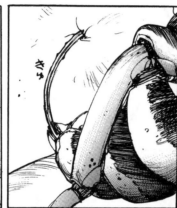

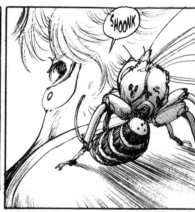

ユルルルル
SHOONK
きゅ
ゴオオオオオオ
ドドン
ドドン
PHEW...
ゴトッ
...
ドドン

I COULD HAVE SHOWN RED BLOOD CORPUSCLES ROARING THROUGH THE INSIDE OF BLOOD VESSELS, A LA *FANTASTIC VOYAGE*, BUT WITH THE SORT OF MICROSURGERY I'M DEPICTING HERE, MILLIMETER-SCALE MACHINES ARE USED, SO RED CORPUSCLES, WHICH ARE NEARLY A THOUSAND TIMES SMALLER, WOULDN'T BE VERY VISIBLE. I DO WORRY THAT THE BLOOD VESSEL I'VE DRAWN LOOKS LIKE SOME SORT OF GRITTY LIQUID, BUT WHAT THE HECK... THE FORWARD PART OF THE TINY MACHINE SHOWN HERE, WITH THE FLAGELLA-LIKE PROTRUSIONS, IS DESIGNED TO HELP THE DEVICE NAVIGATE THE BLOOD FLOW; ADJUSTING ITS LENGTH ALSO ADJUST THE MACHINE'S SPEED. THE LINE PROTRUDING OUT OF THE REAR OF THE DEVICE IS NOT FLAGELLA, BUT A LIFE-LINE. IN THE FIRST PANEL ON THIS PAGE, THE BEE-PROBE IS SHOWN GETTING THE AIR OUT OF ITS STINGER-LIKE TUBE...

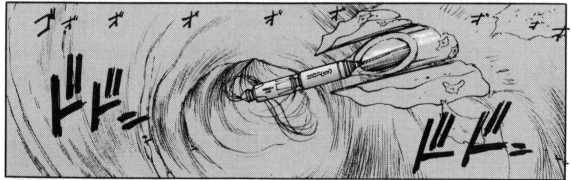

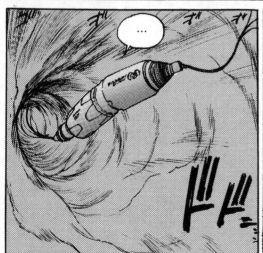

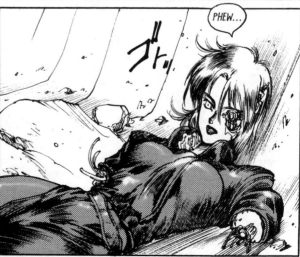

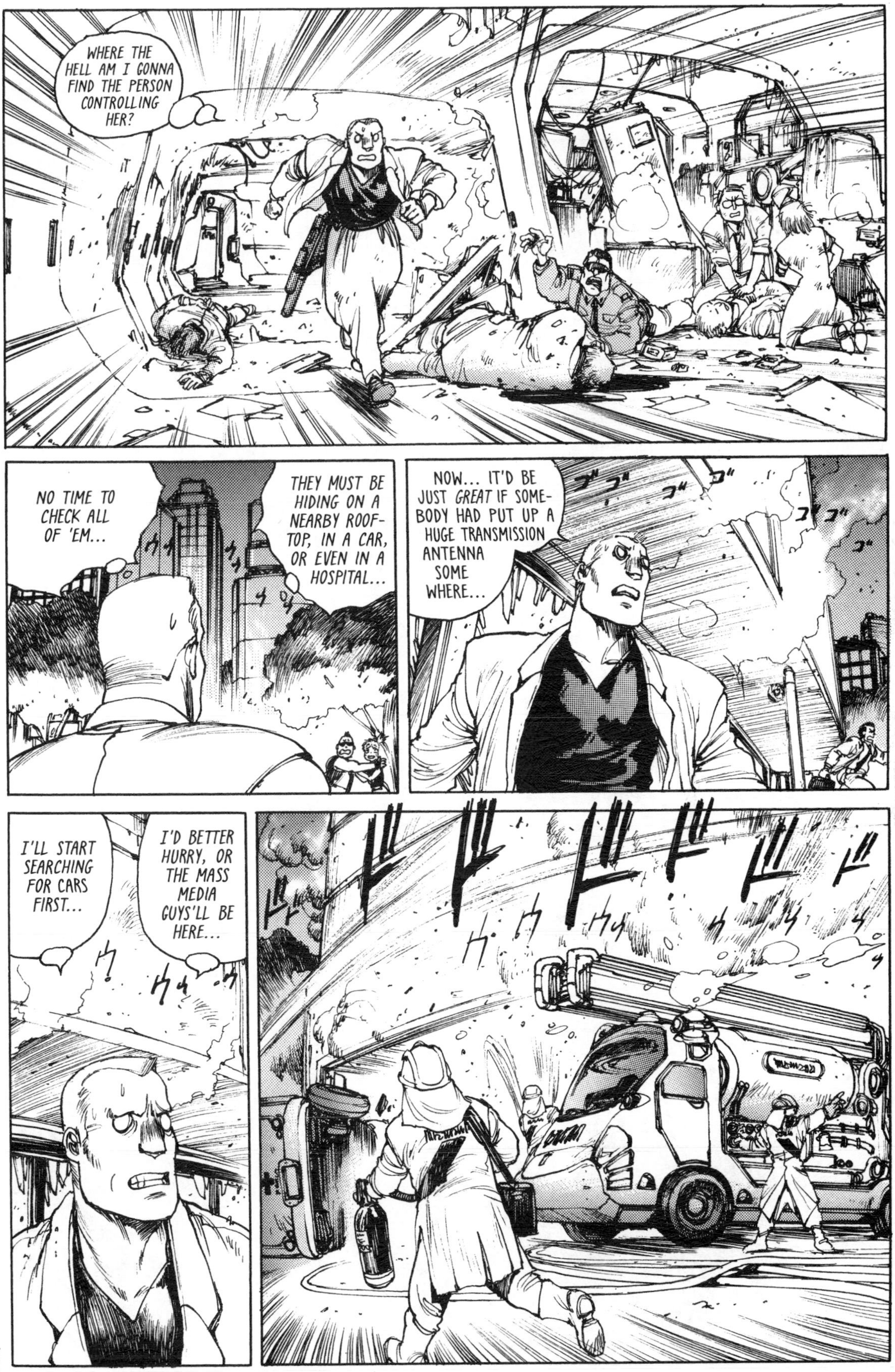
WHERE THE HELL AM I GONNA FIND THE PERSON CONTROLLING HER?
NOW... IT'D BE JUST *GREAT* IF SOMEBODY HAD PUT UP A HUGE TRANSMISSION ANTENNA SOME WHERE...
THEY MUST BE HIDING ON A NEARBY ROOFTOP, IN A CAR, OR EVEN IN A HOSPITAL...
NO TIME TO CHECK ALL OF 'EM...
I'D BETTER HURRY, OR THE MASS MEDIA GUYS'LL BE HERE...
I'LL START SEARCHING FOR CARS FIRST...

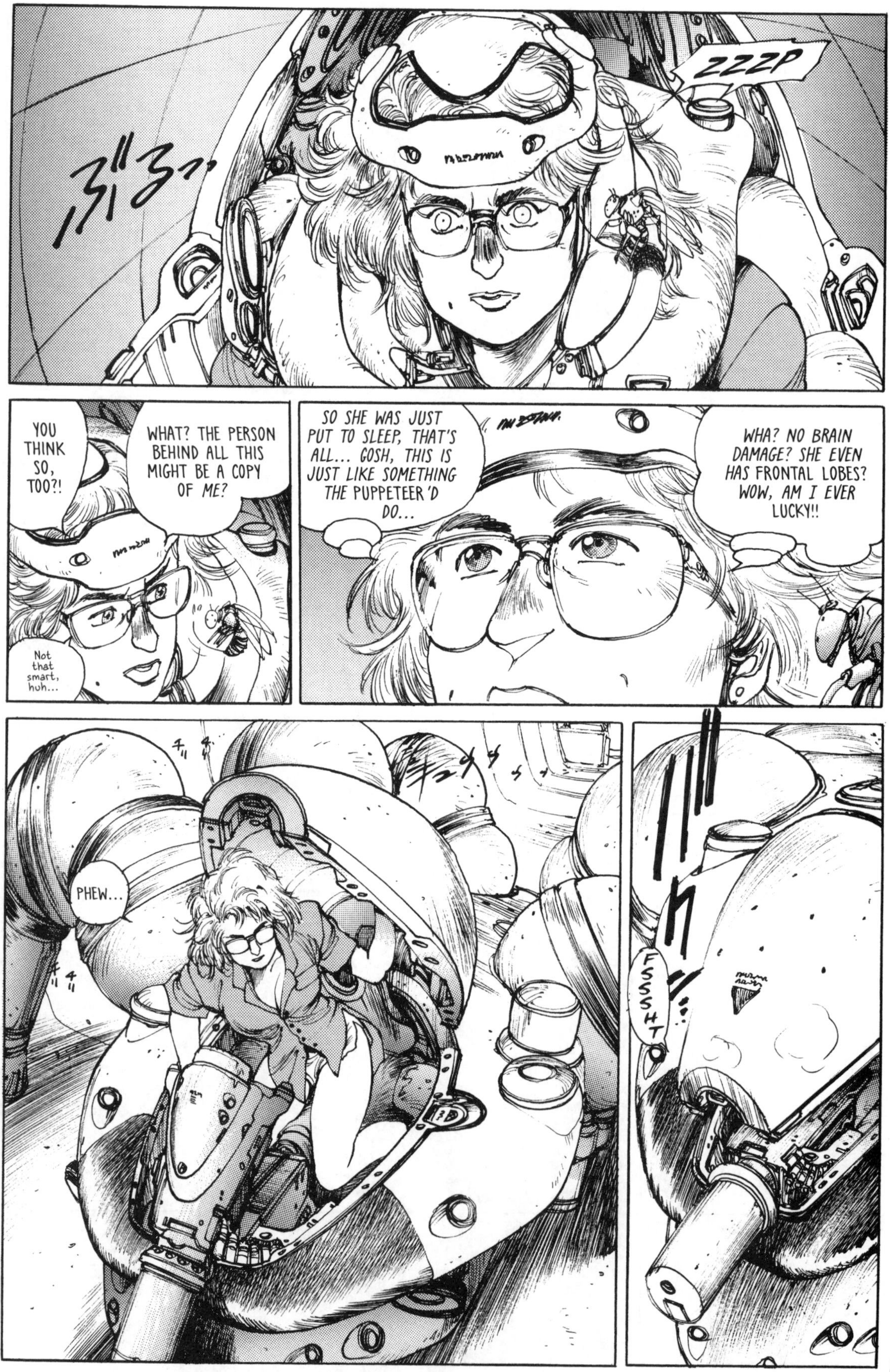
ZZZP
WHA? NO BRAIN DAMAGE? SHE EVEN HAS FRONTAL LOBES? WOW, AM I EVER LUCKY!!
SO SHE WAS JUST PUT TO SLEEP, THAT'S ALL... GOSH, THIS IS JUST LIKE SOMETHING THE PUPPETEER'D DO...
WHAT? THE PERSON BEHIND ALL THIS MIGHT BE A COPY OF ME?
YOU THINK SO, TOO?!
Not that smart, huh...
FSSSHT
PHEW...

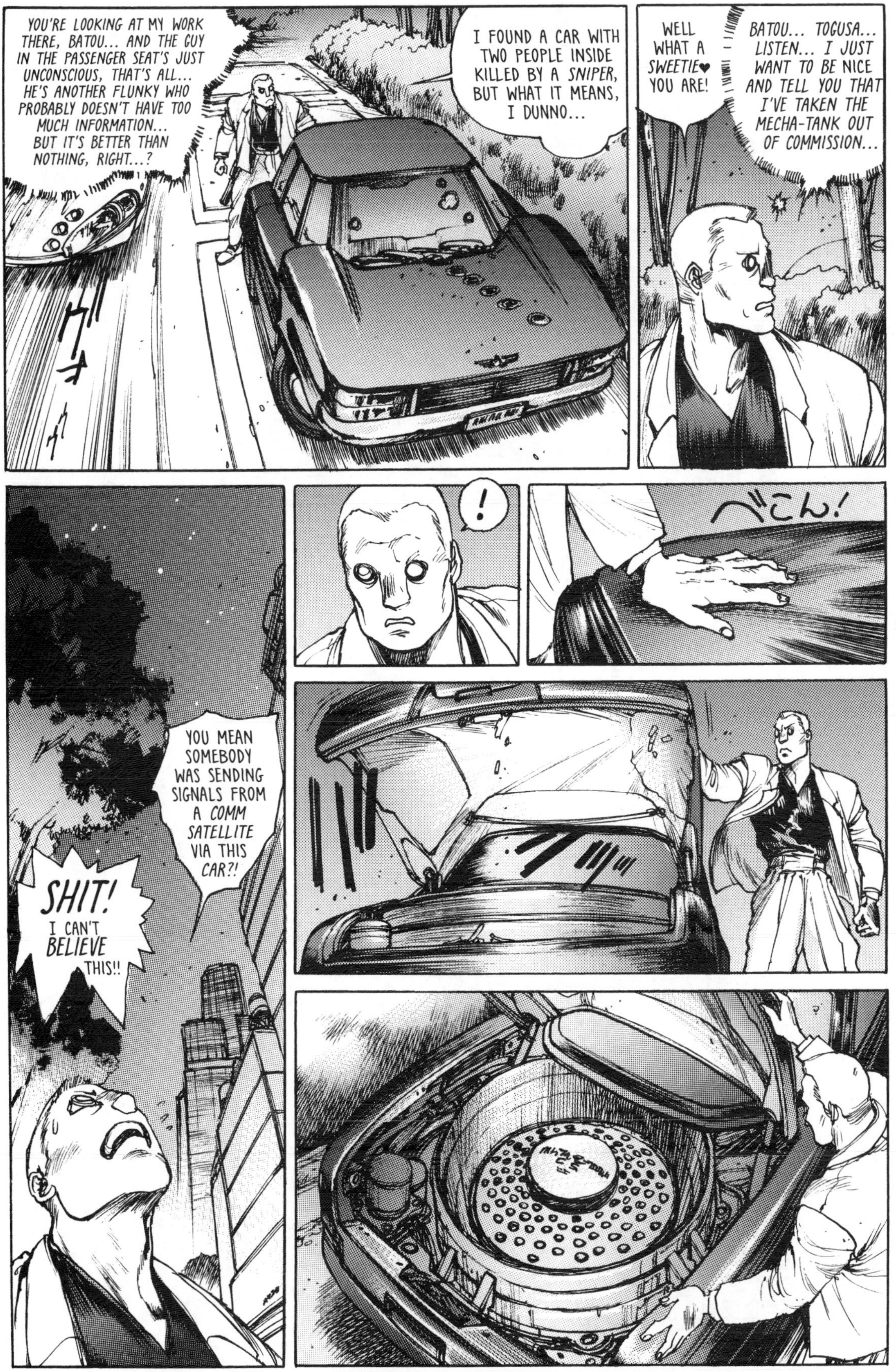
BATOU... TOGUSA... LISTEN... I JUST WANT TO BE NICE AND TELL YOU THAT I'VE TAKEN THE MECHA-TANK OUT OF COMMISSION...
WELL WHAT A SWEETIE❤ YOU ARE!
I FOUND A CAR WITH TWO PEOPLE INSIDE KILLED BY A SNIPER, BUT WHAT IT MEANS, I DUNNO...
YOU'RE LOOKING AT MY WORK THERE, BATOU... AND THE GUY IN THE PASSENGER SEAT'S JUST UNCONSCIOUS, THAT'S ALL... HE'S ANOTHER FLUNKY WHO PROBABLY DOESN'T HAVE TOO MUCH INFORMATION... BUT IT'S BETTER THAN NOTHING, RIGHT...?
べこん!
!
YOU MEAN SOMEBODY WAS SENDING SIGNALS FROM A COMM SATELLITE VIA THIS CAR?!
SHIT! I CAN'T BELIEVE THIS!!

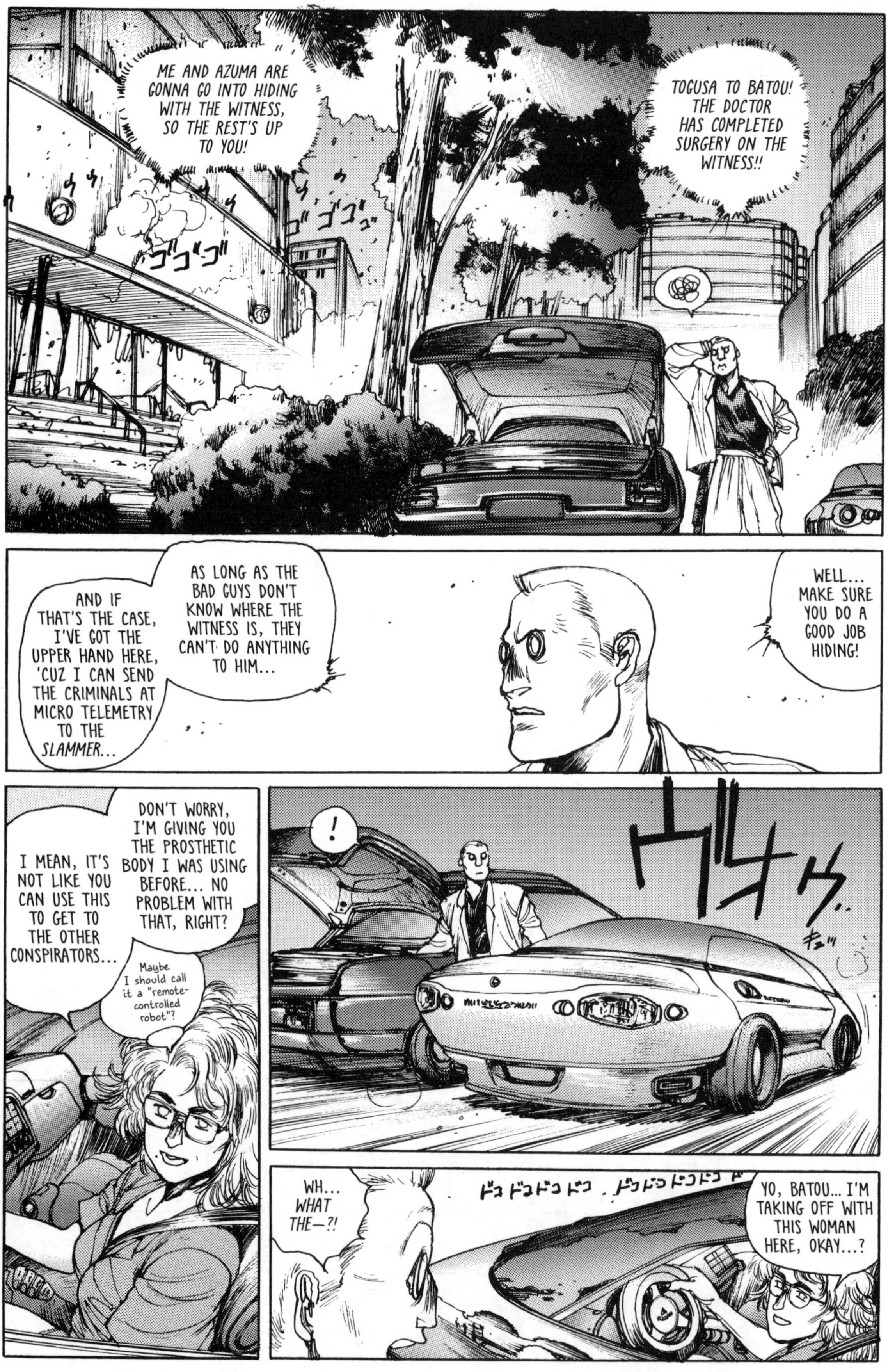
TOGUSA TO BATOU! THE DOCTOR HAS COMPLETED SURGERY ON THE WITNESS!!
ME AND AZUMA ARE GONNA GO INTO HIDING WITH THE WITNESS, SO THE REST'S UP TO YOU!
WELL... MAKE SURE YOU DO A GOOD JOB HIDING!
AS LONG AS THE BAD GUYS DON'T KNOW WHERE THE WITNESS IS, THEY CAN'T DO ANYTHING TO HIM...
AND IF THAT'S THE CASE, I'VE GOT THE UPPER HAND HERE, 'CUZ I CAN SEND THE CRIMINALS AT MICRO TELEMETRY TO THE *SLAMMER*...
!
YO, BATOU... I'M TAKING OFF WITH THIS WOMAN HERE, OKAY...?
WH... WHAT THE—?!
DON'T WORRY, I'M GIVING YOU THE PROSTHETIC BODY I WAS USING BEFORE... NO PROBLEM WITH THAT, RIGHT?
I MEAN, IT'S NOT LIKE YOU CAN USE THIS TO GET TO THE OTHER CONSPIRATORS...
Maybe I should call it a "remote-controlled robot"?

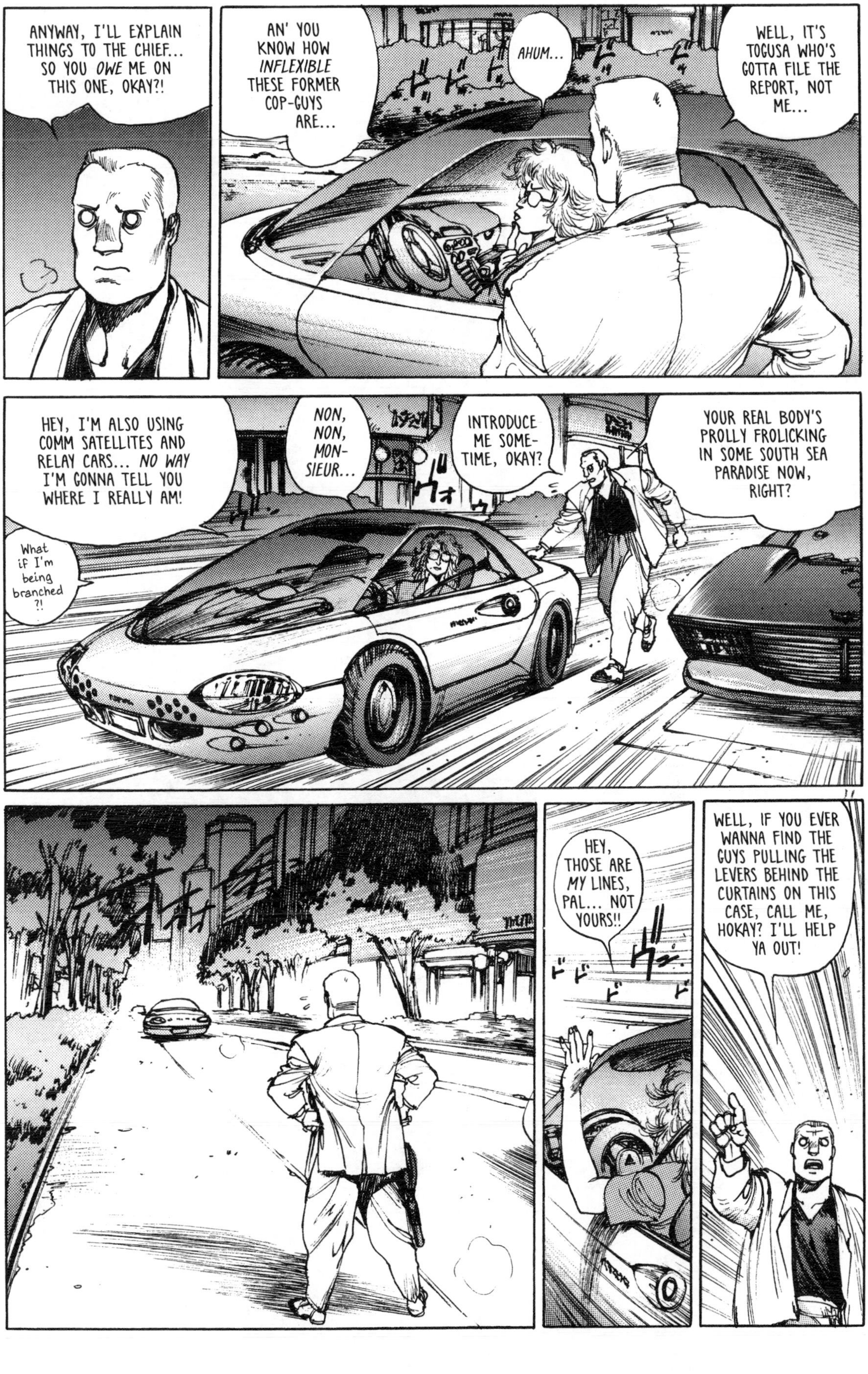
WELL, IT'S TOGUSA WHO'S GOTTA FILE THE REPORT, NOT ME...
AHUM...
AN' YOU KNOW HOW *INFLEXIBLE* THESE FORMER COP-GUYS ARE...
ANYWAY, I'LL EXPLAIN THINGS TO THE CHIEF... SO YOU *OWE* ME ON THIS ONE, OKAY?!
YOUR REAL BODY'S PROLLY FROLICKING IN SOME SOUTH SEA PARADISE NOW, RIGHT?
INTRODUCE ME SOME-TIME, OKAY?
NON, NON, MON-SIEUR...
HEY, I'M ALSO USING COMM SATELLITES AND RELAY CARS... *NO WAY* I'M GONNA TELL YOU WHERE I REALLY AM!
What if I'm being branched ?!
WELL, IF YOU EVER WANNA FIND THE GUYS PULLING THE LEVERS BEHIND THE CURTAINS ON THIS CASE, CALL ME, HOKAY? I'LL HELP YA OUT!
HEY, THOSE ARE *MY* LINES, PAL... NOT YOURS!!

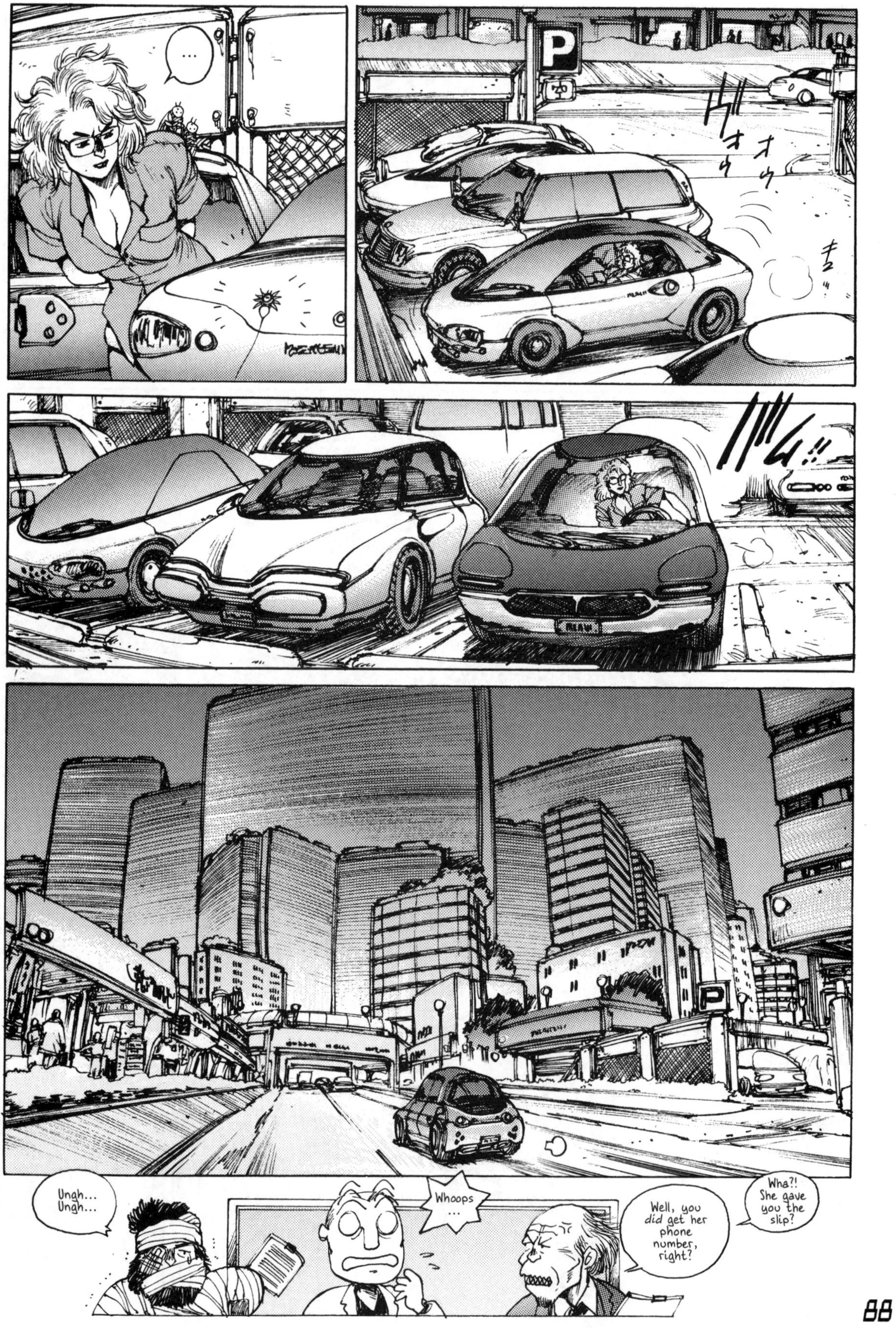
...
Wha?! She gave you the slip?
Well, you did get her phone number, right?
Whoops ...
Ungh... Ungh...

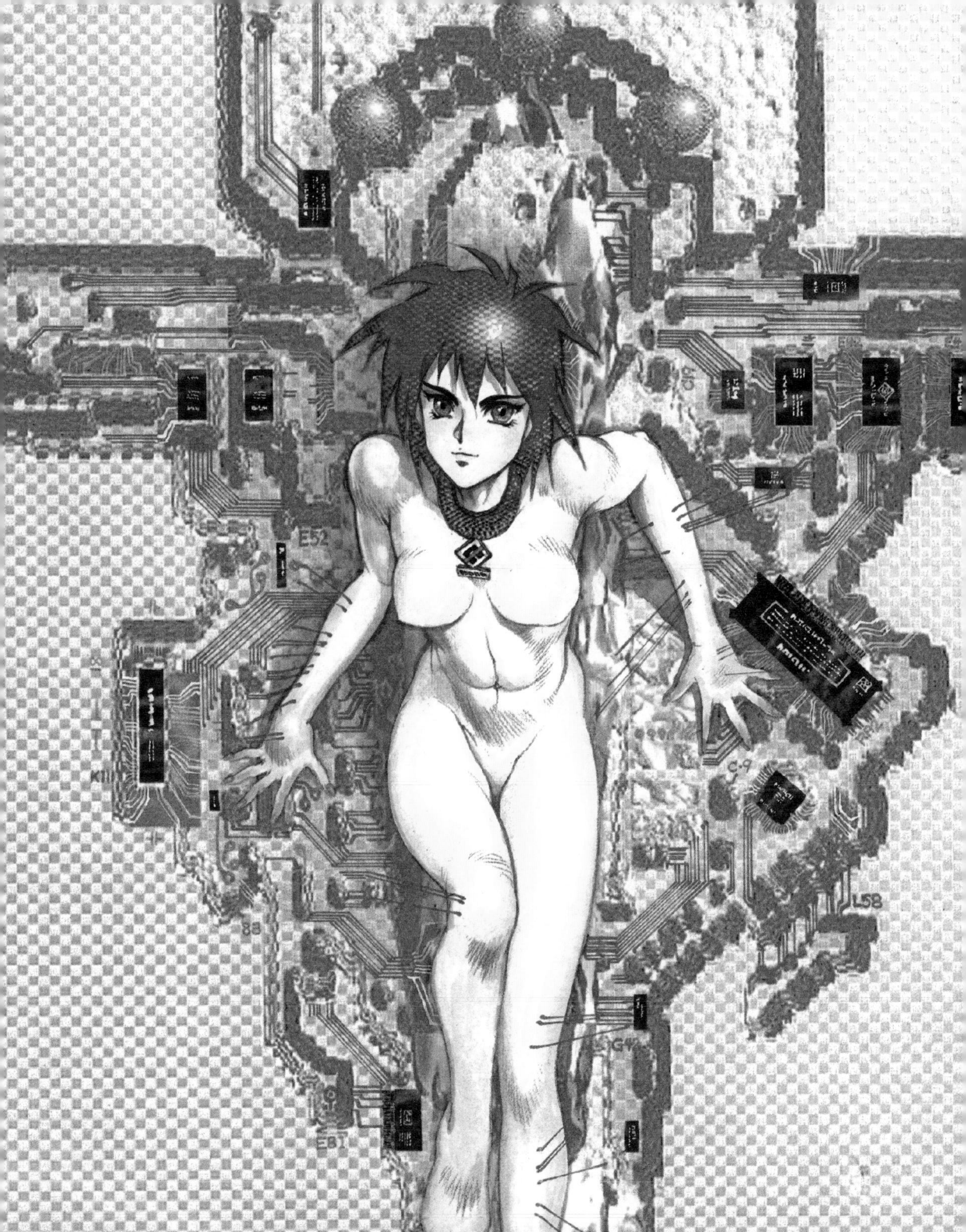

MINES OF MIND Part.1

1995

05

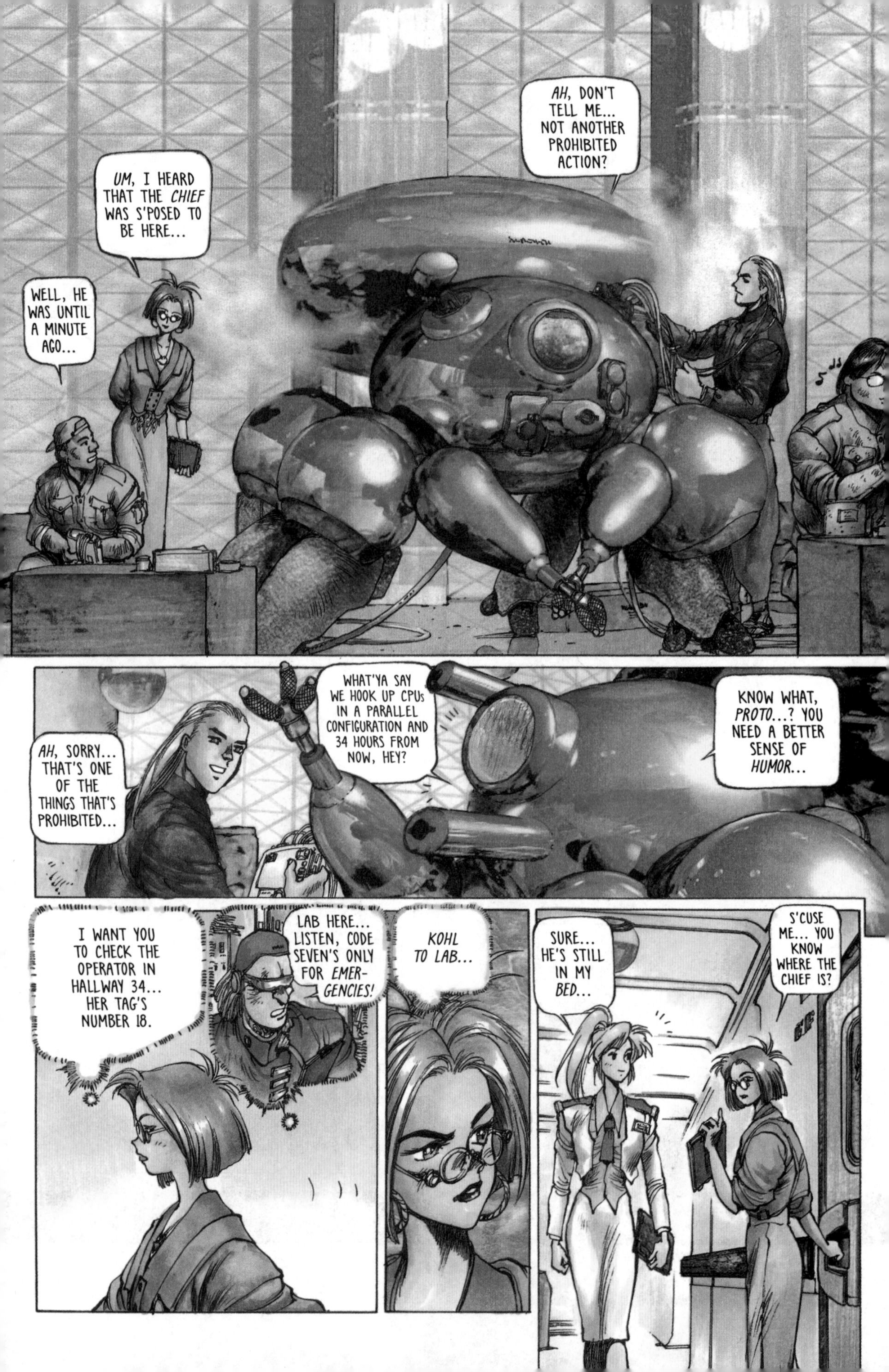

AH, DON'T TELL ME... NOT ANOTHER PROHIBITED ACTION?
UM, I HEARD THAT THE CHIEF WAS S'POSED TO BE HERE...
WELL, HE WAS UNTIL A MINUTE AGO...
KNOW WHAT, PROTO...? YOU NEED A BETTER SENSE OF HUMOR...
WHAT'YA SAY WE HOOK UP CPUs IN A PARALLEL CONFIGURATION AND 34 HOURS FROM NOW, HEY?
AH, SORRY... THAT'S ONE OF THE THINGS THAT'S PROHIBITED...
S'CUSE ME... YOU KNOW WHERE THE CHIEF IS?
SURE... HE'S STILL IN MY BED...
KOHL TO LAB...
LAB HERE... LISTEN, CODE SEVEN'S ONLY FOR EMER-GENCIES!
I WANT YOU TO CHECK THE OPERATOR IN HALLWAY 34... HER TAG'S NUMBER 18.

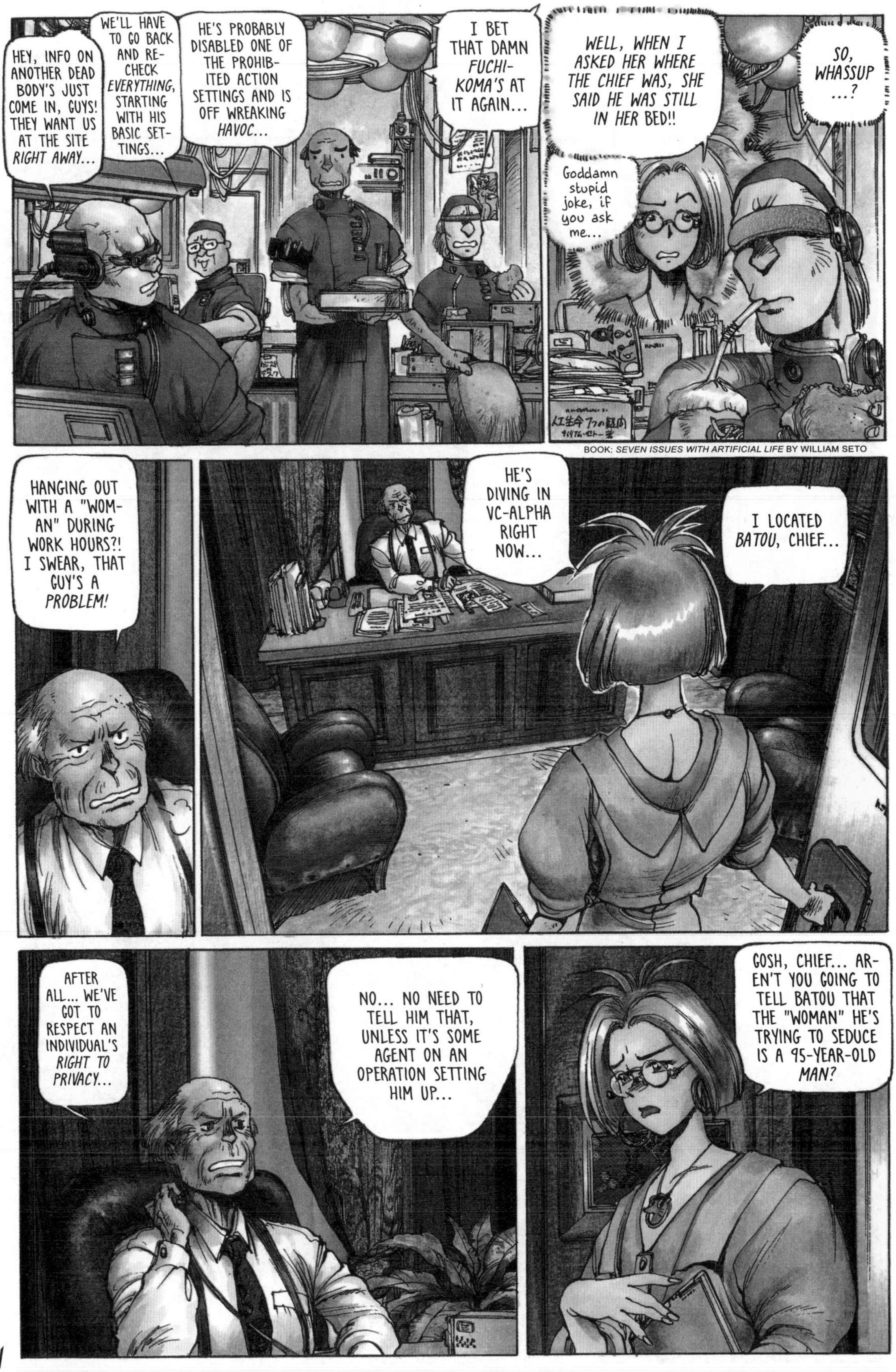

SO, WHASSUP...?
WELL, WHEN I ASKED HER WHERE THE CHIEF WAS, SHE SAID HE WAS STILL IN HER BED!!
Goddamn stupid joke, if you ask me...
I BET THAT DAMN FUCHIKOMA'S AT IT AGAIN...
HE'S PROBABLY DISABLED ONE OF THE PROHIBITED ACTION SETTINGS AND IS OFF WREAKING HAVOC...
WE'LL HAVE TO GO BACK AND RECHECK EVERYTHING, STARTING WITH HIS BASIC SETTINGS...
HEY, INFO ON ANOTHER DEAD BODY'S JUST COME IN, GUYS! THEY WANT US AT THE SITE RIGHT AWAY...
BOOK: SEVEN ISSUES WITH ARTIFICIAL LIFE BY WILLIAM SETO
I LOCATED BATOU, CHIEF...
HE'S DIVING IN VC-ALPHA RIGHT NOW...
HANGING OUT WITH A "WOMAN" DURING WORK HOURS?! I SWEAR, THAT GUY'S A PROBLEM!
GOSH, CHIEF... AREN'T YOU GOING TO TELL BATOU THAT THE "WOMAN" HE'S TRYING TO SEDUCE IS A 95-YEAR-OLD MAN?
NO... NO NEED TO TELL HIM THAT, UNLESS IT'S SOME AGENT ON AN OPERATION SETTING HIM UP...
AFTER ALL... WE'VE GOT TO RESPECT AN INDIVIDUAL'S RIGHT TO PRIVACY...

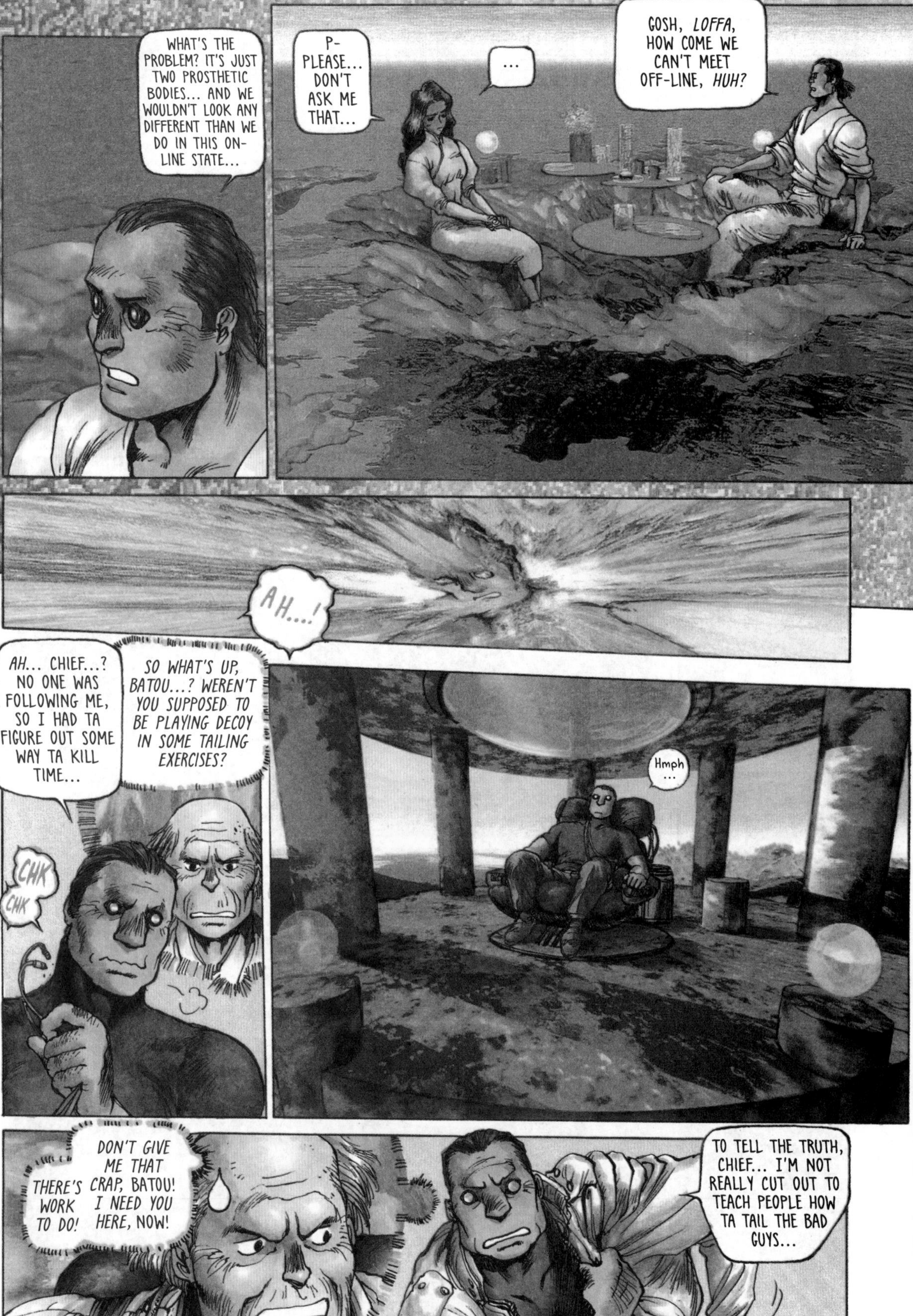
GOSH, *LOFFA*, HOW COME WE CAN'T MEET OFF-LINE, *HUH?*
...
P-PLEASE... DON'T ASK ME THAT...
WHAT'S THE PROBLEM? IT'S JUST TWO PROSTHETIC BODIES... AND WE WOULDN'T LOOK ANY DIFFERENT THAN WE DO IN THIS ON-LINE STATE...
AH...!
Hmph...
SO WHAT'S UP, BATOU...? WEREN'T YOU SUPPOSED TO BE PLAYING DECOY IN SOME TAILING EXERCISES?
AH... CHIEF...? NO ONE WAS FOLLOWING ME, SO I HAD TA FIGURE OUT SOME WAY TA KILL TIME...
CHK
CHK
TO TELL THE TRUTH, CHIEF... I'M NOT REALLY CUT OUT TO TEACH PEOPLE HOW TA TAIL THE BAD GUYS...
DON'T GIVE ME THAT CRAP, BATOU! I NEED YOU HERE, NOW!
THERE'S WORK TO DO!

THE REFERENCE TO "OFF-LINE" HERE MEANS THAT BATOU WANTS TO MEET THE WOMAN(?) OUTSIDE THE E-BRAIN SPACE, IN THE PHYSICAL WORLD. "ON-LINE" MEANS WITHIN THE E-BRAIN SPACE. MEETING OFF-LINE IN THE PHYSICAL WORLD DOESN'T MEAN BATOU WOULD INSTANTLY KNOW LOFFA'S REAL AGE OR SEX, BUT "SHE'S" NONETHELESS AFRAID HE'D FIGURE IT OUT FROM SEEING THE ENVIRONMENT IN WHICH "SHE" LIVES, OR FROM "HER" FRIENDS...

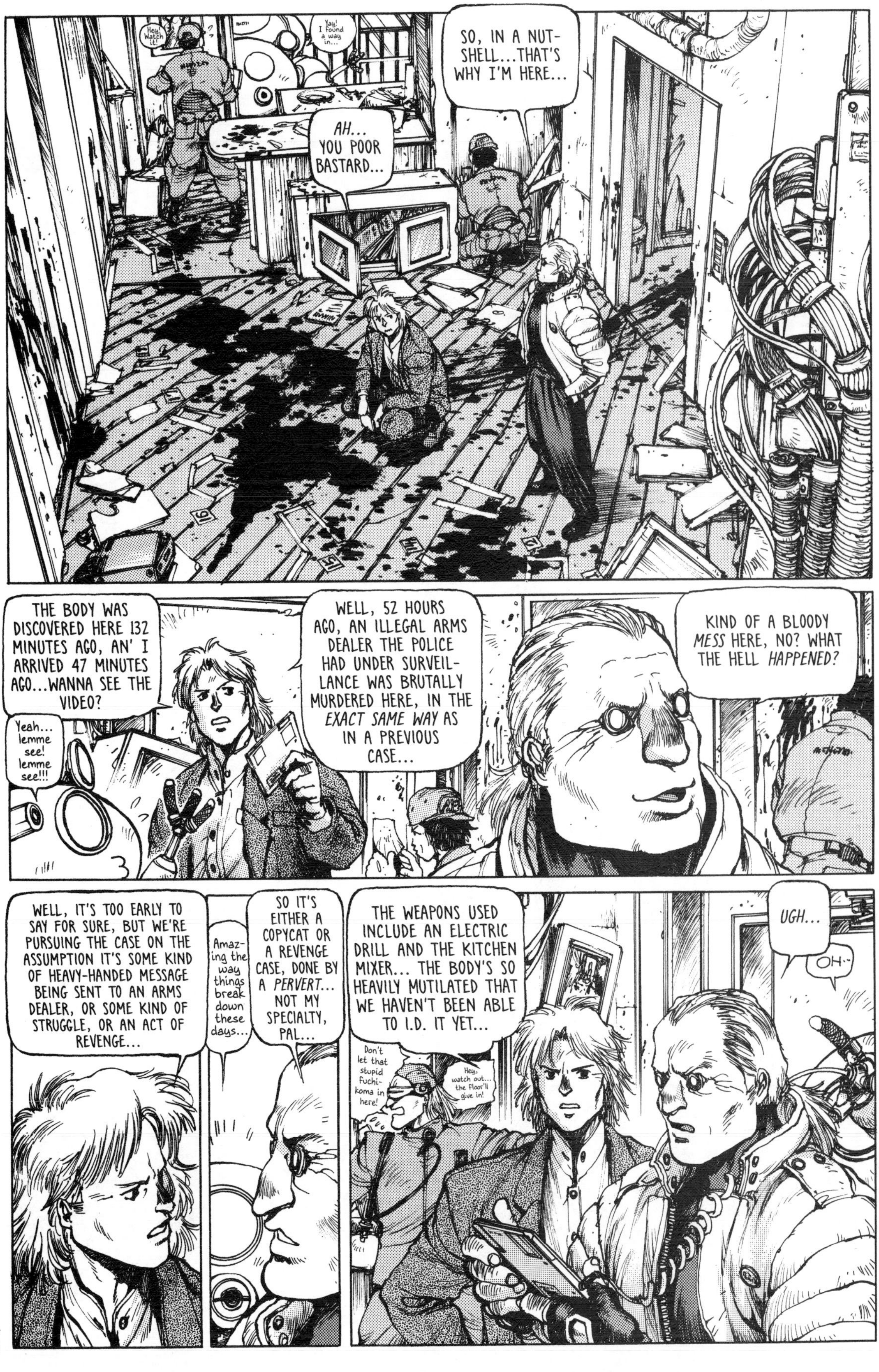
SO, IN A NUT-SHELL...THAT'S WHY I'M HERE...
Yay! I found a way in...
Hey! Watch it!
AH... YOU POOR BASTARD...
KIND OF A BLOODY *MESS* HERE, NO? WHAT THE HELL *HAPPENED?*
WELL, 52 HOURS AGO, AN ILLEGAL ARMS DEALER THE POLICE HAD UNDER SURVEIL-LANCE WAS BRUTALLY MURDERED HERE, IN THE *EXACT SAME WAY* AS IN A PREVIOUS CASE...
THE BODY WAS DISCOVERED HERE 132 MINUTES AGO, AN' I ARRIVED 47 MINUTES AGO...WANNA SEE THE VIDEO?
Yeah... lemme see! lemme see!!!
UGH...
OH..
THE WEAPONS USED INCLUDE AN ELECTRIC DRILL AND THE KITCHEN MIXER... THE BODY'S SO HEAVILY MUTILATED THAT WE HAVEN'T BEEN ABLE TO I.D. IT YET...
Hey, watch out... the floor'll give in!
Don't let that stupid Fuchi-koma in here!
SO IT'S EITHER A COPYCAT OR A REVENGE CASE, DONE BY A *PERVERT*... NOT MY SPECIALTY, PAL...
Amaz-ing the way things break down these days...
WELL, IT'S TOO EARLY TO SAY FOR SURE, BUT WE'RE PURSUING THE CASE ON THE ASSUMPTION IT'S SOME KIND OF HEAVY-HANDED MESSAGE BEING SENT TO AN ARMS DEALER, OR SOME KIND OF STRUGGLE, OR AN ACT OF REVENGE...

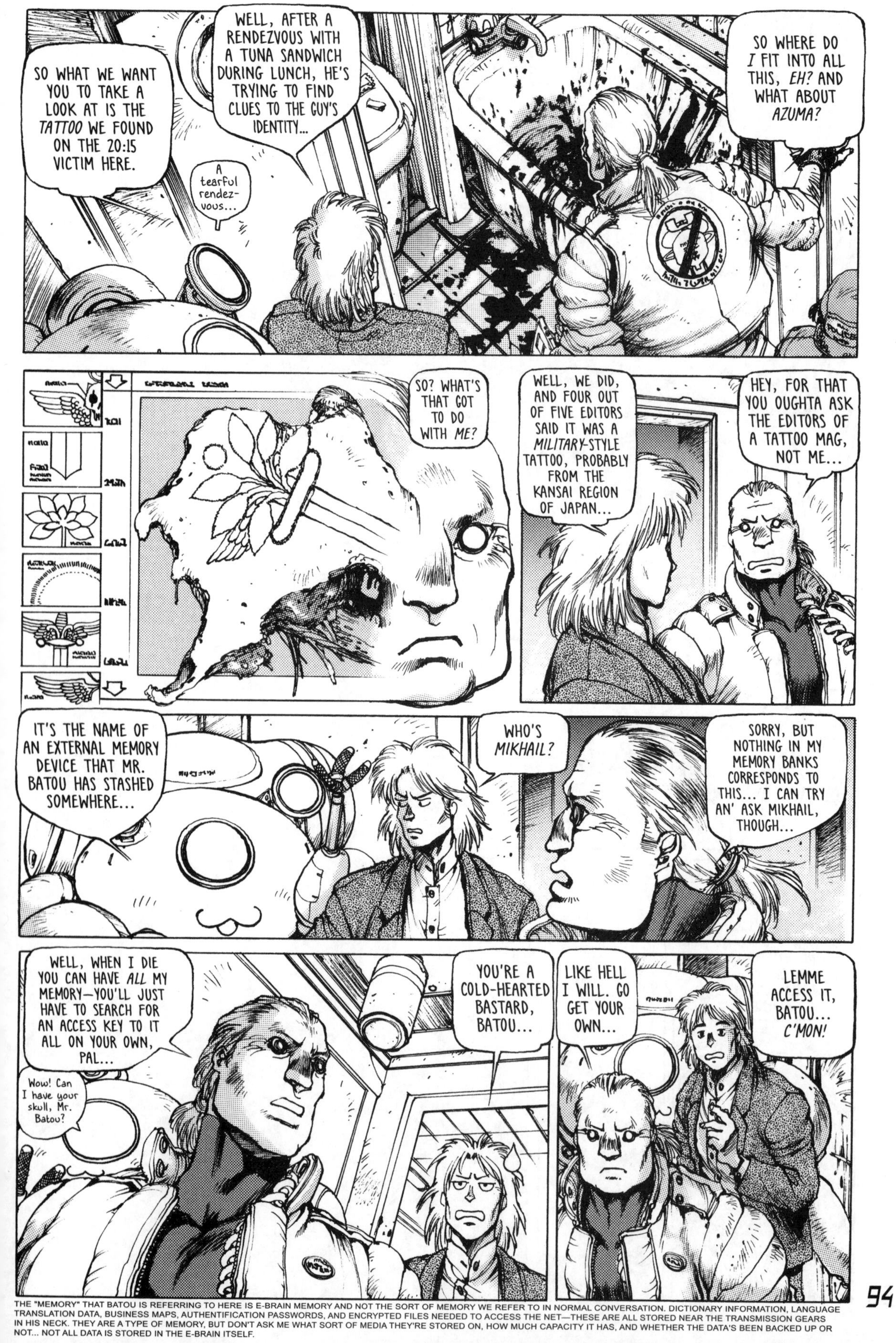
SO WHERE DO *I* FIT INTO ALL THIS, *EH?* AND WHAT ABOUT *AZUMA?*
WELL, AFTER A RENDEZVOUS WITH A TUNA SANDWICH DURING LUNCH, HE'S TRYING TO FIND CLUES TO THE GUY'S IDENTITY...
A tearful rendez-vous...
SO WHAT WE WANT YOU TO TAKE A LOOK AT IS THE *TATTOO* WE FOUND ON THE 20:15 VICTIM HERE.
HEY, FOR THAT YOU OUGHTA ASK THE EDITORS OF A TATTOO MAG, NOT ME...
WELL, WE DID, AND FOUR OUT OF FIVE EDITORS SAID IT WAS A *MILITARY*-STYLE TATTOO, PROBABLY FROM THE KANSAI REGION OF JAPAN...
SO? WHAT'S THAT GOT TO DO WITH *ME?*
SORRY, BUT NOTHING IN MY MEMORY BANKS CORRESPONDS TO THIS... I CAN TRY AN' ASK MIKHAIL, THOUGH...
WHO'S *MIKHAIL?*
IT'S THE NAME OF AN EXTERNAL MEMORY DEVICE THAT MR. BATOU HAS STASHED SOMEWHERE...
LEMME ACCESS IT, BATOU... *C'MON!*
LIKE HELL I WILL. GO GET YOUR OWN...
YOU'RE A COLD-HEARTED BASTARD, BATOU...
WELL, WHEN I DIE YOU CAN HAVE *ALL* MY MEMORY—YOU'LL JUST HAVE TO SEARCH FOR AN ACCESS KEY TO IT ALL ON YOUR OWN, PAL...
Wow! Can I have your skull, Mr. Batou?

THE "MEMORY" THAT BATOU IS REFERRING TO HERE IS E-BRAIN MEMORY AND NOT THE SORT OF MEMORY WE REFER TO IN NORMAL CONVERSATION. DICTIONARY INFORMATION, LANGUAGE TRANSLATION DATA, BUSINESS MAPS, AUTHENTIFICATION PASSWORDS, AND ENCRYPTED FILES NEEDED TO ACCESS THE NET—THESE ARE ALL STORED NEAR THE TRANSMISSION GEARS IN HIS NECK. THEY ARE A TYPE OF MEMORY, BUT DON'T ASK ME WHAT SORT OF MEDIA THEY'RE STORED ON, HOW MUCH CAPACITY IT HAS, AND WHETHER THE DATA'S BEEN BACKED UP OR NOT... NOT ALL DATA IS STORED IN THE E-BRAIN ITSELF.

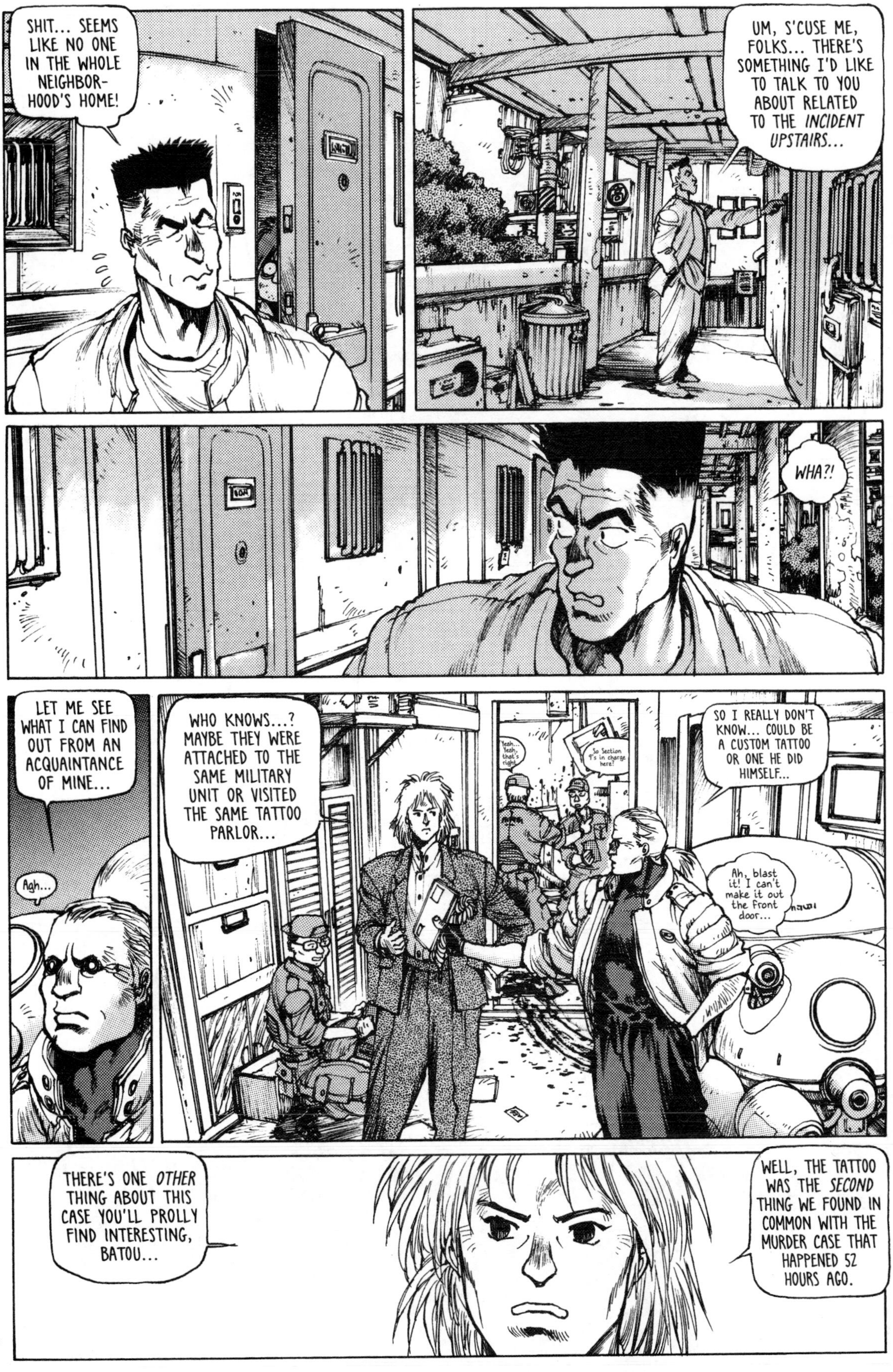
UM, S'CUSE ME, FOLKS... THERE'S SOMETHING I'D LIKE TO TALK TO YOU ABOUT RELATED TO THE *INCIDENT UPSTAIRS*...
SHIT... SEEMS LIKE NO ONE IN THE WHOLE NEIGHBOR-HOOD'S HOME!
WHA?!
SO I REALLY DON'T KNOW... COULD BE A CUSTOM TATTOO OR ONE HE DID HIMSELF...
Ah, blast it! I can't make it out the front door...
So Section 9's in charge here?
Yeah... Yeah, that's right
WHO KNOWS...? MAYBE THEY WERE ATTACHED TO THE SAME MILITARY UNIT OR VISITED THE SAME TATTOO PARLOR...
LET ME SEE WHAT I CAN FIND OUT FROM AN ACQUAINTANCE OF MINE...
Agh...
WELL, THE TATTOO WAS THE *SECOND* THING WE FOUND IN COMMON WITH THE MURDER CASE THAT HAPPENED 52 HOURS AGO.
THERE'S ONE *OTHER* THING ABOUT THIS CASE YOU'LL PROLLY FIND INTERESTING, BATOU...

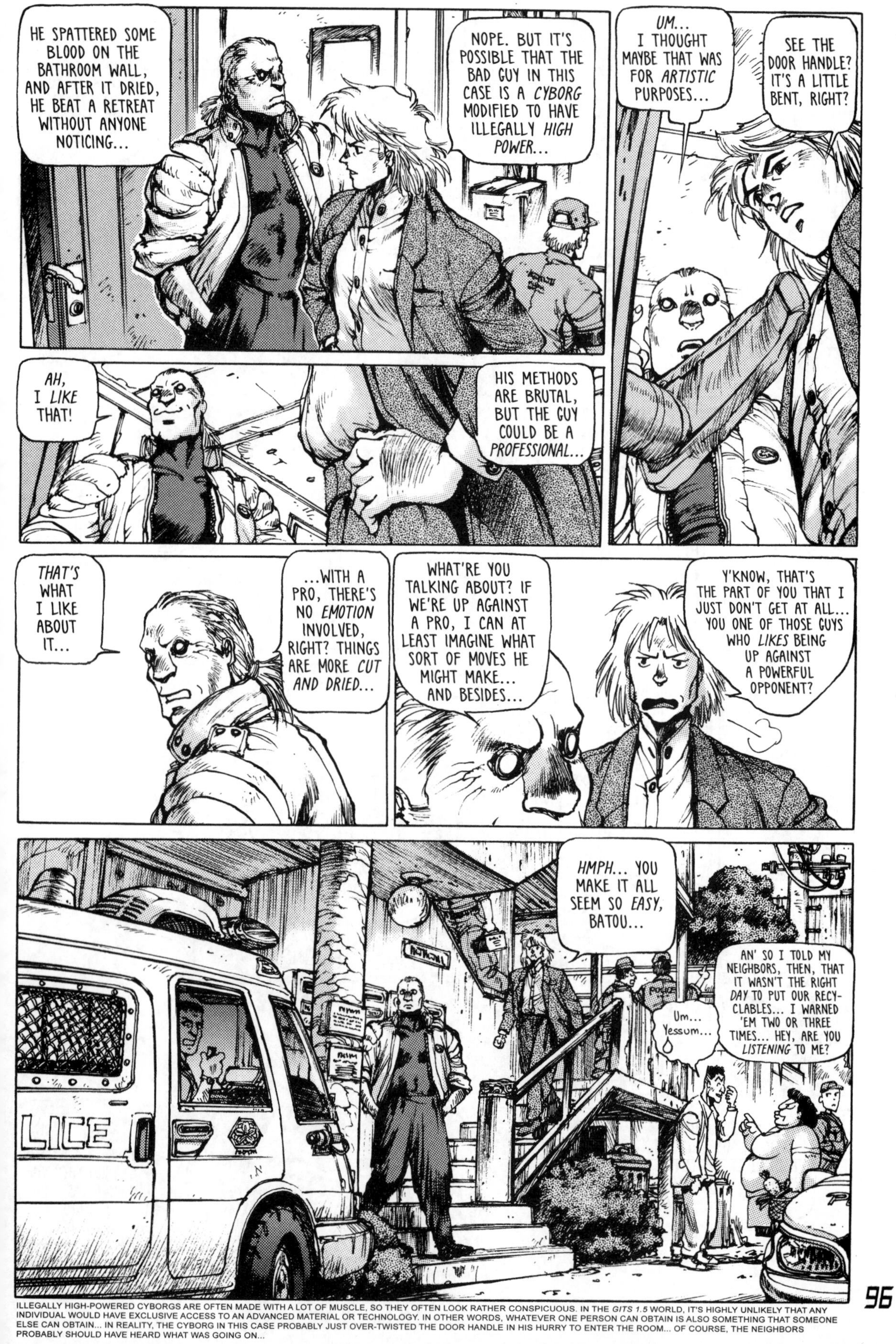
SEE THE DOOR HANDLE? IT'S A LITTLE BENT, RIGHT?
UM... I THOUGHT MAYBE THAT WAS FOR *ARTISTIC* PURPOSES...
NOPE. BUT IT'S POSSIBLE THAT THE BAD GUY IN THIS CASE IS A *CYBORG* MODIFIED TO HAVE ILLEGALLY *HIGH POWER*...
HE SPATTERED SOME BLOOD ON THE BATHROOM WALL, AND AFTER IT DRIED, HE BEAT A RETREAT WITHOUT ANYONE NOTICING...
HIS METHODS ARE BRUTAL, BUT THE GUY COULD BE A *PROFESSIONAL*...
AH, I *LIKE* THAT!
Y'KNOW, THAT'S THE PART OF YOU THAT I JUST DON'T GET AT ALL... YOU ONE OF THOSE GUYS WHO *LIKES* BEING UP AGAINST A POWERFUL OPPONENT?
WHAT'RE YOU TALKING ABOUT? IF WE'RE UP AGAINST A PRO, I CAN AT LEAST IMAGINE WHAT SORT OF MOVES HE MIGHT MAKE... AND BESIDES...
...WITH A PRO, THERE'S NO *EMOTION* INVOLVED, RIGHT? THINGS ARE MORE *CUT AND DRIED*...
THAT'S WHAT I LIKE ABOUT IT...
HMPH... YOU MAKE IT ALL SEEM SO *EASY*, BATOU...
AN' SO I TOLD MY NEIGHBORS, THEN, THAT IT WASN'T THE RIGHT *DAY* TO PUT OUR RECYCLABLES... I WARNED 'EM TWO OR THREE TIMES... HEY, ARE YOU *LISTENING* TO ME?
Um... Yessum...
LICE

ILLEGALLY HIGH-POWERED CYBORGS ARE OFTEN MADE WITH A LOT OF MUSCLE, SO THEY OFTEN LOOK RATHER CONSPICUOUS. IN THE *GITS 1.5* WORLD, IT'S HIGHLY UNLIKELY THAT ANY INDIVIDUAL WOULD HAVE EXCLUSIVE ACCESS TO AN ADVANCED MATERIAL OR TECHNOLOGY. IN OTHER WORDS, WHATEVER ONE PERSON CAN OBTAIN IS ALSO SOMETHING THAT SOMEONE ELSE CAN OBTAIN... IN REALITY, THE CYBORG IN THIS CASE PROBABLY JUST OVER-TWISTED THE DOOR HANDLE IN HIS HURRY TO ENTER THE ROOM... OF COURSE, THE NEIGHBORS PROBABLY SHOULD HAVE HEARD WHAT WAS GOING ON...

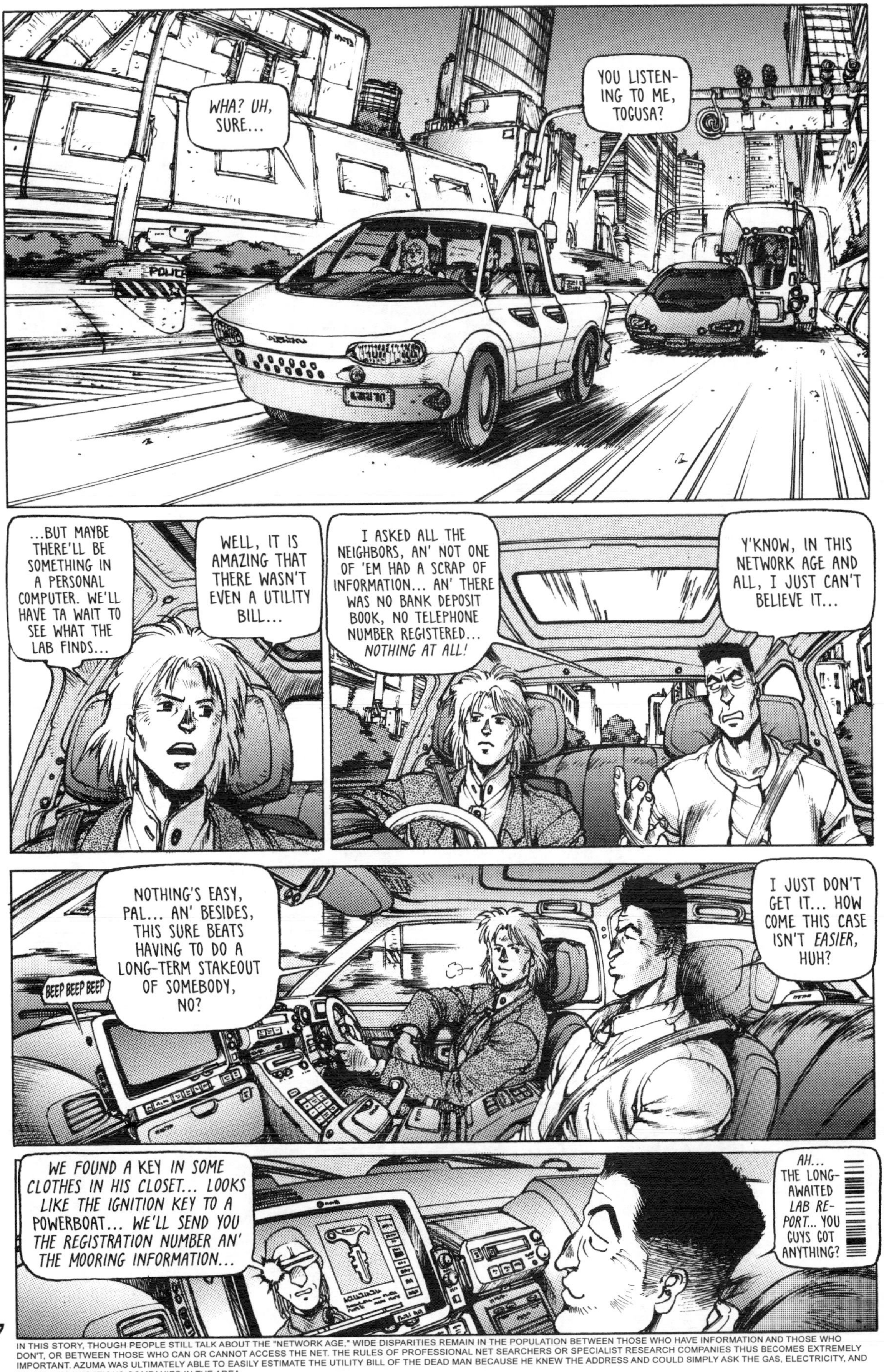
YOU LISTENING TO ME, TOGUSA?
WHA? UH, SURE...
Y'KNOW, IN THIS NETWORK AGE AND ALL, I JUST CAN'T BELIEVE IT...
I ASKED ALL THE NEIGHBORS, AN' NOT ONE OF 'EM HAD A SCRAP OF INFORMATION... AN' THERE WAS NO BANK DEPOSIT BOOK, NO TELEPHONE NUMBER REGISTERED... *NOTHING AT ALL!*
WELL, IT IS AMAZING THAT THERE WASN'T EVEN A UTILITY BILL...
...BUT MAYBE THERE'LL BE SOMETHING IN A PERSONAL COMPUTER. WE'LL HAVE TA WAIT TO SEE WHAT THE LAB FINDS...
I JUST DON'T GET IT... HOW COME THIS CASE ISN'T *EASIER*, HUH?
NOTHING'S EASY, PAL... AN' BESIDES, THIS SURE BEATS HAVING TO DO A LONG-TERM STAKEOUT OF SOMEBODY, NO?
BEEP BEEP BEEP
AH... THE LONG-AWAITED *LAB REPORT*... YOU GUYS GOT ANYTHING?
WE FOUND A KEY IN SOME CLOTHES IN HIS CLOSET... LOOKS LIKE THE IGNITION KEY TO A POWERBOAT... WE'LL SEND YOU THE REGISTRATION NUMBER AN' THE MOORING INFORMATION...

IN THIS STORY, THOUGH PEOPLE STILL TALK ABOUT THE "NETWORK AGE," WIDE DISPARITIES REMAIN IN THE POPULATION BETWEEN THOSE WHO HAVE INFORMATION AND THOSE WHO DON'T, OR BETWEEN THOSE WHO CAN OR CANNOT ACCESS THE NET. THE RULES OF PROFESSIONAL NET SEARCHERS OR SPECIALIST RESEARCH COMPANIES THUS BECOMES EXTREMELY IMPORTANT. AZUMA WAS ULTIMATELY ABLE TO EASILY ESTIMATE THE UTILITY BILL OF THE DEAD MAN BECAUSE HE KNEW THE ADDRESS AND COULD SIMPLY ASK THE GAS, ELECTRICITY, AND TELECOMMUNICATIONS COMPANIES IN THE AREA.

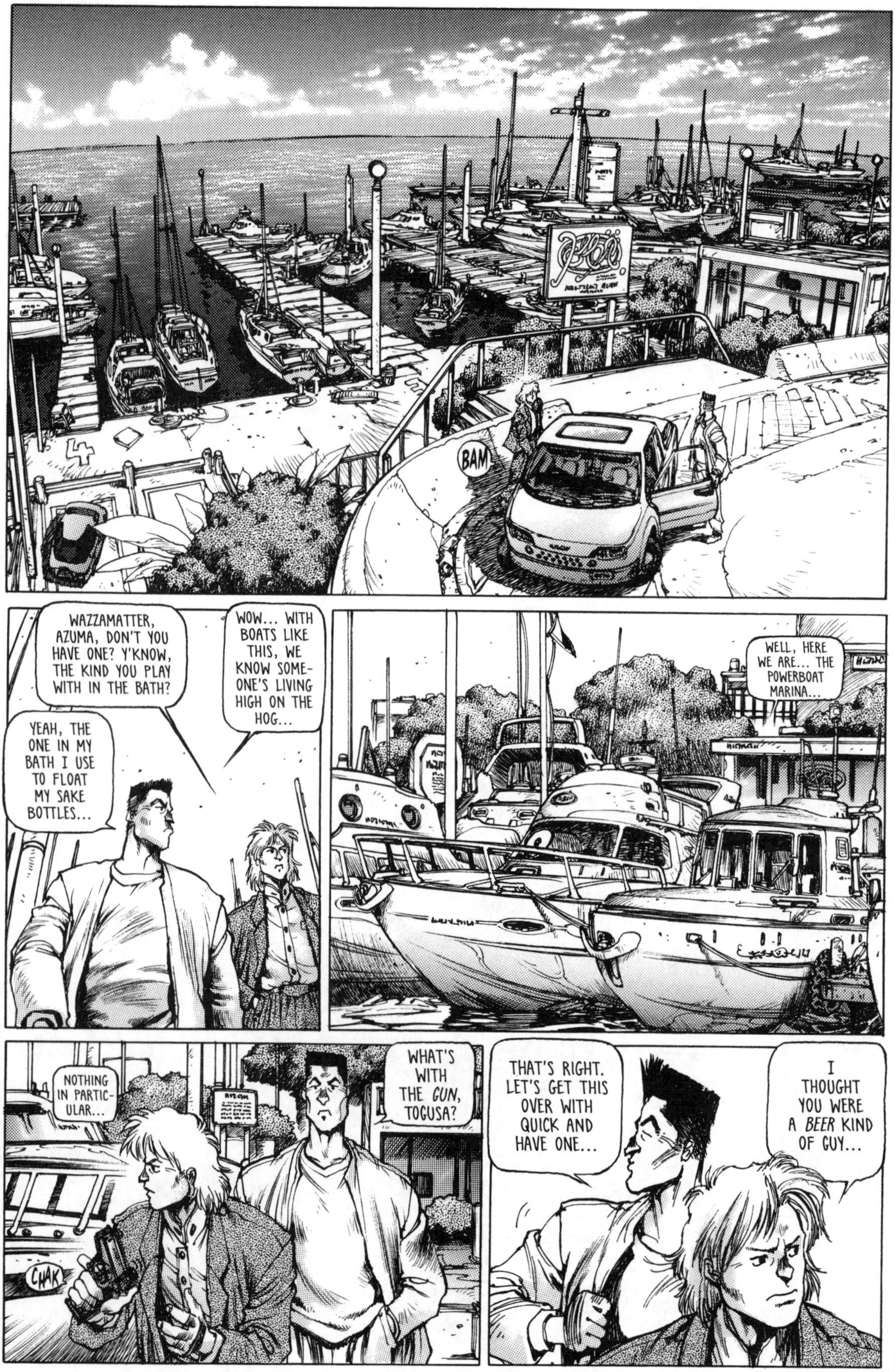
BAM
WELL, HERE WE ARE... THE POWERBOAT MARINA...
WOW... WITH BOATS LIKE THIS, WE KNOW SOMEONE'S LIVING HIGH ON THE HOG...
WAZZAMATTER, AZUMA, DON'T YOU HAVE ONE? Y'KNOW, THE KIND YOU PLAY WITH IN THE BATH?
YEAH, THE ONE IN MY BATH I USE TO FLOAT MY SAKE BOTTLES...
I THOUGHT YOU WERE A *BEER* KIND OF GUY...
THAT'S RIGHT. LET'S GET THIS OVER WITH QUICK AND HAVE ONE...
WHAT'S WITH THE *GUN*, TOGUSA?
NOTHING IN PARTICULAR...
CHAK

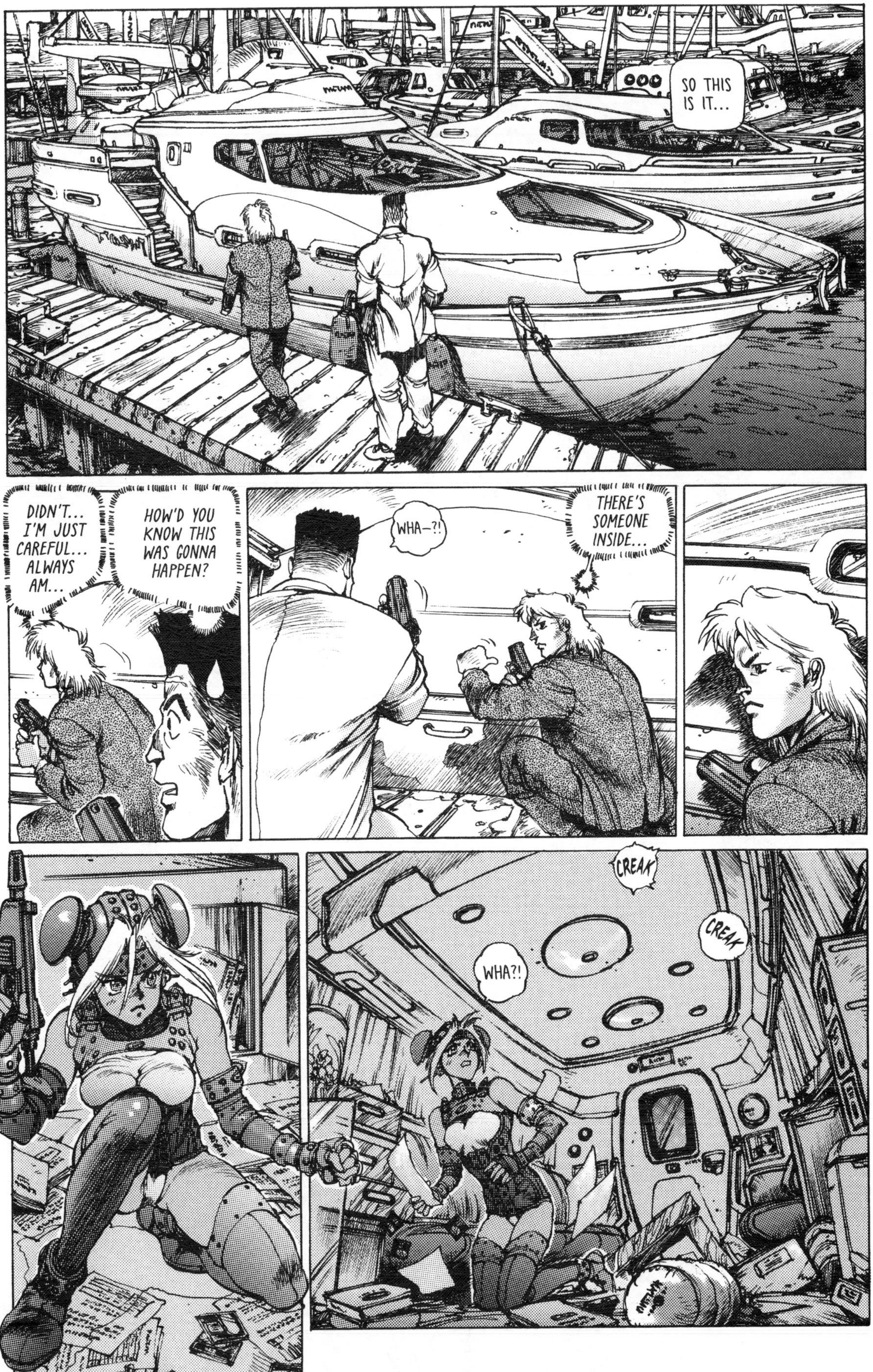
SO THIS IS IT...
THERE'S SOMEONE INSIDE...
WHA–?!
HOW'D YOU KNOW THIS WAS GONNA HAPPEN?
DIDN'T... I'M JUST CAREFUL... ALWAYS AM...
CREAK
CREAK
WHA?!

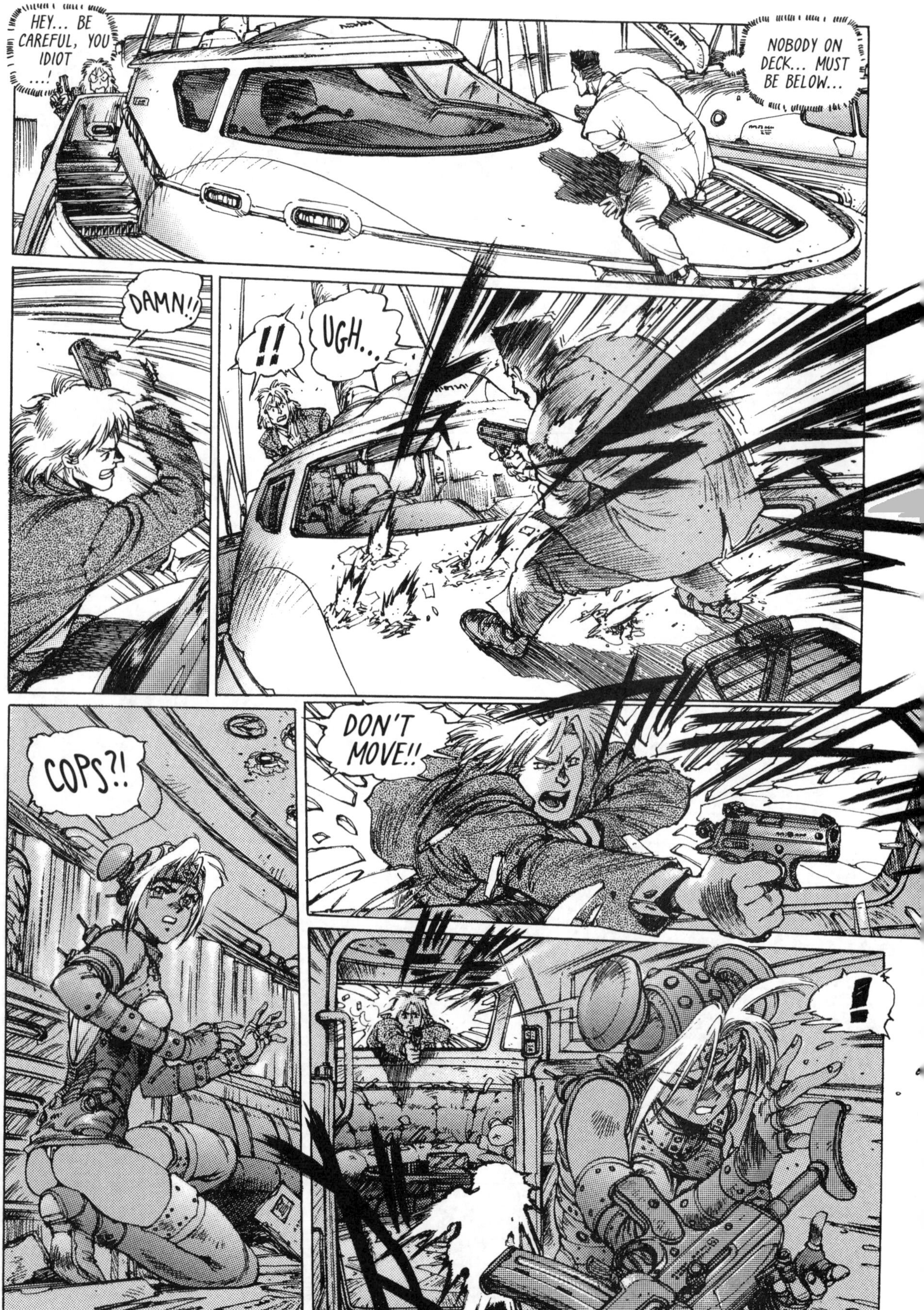
NOBODY ON DECK... MUST BE BELOW...
HEY... BE CAREFUL, YOU IDIOT ...!
UGH...
!!
DAMN!!
DON'T MOVE!!
!
COPS?!

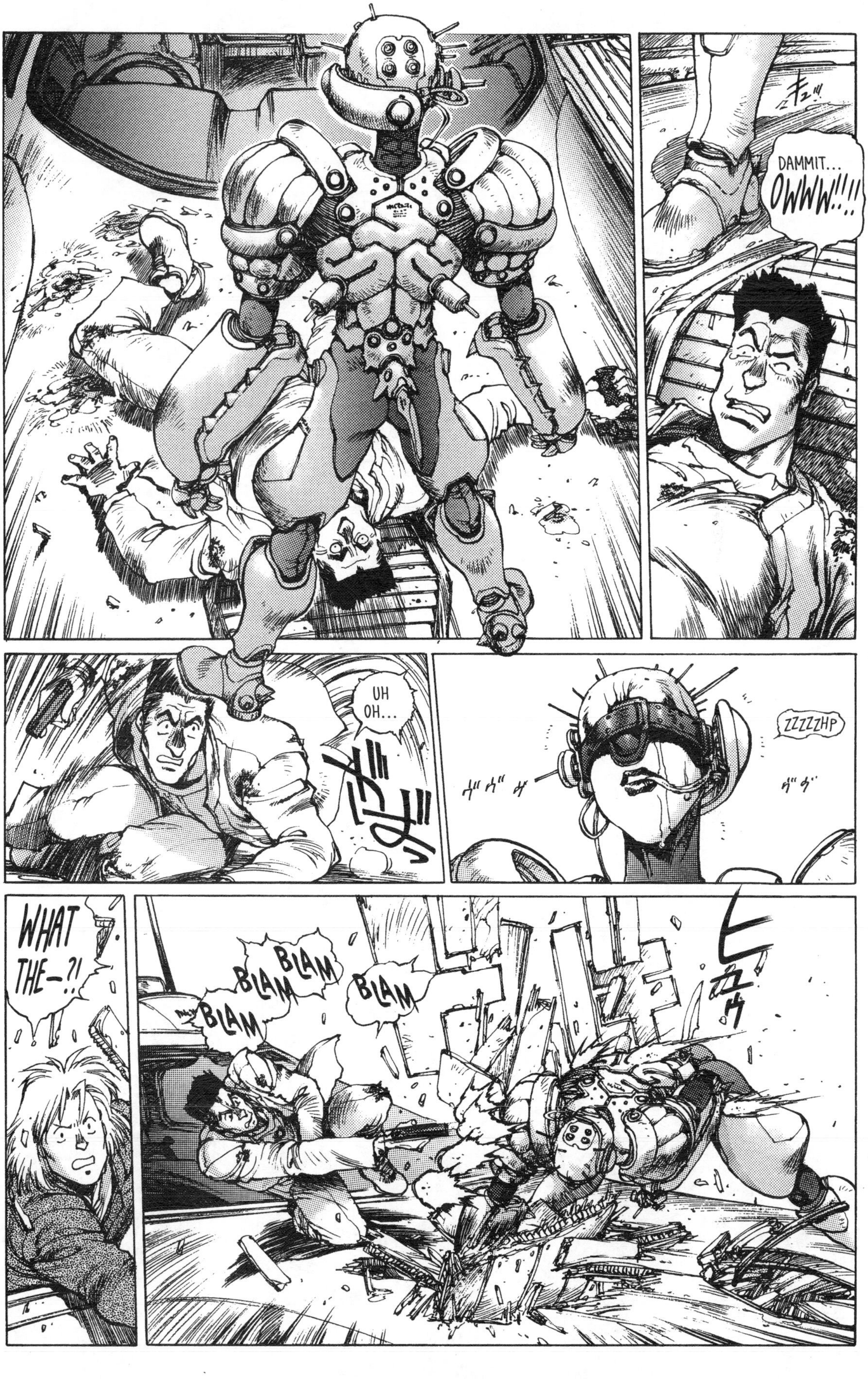

DAMMIT... OWWW!!!!
ZZZZZHP
UH OH...
BLAM
BLAM
BLAM
BLAM
BLAM
WHAT THE—?!

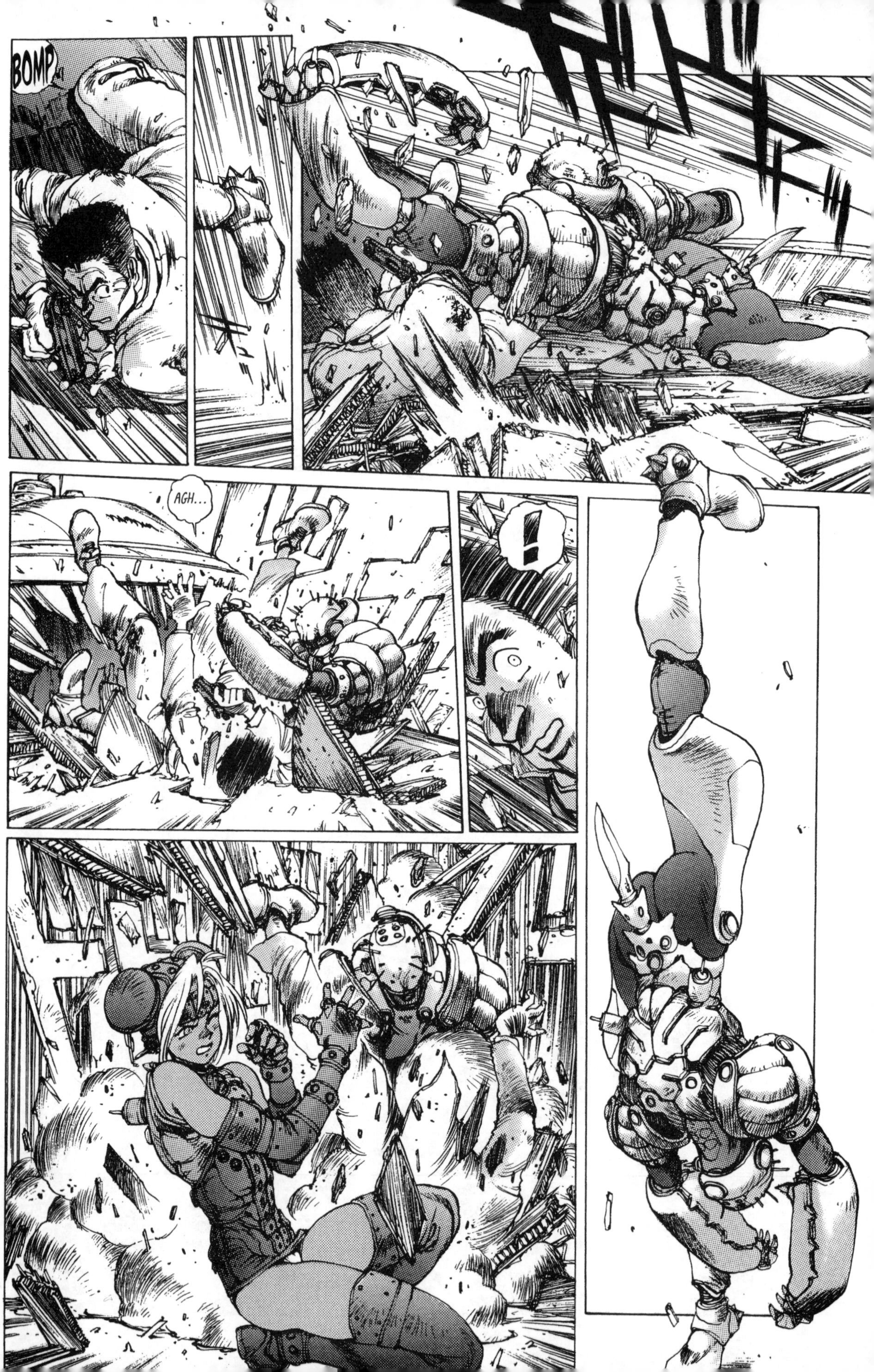
BOMP
!
AGH...

AGHAH...

HACK HACK

AZUMA!!!

SHWIP

CHAK

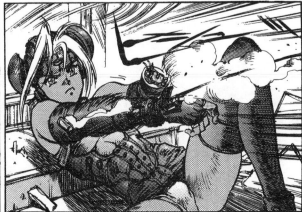

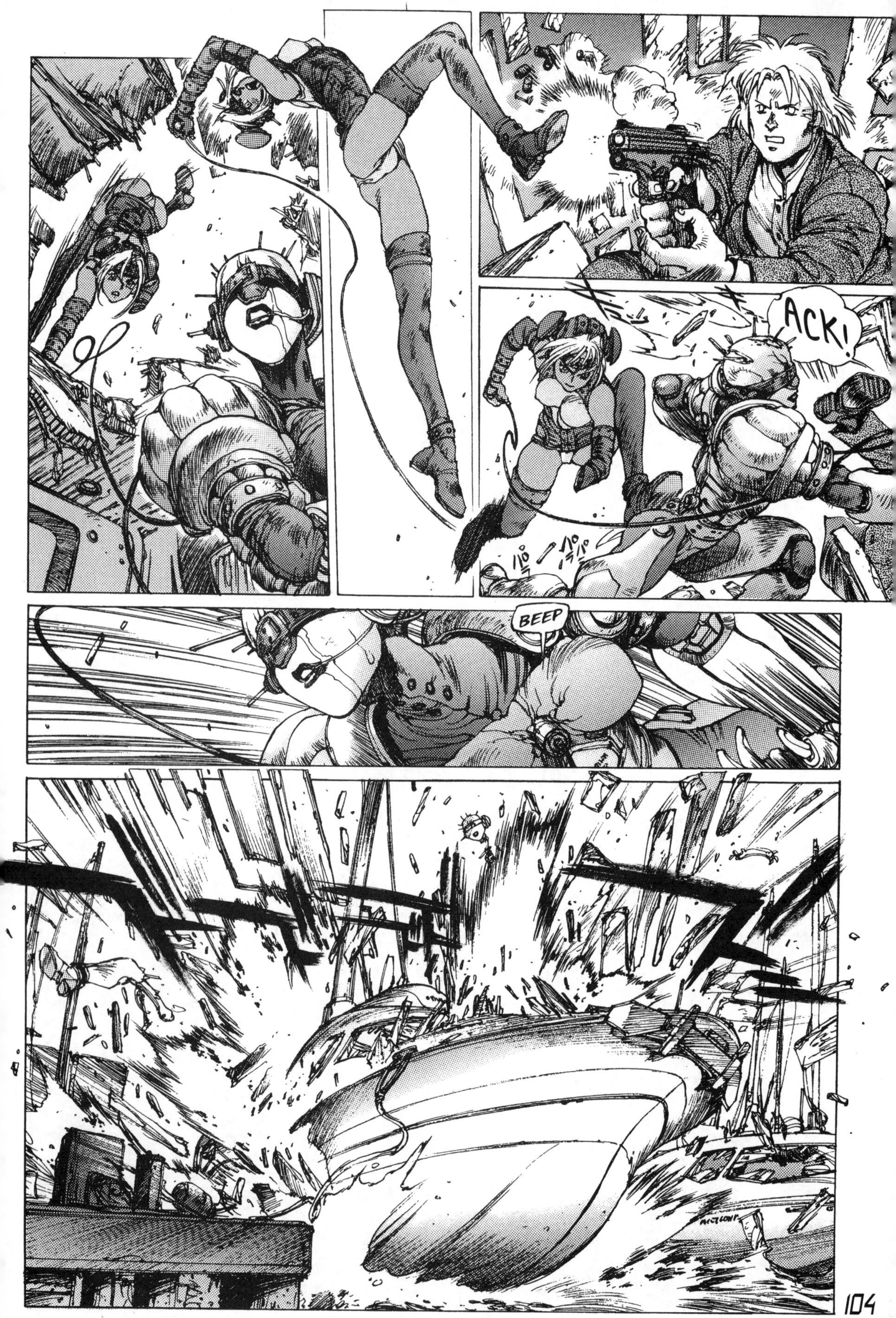
ACK!
BEEP

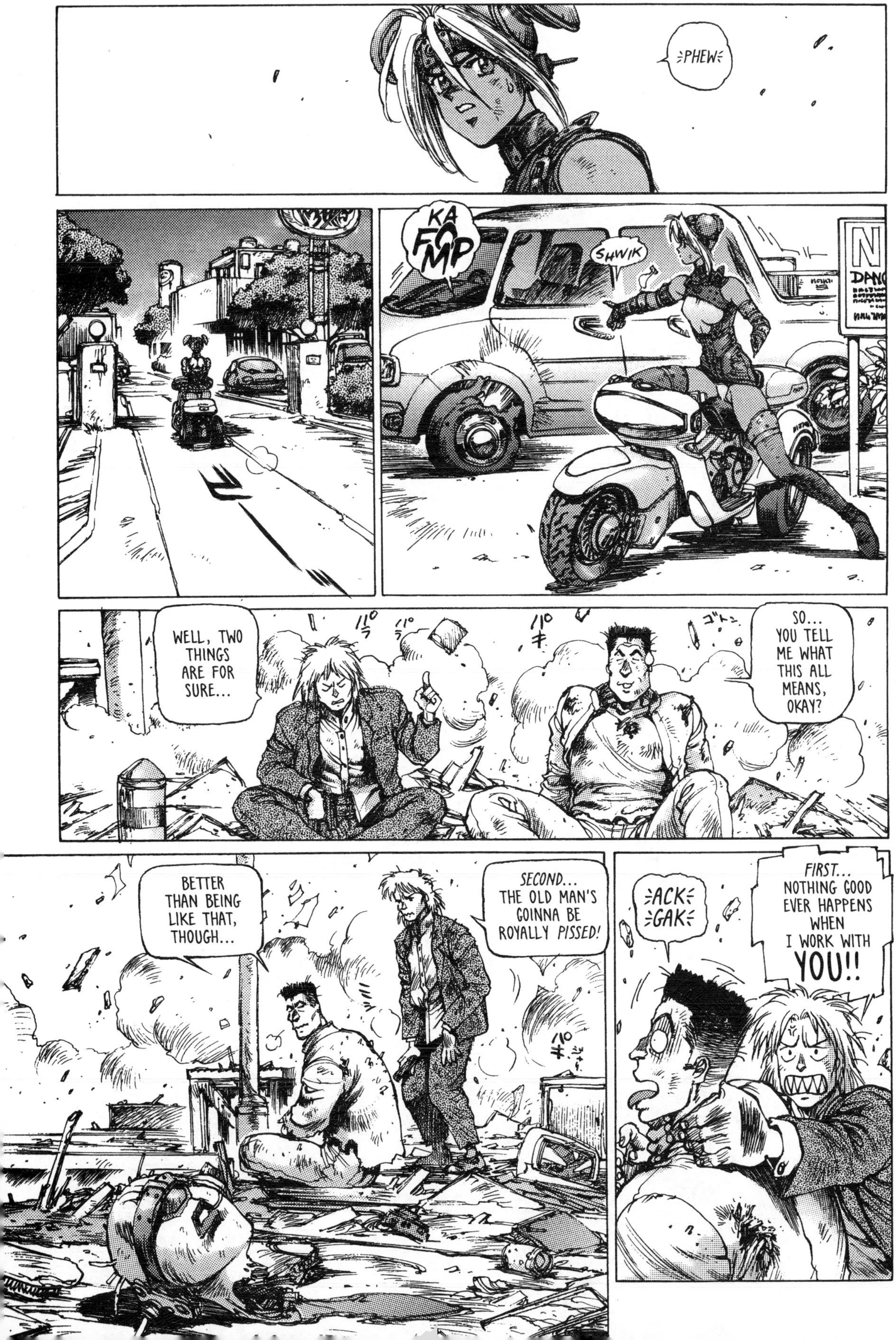
PHEW
KA FOMP
SHWIK
SO... YOU TELL ME WHAT THIS ALL MEANS, OKAY?
WELL, TWO THINGS ARE FOR SURE...
FIRST... NOTHING GOOD EVER HAPPENS WHEN I WORK WITH YOU!!
ACK GAK
SECOND... THE OLD MAN'S GOINNA BE ROYALLY PISSED!
BETTER THAN BEING LIKE THAT, THOUGH...

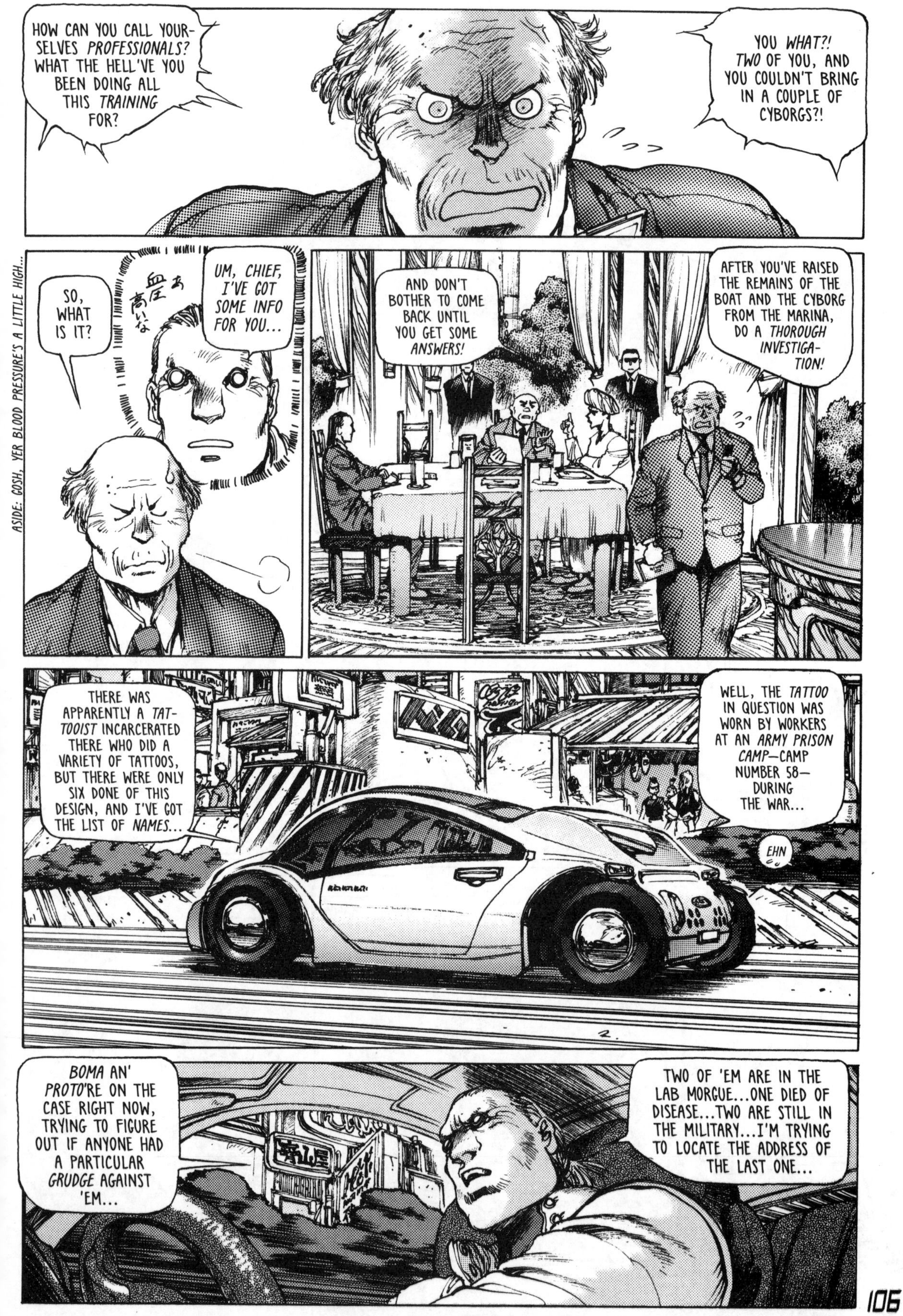
YOU WHAT?! TWO OF YOU, AND YOU COULDN'T BRING IN A COUPLE OF CYBORGS?!
HOW CAN YOU CALL YOURSELVES PROFESSIONALS? WHAT THE HELL'VE YOU BEEN DOING ALL THIS TRAINING FOR?
AFTER YOU'VE RAISED THE REMAINS OF THE BOAT AND THE CYBORG FROM THE MARINA, DO A THOROUGH INVESTIGATION!
AND DON'T BOTHER TO COME BACK UNTIL YOU GET SOME ANSWERS!
UM, CHIEF, I'VE GOT SOME INFO FOR YOU...
血圧高いなあ
SO, WHAT IS IT?
ASIDE: GOSH, YER BLOOD PRESSURE'S A LITTLE HIGH...
WELL, THE TATTOO IN QUESTION WAS WORN BY WORKERS AT AN ARMY PRISON CAMP—CAMP NUMBER 58—DURING THE WAR...
EHN
THERE WAS APPARENTLY A TATTOOIST INCARCERATED THERE WHO DID A VARIETY OF TATTOOS, BUT THERE WERE ONLY SIX DONE OF THIS DESIGN, AND I'VE GOT THE LIST OF NAMES...
TWO OF 'EM ARE IN THE LAB MORGUE...ONE DIED OF DISEASE...TWO ARE STILL IN THE MILITARY...I'M TRYING TO LOCATE THE ADDRESS OF THE LAST ONE...
BOMA AN' PROTO'RE ON THE CASE RIGHT NOW, TRYING TO FIGURE OUT IF ANYONE HAD A PARTICULAR GRUDGE AGAINST 'EM...

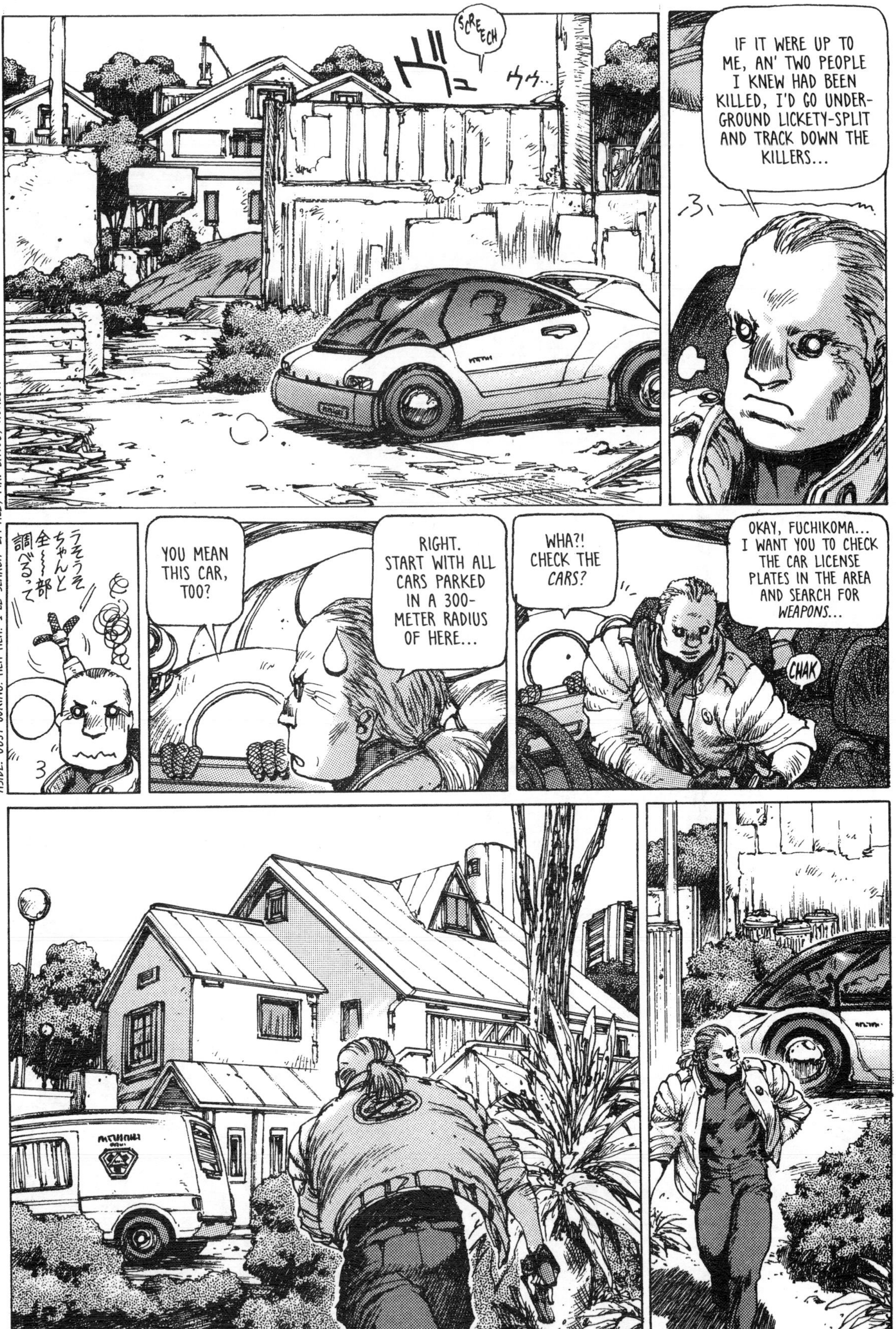
IF IT WERE UP TO ME, AN' TWO PEOPLE I KNEW HAD BEEN KILLED, I'D GO UNDERGROUND LICKETY-SPLIT AND TRACK DOWN THE KILLERS...
SCREECH
OKAY, FUCHIKOMA... I WANT YOU TO CHECK THE CAR LICENSE PLATES IN THE AREA AND SEARCH FOR *WEAPONS*...
CHAK
WHA?! CHECK THE *CARS*?
RIGHT. START WITH ALL CARS PARKED IN A 300-METER RADIUS OF HERE...
YOU MEAN THIS CAR, TOO?
うそうそ ちゃんと 全〜〜部 調べるって

ASIDE: JUST JOKING! HEH HEH! I'LL SEARCH 'EM ALL, MR. BATOU, HONEST!

RE: PANEL THREE—BATOU HAS RECENTLY TAKEN TO WEARING HIS SEATBELT WHILE DRIVING, BUT HE STILL DOESN'T LOCK THE CAR DOOR. THIS ISN'T A SPECIAL FORCES PROCEDURE, BUT SOMETHING BATOU JUST DOES ON HIS OWN... OF COURSE, HE UNLOCKS HIS SEATBELT BEFORE AND AFTER ANY GUNFIGHTS, AND HE DOESN'T WEAR HIS SEATBELT WHEN GUARDING VIPs, EITHER. IN THE FINAL PANELS ON THIS PAGE, BATOU IS VISUALLY CHECKING TO MAKE SURE NO ONE IS IN THE HOUSE OR IN THE VEHICLE IN FRONT OF IT. BUT, OF COURSE, HE COULD STILL BE SPOTTED ANYWAY...

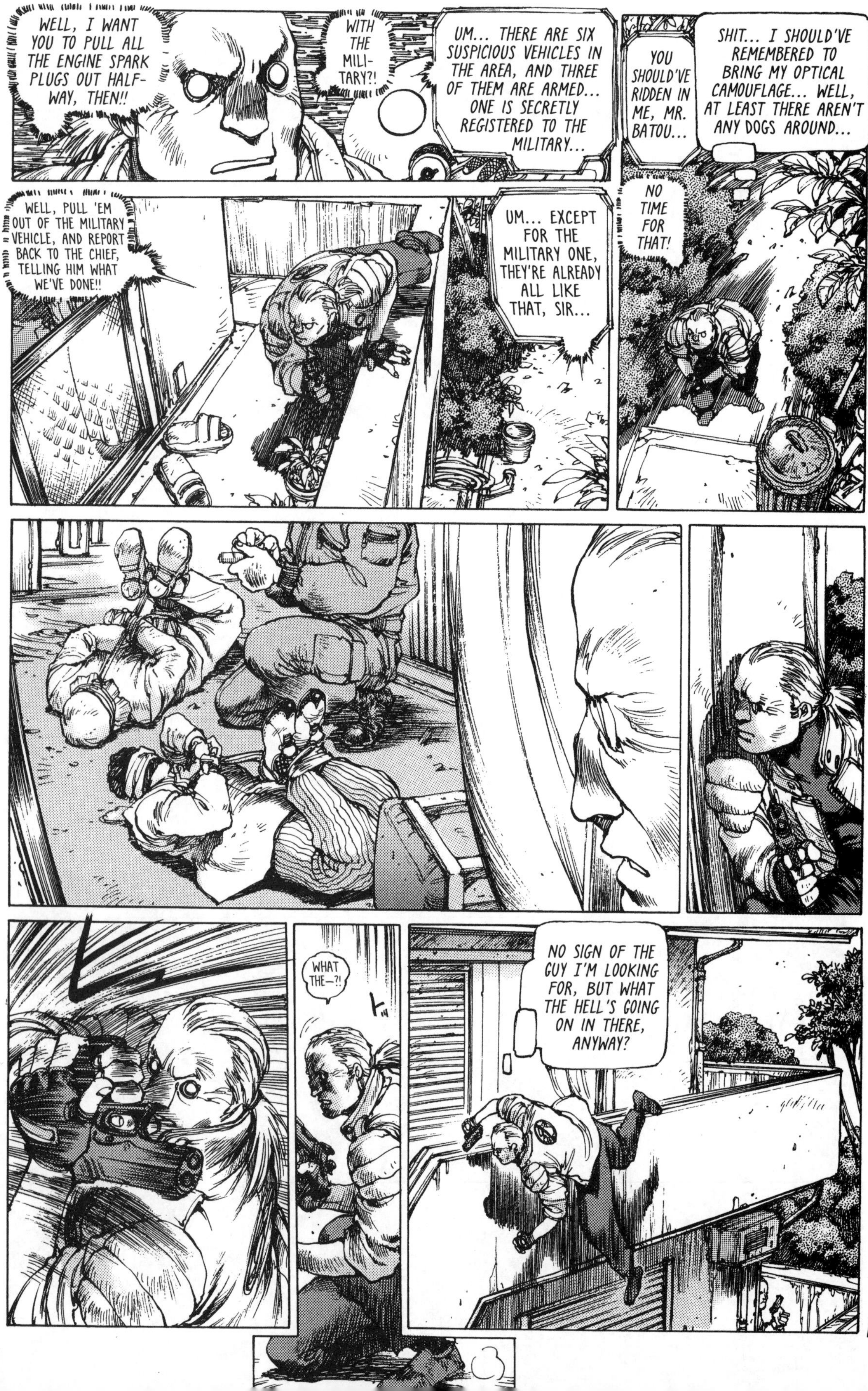

SHIT... I SHOULD'VE REMEMBERED TO BRING MY OPTICAL CAMOUFLAGE... WELL, AT LEAST THERE AREN'T ANY DOGS AROUND...
YOU SHOULD'VE RIDDEN IN ME, MR. BATOU...
NO TIME FOR THAT!
UM... THERE ARE SIX SUSPICIOUS VEHICLES IN THE AREA, AND THREE OF THEM ARE ARMED... ONE IS SECRETLY REGISTERED TO THE MILITARY...
WITH THE MILITARY?!
WELL, I WANT YOU TO PULL ALL THE ENGINE SPARK PLUGS OUT HALF-WAY, THEN!!
UM... EXCEPT FOR THE MILITARY ONE, THEY'RE ALREADY ALL LIKE THAT, SIR...
WELL, PULL 'EM OUT OF THE MILITARY VEHICLE, AND REPORT BACK TO THE CHIEF, TELLING HIM WHAT WE'VE DONE!!
NO SIGN OF THE GUY I'M LOOKING FOR, BUT WHAT THE HELL'S GOING ON IN THERE, ANYWAY?
WHAT THE—?!

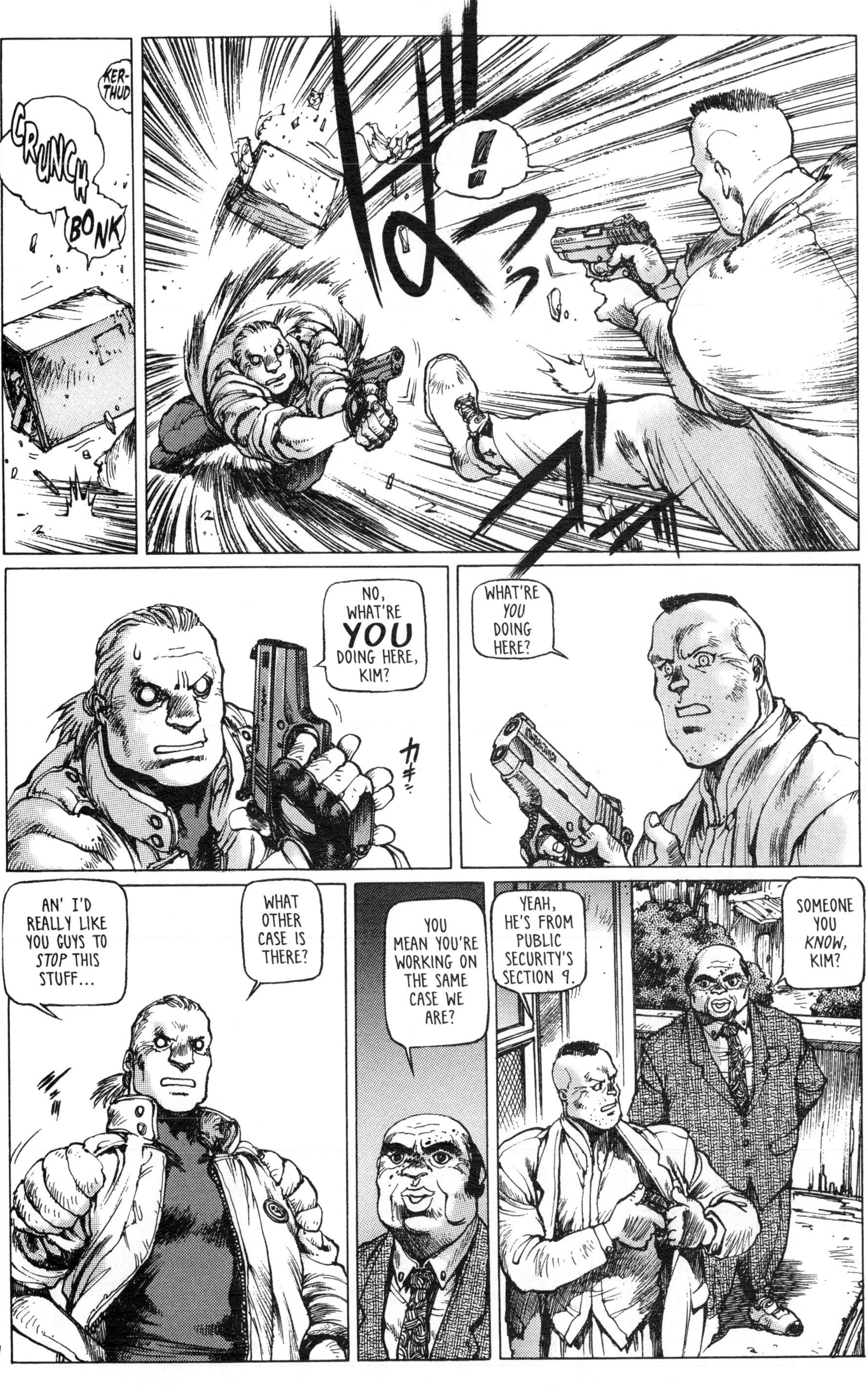
!
KER-THUD
CRUNCH BONK
WHAT'RE YOU DOING HERE?
NO, WHAT'RE YOU DOING HERE, KIM?
カチ
SOMEONE YOU KNOW, KIM?
YEAH, HE'S FROM PUBLIC SECURITY'S SECTION 9.
YOU MEAN YOU'RE WORKING ON THE SAME CASE WE ARE?
WHAT OTHER CASE IS THERE?
AN' I'D REALLY LIKE YOU GUYS TO STOP THIS STUFF...

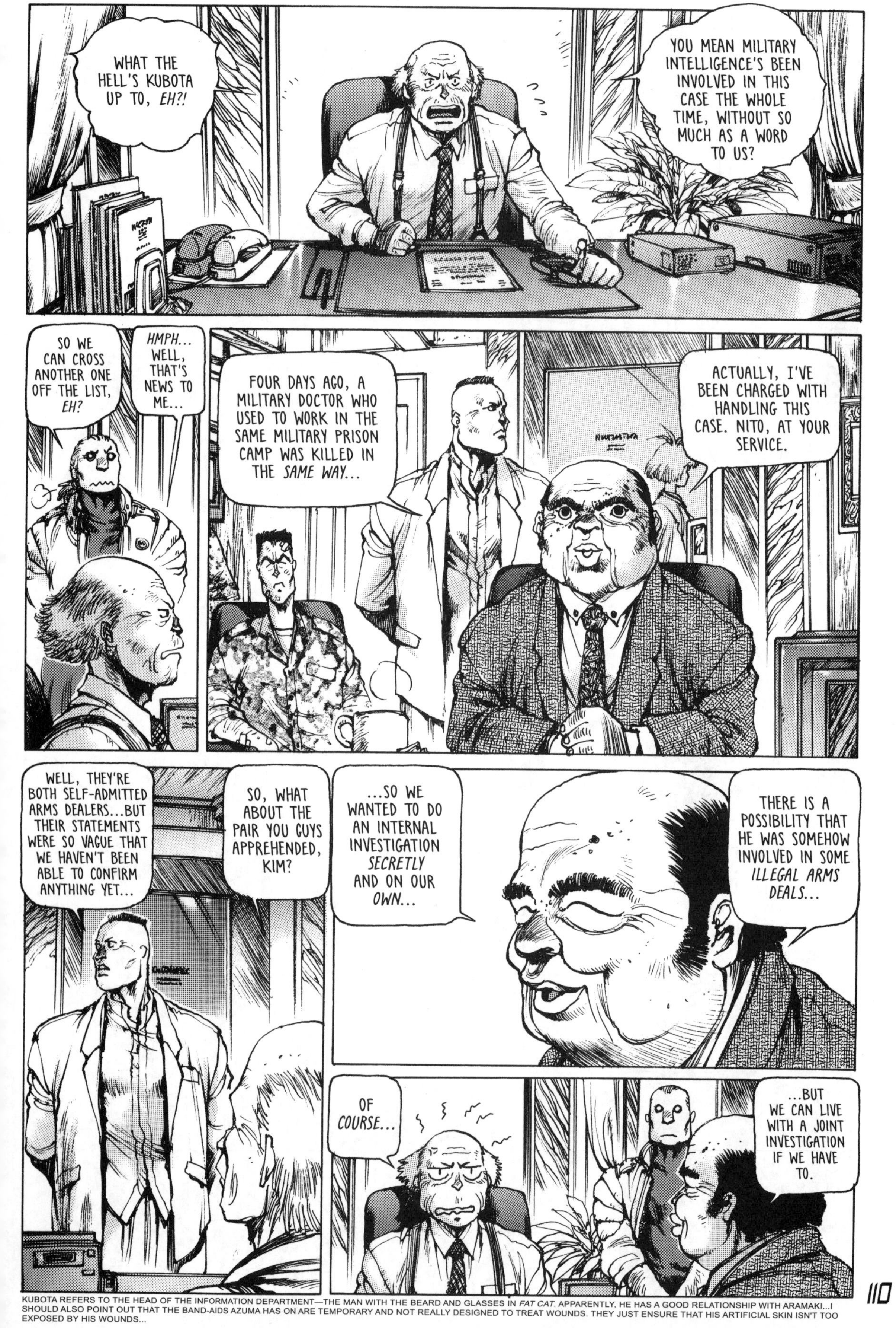
YOU MEAN MILITARY INTELLIGENCE'S BEEN INVOLVED IN THIS CASE THE WHOLE TIME, WITHOUT SO MUCH AS A WORD TO US?
WHAT THE HELL'S KUBOTA UP TO, *EH?!*
ACTUALLY, I'VE BEEN CHARGED WITH HANDLING THIS CASE. NITO, AT YOUR SERVICE.
FOUR DAYS AGO, A MILITARY DOCTOR WHO USED TO WORK IN THE SAME MILITARY PRISON CAMP WAS KILLED IN THE *SAME WAY*...
HMPH... WELL, THAT'S NEWS TO ME...
SO WE CAN CROSS ANOTHER ONE OFF THE LIST, *EH?*
THERE IS A POSSIBILITY THAT HE WAS SOMEHOW INVOLVED IN SOME *ILLEGAL ARMS* DEALS...
...SO WE WANTED TO DO AN INTERNAL INVESTIGATION *SECRETLY* AND ON OUR *OWN*...
...BUT WE CAN LIVE WITH A JOINT INVESTIGATION IF WE HAVE TO.
OF *COURSE*...
SO, WHAT ABOUT THE PAIR YOU GUYS APPREHENDED, KIM?
WELL, THEY'RE BOTH SELF-ADMITTED ARMS DEALERS...BUT THEIR STATEMENTS WERE SO VAGUE THAT WE HAVEN'T BEEN ABLE TO CONFIRM ANYTHING YET...

KUBOTA REFERS TO THE HEAD OF THE INFORMATION DEPARTMENT—THE MAN WITH THE BEARD AND GLASSES IN *FAT CAT*. APPARENTLY, HE HAS A GOOD RELATIONSHIP WITH ARAMAKI...I SHOULD ALSO POINT OUT THAT THE BAND-AIDS AZUMA HAS ON ARE TEMPORARY AND NOT REALLY DESIGNED TO TREAT WOUNDS. THEY JUST ENSURE THAT HIS ARTIFICIAL SKIN ISN'T TOO EXPOSED BY HIS WOUNDS...

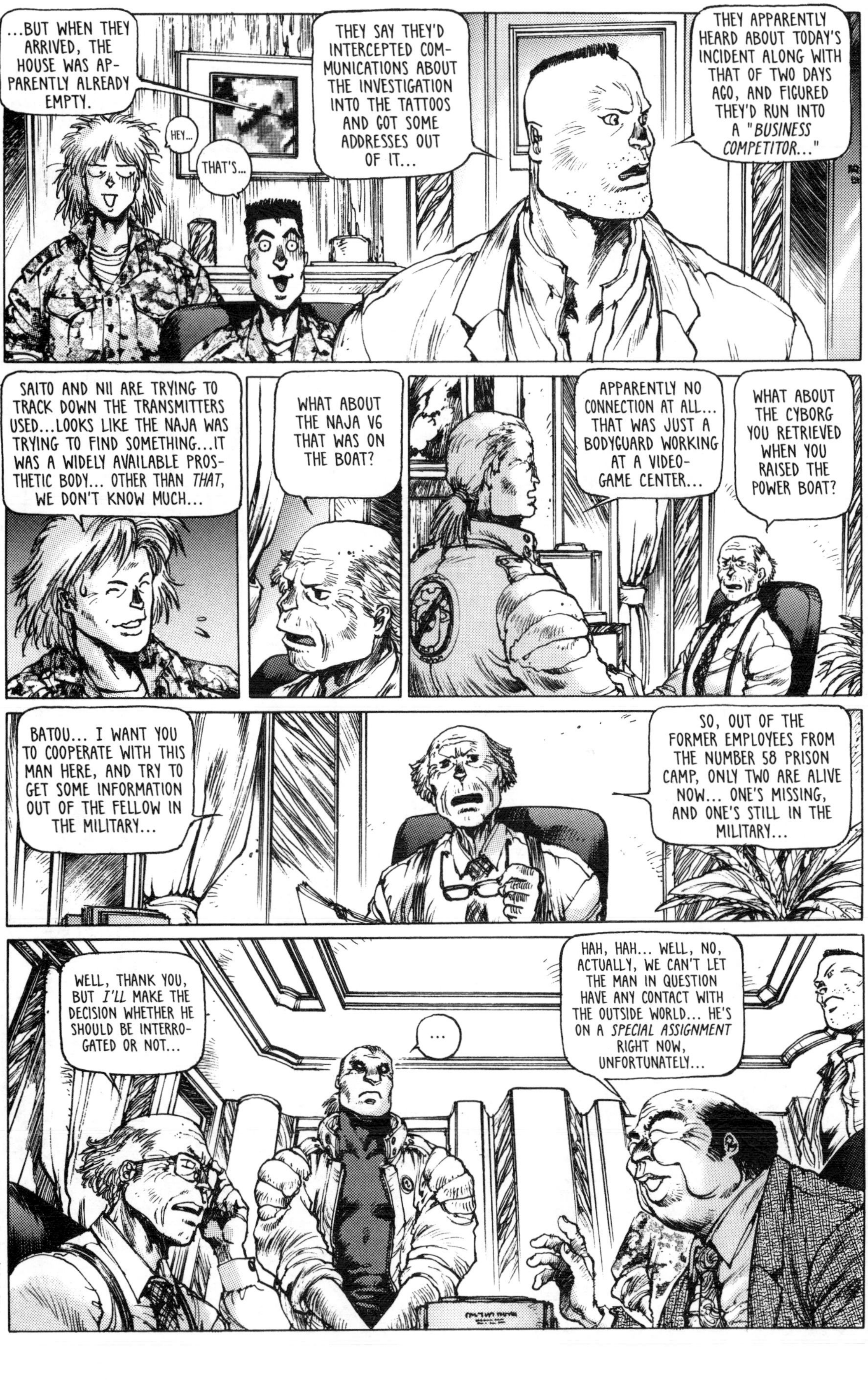
THEY APPARENTLY HEARD ABOUT TODAY'S INCIDENT ALONG WITH THAT OF TWO DAYS AGO, AND FIGURED THEY'D RUN INTO A "*BUSINESS COMPETITOR...*"
THEY SAY THEY'D INTERCEPTED COMMUNICATIONS ABOUT THE INVESTIGATION INTO THE TATTOOS AND GOT SOME ADDRESSES OUT OF IT...
...BUT WHEN THEY ARRIVED, THE HOUSE WAS APPARENTLY ALREADY EMPTY.
HEY...
THAT'S...
WHAT ABOUT THE CYBORG YOU RETRIEVED WHEN YOU RAISED THE POWER BOAT?
APPARENTLY NO CONNECTION AT ALL... THAT WAS JUST A BODYGUARD WORKING AT A VIDEO-GAME CENTER...
WHAT ABOUT THE NAJA V6 THAT WAS ON THE BOAT?
SAITO AND NII ARE TRYING TO TRACK DOWN THE TRANSMITTERS USED...LOOKS LIKE THE NAJA WAS TRYING TO FIND SOMETHING...IT WAS A WIDELY AVAILABLE PROSTHETIC BODY... OTHER THAN *THAT*, WE DON'T KNOW MUCH...
SO, OUT OF THE FORMER EMPLOYEES FROM THE NUMBER 58 PRISON CAMP, ONLY TWO ARE ALIVE NOW... ONE'S MISSING, AND ONE'S STILL IN THE MILITARY...
BATOU... I WANT YOU TO COOPERATE WITH THIS MAN HERE, AND TRY TO GET SOME INFORMATION OUT OF THE FELLOW IN THE MILITARY...
HAH, HAH... WELL, NO, ACTUALLY, WE CAN'T LET THE MAN IN QUESTION HAVE ANY CONTACT WITH THE OUTSIDE WORLD... HE'S ON A *SPECIAL ASSIGNMENT* RIGHT NOW, UNFORTUNATELY...
...
WELL, THANK YOU, BUT *I'LL* MAKE THE DECISION WHETHER HE SHOULD BE INTERROGATED OR NOT...

ONE OBVIOUSLY CAN'T USE A SECRET CODE NUMBER OR ENCRYPTION SYSTEM WHEN COMMUNICATING WITH SOMEONE, UNLESS THAT SOMEONE IS PARTY TO THE CODE OR THERE HAS BEEN SOME PRIOR AGREEMENT ON THE CODE BEING USED (WE'RE NOT TALKING ABOUT CODE CRACKING HERE). TO PREVENT ELECTRONIC COMMUNICATIONS FROM BEING INTERCEPTED OR OVERHEARD, THE BEST THING WOULD ACTUALLY BE TO PHYSICALLY MEET THE PARTY WITH WHOM ONE IS TRYING TO COMMUNICATE, BUT THAT TAKES TIME, OF COURSE...IN THIS CASE, THE TRANSMITTERS WERE IN THE MARINA OR PORT, AND ATTACHED TO THE MOST SUSPICIOUS OF THE VEHICLES AFTER THEIR PLATES AND OWNER REGISTRATIONS HAD BEEN CHECKED. I JUST HAVEN'T DRAWN THE SCENES SHOWING THE VEHICLES BEING TAGGED...

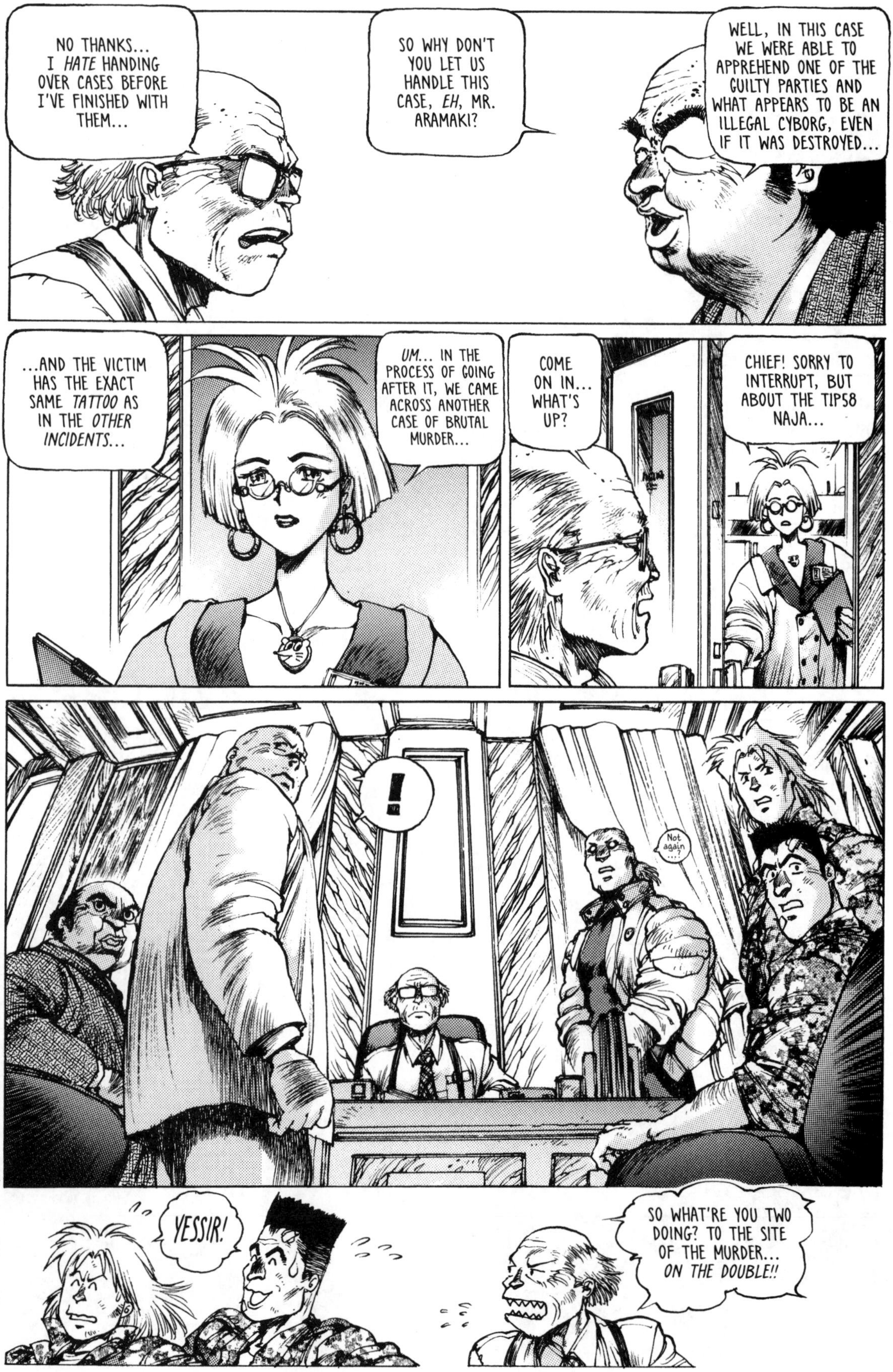
WELL, IN THIS CASE WE WERE ABLE TO APPREHEND ONE OF THE GUILTY PARTIES AND WHAT APPEARS TO BE AN ILLEGAL CYBORG, EVEN IF IT WAS DESTROYED...
SO WHY DON'T YOU LET US HANDLE THIS CASE, *EH*, MR. ARAMAKI?
NO THANKS... I *HATE* HANDING OVER CASES BEFORE I'VE FINISHED WITH THEM...
CHIEF! SORRY TO INTERRUPT, BUT ABOUT THE TIP58 NAJA...
COME ON IN... WHAT'S UP?
UM... IN THE PROCESS OF GOING AFTER IT, WE CAME ACROSS ANOTHER CASE OF BRUTAL MURDER...
...AND THE VICTIM HAS THE EXACT SAME *TATTOO* AS IN THE *OTHER INCIDENTS*...
!
Not again...?
SO WHAT'RE YOU TWO DOING? TO THE SITE OF THE MURDER... *ON THE DOUBLE!!*
YESSIR!

MINES OF MIND Part.2

1995

06

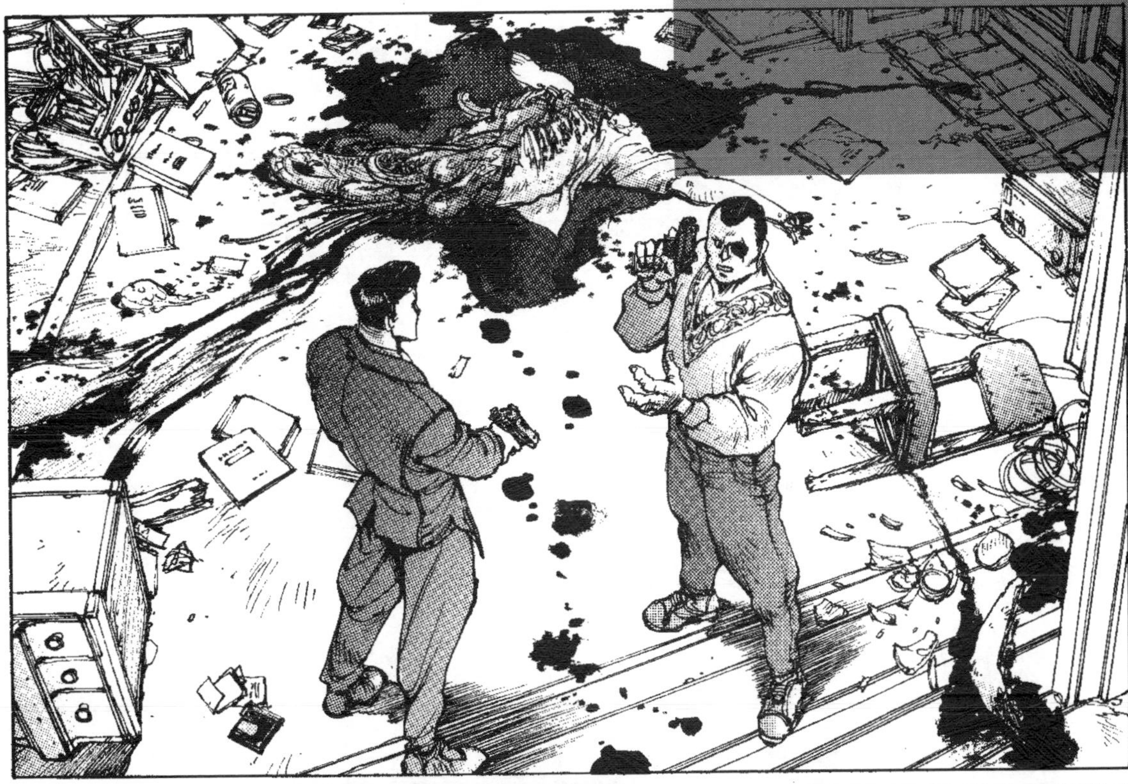

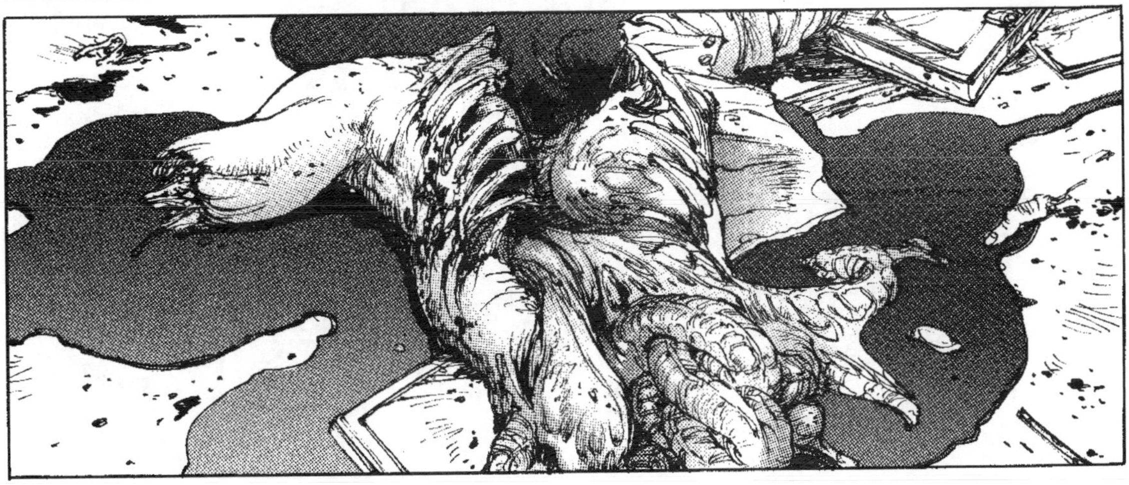

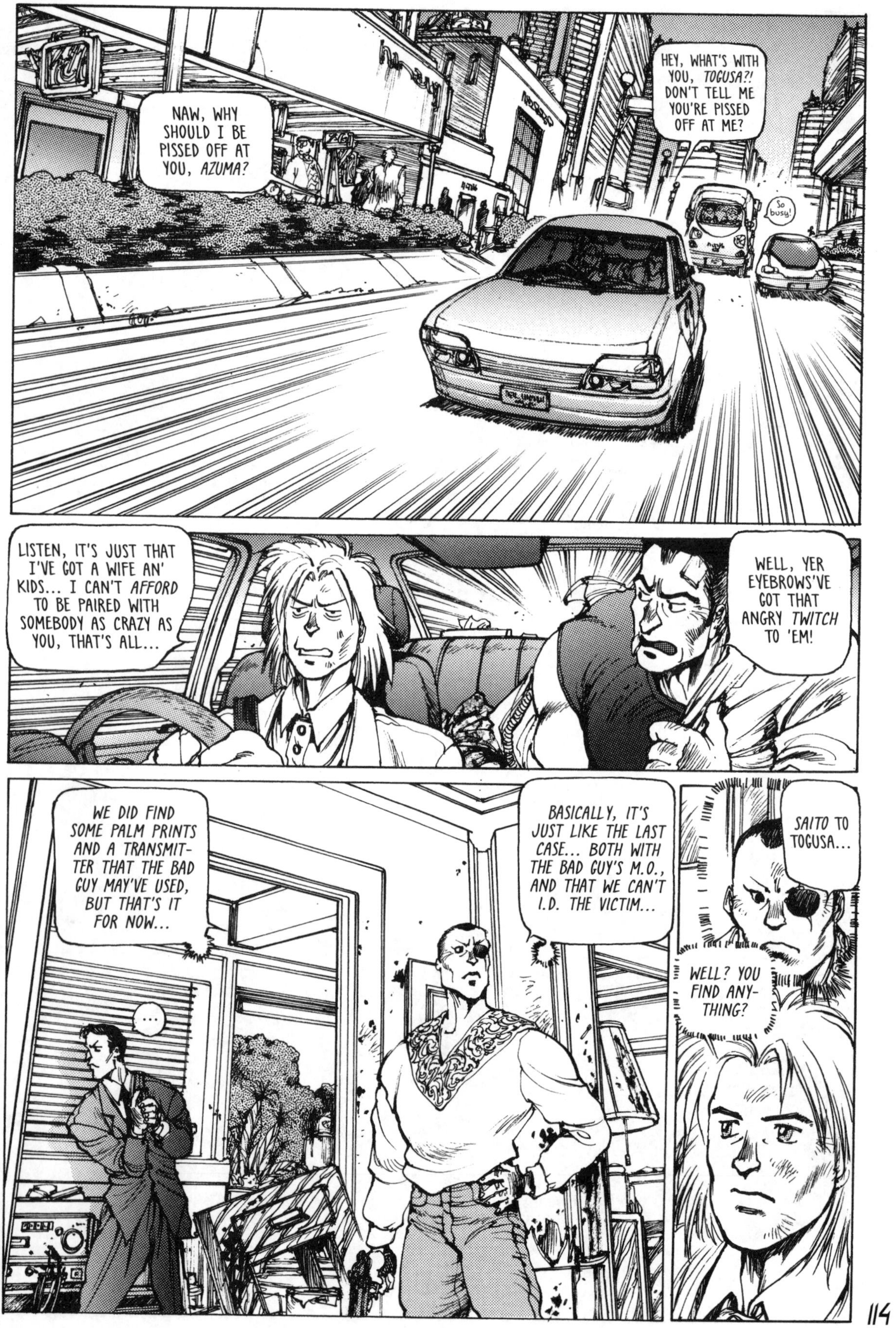
HEY, WHAT'S WITH YOU, *TOGUSA?!* DON'T TELL ME YOU'RE PISSED OFF AT ME?
So busy!
NAW, WHY SHOULD I BE PISSED OFF AT YOU, *AZUMA?*
WELL, YER EYEBROWS'VE GOT THAT ANGRY *TWITCH* TO 'EM!
LISTEN, IT'S JUST THAT I'VE GOT A WIFE AN' KIDS... I CAN'T *AFFORD* TO BE PAIRED WITH SOMEBODY AS CRAZY AS YOU, THAT'S ALL...
SAITO TO TOGUSA...
WELL? YOU FIND ANY-THING?
BASICALLY, IT'S JUST LIKE THE LAST CASE... BOTH WITH THE BAD GUY'S M.O., AND THAT WE CAN'T I.D. THE VICTIM...
WE DID FIND SOME PALM PRINTS AND A TRANSMIT-TER THAT THE BAD GUY MAY'VE USED, BUT THAT'S IT FOR NOW...
...

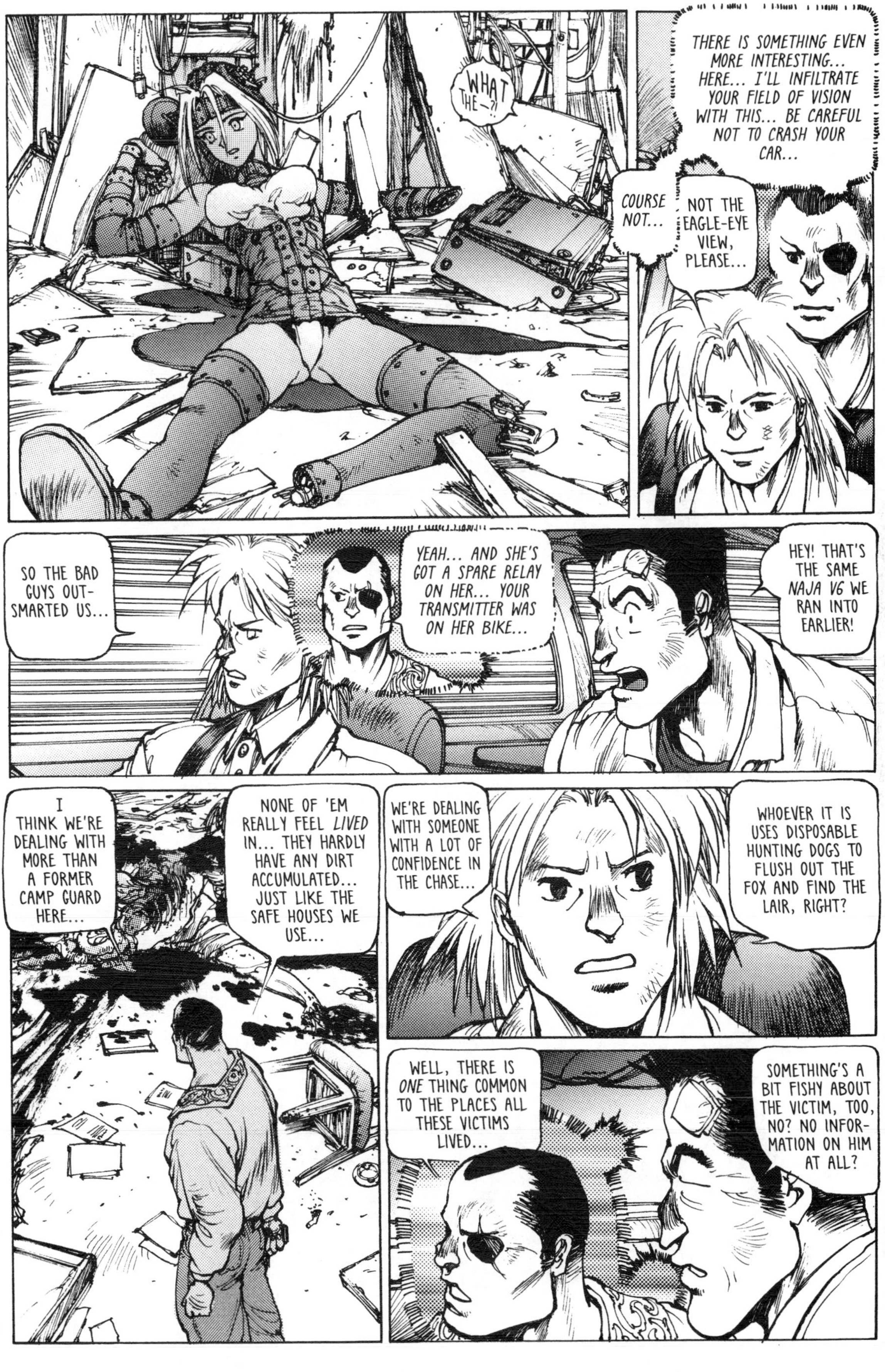
THERE IS SOMETHING EVEN MORE INTERESTING... HERE... I'LL INFILTRATE YOUR FIELD OF VISION WITH THIS... BE CAREFUL NOT TO CRASH YOUR CAR...
NOT THE EAGLE-EYE VIEW, PLEASE...
COURSE NOT...
WHAT THE—?!
HEY! THAT'S THE SAME *NAJA V6* WE RAN INTO EARLIER!
YEAH... AND SHE'S GOT A SPARE RELAY ON HER... YOUR TRANSMITTER WAS ON HER BIKE...
SO THE BAD GUYS OUT-SMARTED US...
WHOEVER IT IS USES DISPOSABLE HUNTING DOGS TO FLUSH OUT THE FOX AND FIND THE LAIR, RIGHT?
WE'RE DEALING WITH SOMEONE WITH A LOT OF CONFIDENCE IN THE CHASE...
SOMETHING'S A BIT FISHY ABOUT THE VICTIM, TOO, NO? NO INFOR-MATION ON HIM AT ALL?
WELL, THERE IS *ONE* THING COMMON TO THE PLACES ALL THESE VICTIMS LIVED...
NONE OF 'EM REALLY FEEL *LIVED* IN... THEY HARDLY HAVE ANY DIRT ACCUMULATED... JUST LIKE THE SAFE HOUSES WE USE...
I THINK WE'RE DEALING WITH MORE THAN A FORMER CAMP GUARD HERE...

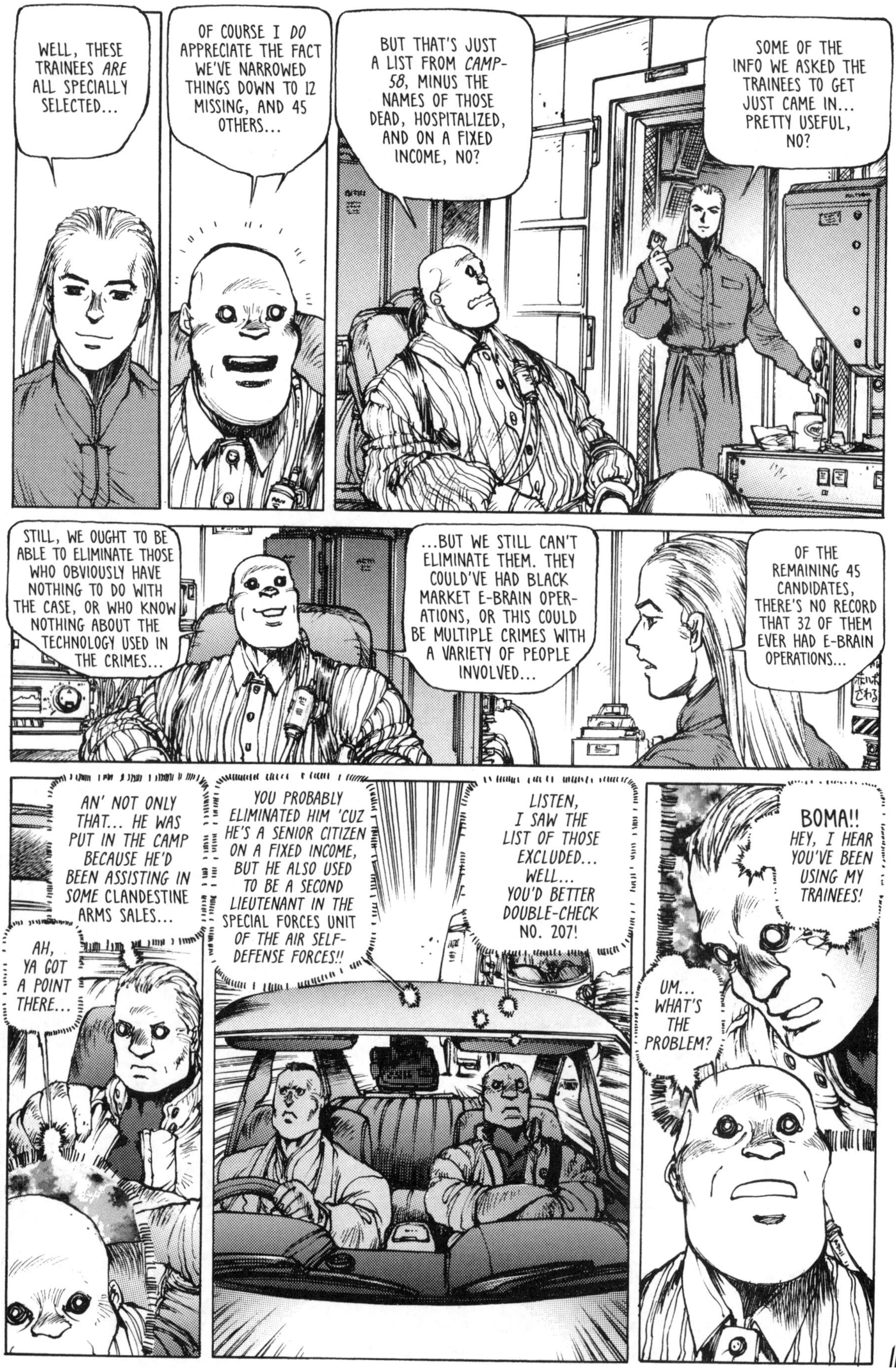

SOME OF THE INFO WE ASKED THE TRAINEES TO GET JUST CAME IN... PRETTY USEFUL, NO?
BUT THAT'S JUST A LIST FROM *CAMP-58*, MINUS THE NAMES OF THOSE DEAD, HOSPITALIZED, AND ON A FIXED INCOME, NO?
OF COURSE I *DO* APPRECIATE THE FACT WE'VE NARROWED THINGS DOWN TO 12 MISSING, AND 45 OTHERS...
WELL, THESE TRAINEES *ARE* ALL SPECIALLY SELECTED...
OF THE REMAINING 45 CANDIDATES, THERE'S NO RECORD THAT 32 OF THEM EVER HAD E-BRAIN OPERATIONS...
...BUT WE STILL CAN'T ELIMINATE THEM. THEY COULD'VE HAD BLACK MARKET E-BRAIN OPERATIONS, OR THIS COULD BE MULTIPLE CRIMES WITH A VARIETY OF PEOPLE INVOLVED...
STILL, WE OUGHT TO BE ABLE TO ELIMINATE THOSE WHO OBVIOUSLY HAVE NOTHING TO DO WITH THE CASE, OR WHO KNOW NOTHING ABOUT THE TECHNOLOGY USED IN THE CRIMES...
BOMA!! HEY, I HEAR YOU'VE BEEN USING MY TRAINEES!
UM... WHAT'S THE PROBLEM?
LISTEN, I SAW THE LIST OF THOSE EXCLUDED... WELL... YOU'D BETTER DOUBLE-CHECK NO. 207!
YOU PROBABLY ELIMINATED HIM 'CUZ HE'S A SENIOR CITIZEN ON A FIXED INCOME, BUT HE ALSO USED TO BE A SECOND LIEUTENANT IN THE SPECIAL FORCES UNIT OF THE AIR SELF-DEFENSE FORCES!!
AN' NOT ONLY THAT... HE WAS PUT IN THE CAMP BECAUSE HE'D BEEN ASSISTING IN SOME CLANDESTINE ARMS SALES...
AH, YA GOT A POINT THERE...

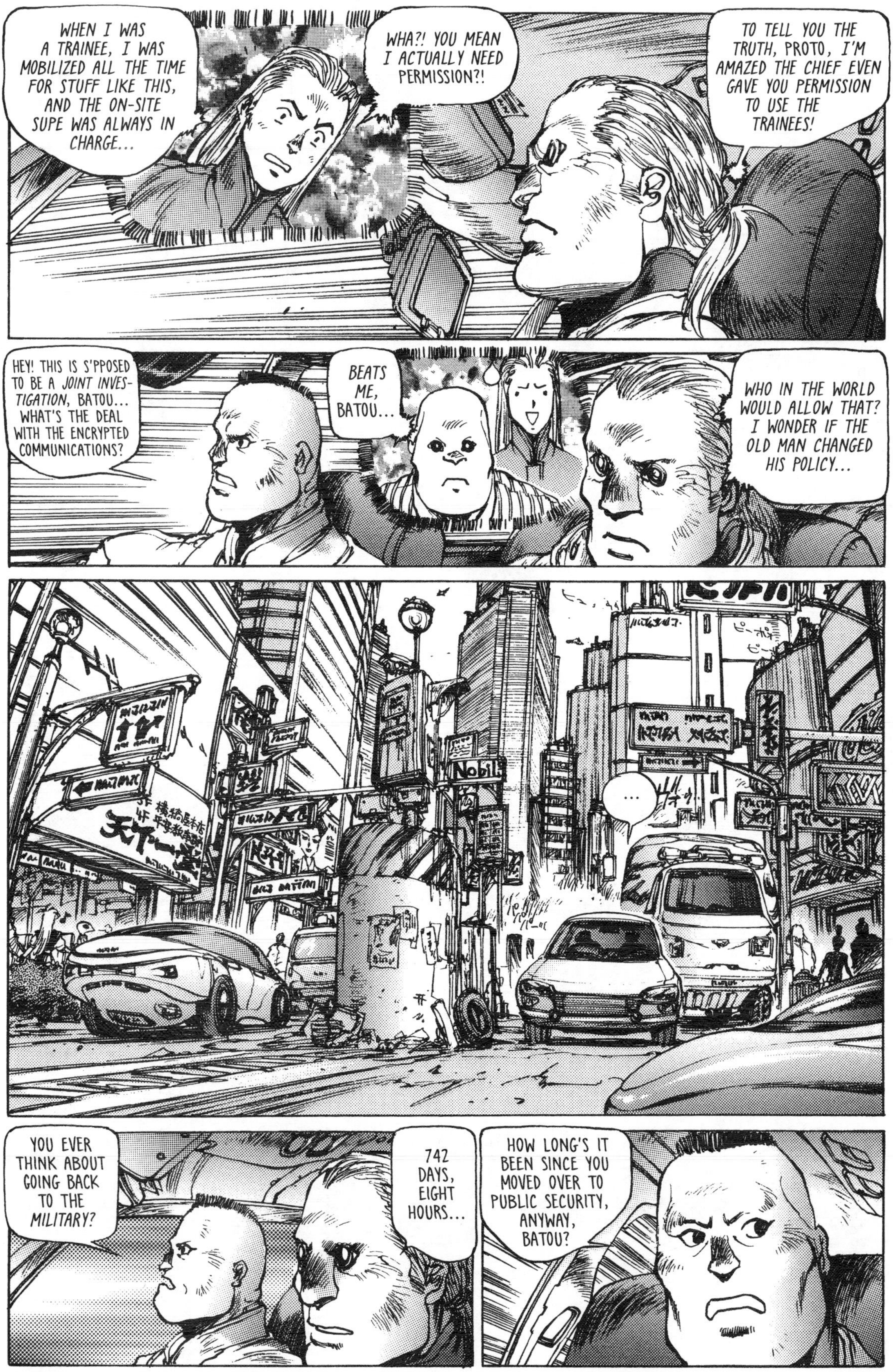
TO TELL YOU THE TRUTH, PROTO, I'M AMAZED THE CHIEF EVEN GAVE YOU PERMISSION TO USE THE TRAINEES!
WHA?! YOU MEAN I ACTUALLY NEED PERMISSION?!
WHEN I WAS A TRAINEE, I WAS MOBILIZED ALL THE TIME FOR STUFF LIKE THIS, AND THE ON-SITE SUPE WAS ALWAYS IN CHARGE...
WHO IN THE WORLD WOULD ALLOW THAT? I WONDER IF THE OLD MAN CHANGED HIS POLICY...
BEATS ME, BATOU...
HEY! THIS IS S'PPOSED TO BE A *JOINT INVESTIGATION*, BATOU... WHAT'S THE DEAL WITH THE ENCRYPTED COMMUNICATIONS?
Nobil
...
HOW LONG'S IT BEEN SINCE YOU MOVED OVER TO PUBLIC SECURITY, ANYWAY, BATOU?
742 DAYS, EIGHT HOURS...
YOU EVER THINK ABOUT GOING BACK TO THE MILITARY?

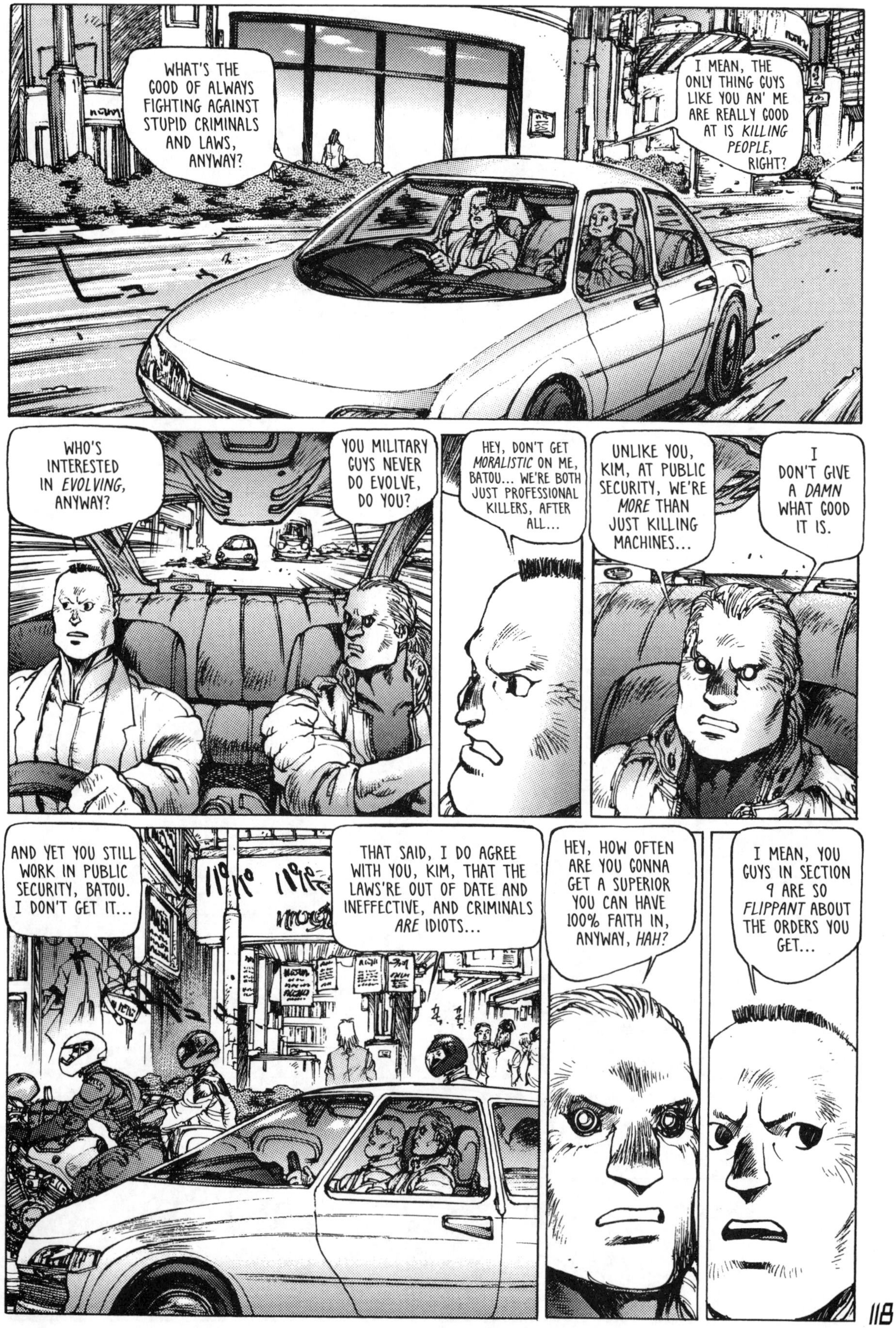
I MEAN, THE ONLY THING GUYS LIKE YOU AN' ME ARE REALLY GOOD AT IS *KILLING PEOPLE*, RIGHT?
WHAT'S THE GOOD OF ALWAYS FIGHTING AGAINST STUPID CRIMINALS AND LAWS, ANYWAY?
I DON'T GIVE A *DAMN* WHAT GOOD IT IS.
UNLIKE YOU, KIM, AT PUBLIC SECURITY, WE'RE *MORE* THAN JUST KILLING MACHINES...
HEY, DON'T GET *MORALISTIC* ON ME, BATOU... WE'RE BOTH JUST PROFESSIONAL KILLERS, AFTER ALL...
YOU MILITARY GUYS NEVER DO EVOLVE, DO YOU?
WHO'S INTERESTED IN *EVOLVING*, ANYWAY?
I MEAN, YOU GUYS IN SECTION 9 ARE SO *FLIPPANT* ABOUT THE ORDERS YOU GET...
HEY, HOW OFTEN ARE YOU GONNA GET A SUPERIOR YOU CAN HAVE 100% FAITH IN, ANYWAY, *HAH?*
THAT SAID, I DO AGREE WITH YOU, KIM, THAT THE LAWS'RE OUT OF DATE AND INEFFECTIVE, AND CRIMINALS *ARE* IDIOTS...
AND YET YOU STILL WORK IN PUBLIC SECURITY, BATOU. I DON'T GET IT...

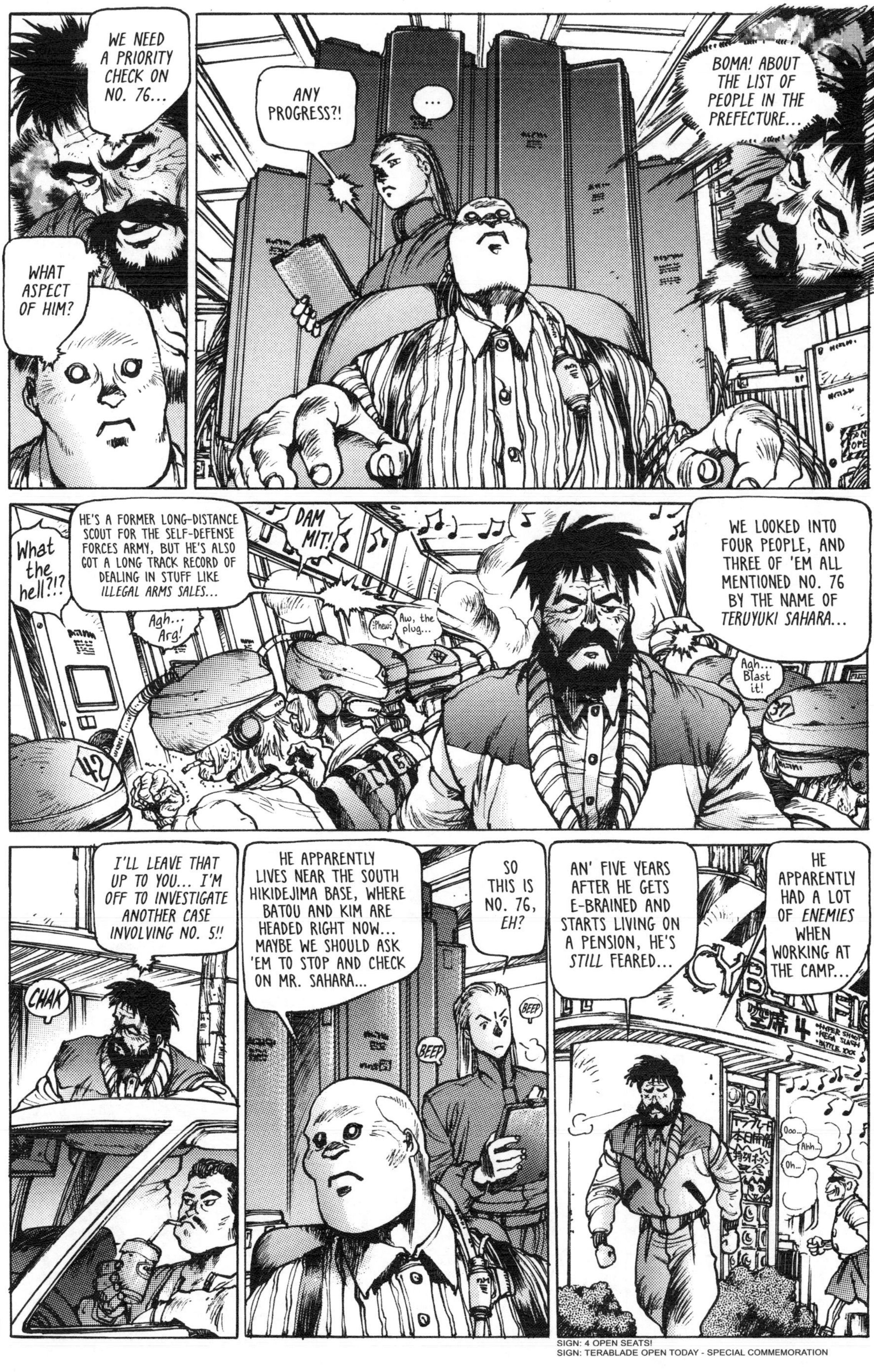
BOMA! ABOUT THE LIST OF PEOPLE IN THE PREFECTURE...
ANY PROGRESS?!
...
WE NEED A PRIORITY CHECK ON NO. 76...
WHAT ASPECT OF HIM?
WE LOOKED INTO FOUR PEOPLE, AND THREE OF 'EM ALL MENTIONED NO. 76 BY THE NAME OF *TERUYUKI SAHARA*...
Agh... Blast it!
Aw, the plug...
:Phew:
DAM MIT!
HE'S A FORMER LONG-DISTANCE SCOUT FOR THE SELF-DEFENSE FORCES ARMY, BUT HE'S ALSO GOT A LONG TRACK RECORD OF DEALING IN STUFF LIKE *ILLEGAL ARMS SALES*...
Agh... Arg!
What the hell?!?
HE APPARENTLY HAD A LOT OF *ENEMIES* WHEN WORKING AT THE CAMP...
AN' FIVE YEARS AFTER HE GETS E-BRAINED AND STARTS LIVING ON A PENSION, HE'S *STILL* FEARED...
空席4
Ooo...
Ahh...
Oh...
SO THIS IS NO. 76, *EH?*
HE APPARENTLY LIVES NEAR THE SOUTH HIKIDEJIMA BASE, WHERE BATOU AND KIM ARE HEADED RIGHT NOW... MAYBE WE SHOULD ASK 'EM TO STOP AND CHECK ON MR. SAHARA...
BEEP
BEEP
I'LL LEAVE THAT UP TO YOU... I'M OFF TO INVESTIGATE ANOTHER CASE INVOLVING NO. 5!!
CHAK

SIGN: 4 OPEN SEATS!
SIGN: TERABLADE OPEN TODAY - SPECIAL COMMEMORATION

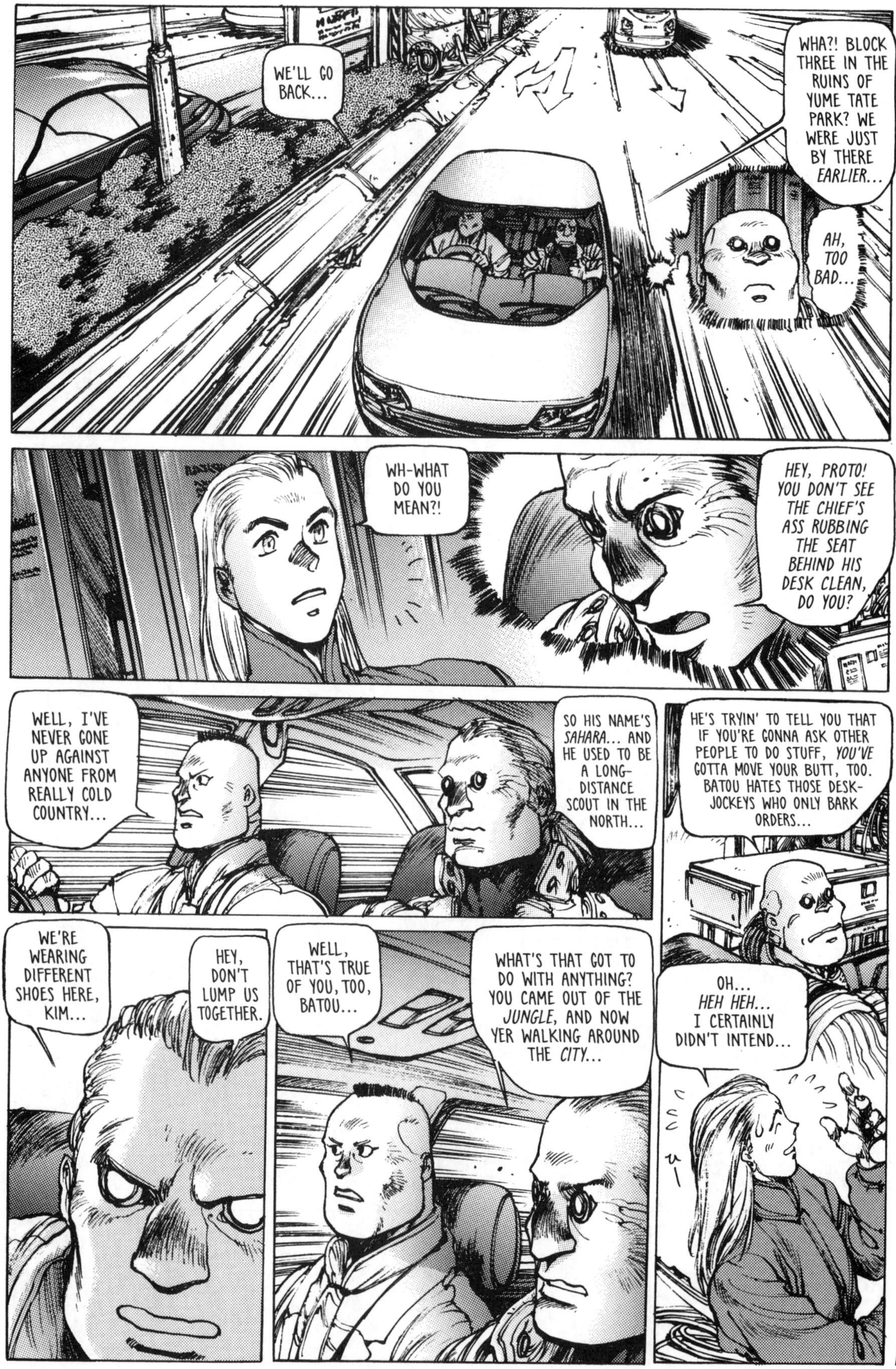
WHA?! BLOCK THREE IN THE RUINS OF YUME TATE PARK? WE WERE JUST BY THERE *EARLIER*...
AH, TOO BAD...
WE'LL GO BACK...
HEY, PROTO! YOU DON'T SEE THE CHIEF'S ASS RUBBING THE SEAT BEHIND HIS DESK CLEAN, DO YOU?
WH-WHAT DO YOU MEAN?!
HE'S TRYIN' TO TELL YOU THAT IF YOU'RE GONNA ASK OTHER PEOPLE TO DO STUFF, *YOU'VE* GOTTA MOVE YOUR BUTT, TOO. BATOU HATES THOSE DESK-JOCKEYS WHO ONLY BARK ORDERS...
OH... *HEH HEH*... I CERTAINLY DIDN'T INTEND...
SO HIS NAME'S *SAHARA*... AND HE USED TO BE A LONG-DISTANCE SCOUT IN THE NORTH...
WELL, I'VE NEVER GONE UP AGAINST ANYONE FROM REALLY COLD COUNTRY...
WHAT'S THAT GOT TO DO WITH ANYTHING? YOU CAME OUT OF THE *JUNGLE*, AND NOW YER WALKING AROUND THE *CITY*...
WELL, THAT'S TRUE OF YOU, TOO, BATOU...
HEY, DON'T LUMP US TOGETHER.
WE'RE WEARING DIFFERENT SHOES HERE, KIM...

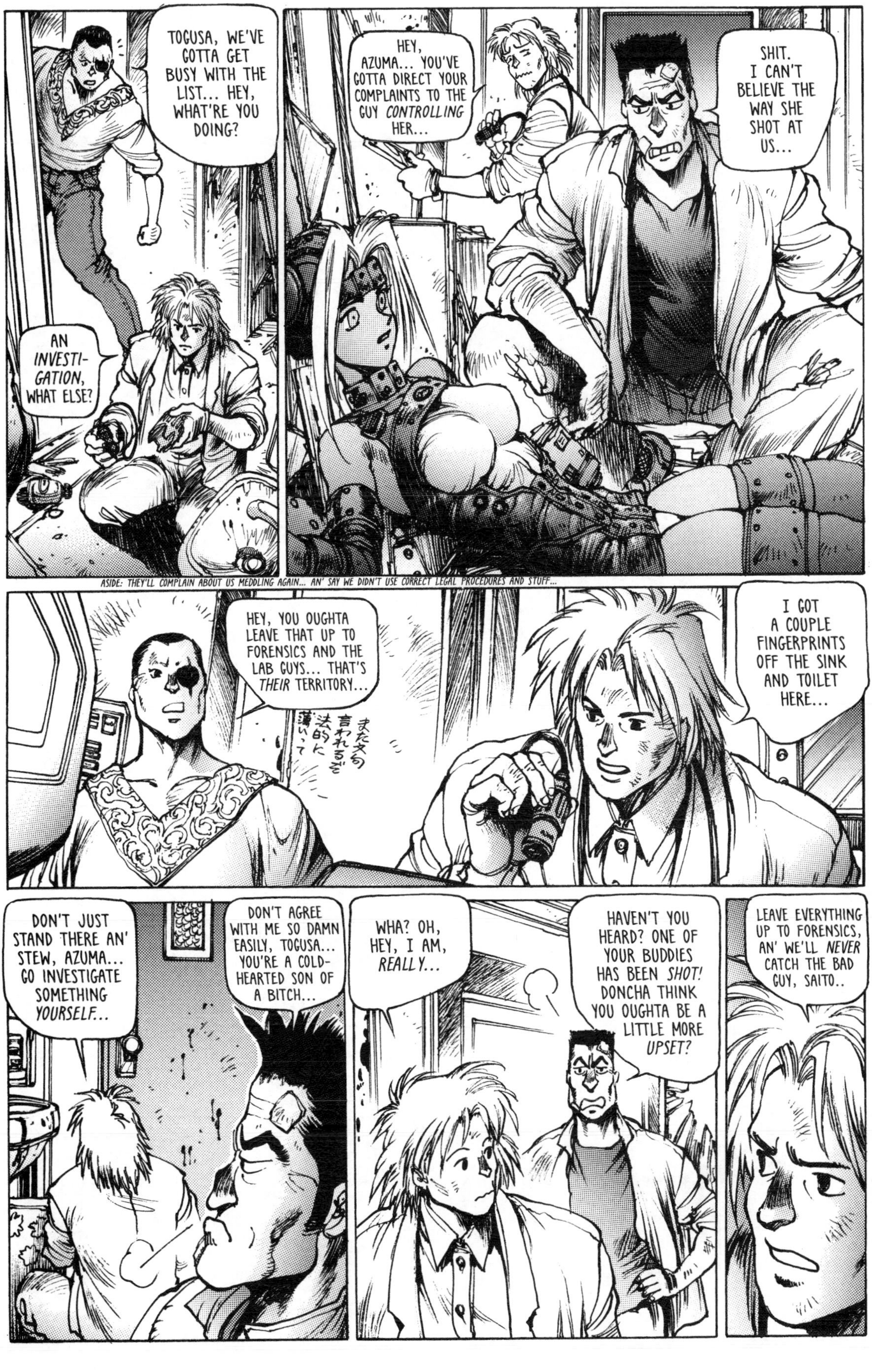
TOGUSA, WE'VE GOTTA GET BUSY WITH THE LIST... HEY, WHAT'RE YOU DOING?
AN *INVESTIGATION*, WHAT ELSE?
SHIT. I CAN'T BELIEVE THE WAY SHE SHOT AT US...
HEY, AZUMA... YOU'VE GOTTA DIRECT YOUR COMPLAINTS TO THE GUY *CONTROLLING* HER...
ASIDE: THEY'LL COMPLAIN ABOUT US MEDDLING AGAIN... AN' SAY WE DIDN'T USE CORRECT LEGAL PROCEDURES AND STUFF...
HEY, YOU OUGHTA LEAVE THAT UP TO FORENSICS AND THE LAB GUYS... THAT'S *THEIR* TERRITORY...
また文句言われるぞ法的に薄いって
I GOT A COUPLE FINGERPRINTS OFF THE SINK AND TOILET HERE...
DON'T JUST STAND THERE AN' STEW, AZUMA... GO INVESTIGATE SOMETHING *YOURSELF*...
DON'T AGREE WITH ME SO DAMN EASILY, TOGUSA... YOU'RE A COLD-HEARTED SON OF A BITCH...
WHA? OH, HEY, I AM, *REALLY*...
HAVEN'T YOU HEARD? ONE OF YOUR BUDDIES HAS BEEN *SHOT!* DONCHA THINK YOU OUGHTA BE A LITTLE MORE *UPSET?*
LEAVE EVERYTHING UP TO FORENSICS, AN' WE'LL *NEVER* CATCH THE BAD GUY, SAITO..

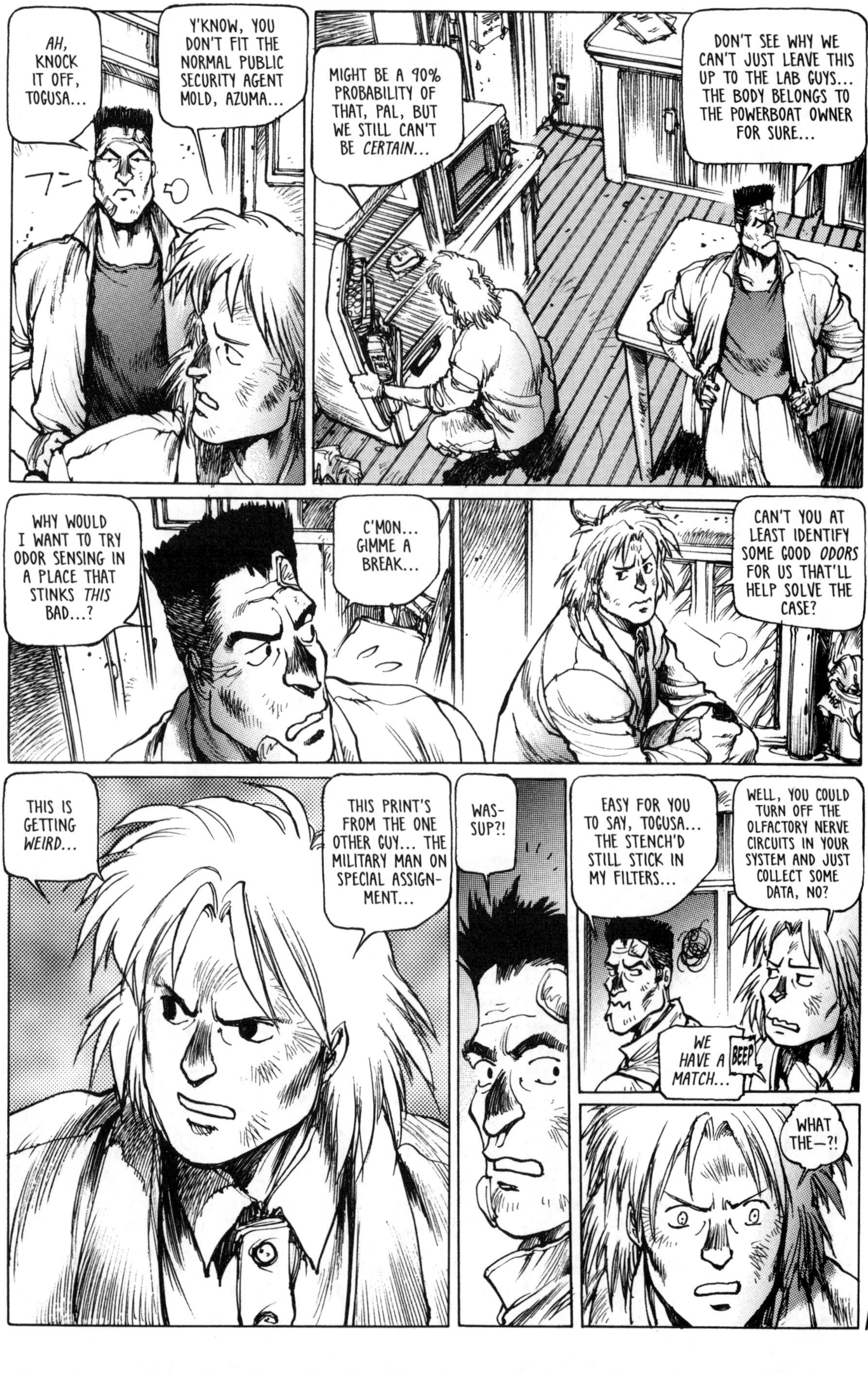
DON'T SEE WHY WE CAN'T JUST LEAVE THIS UP TO THE LAB GUYS... THE BODY BELONGS TO THE POWERBOAT OWNER FOR SURE...
MIGHT BE A 90% PROBABILITY OF THAT, PAL, BUT WE STILL CAN'T BE *CERTAIN*...
Y'KNOW, YOU DON'T FIT THE NORMAL PUBLIC SECURITY AGENT MOLD, AZUMA...
AH, KNOCK IT OFF, TOGUSA...
フン
CAN'T YOU AT LEAST IDENTIFY SOME GOOD *ODORS* FOR US THAT'LL HELP SOLVE THE CASE?
C'MON... GIMME A BREAK...
WHY WOULD I WANT TO TRY ODOR SENSING IN A PLACE THAT STINKS *THIS* BAD...?
WELL, YOU COULD TURN OFF THE OLFACTORY NERVE CIRCUITS IN YOUR SYSTEM AND JUST COLLECT SOME DATA, NO?
EASY FOR YOU TO SAY, TOGUSA... THE STENCH'D STILL STICK IN MY FILTERS...
BEEP
WE HAVE A MATCH...
WHAT THE—?!
WAS-SUP?!
THIS PRINT'S FROM THE ONE OTHER GUY... THE MILITARY MAN ON SPECIAL ASSIGN-MENT...
THIS IS GETTING *WEIRD*...

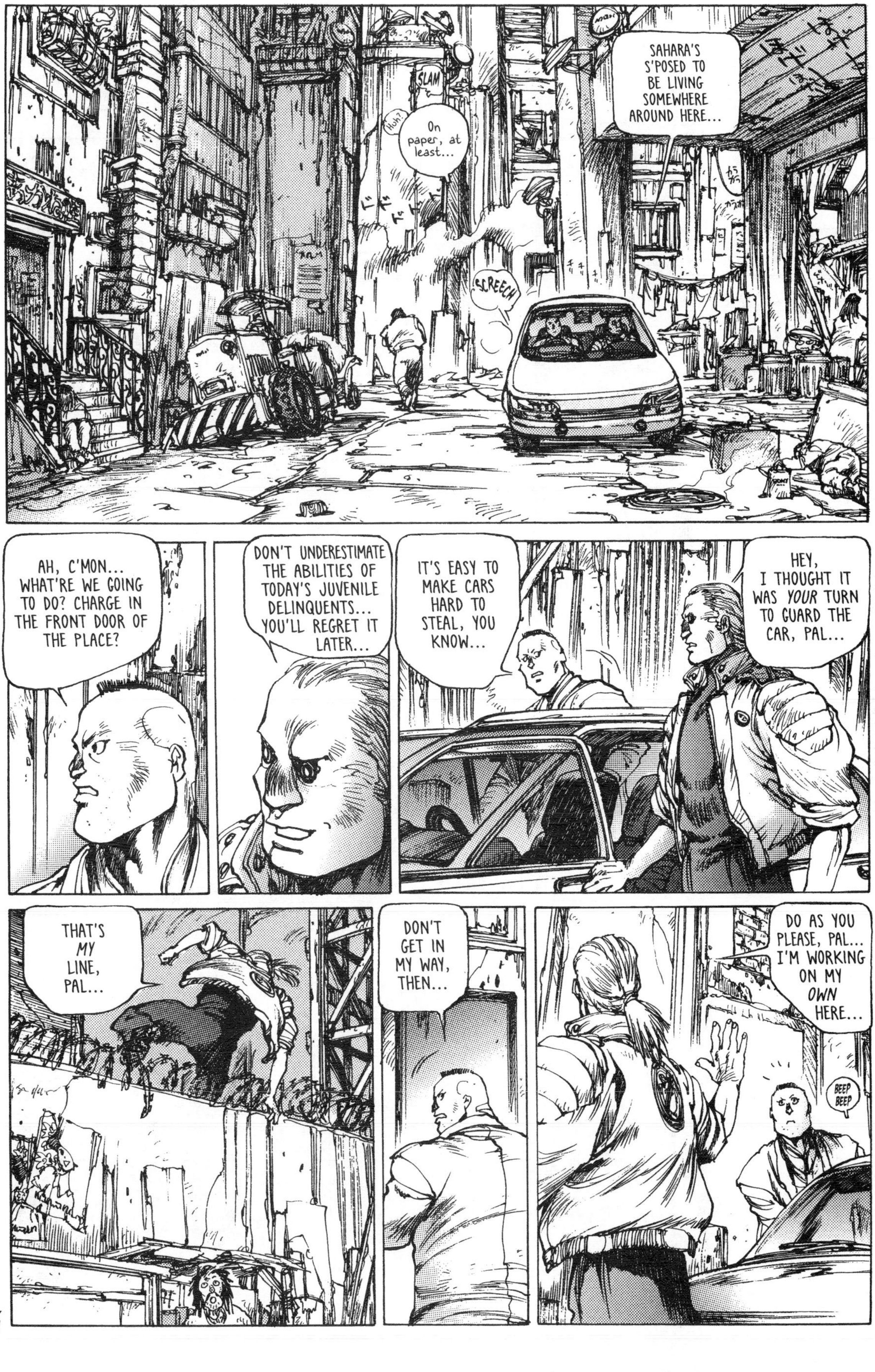
SAHARA'S S'POSED TO BE LIVING SOMEWHERE AROUND HERE...
SLAM
Huh?
On paper, at least...
SCREECH
HEY, I THOUGHT IT WAS *YOUR* TURN TO GUARD THE CAR, PAL...
IT'S EASY TO MAKE CARS HARD TO STEAL, YOU KNOW...
DON'T UNDERESTIMATE THE ABILITIES OF TODAY'S JUVENILE DELINQUENTS... YOU'LL REGRET IT LATER...
AH, C'MON... WHAT'RE WE GOING TO DO? CHARGE IN THE FRONT DOOR OF THE PLACE?
DO AS YOU PLEASE, PAL... I'M WORKING ON MY *OWN* HERE...
BEEP BEEP
DON'T GET IN MY WAY, THEN...
THAT'S *MY* LINE, PAL...

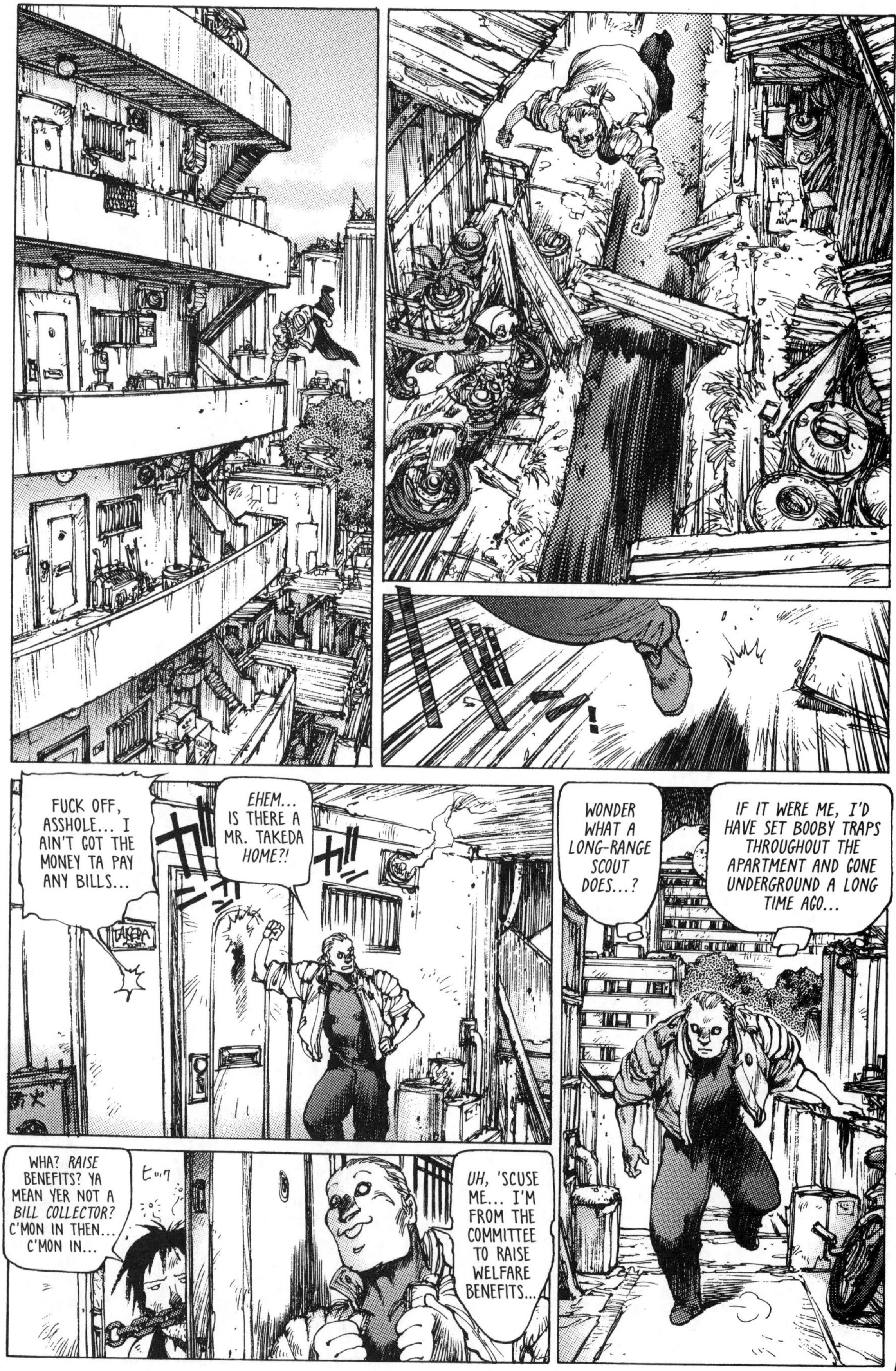

!
IF IT WERE ME, I'D HAVE SET BOOBY TRAPS THROUGHOUT THE APARTMENT AND GONE UNDERGROUND A LONG TIME AGO...
WONDER WHAT A LONG-RANGE SCOUT DOES...?
EHEM... IS THERE A MR. TAKEDA HOME?!
FUCK OFF, ASSHOLE... I AIN'T GOT THE MONEY TA PAY ANY BILLS...
TAKEDA
UH, 'SCUSE ME... I'M FROM THE COMMITTEE TO RAISE WELFARE BENEFITS...
WHA? *RAISE* BENEFITS? YA MEAN YER NOT A *BILL COLLECTOR?* C'MON IN THEN... C'MON IN...
ヒック

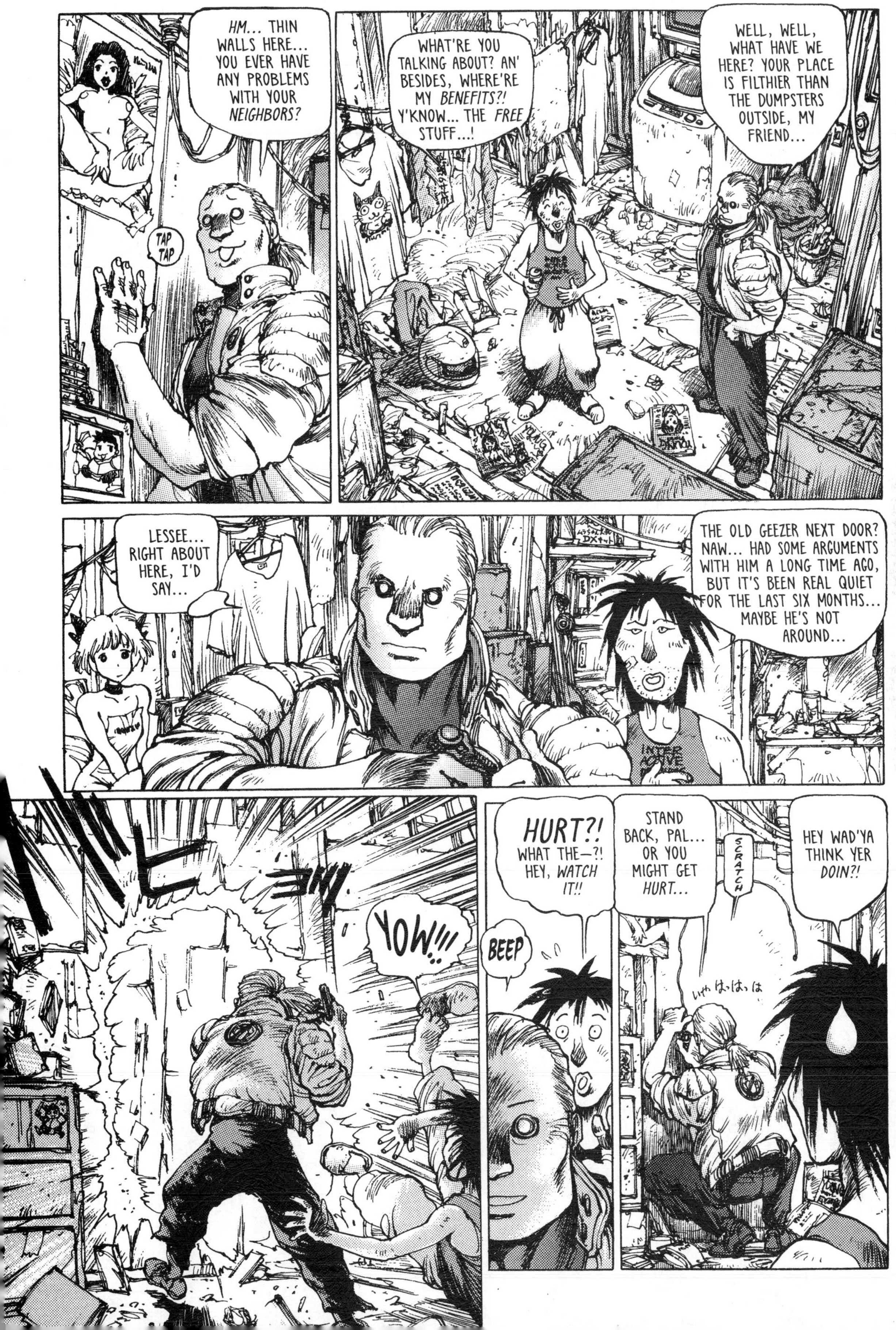
WELL, WELL, WHAT HAVE WE HERE? YOUR PLACE IS FILTHIER THAN THE DUMPSTERS OUTSIDE, MY FRIEND...
WHAT'RE YOU TALKING ABOUT? AN' BESIDES, WHERE'RE MY BENEFITS?! Y'KNOW... THE FREE STUFF...!
HM... THIN WALLS HERE... YOU EVER HAVE ANY PROBLEMS WITH YOUR NEIGHBORS?
TAP TAP
THE OLD GEEZER NEXT DOOR? NAW... HAD SOME ARGUMENTS WITH HIM A LONG TIME AGO, BUT IT'S BEEN REAL QUIET FOR THE LAST SIX MONTHS... MAYBE HE'S NOT AROUND...
LESSEE... RIGHT ABOUT HERE, I'D SAY...
HEY WAD'YA THINK YER DOIN?!
SCRATCH
STAND BACK, PAL... OR YOU MIGHT GET HURT...
HURT?! WHAT THE—?! HEY, WATCH IT!!
BEEP
YOW!!!

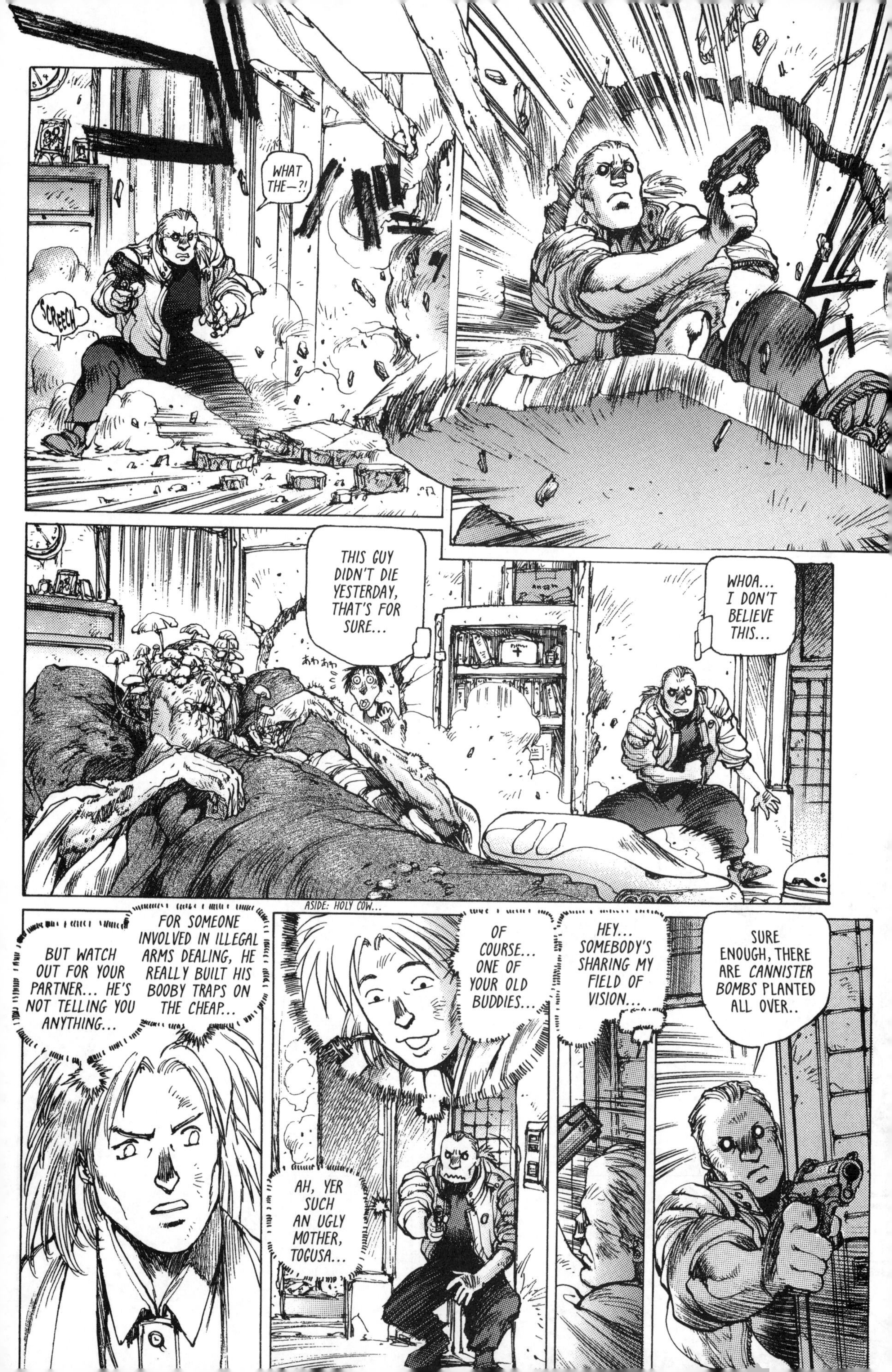
WHAT THE—?!
SCREECH
WHOA... I DON'T BELIEVE THIS...
THIS GUY DIDN'T DIE YESTERDAY, THAT'S FOR SURE...
あわあわ
ASIDE: HOLY COW...
SURE ENOUGH, THERE ARE CANNISTER BOMBS PLANTED ALL OVER..
HEY... SOMEBODY'S SHARING MY FIELD OF VISION...
OF COURSE... ONE OF YOUR OLD BUDDIES...
AH, YER SUCH AN UGLY MOTHER, TOGUSA...
FOR SOMEONE INVOLVED IN ILLEGAL ARMS DEALING, HE REALLY BUILT HIS BOOBY TRAPS ON THE CHEAP...
BUT WATCH OUT FOR YOUR PARTNER... HE'S NOT TELLING YOU ANYTHING...

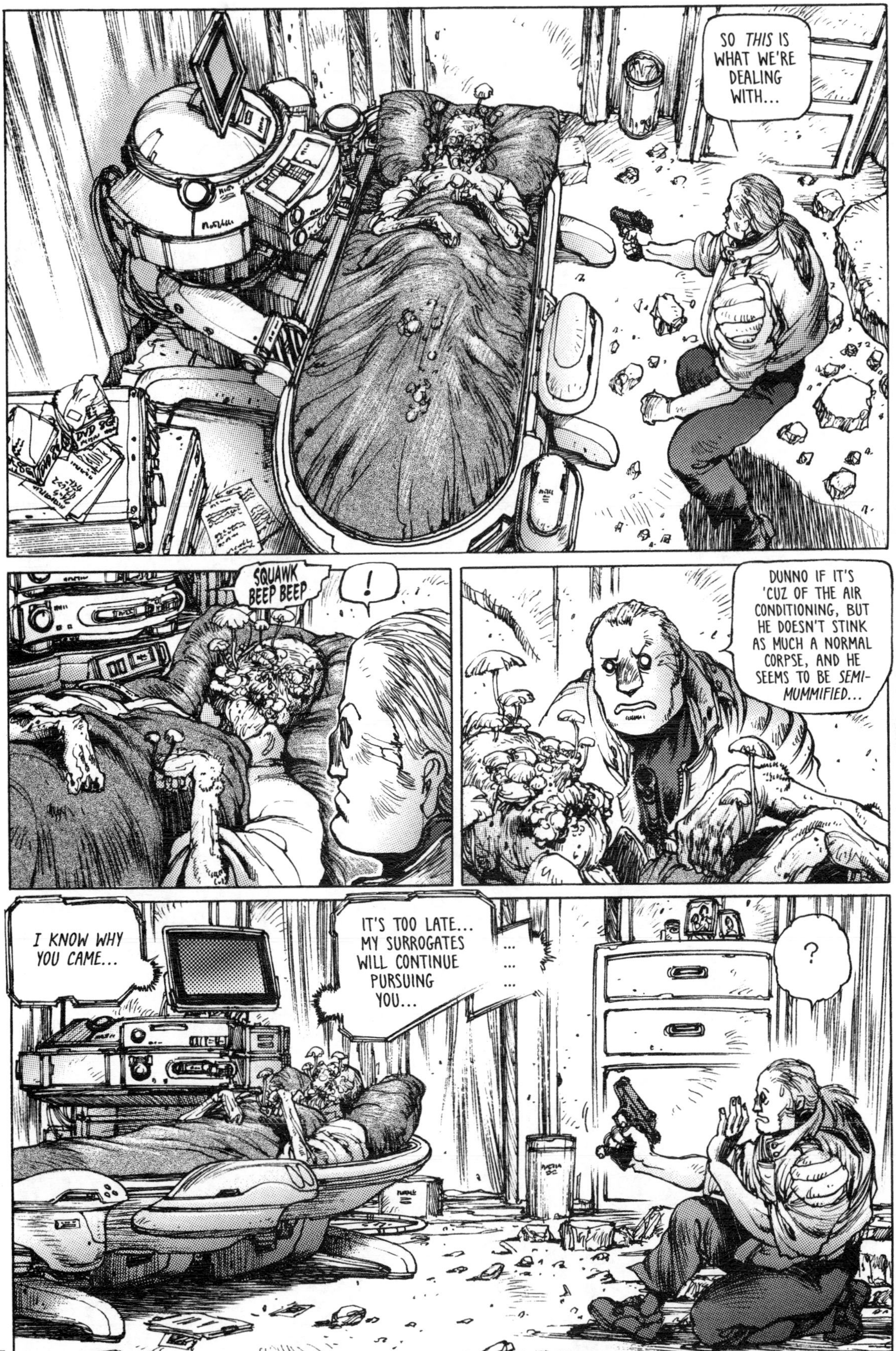
SO *THIS* IS WHAT WE'RE DEALING WITH...
DUNNO IF IT'S 'CUZ OF THE AIR CONDITIONING, BUT HE DOESN'T STINK AS MUCH A NORMAL CORPSE, AND HE SEEMS TO BE *SEMI-MUMMIFIED*...
!
SQUAWK BEEP BEEP
?
IT'S TOO LATE... MY SURROGATES WILL CONTINUE PURSUING YOU...
I KNOW WHY YOU CAME...

ASIDE: SHIT! HELLO? HELLO? POLICE? AW MAN, MY PHONE'S BEEN CUT OFF FOR NON-PAYMENT!

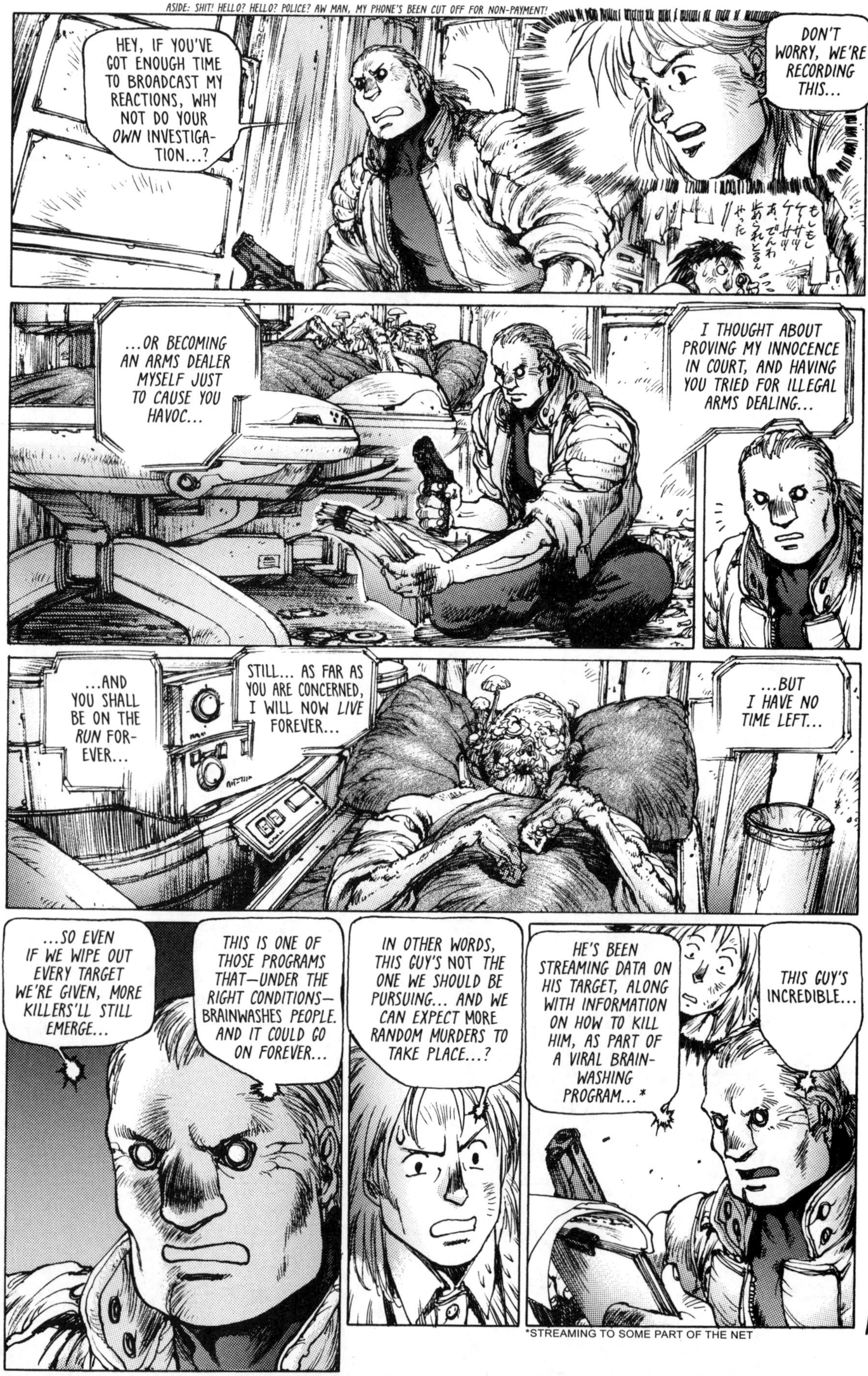
DON'T WORRY, WE'RE RECORDING THIS...
もしもし ケーサツ!! あ、でんわ止められとるん やった!!
HEY, IF YOU'VE GOT ENOUGH TIME TO BROADCAST MY REACTIONS, WHY NOT DO YOUR *OWN* INVESTIGATION...?
I THOUGHT ABOUT PROVING MY INNOCENCE IN COURT, AND HAVING YOU TRIED FOR ILLEGAL ARMS DEALING...
...OR BECOMING AN ARMS DEALER MYSELF JUST TO CAUSE YOU HAVOC...
...BUT I HAVE NO TIME LEFT...
STILL... AS FAR AS YOU ARE CONCERNED, I WILL NOW *LIVE* FOREVER...
...AND YOU SHALL BE ON THE *RUN* FOREVER...
THIS GUY'S INCREDIBLE...
HE'S BEEN STREAMING DATA ON HIS TARGET, ALONG WITH INFORMATION ON HOW TO KILL HIM, AS PART OF A VIRAL BRAINWASHING PROGRAM...*
IN OTHER WORDS, THIS GUY'S NOT THE ONE WE SHOULD BE PURSUING... AND WE CAN EXPECT MORE RANDOM MURDERS TO TAKE PLACE...?
THIS IS ONE OF THOSE PROGRAMS THAT—UNDER THE RIGHT CONDITIONS—BRAINWASHES *PEOPLE*. AND IT COULD GO ON FOREVER...
...SO EVEN IF WE WIPE OUT EVERY TARGET WE'RE GIVEN, MORE KILLERS'LL STILL EMERGE...

*STREAMING TO SOME PART OF THE NET

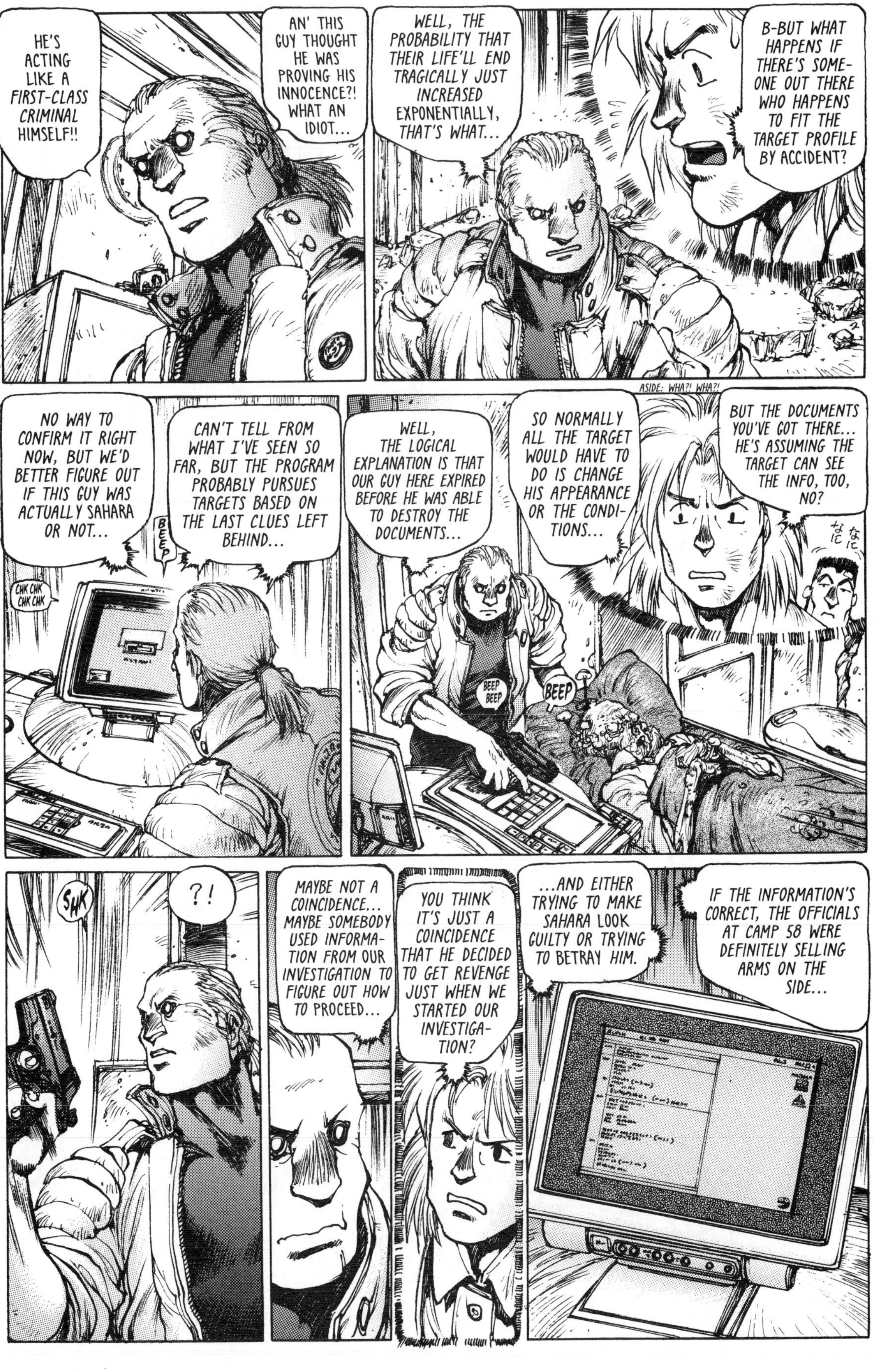
B-BUT WHAT HAPPENS IF THERE'S SOME-ONE OUT THERE WHO HAPPENS TO FIT THE TARGET PROFILE BY ACCIDENT?
WELL, THE PROBABILITY THAT THEIR LIFE'LL END TRAGICALLY JUST INCREASED EXPONENTIALLY, THAT'S WHAT...
AN' THIS GUY THOUGHT HE WAS PROVING HIS INNOCENCE?! WHAT AN IDIOT...
HE'S ACTING LIKE A FIRST-CLASS CRIMINAL HIMSELF!!
ASIDE: WHA?! WHA?!
BUT THE DOCUMENTS YOU'VE GOT THERE... HE'S ASSUMING THE TARGET CAN SEE THE INFO, TOO, NO?
なに なに
SO NORMALLY ALL THE TARGET WOULD HAVE TO DO IS CHANGE HIS APPEARANCE OR THE CONDI-TIONS...
WELL, THE LOGICAL EXPLANATION IS THAT OUR GUY HERE EXPIRED BEFORE HE WAS ABLE TO DESTROY THE DOCUMENTS...
BEEP
BEEP BEEP
CAN'T TELL FROM WHAT I'VE SEEN SO FAR, BUT THE PROGRAM PROBABLY PURSUES TARGETS BASED ON THE LAST CLUES LEFT BEHIND...
BEEP
NO WAY TO CONFIRM IT RIGHT NOW, BUT WE'D BETTER FIGURE OUT IF THIS GUY WAS ACTUALLY SAHARA OR NOT...
CHK CHK CHK CHK
IF THE INFORMATION'S CORRECT, THE OFFICIALS AT CAMP 58 WERE DEFINITELY SELLING ARMS ON THE SIDE...
...AND EITHER TRYING TO MAKE SAHARA LOOK GUILTY OR TRYING TO BETRAY HIM.
YOU THINK IT'S JUST A COINCIDENCE THAT HE DECIDED TO GET REVENGE JUST WHEN WE STARTED OUR INVESTIGA-TION?
MAYBE NOT A COINCIDENCE... MAYBE SOMEBODY USED INFORMA-TION FROM OUR INVESTIGATION TO FIGURE OUT HOW TO PROCEED...
?!
SHK

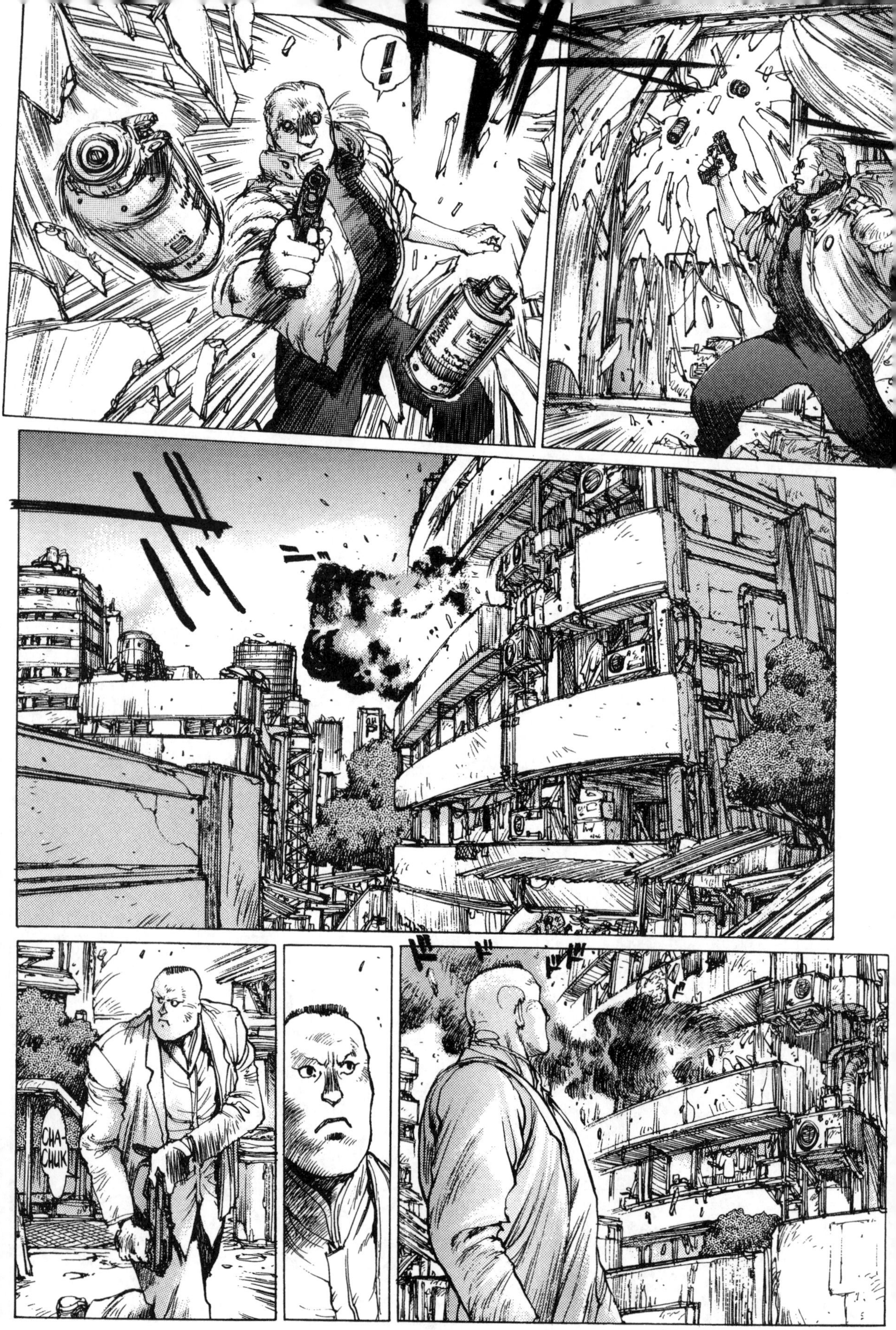
!
CHA-CHUK

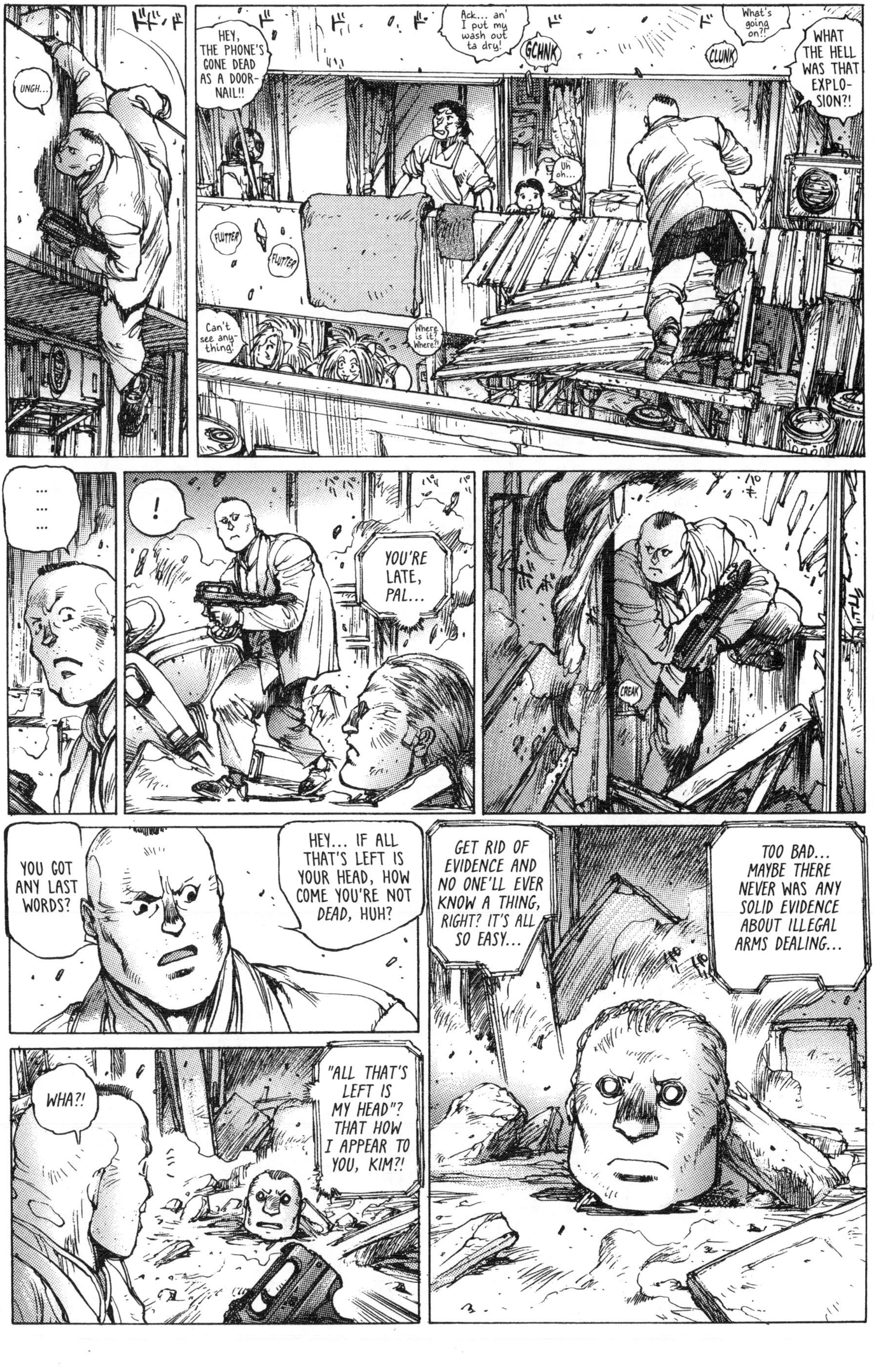
What's going on?!
WHAT THE HELL WAS THAT EXPLO-SION?!
CLUNK
Ack... an' I put my wash out ta dry!
GCHNK
HEY, THE PHONE'S GONE DEAD AS A DOOR-NAIL!!
Uh oh...
FLUTTER
FLUTTER
Where is it? Where?!
Can't see any-thing!
UNGH...
CREAK
YOU'RE LATE, PAL...
!
...
...
...
TOO BAD... MAYBE THERE NEVER WAS ANY SOLID EVIDENCE ABOUT ILLEGAL ARMS DEALING...
GET RID OF EVIDENCE AND NO ONE'LL EVER KNOW A THING, RIGHT? IT'S ALL SO EASY...
HEY... IF ALL THAT'S LEFT IS YOUR HEAD, HOW COME YOU'RE NOT DEAD, HUH?
YOU GOT ANY LAST WORDS?
"ALL THAT'S LEFT IS MY HEAD"? THAT HOW I APPEAR TO YOU, KIM?!
WHA?!

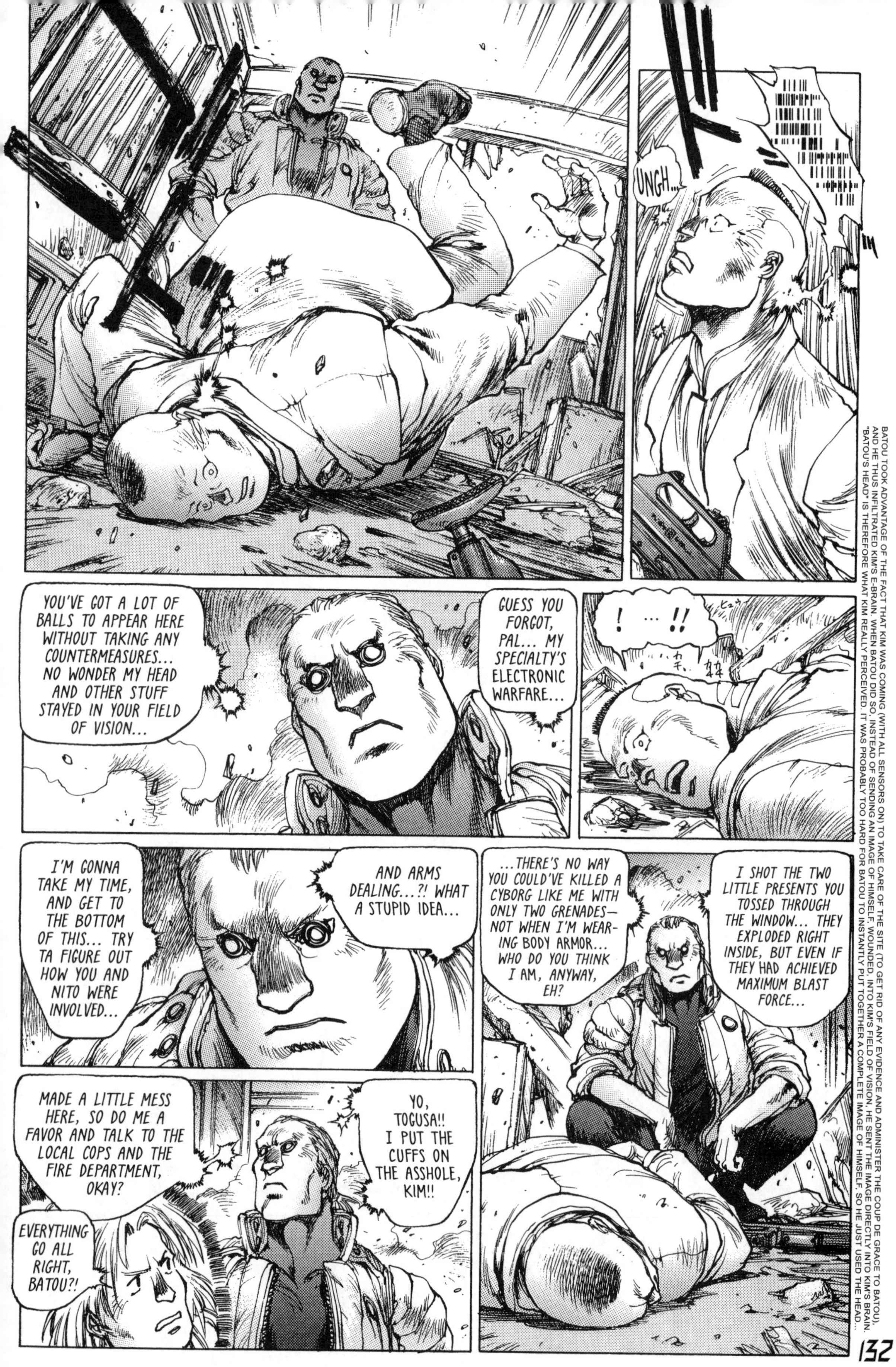
UNGH...
! ... !!
GUESS YOU FORGOT, PAL... MY SPECIALTY'S ELECTRONIC WARFARE...
YOU'VE GOT A LOT OF BALLS TO APPEAR HERE WITHOUT TAKING ANY COUNTERMEASURES... NO WONDER MY HEAD AND OTHER STUFF STAYED IN YOUR FIELD OF VISION...
I SHOT THE TWO LITTLE PRESENTS YOU TOSSED THROUGH THE WINDOW... THEY EXPLODED RIGHT INSIDE, BUT EVEN IF THEY HAD ACHIEVED MAXIMUM BLAST FORCE...
...THERE'S NO WAY YOU COULD'VE KILLED A CYBORG LIKE ME WITH ONLY TWO GRENADES—NOT WHEN I'M WEARING BODY ARMOR... WHO DO YOU THINK I AM, ANYWAY, EH?
AND ARMS DEALING...?! WHAT A STUPID IDEA...
I'M GONNA TAKE MY TIME, AND GET TO THE BOTTOM OF THIS... TRY TA FIGURE OUT HOW YOU AND NITO WERE INVOLVED...
YO, TOGUSA!! I PUT THE CUFFS ON THE ASSHOLE, KIM!!
MADE A LITTLE MESS HERE, SO DO ME A FAVOR AND TALK TO THE LOCAL COPS AND THE FIRE DEPARTMENT, OKAY?
EVERYTHING GO ALL RIGHT, BATOU?!

BATOU TOOK ADVANTAGE OF THE FACT THAT KIM WAS COMING (WITH ALL SENSORS ON) TO TAKE CARE OF THE SITE (TO GET RID OF ANY EVIDENCE AND ADMINISTER THE COUP DE GRACE TO BATOU), AND HE THUS INFILTRATED KIM'S E-BRAIN. WHEN BATOU DID SO, INSTEAD OF SENDING AN IMAGE OF HIMSELF, WOUNDED, INTO KIM'S FIELD OF VISION, HE SENT THE IMAGE DIRECTLY INTO KIM'S BRAIN. "BATOU'S HEAD" IS THEREFORE WHAT KIM REALLY PERCEIVED. IT WAS PROBABLY TOO HARD FOR BATOU TO INSTANTLY PUT TOGETHER A COMPLETE IMAGE OF HIMSELF, SO HE JUST USED THE HEAD...

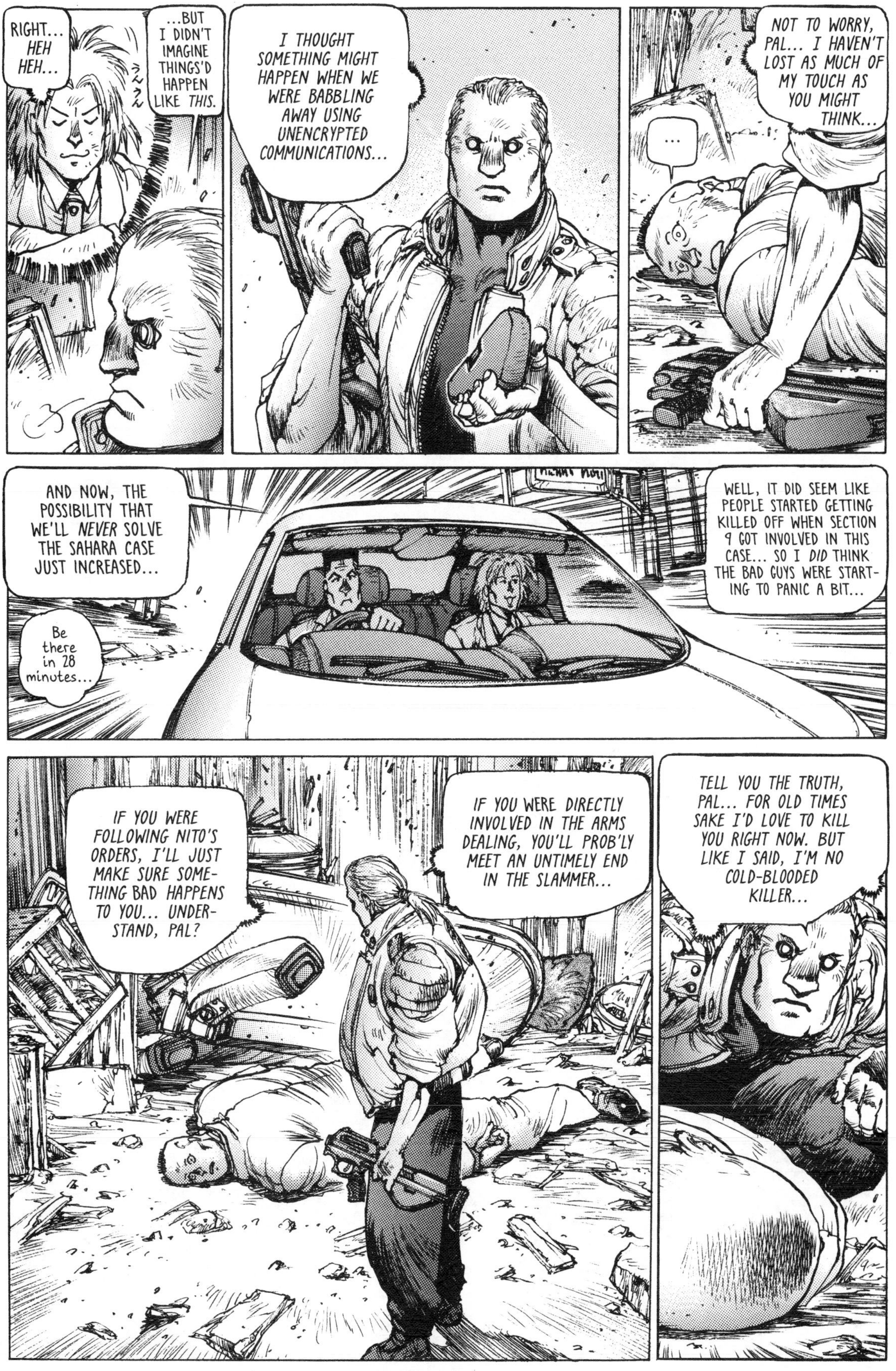
NOT TO WORRY, PAL... I HAVEN'T LOST AS MUCH OF MY TOUCH AS YOU MIGHT THINK...
...
I THOUGHT SOMETHING MIGHT HAPPEN WHEN WE WERE BABBLING AWAY USING UNENCRYPTED COMMUNICATIONS...
...BUT I DIDN'T IMAGINE THINGS'D HAPPEN LIKE *THIS*.
RIGHT... *HEH HEH*...
WELL, IT DID SEEM LIKE PEOPLE STARTED GETTING KILLED OFF WHEN SECTION 9 GOT INVOLVED IN THIS CASE... SO I *DID* THINK THE BAD GUYS WERE STARTING TO PANIC A BIT...
AND NOW, THE POSSIBILITY THAT WE'LL *NEVER* SOLVE THE SAHARA CASE JUST INCREASED...
Be there in 28 minutes...
TELL YOU THE TRUTH, PAL... FOR OLD TIMES SAKE I'D LOVE TO KILL YOU RIGHT NOW. BUT LIKE I SAID, I'M NO COLD-BLOODED KILLER...
IF YOU WERE DIRECTLY INVOLVED IN THE ARMS DEALING, YOU'LL PROB'LY MEET AN UNTIMELY END IN THE SLAMMER...
IF YOU WERE FOLLOWING NITO'S ORDERS, I'LL JUST MAKE SURE SOMETHING BAD HAPPENS TO YOU... UNDERSTAND, PAL?

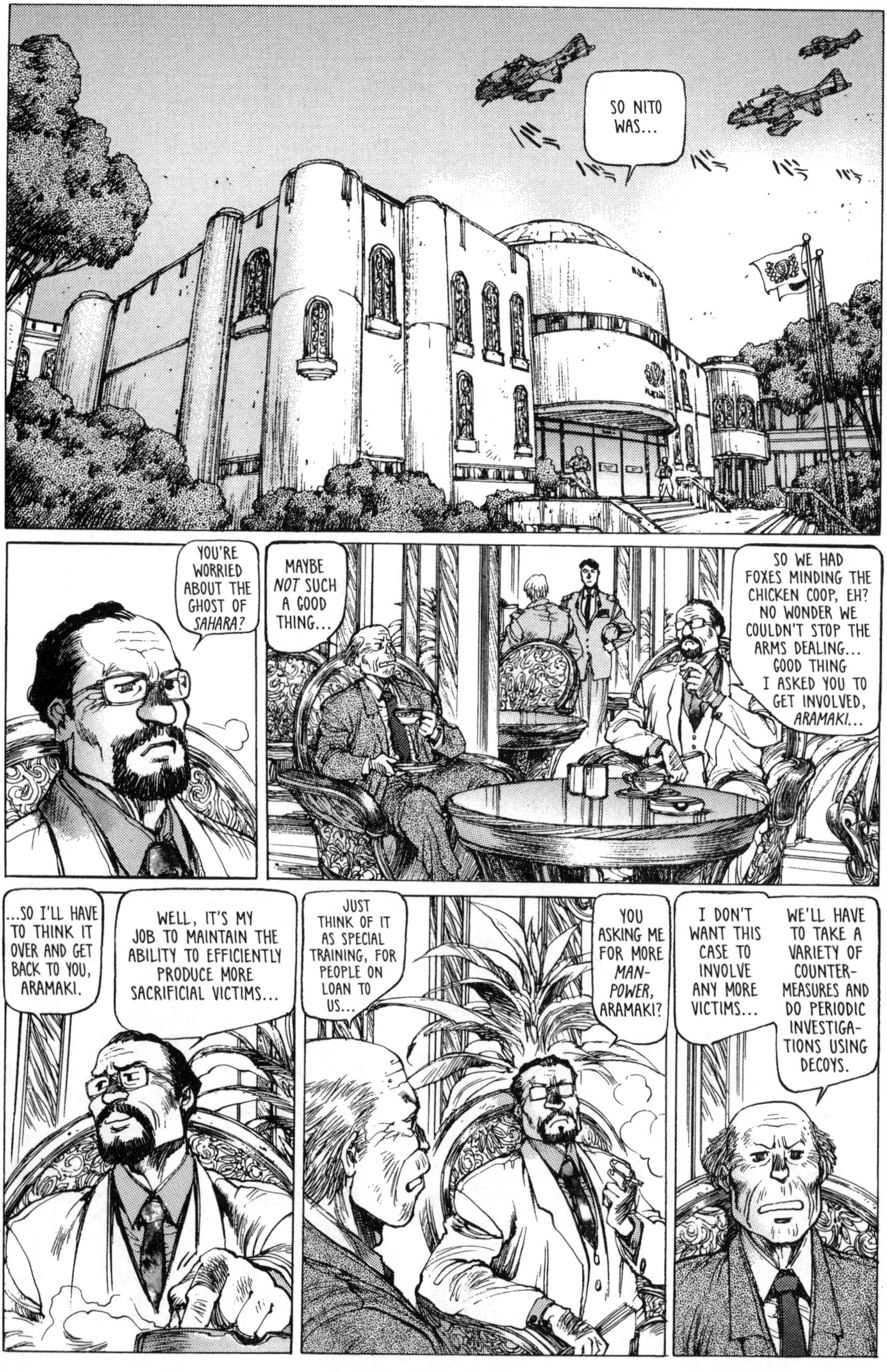
SO NITO WAS...
SO WE HAD FOXES MINDING THE CHICKEN COOP, EH? NO WONDER WE COULDN'T STOP THE ARMS DEALING... GOOD THING I ASKED YOU TO GET INVOLVED, *ARAMAKI*...
MAYBE *NOT* SUCH A GOOD THING...
YOU'RE WORRIED ABOUT THE GHOST OF *SAHARA?*
WE'LL HAVE TO TAKE A VARIETY OF COUNTER-MEASURES AND DO PERIODIC INVESTIGA-TIONS USING DECOYS.
I DON'T WANT THIS CASE TO INVOLVE ANY MORE VICTIMS...
YOU ASKING ME FOR MORE *MAN-POWER*, ARAMAKI?
JUST THINK OF IT AS SPECIAL TRAINING, FOR PEOPLE ON LOAN TO US...
WELL, IT'S MY JOB TO MAINTAIN THE ABILITY TO EFFICIENTLY PRODUCE MORE SACRIFICIAL VICTIMS...
...SO I'LL HAVE TO THINK IT OVER AND GET BACK TO YOU, ARAMAKI.

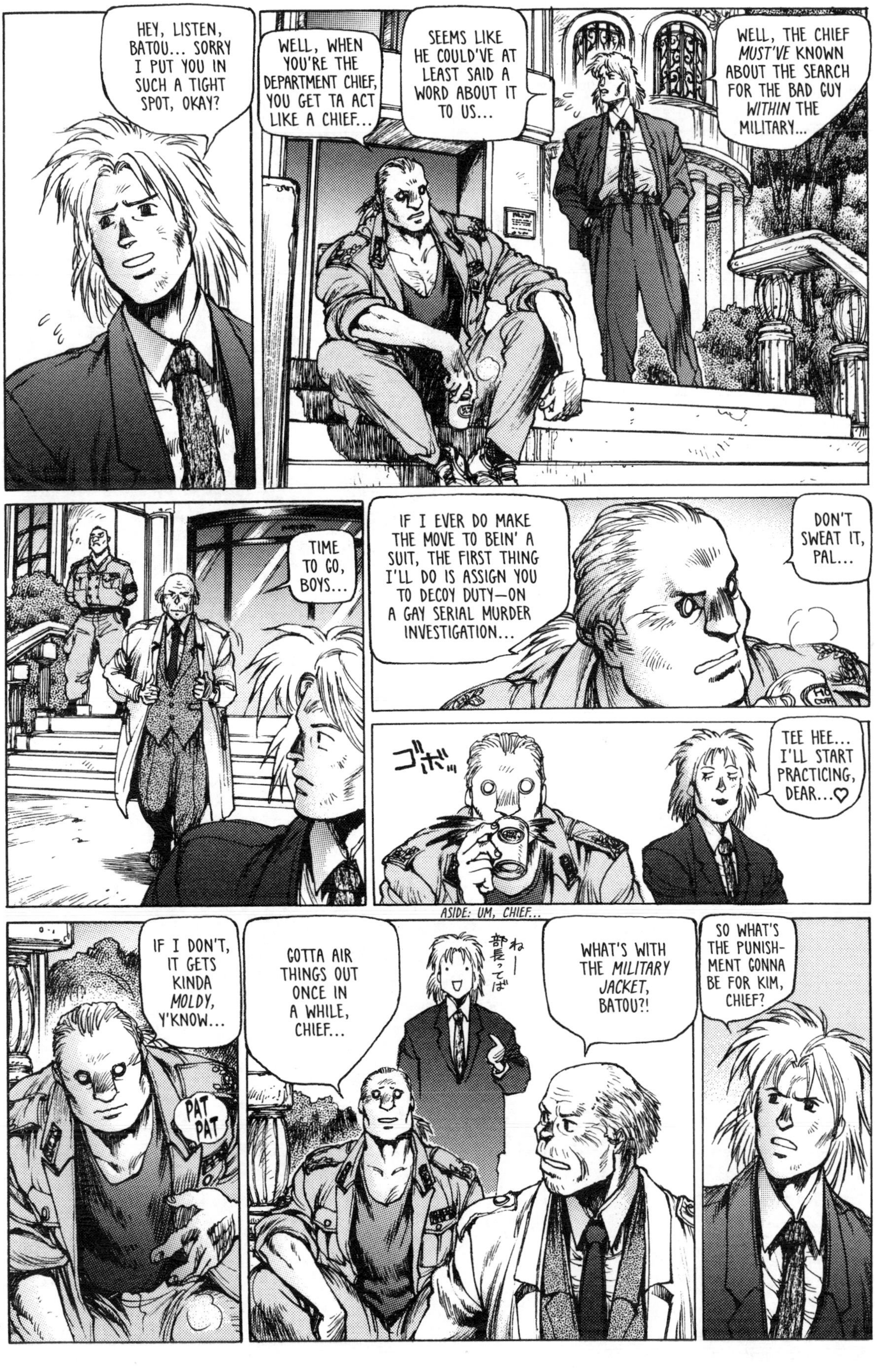
WELL, THE CHIEF *MUST'VE* KNOWN ABOUT THE SEARCH FOR THE BAD GUY *WITHIN* THE MILITARY...
SEEMS LIKE HE COULD'VE AT LEAST SAID A WORD ABOUT IT TO US...
WELL, WHEN YOU'RE THE DEPARTMENT CHIEF, YOU GET TA ACT LIKE A CHIEF...
HEY, LISTEN, BATOU... SORRY I PUT YOU IN SUCH A TIGHT SPOT, OKAY?
DON'T SWEAT IT, PAL...
IF I EVER DO MAKE THE MOVE TO BEIN' A SUIT, THE FIRST THING I'LL DO IS ASSIGN YOU TO DECOY DUTY—ON A GAY SERIAL MURDER INVESTIGATION...
TEE HEE... I'LL START PRACTICING, DEAR...♡
ゴボッ
TIME TO GO, BOYS...
ASIDE: UM, CHIEF...
SO WHAT'S THE PUNISHMENT GONNA BE FOR KIM, CHIEF?
WHAT'S WITH THE *MILITARY JACKET*, BATOU?!
ねー部長ってば
GOTTA AIR THINGS OUT ONCE IN A WHILE, CHIEF...
IF I DON'T, IT GETS KINDA *MOLDY*, Y'KNOW...
PAT PAT

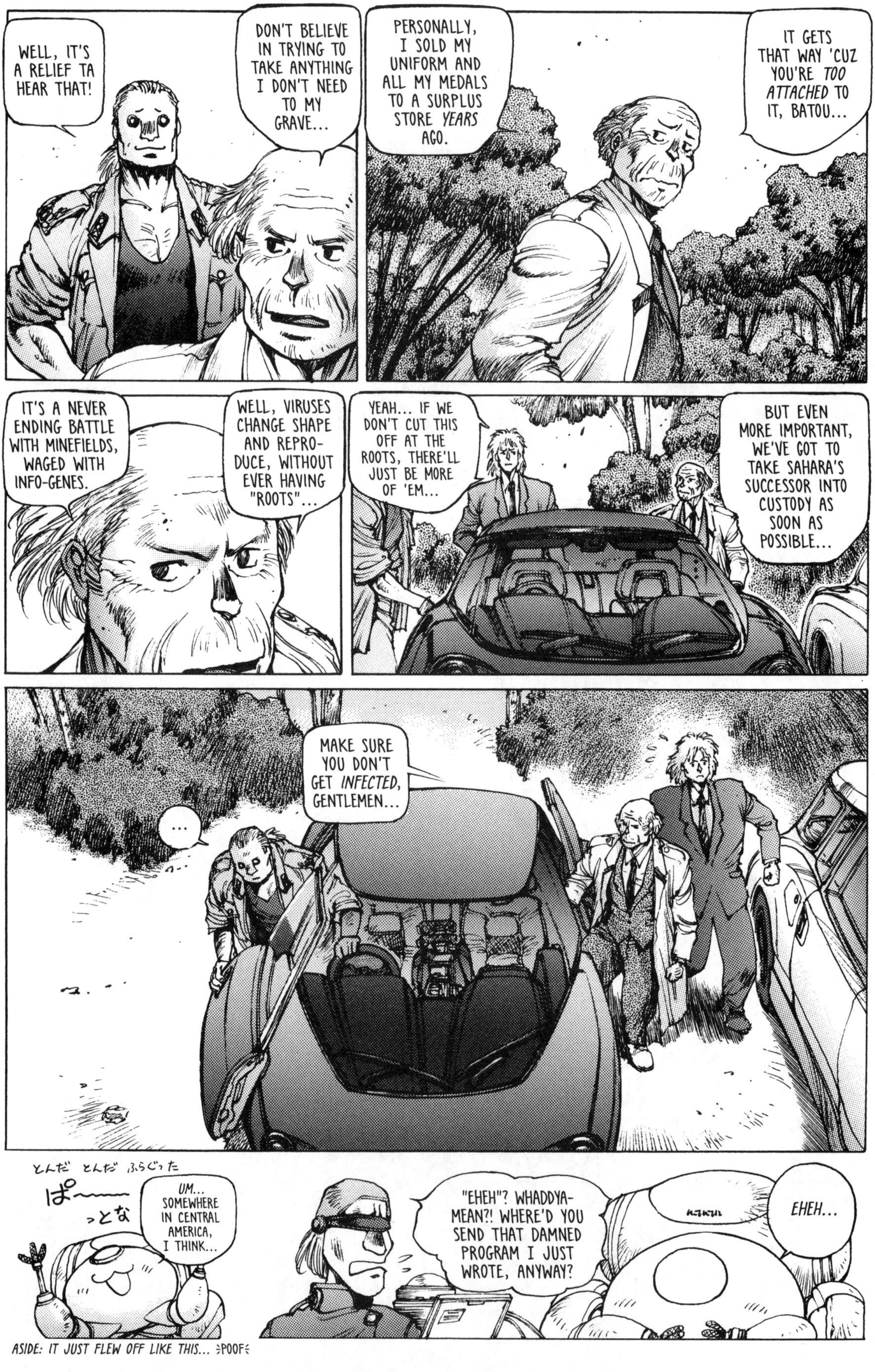

WELL, IT'S A RELIEF TA HEAR THAT!
DON'T BELIEVE IN TRYING TO TAKE ANYTHING I DON'T NEED TO MY GRAVE...
PERSONALLY, I SOLD MY UNIFORM AND ALL MY MEDALS TO A SURPLUS STORE *YEARS* AGO.
IT GETS THAT WAY 'CUZ YOU'RE *TOO ATTACHED* TO IT, BATOU...
IT'S A NEVER ENDING BATTLE WITH MINEFIELDS, WAGED WITH INFO-GENES.
WELL, VIRUSES CHANGE SHAPE AND REPRODUCE, WITHOUT EVER HAVING "ROOTS"...
YEAH... IF WE DON'T CUT THIS OFF AT THE ROOTS, THERE'LL JUST BE MORE OF 'EM...
BUT EVEN MORE IMPORTANT, WE'VE GOT TO TAKE SAHARA'S SUCCESSOR INTO CUSTODY AS SOON AS POSSIBLE...
MAKE SURE YOU DON'T GET *INFECTED*, GENTLEMEN...
...
EHEH...
"EHEH"? WHADDYA-MEAN?! WHERE'D YOU SEND THAT DAMNED PROGRAM I JUST WROTE, ANYWAY?
UM... SOMEWHERE IN CENTRAL AMERICA, I THINK...
とんだ とんだ ふらぐった
ぱ〜〜〜っとな

ASIDE: IT JUST FLEW OFF LIKE THIS... ≥POOF≤

LOST PAST 07

1996

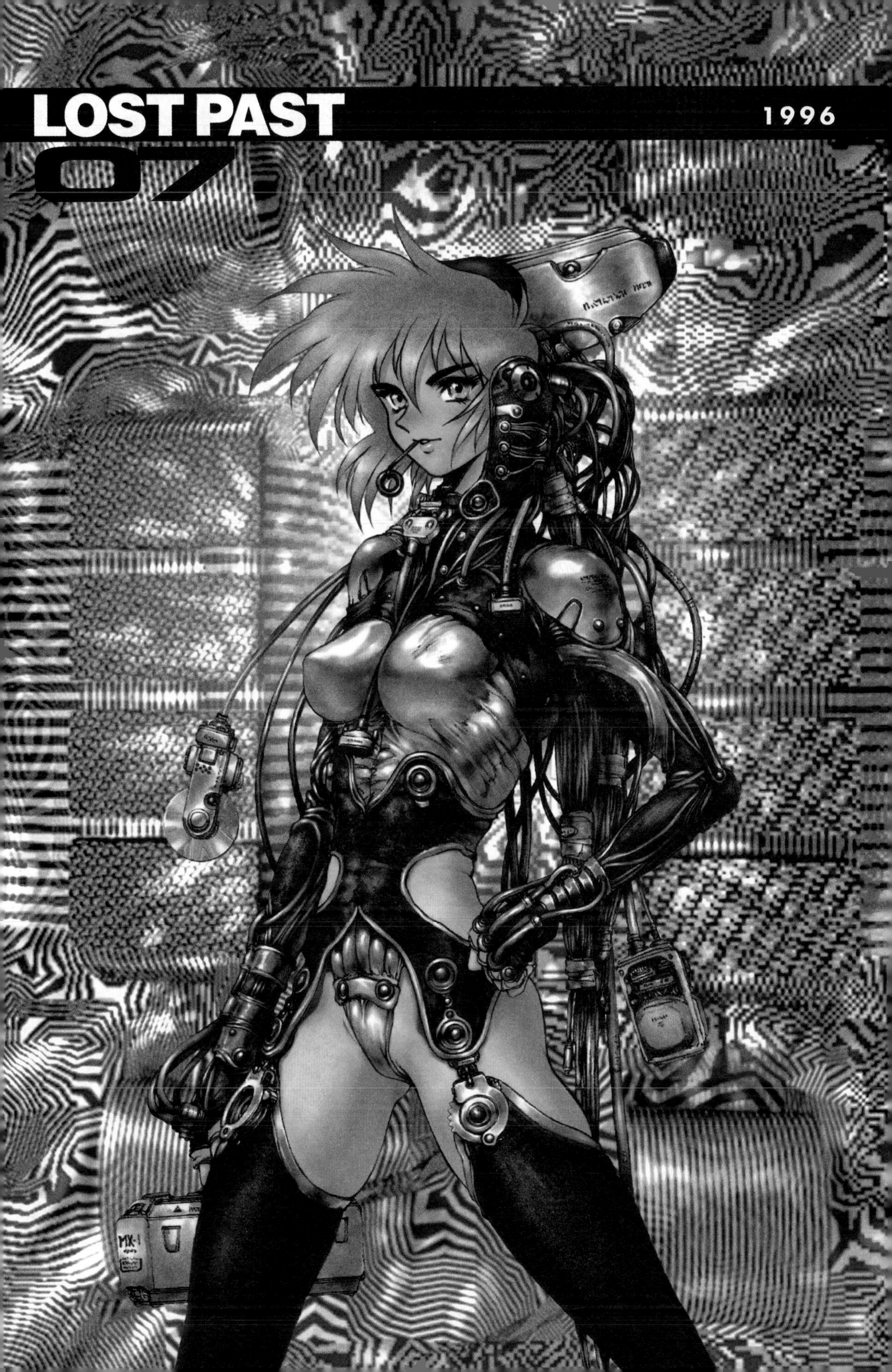
MX-1

DAMMIT...

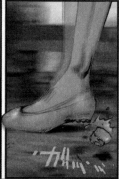

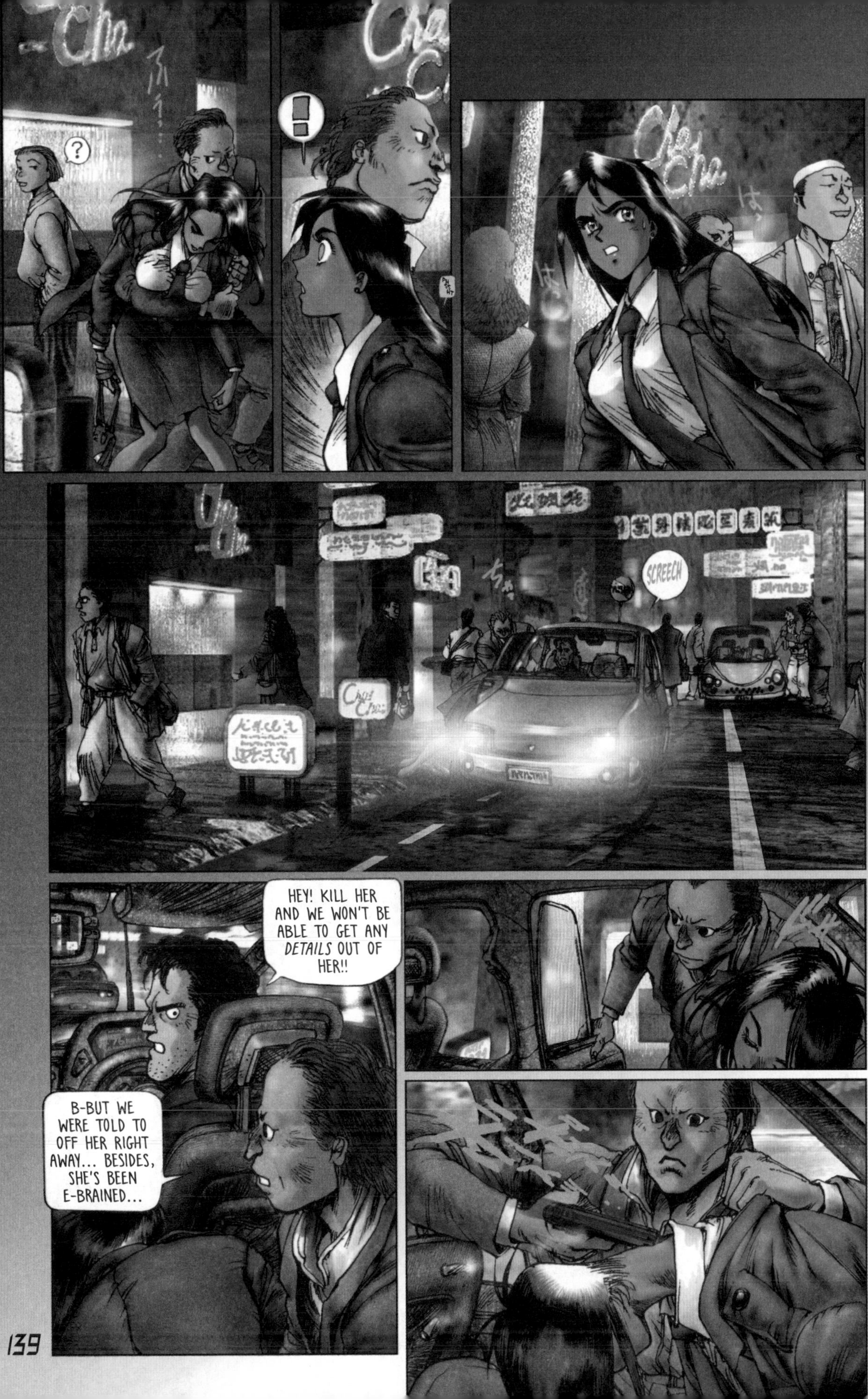

!
?
SCREECH
HEY! KILL HER AND WE WON'T BE ABLE TO GET ANY *DETAILS* OUT OF HER!!
B-BUT WE WERE TOLD TO OFF HER RIGHT AWAY... BESIDES, SHE'S BEEN E-BRAINED...

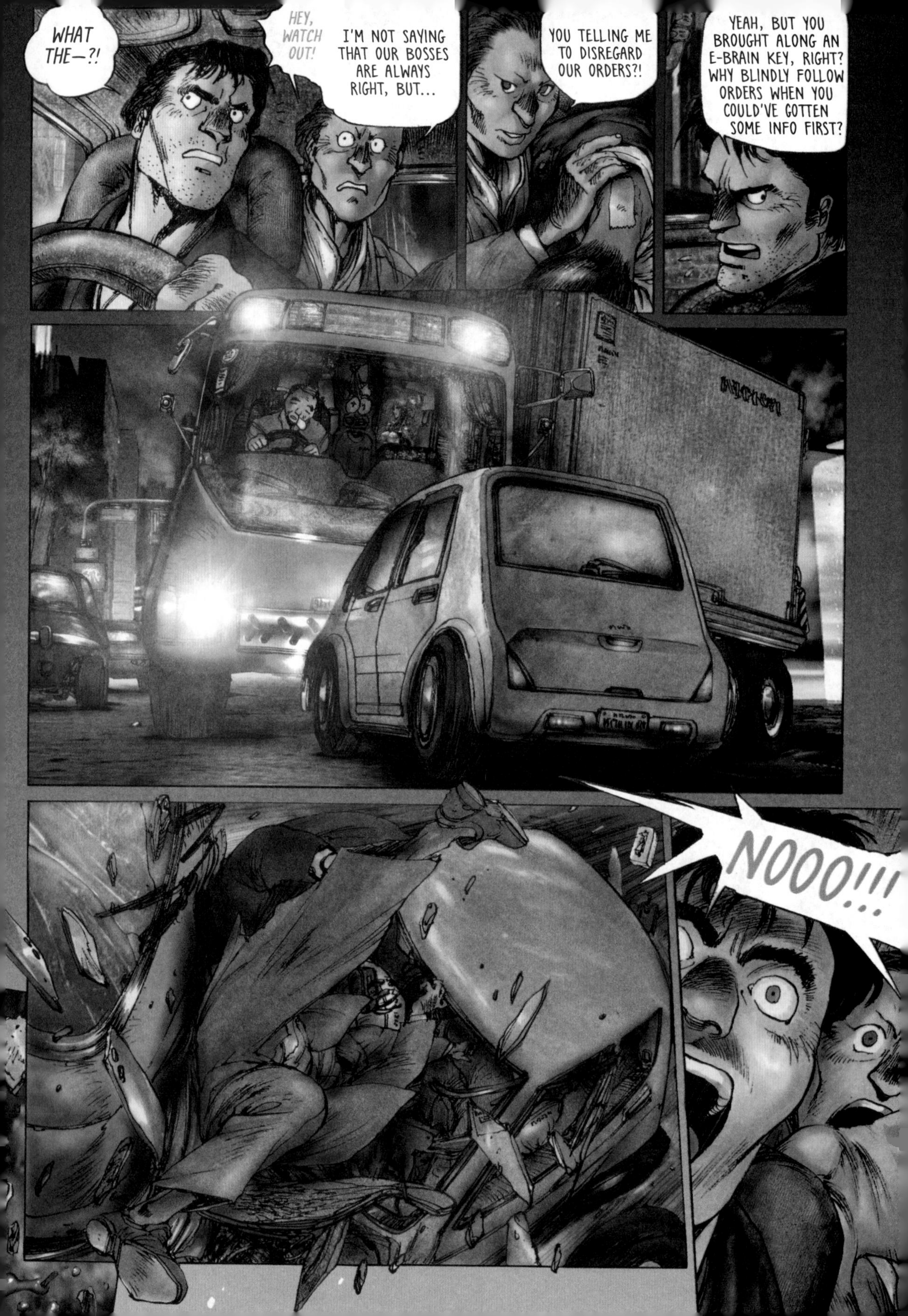
YEAH, BUT YOU BROUGHT ALONG AN E-BRAIN KEY, RIGHT? WHY BLINDLY FOLLOW ORDERS WHEN YOU COULD'VE GOTTEN SOME INFO FIRST?
YOU TELLING ME TO DISREGARD OUR ORDERS?!
I'M NOT SAYING THAT OUR BOSSES ARE ALWAYS RIGHT, BUT...
HEY, WATCH OUT!
WHAT THE—?!
NOOO!!!

TRUCK: YAMAMURA TRANSPORT

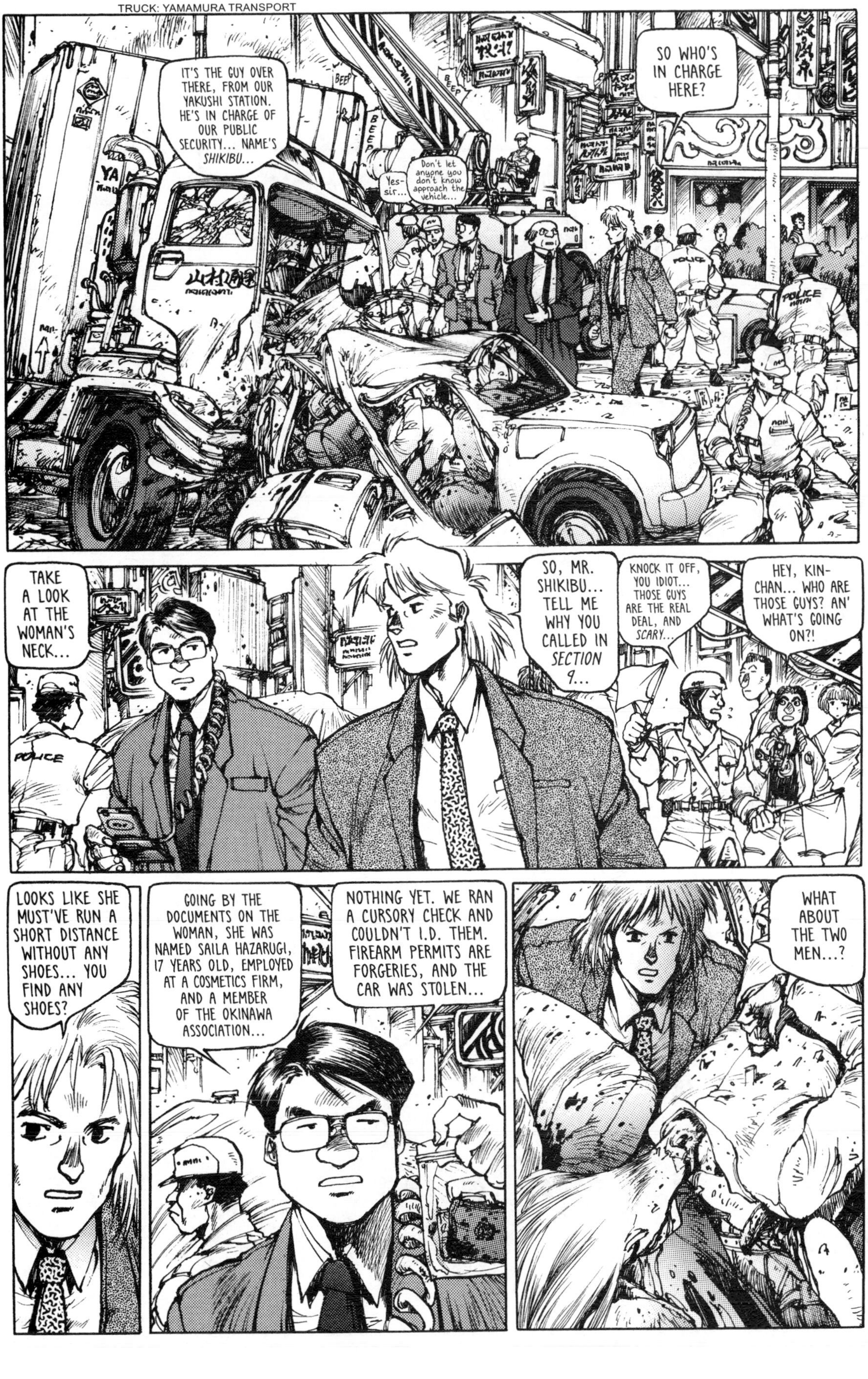

SO WHO'S IN CHARGE HERE?
IT'S THE GUY OVER THERE, FROM OUR YAKUSHI STATION. HE'S IN CHARGE OF OUR PUBLIC SECURITY... NAME'S *SHIKIBU*...
BEEP
BEEP
BEEP
Don't let anyone you don't know approach the vehicle...
Yes-sir...
HEY, KIN-CHAN... WHO ARE THOSE GUYS? AN' WHAT'S GOING ON?!
KNOCK IT OFF, YOU IDIOT... THOSE GUYS ARE THE REAL DEAL, AND *SCARY*...
SO, MR. SHIKIBU... TELL ME WHY YOU CALLED IN *SECTION 9*...
TAKE A LOOK AT THE WOMAN'S NECK...
WHAT ABOUT THE TWO MEN...?
NOTHING YET. WE RAN A CURSORY CHECK AND COULDN'T I.D. THEM. FIREARM PERMITS ARE FORGERIES, AND THE CAR WAS STOLEN...
GOING BY THE DOCUMENTS ON THE WOMAN, SHE WAS NAMED SAILA HAZARUGI, 17 YEARS OLD, EMPLOYED AT A COSMETICS FIRM, AND A MEMBER OF THE OKINAWA ASSOCIATION...
LOOKS LIKE SHE MUST'VE RUN A SHORT DISTANCE WITHOUT ANY SHOES... YOU FIND ANY SHOES?

SIGN: POLICE LINE - DO NOT CROSS

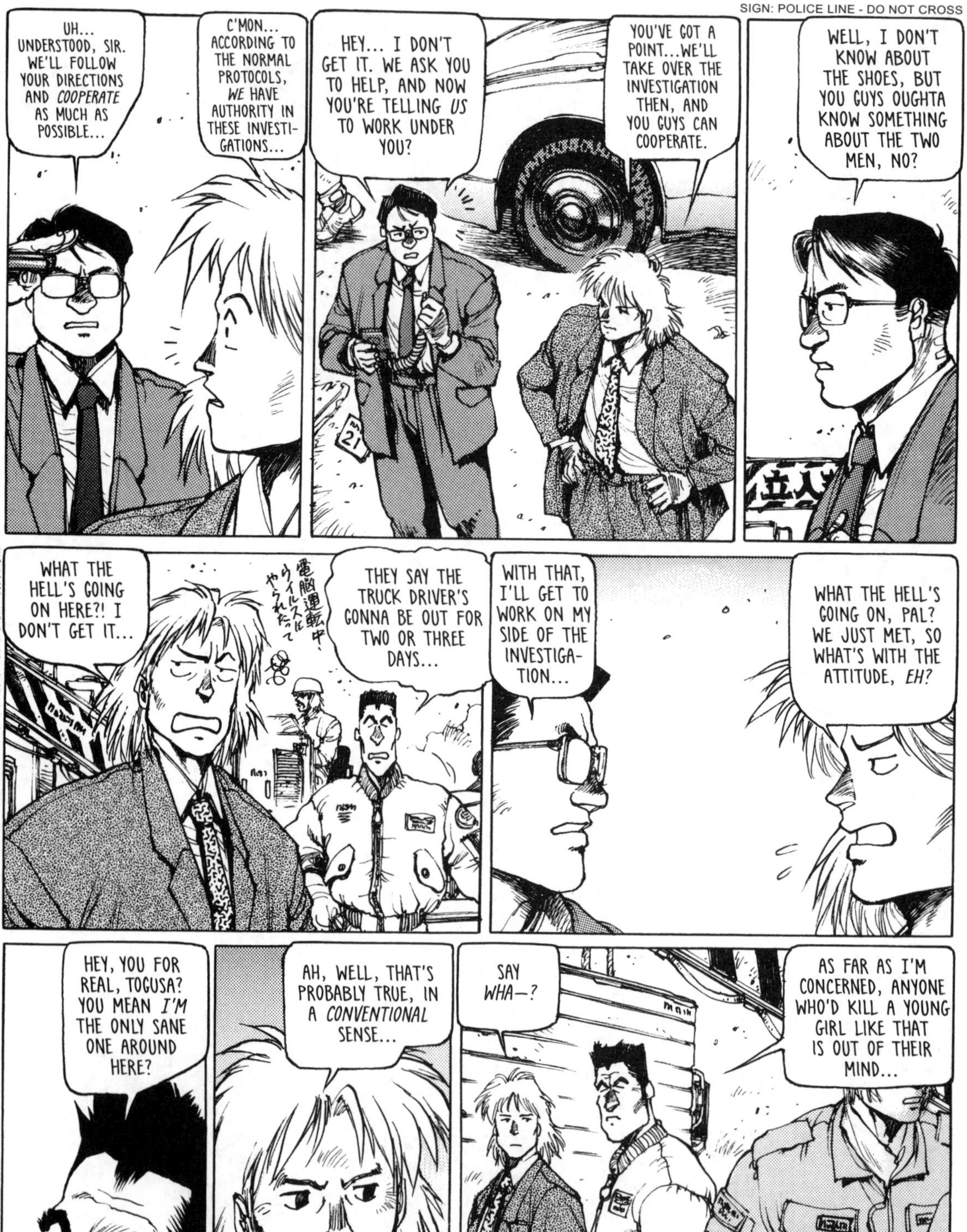

WELL, I DON'T KNOW ABOUT THE SHOES, BUT YOU GUYS OUGHTA KNOW SOMETHING ABOUT THE TWO MEN, NO?
YOU'VE GOT A POINT...WE'LL TAKE OVER THE INVESTIGATION THEN, AND YOU GUYS CAN COOPERATE.
HEY... I DON'T GET IT. WE ASK YOU TO HELP, AND NOW YOU'RE TELLING *US* TO WORK UNDER YOU?
C'MON... ACCORDING TO THE NORMAL PROTOCOLS, *WE* HAVE AUTHORITY IN THESE INVESTIGATIONS...
UH... UNDERSTOOD, SIR. WE'LL FOLLOW YOUR DIRECTIONS AND *COOPERATE* AS MUCH AS POSSIBLE...
WHAT THE HELL'S GOING ON, PAL? WE JUST MET, SO WHAT'S WITH THE ATTITUDE, *EH?*
WITH THAT, I'LL GET TO WORK ON MY SIDE OF THE INVESTIGATION...
THEY SAY THE TRUCK DRIVER'S GONNA BE OUT FOR TWO OR THREE DAYS...
電脳運転中、ウイルスにやられたって
WHAT THE HELL'S GOING ON HERE?! I DON'T GET IT...
AS FAR AS I'M CONCERNED, ANYONE WHO'D KILL A YOUNG GIRL LIKE THAT IS OUT OF THEIR MIND...
SAY *WHA—?*
AH, WELL, THAT'S PROBABLY TRUE, IN A *CONVENTIONAL* SENSE...
HEY, YOU FOR REAL, TOGUSA? YOU MEAN *I'M* THE ONLY SANE ONE AROUND HERE?

ASIDE: HE WAS APPARENTLY ATTACKED BY A VIRUS WHILE E-BRAIN DRIVING...

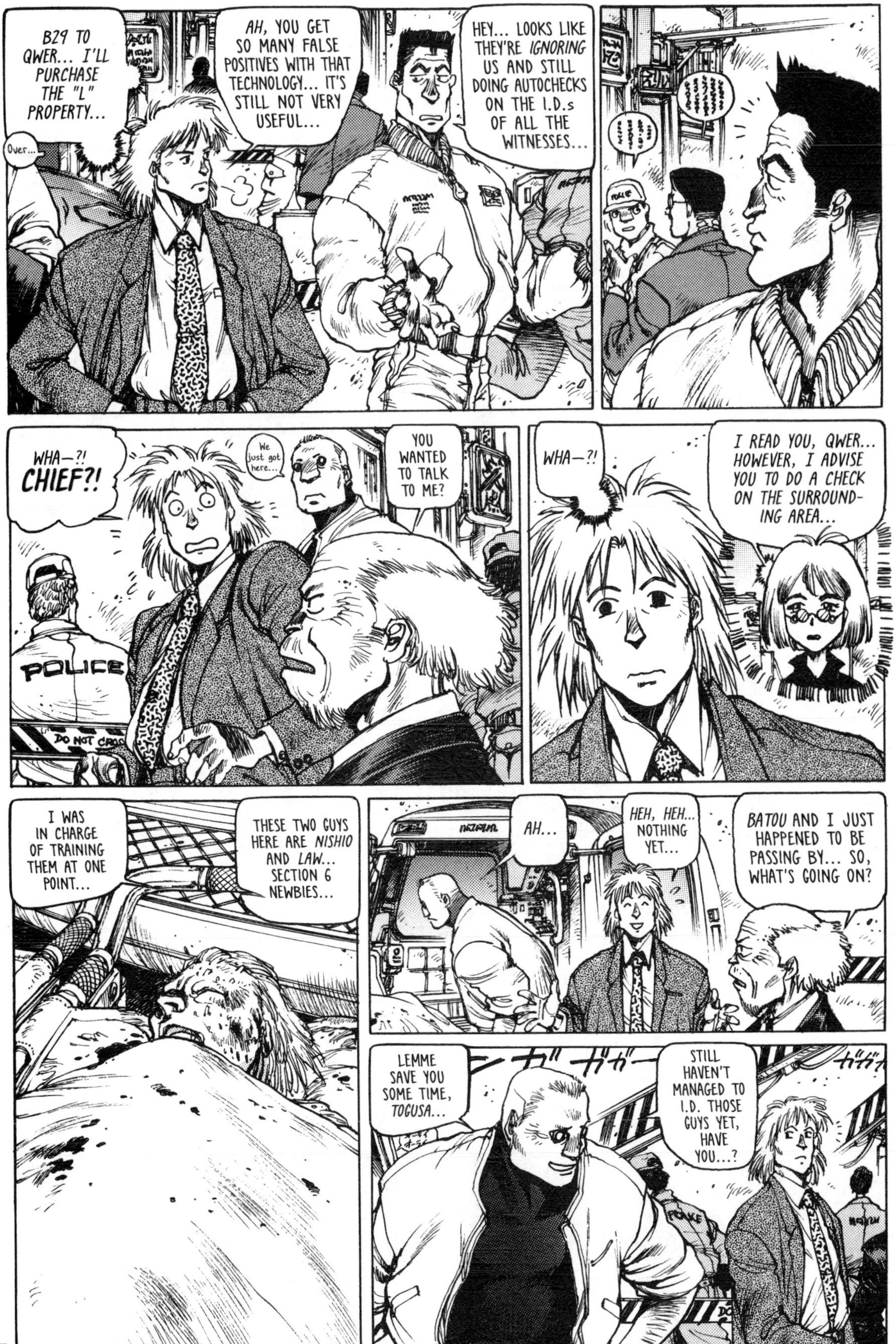
HEY... LOOKS LIKE THEY'RE *IGNORING* US AND STILL DOING AUTOCHECKS ON THE I.D.s OF ALL THE WITNESSES...
AH, YOU GET SO MANY FALSE POSITIVES WITH THAT TECHNOLOGY... IT'S STILL NOT VERY USEFUL...
B29 TO QWER... I'LL PURCHASE THE "L" PROPERTY...
Over...
I READ YOU, QWER... HOWEVER, I ADVISE YOU TO DO A CHECK ON THE SURROUNDING AREA...
WHA—?!
YOU WANTED TO TALK TO ME?
We just got here...
WHA—?! **CHIEF?!**
POLICE
DO NOT CROSS
BATOU AND I JUST HAPPENED TO BE PASSING BY... SO, WHAT'S GOING ON?
HEH, HEH... NOTHING YET...
AH...
STILL HAVEN'T MANAGED TO I.D. THOSE GUYS YET, HAVE YOU...?
LEMME SAVE YOU SOME TIME, *TOGUSA*...
THESE TWO GUYS HERE ARE *NISHIO* AND *LAW*... SECTION 6 NEWBIES...
I WAS IN CHARGE OF TRAINING THEM AT ONE POINT...

SECTION 6 OF PUBLIC SECURITY IS ALSO KNOWN AS THE FOREIGN MINISTRY'S "TREATY DELIBERATION SECTION" AND IS MAINLY RESPONSIBLE FOR SECURITY OUTSIDE OF JAPAN. DURING THE "PUPPETEER" INCIDENT IN *GHOST IN THE SHELL*, SECTION 6 WAS INVOLVED IN VARIOUS BEHIND THE SCENES MACHINATIONS AND CAME INTO CONFLICT WITH SECTION 9...

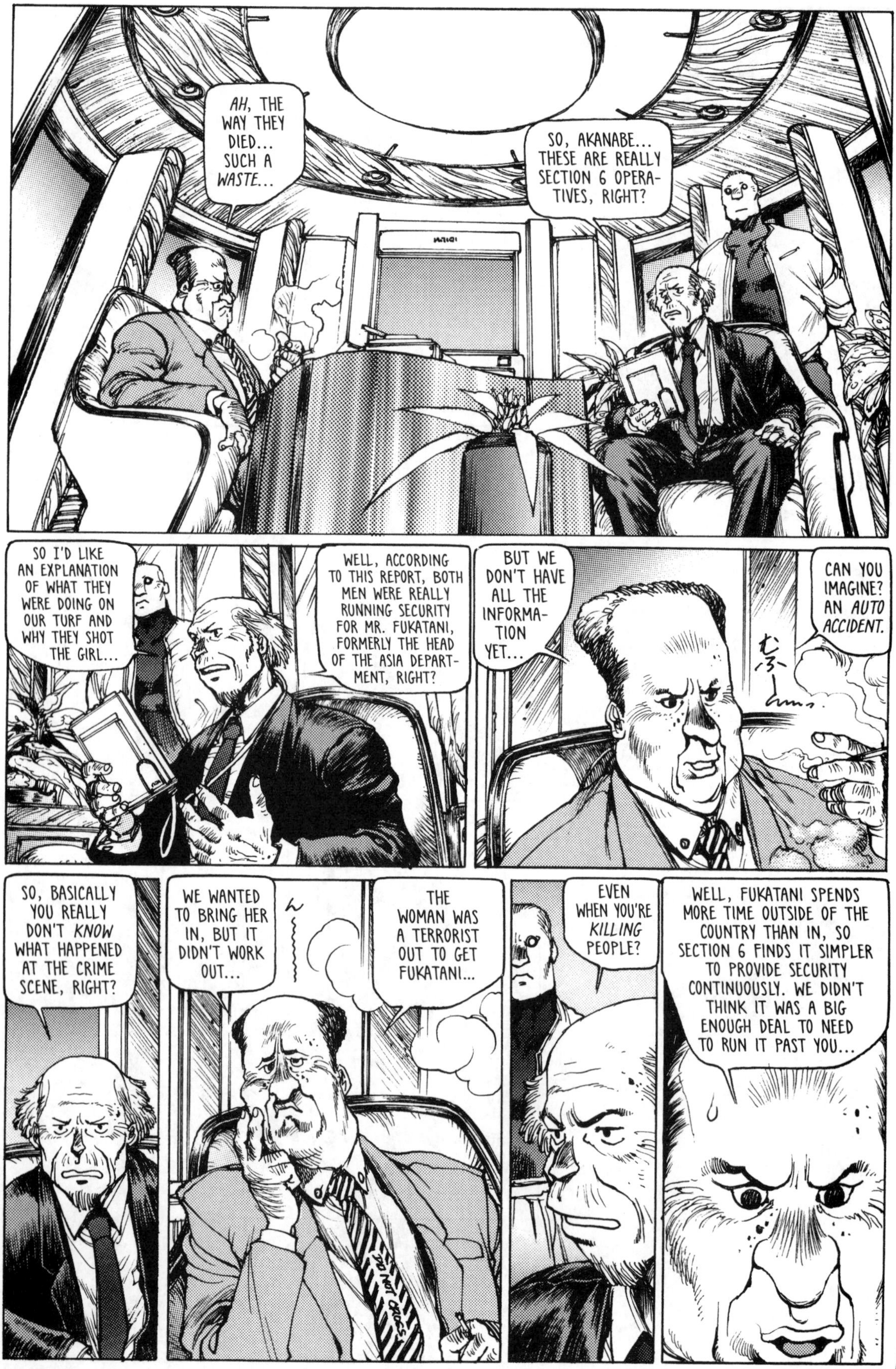
SO, AKANABE... THESE ARE REALLY SECTION 6 OPERATIVES, RIGHT?
AH, THE WAY THEY DIED... SUCH A *WASTE*...
CAN YOU IMAGINE? AN *AUTO ACCIDENT.*
BUT WE DON'T HAVE ALL THE INFORMATION YET...
WELL, ACCORDING TO THIS REPORT, BOTH MEN WERE REALLY RUNNING SECURITY FOR MR. FUKATANI, FORMERLY THE HEAD OF THE ASIA DEPARTMENT, RIGHT?
SO I'D LIKE AN EXPLANATION OF WHAT THEY WERE DOING ON OUR TURF AND WHY THEY SHOT THE GIRL...
WELL, FUKATANI SPENDS MORE TIME OUTSIDE OF THE COUNTRY THAN IN, SO SECTION 6 FINDS IT SIMPLER TO PROVIDE SECURITY CONTINUOUSLY. WE DIDN'T THINK IT WAS A BIG ENOUGH DEAL TO NEED TO RUN IT PAST YOU...
EVEN WHEN YOU'RE *KILLING* PEOPLE?
THE WOMAN WAS A TERRORIST OUT TO GET FUKATANI...
WE WANTED TO BRING HER IN, BUT IT DIDN'T WORK OUT...
SO, BASICALLY YOU REALLY DON'T *KNOW* WHAT HAPPENED AT THE CRIME SCENE, RIGHT?

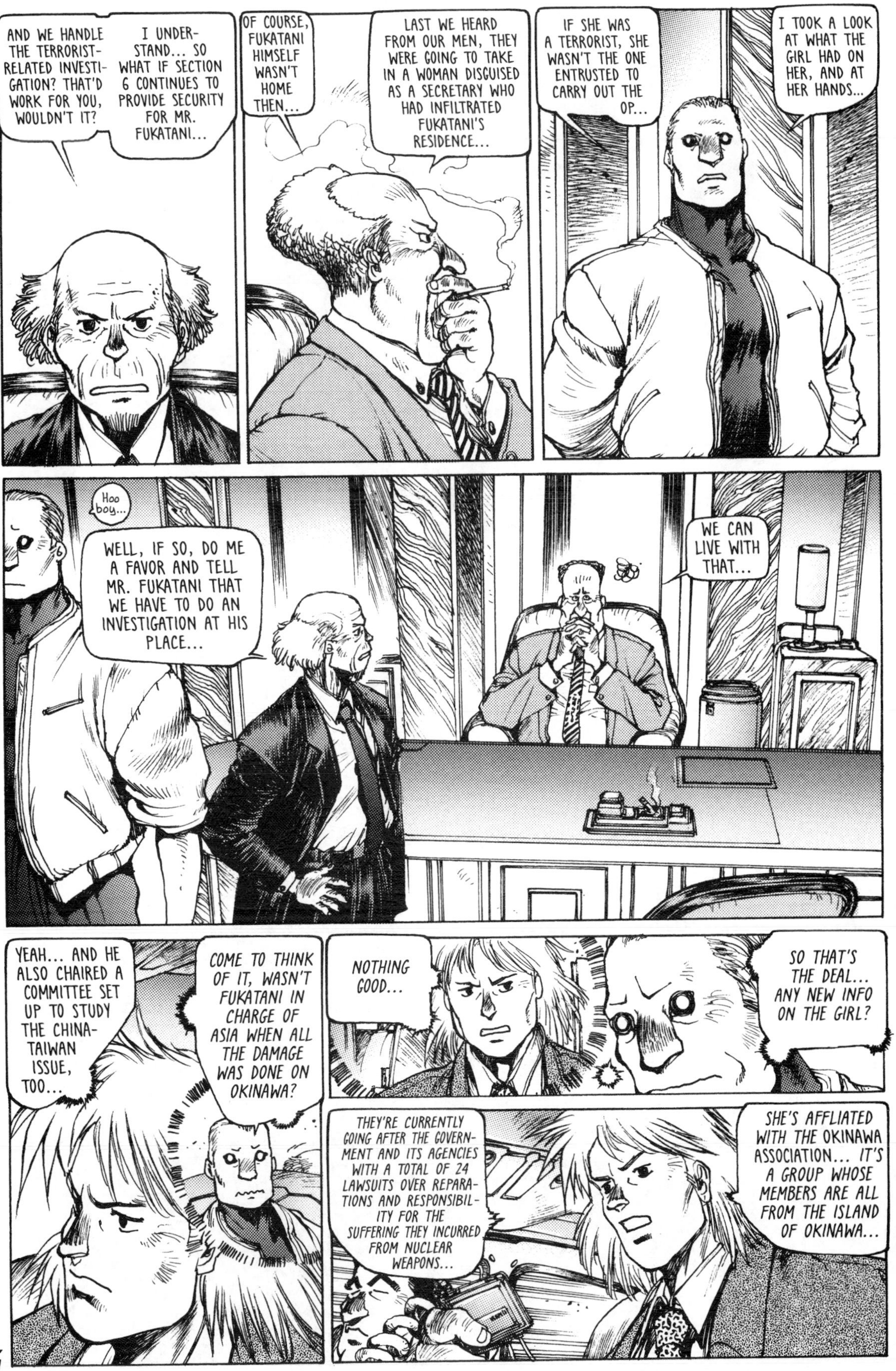
I TOOK A LOOK AT WHAT THE GIRL HAD ON HER, AND AT HER HANDS...
IF SHE WAS A TERRORIST, SHE WASN'T THE ONE ENTRUSTED TO CARRY OUT THE OP...
LAST WE HEARD FROM OUR MEN, THEY WERE GOING TO TAKE IN A WOMAN DISGUISED AS A SECRETARY WHO HAD INFILTRATED FUKATANI'S RESIDENCE...
OF COURSE, FUKATANI HIMSELF WASN'T HOME THEN...
I UNDERSTAND... SO WHAT IF SECTION 6 CONTINUES TO PROVIDE SECURITY FOR MR. FUKATANI...
AND WE HANDLE THE TERRORIST-RELATED INVESTIGATION? THAT'D WORK FOR YOU, WOULDN'T IT?
WE CAN LIVE WITH THAT...
WELL, IF SO, DO ME A FAVOR AND TELL MR. FUKATANI THAT WE HAVE TO DO AN INVESTIGATION AT HIS PLACE...
Hoo boy...
SO THAT'S THE DEAL... ANY NEW INFO ON THE GIRL?
NOTHING GOOD...
SHE'S AFFLIATED WITH THE OKINAWA ASSOCIATION... IT'S A GROUP WHOSE MEMBERS ARE ALL FROM THE ISLAND OF OKINAWA...
THEY'RE CURRENTLY GOING AFTER THE GOVERNMENT AND ITS AGENCIES WITH A TOTAL OF 24 LAWSUITS OVER REPARATIONS AND RESPONSIBILITY FOR THE SUFFERING THEY INCURRED FROM NUCLEAR WEAPONS...
COME TO THINK OF IT, WASN'T FUKATANI IN CHARGE OF ASIA WHEN ALL THE DAMAGE WAS DONE ON OKINAWA?
YEAH... AND HE ALSO CHAIRED A COMMITTEE SET UP TO STUDY THE CHINA-TAIWAN ISSUE, TOO...

SIGN: OKINAWA ASSOCIATION OFFICE

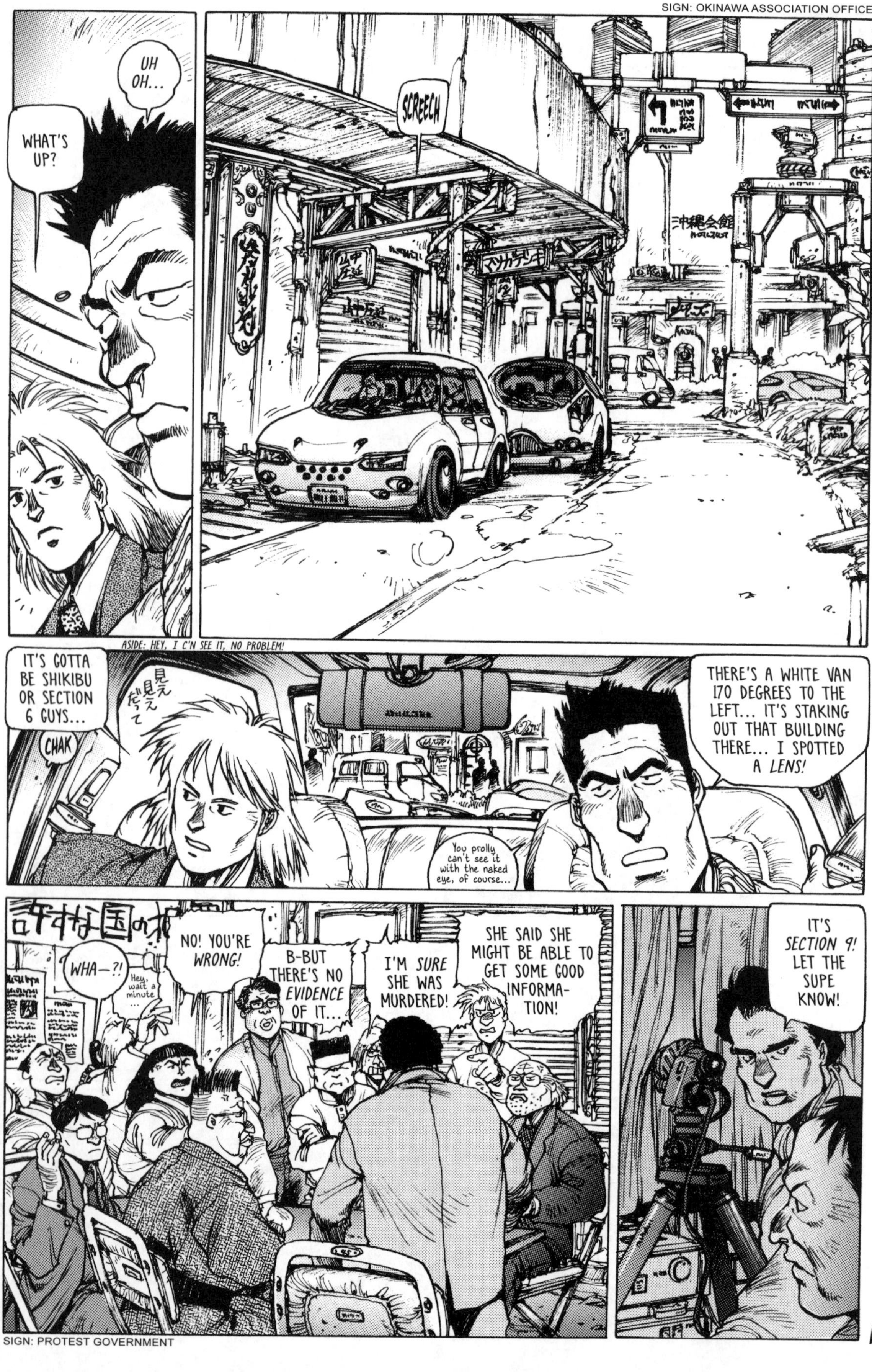
SCREECH
沖縄会館
UH OH...
WHAT'S UP?
THERE'S A WHITE VAN 170 DEGREES TO THE LEFT... IT'S STAKING OUT THAT BUILDING THERE... I SPOTTED A *LENS!*
You prolly can't see it with the naked eye, of course...
ASIDE: HEY, I C'N SEE IT, NO PROBLEM!
見え見えだって
IT'S GOTTA BE SHIKIBU OR SECTION 6 GUYS...
CHAK
IT'S *SECTION 9!* LET THE SUPE KNOW!
SHE SAID SHE MIGHT BE ABLE TO GET SOME GOOD INFORMATION!
I'M *SURE* SHE WAS MURDERED!
B-BUT THERE'S NO *EVIDENCE* OF IT...
NO! YOU'RE *WRONG!*
Hey, wait a minute...
WHA—?!
許すな国の

SIGN: PROTEST GOVERNMENT

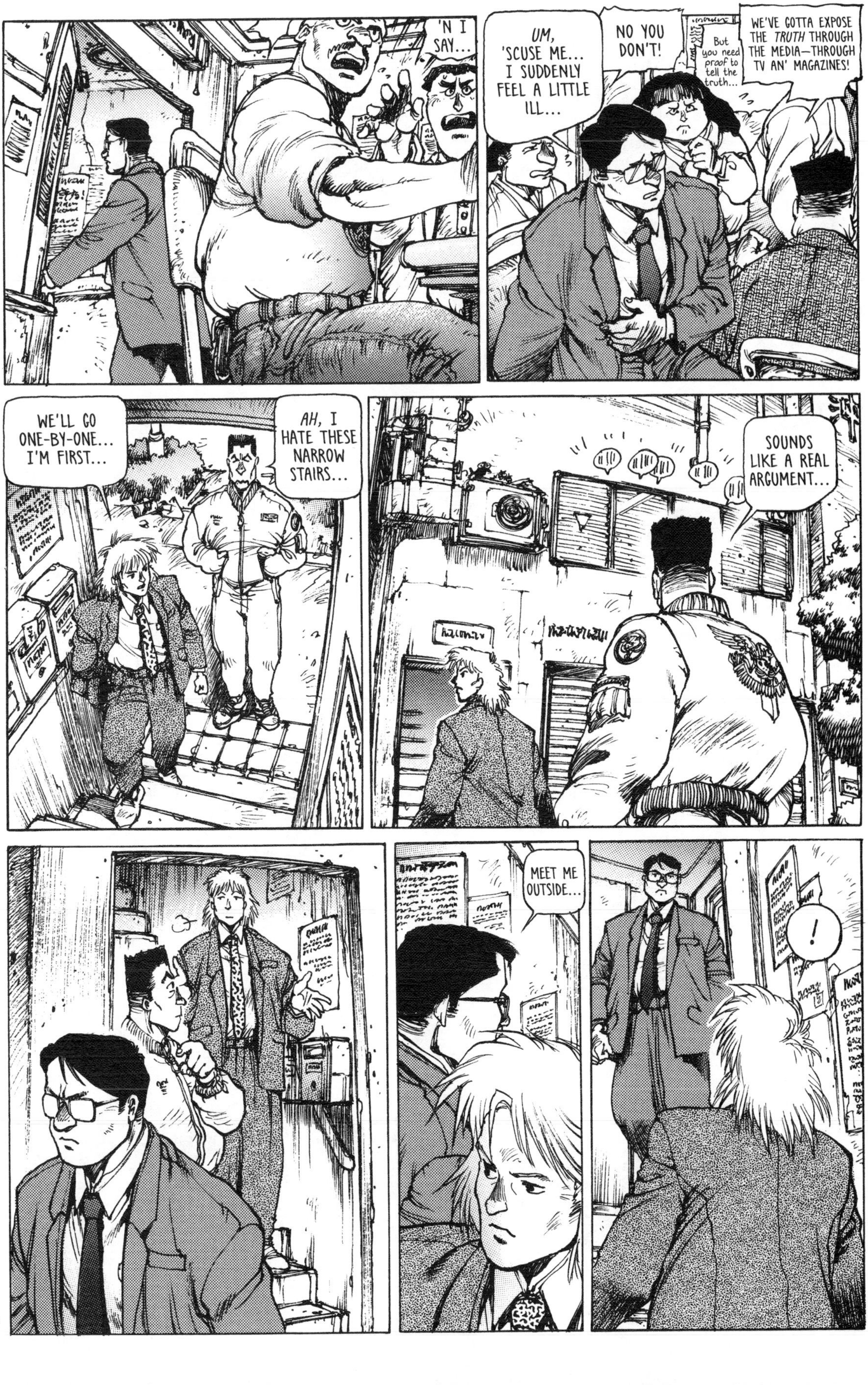

WE'VE GOTTA EXPOSE THE *TRUTH* THROUGH THE MEDIA—THROUGH TV AN' MAGAZINES!
But you need proof to tell the truth...
NO YOU DON'T!
UM, 'SCUSE ME... I SUDDENLY FEEL A LITTLE ILL...
'N I SAY...
SOUNDS LIKE A REAL ARGUMENT...
AH, I HATE THESE NARROW STAIRS...
WE'LL GO ONE-BY-ONE... I'M FIRST...
!
MEET ME OUTSIDE...

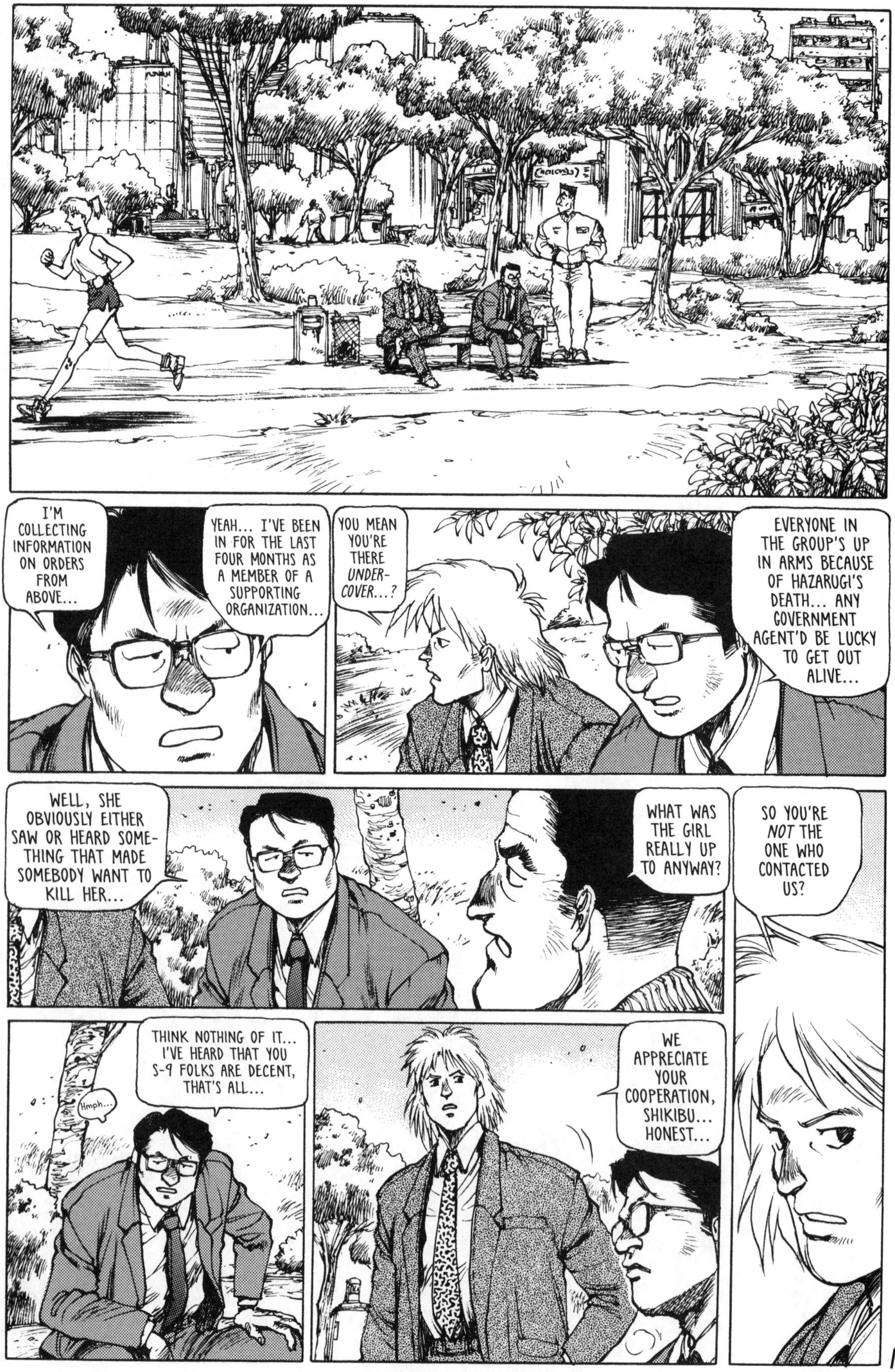
EVERYONE IN THE GROUP'S UP IN ARMS BECAUSE OF HAZARUGI'S DEATH... ANY GOVERNMENT AGENT'D BE LUCKY TO GET OUT ALIVE...
YOU MEAN YOU'RE THERE *UNDER-COVER*...?
YEAH... I'VE BEEN IN FOR THE LAST FOUR MONTHS AS A MEMBER OF A SUPPORTING ORGANIZATION...
I'M COLLECTING INFORMATION ON ORDERS FROM ABOVE...
SO YOU'RE *NOT* THE ONE WHO CONTACTED US?
WHAT WAS THE GIRL REALLY UP TO ANYWAY?
WELL, SHE OBVIOUSLY EITHER SAW OR HEARD SOME-THING THAT MADE SOMEBODY WANT TO KILL HER...
WE APPRECIATE YOUR COOPERATION, SHIKIBU... HONEST...
THINK NOTHING OF IT... I'VE HEARD THAT YOU S-9 FOLKS ARE DECENT, THAT'S ALL...
Hmph...

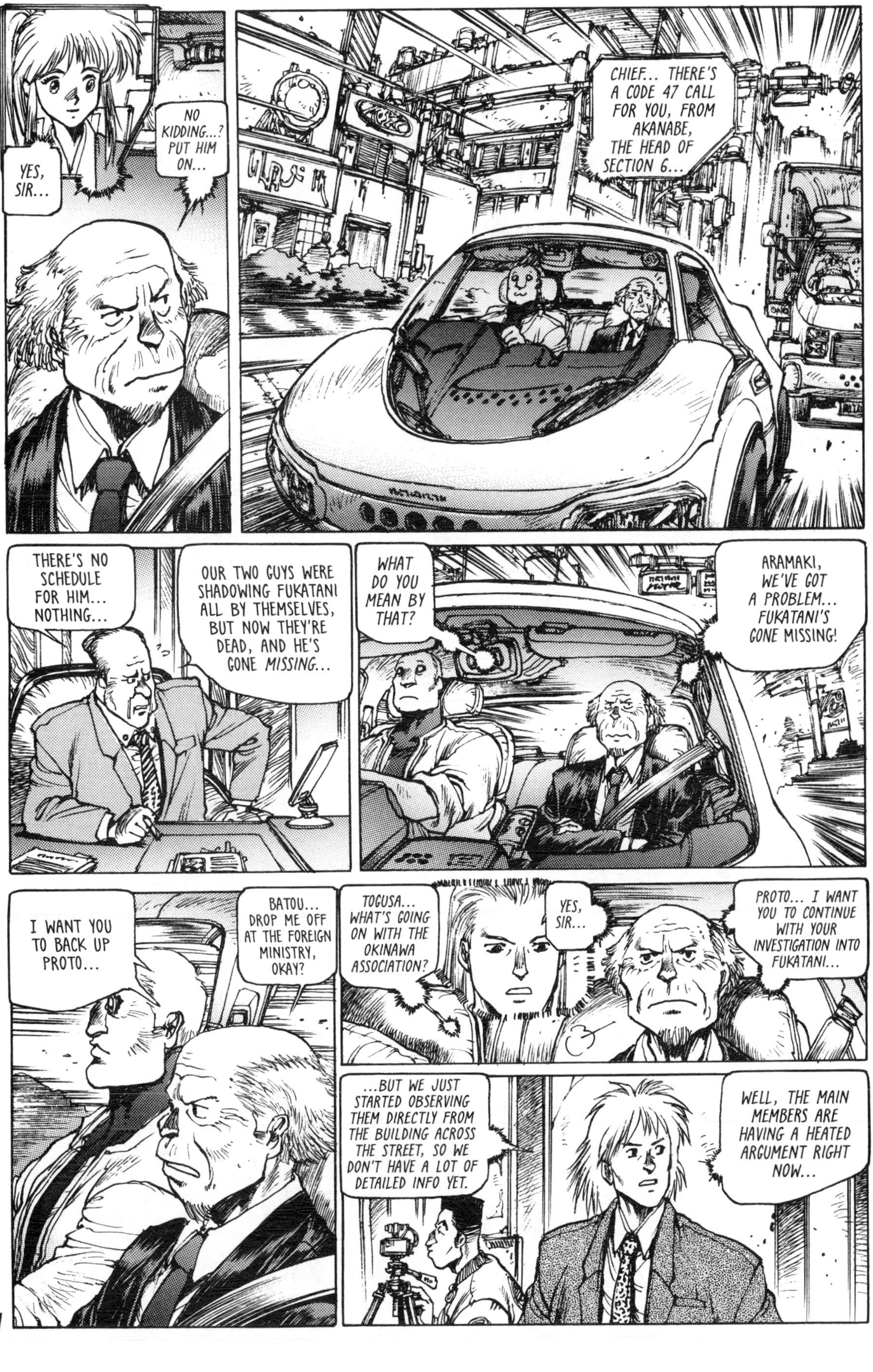
CHIEF... THERE'S A CODE 47 CALL FOR YOU, FROM AKANABE, THE HEAD OF SECTION 6...
NO KIDDING...? PUT HIM ON...
YES, SIR...
ARAMAKI, WE'VE GOT A PROBLEM... FUKATANI'S GONE MISSING!
WHAT DO YOU MEAN BY THAT?
OUR TWO GUYS WERE SHADOWING FUKATANI ALL BY THEMSELVES, BUT NOW THEY'RE DEAD, AND HE'S GONE *MISSING*...
THERE'S NO SCHEDULE FOR HIM... NOTHING...
PROTO... I WANT YOU TO CONTINUE WITH YOUR INVESTIGATION INTO FUKATANI...
YES, SIR...
TOGUSA... WHAT'S GOING ON WITH THE OKINAWA ASSOCIATION?
WELL, THE MAIN MEMBERS ARE HAVING A HEATED ARGUMENT RIGHT NOW...
...BUT WE JUST STARTED OBSERVING THEM DIRECTLY FROM THE BUILDING ACROSS THE STREET, SO WE DON'T HAVE A LOT OF DETAILED INFO YET.
BATOU... DROP ME OFF AT THE FOREIGN MINISTRY, OKAY?
I WANT YOU TO BACK UP PROTO...

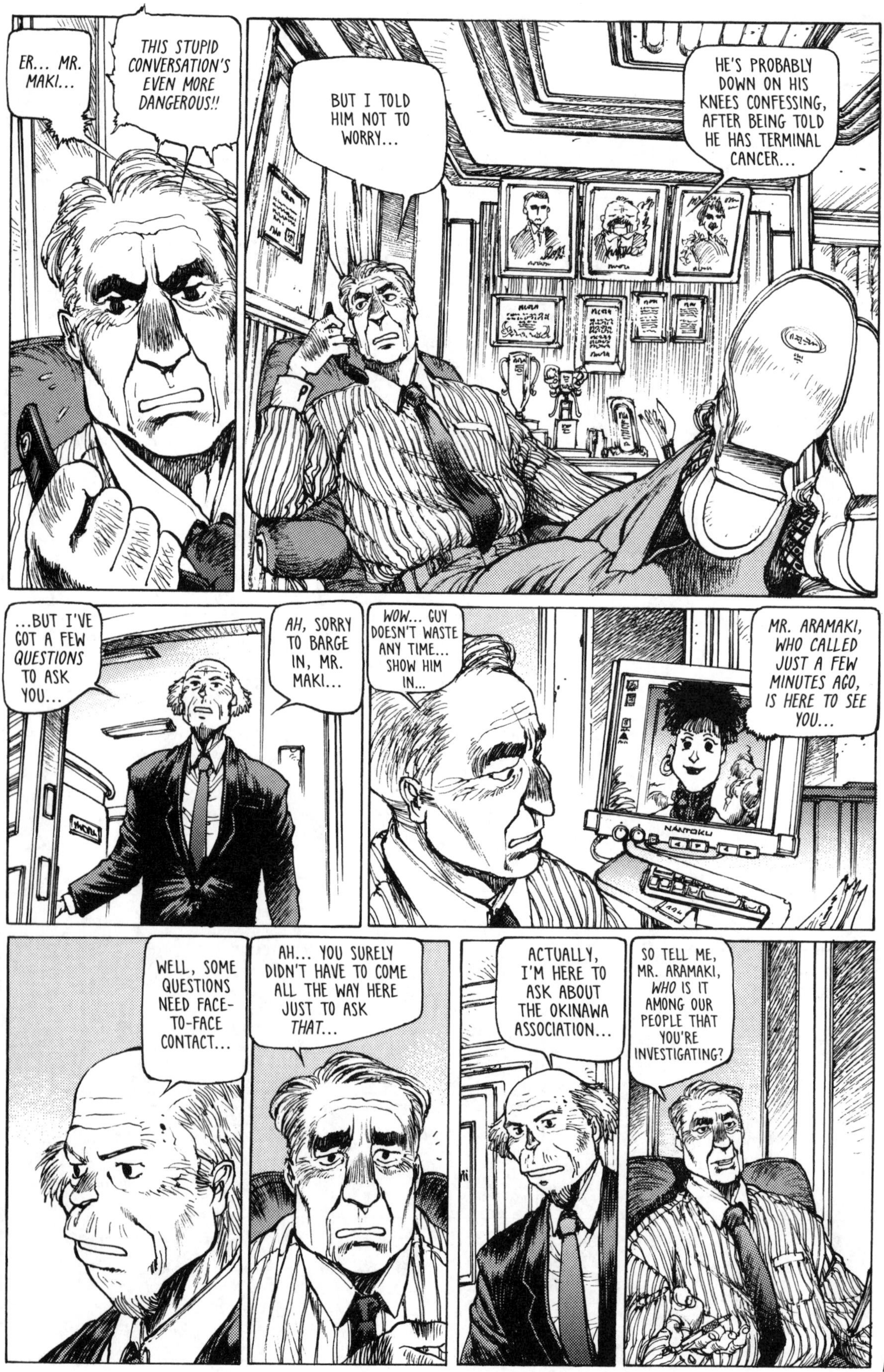

HE'S PROBABLY DOWN ON HIS KNEES CONFESSING, AFTER BEING TOLD HE HAS TERMINAL CANCER...
BUT I TOLD HIM NOT TO WORRY...
THIS STUPID CONVERSATION'S EVEN MORE DANGEROUS!!
ER... MR. MAKI...
MR. ARAMAKI, WHO CALLED JUST A FEW MINUTES AGO, IS HERE TO SEE YOU...
WOW... GUY DOESN'T WASTE ANY TIME... SHOW HIM IN...
NANTOKU
AH, SORRY TO BARGE IN, MR. MAKI...
...BUT I'VE GOT A FEW *QUESTIONS* TO ASK YOU...
SO TELL ME, MR. ARAMAKI, *WHO* IS IT AMONG OUR PEOPLE THAT YOU'RE INVESTIGATING?
ACTUALLY, I'M HERE TO ASK ABOUT THE OKINAWA ASSOCIATION...
AH... YOU SURELY DIDN'T HAVE TO COME ALL THE WAY HERE JUST TO ASK *THAT*...
WELL, SOME QUESTIONS NEED FACE-TO-FACE CONTACT...

DURING THE ERA IN WHICH THIS STORY IS SET, U.S. FORCES IN THE FAR EAST ARE NO LONGER MAINLY BASED IN JAPAN AND A UNIFIED KOREA (I KNOW THIS NOMENCLATURE ISN'T PROPER, BUT FORGIVE ME; IT'S THE ONLY THING I COULD COME UP WITH). U.S. FORCES ARE INSTEAD ON A LANDFILL AREA NEAR TAKESHIMA ISLAND (AH, AGAIN FORGIVE ME. I KNOW THERE ARE POLITICAL PROBLEMS WITH THIS NAME, BUT IT'S TOO DIFFICULT TO GO INTO THE DETAILS, SO PLEASE FORGIVE ME). NOW, I KNOW THAT MOVING U.S. FORCES TO A LANDFILL AREA IS PROBABLY IMPOSSIBLE, BUT WE ARE DEALING WITH A MANGA, AFTER ALL, SO PLEASE HUMOR ME. I DO WISH SOMETHING COULD BE DONE ABOUT THIS ISSUE, THOUGH. WHAT PROBABLY CAN BE DONE IS TO HAVE U.S. FORCES DISPERSE OFF JAPAN'S MAIN ISLANDS, AND BUILD UP THE DEFENSE CAPABILITIES OF THE JAPANESE SELF-DEFENSE FORCES. BUT THAT'S A SCARY IDEA IN AND OF ITSELF... AH, EXCUSE THE POLITICAL DIVERSION...

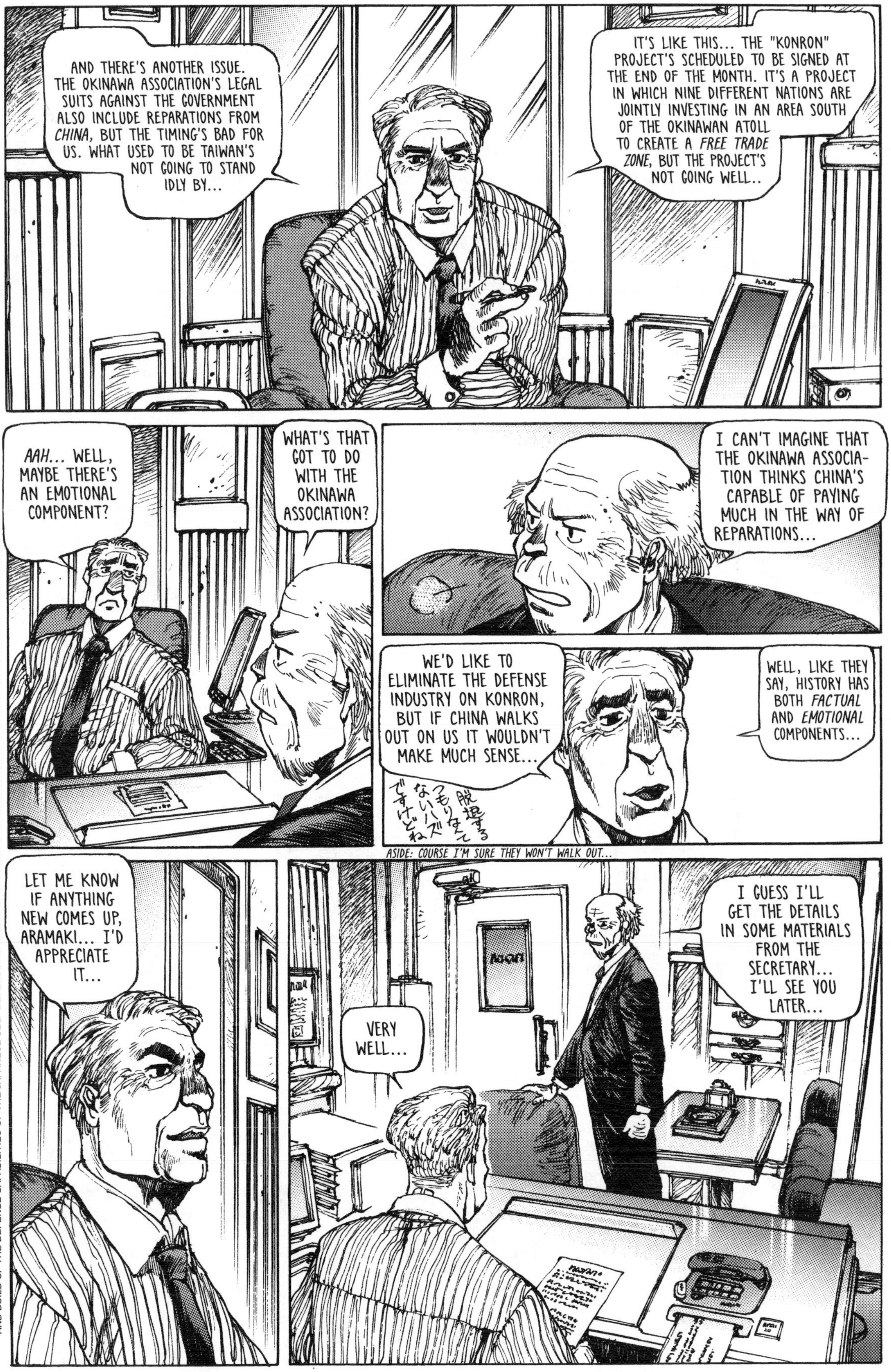
IT'S LIKE THIS... THE "KONRON" PROJECT'S SCHEDULED TO BE SIGNED AT THE END OF THE MONTH. IT'S A PROJECT IN WHICH NINE DIFFERENT NATIONS ARE JOINTLY INVESTING IN AN AREA SOUTH OF THE OKINAWAN ATOLL TO CREATE A *FREE TRADE ZONE*, BUT THE PROJECT'S NOT GOING WELL..
AND THERE'S ANOTHER ISSUE. THE OKINAWA ASSOCIATION'S LEGAL SUITS AGAINST THE GOVERNMENT ALSO INCLUDE REPARATIONS FROM *CHINA*, BUT THE TIMING'S BAD FOR US. WHAT USED TO BE TAIWAN'S NOT GOING TO STAND IDLY BY...
I CAN'T IMAGINE THAT THE OKINAWA ASSOCIATION THINKS CHINA'S CAPABLE OF PAYING MUCH IN THE WAY OF REPARATIONS...
WELL, LIKE THEY SAY, HISTORY HAS BOTH *FACTUAL* AND *EMOTIONAL* COMPONENTS...
WE'D LIKE TO ELIMINATE THE DEFENSE INDUSTRY ON KONRON, BUT IF CHINA WALKS OUT ON US IT WOULDN'T MAKE MUCH SENSE...
脱退するつもりなんてないハズですけどね
ASIDE: COURSE I'M SURE THEY WON'T WALK OUT...
WHAT'S THAT GOT TO DO WITH THE OKINAWA ASSOCIATION?
AAH... WELL, MAYBE THERE'S AN EMOTIONAL COMPONENT?
I GUESS I'LL GET THE DETAILS IN SOME MATERIALS FROM THE SECRETARY... I'LL SEE YOU LATER...
VERY WELL...
LET ME KNOW IF ANYTHING NEW COMES UP, ARAMAKI... I'D APPRECIATE IT...

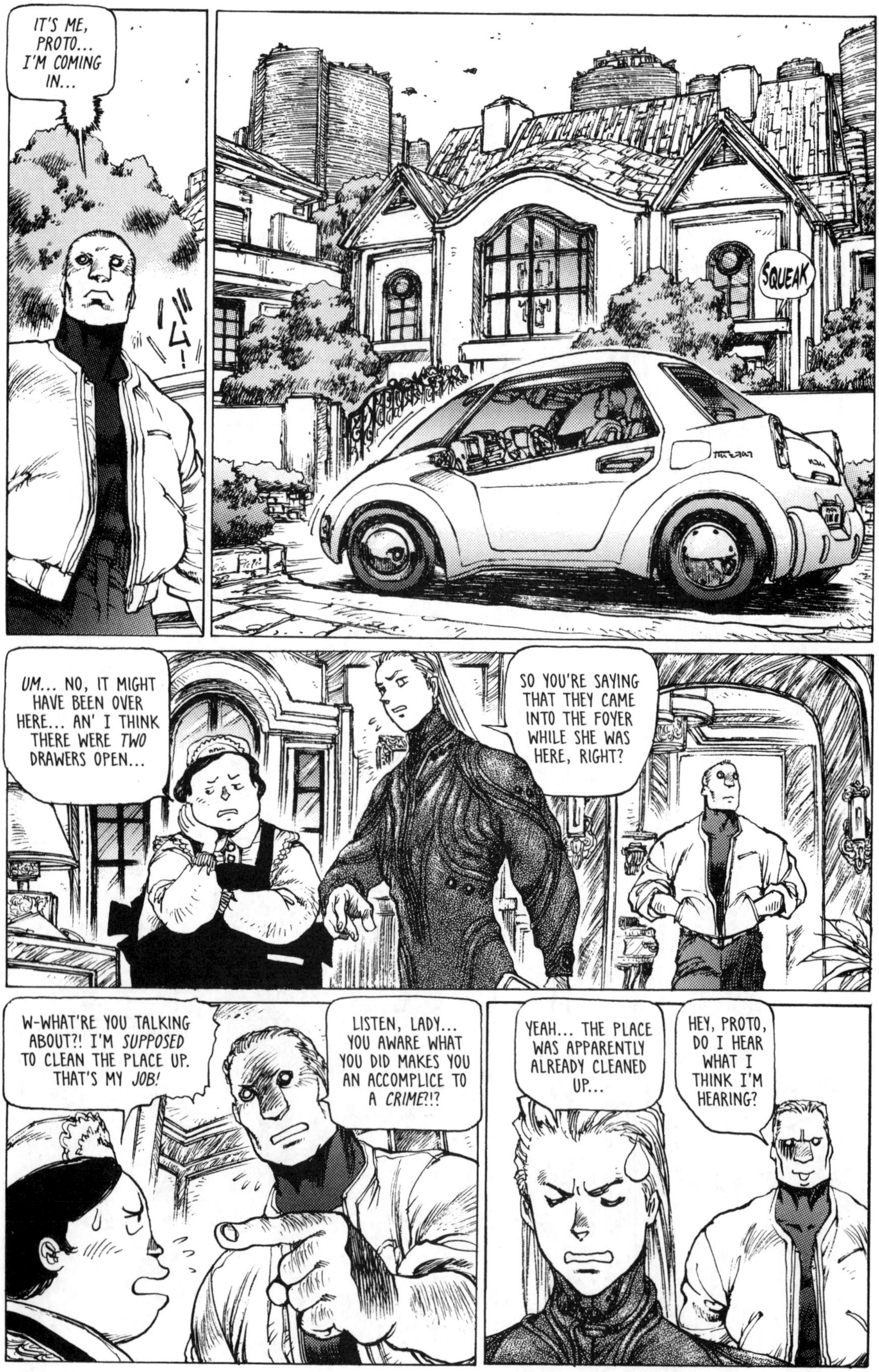
SQUEAK
IT'S ME, PROTO... I'M COMING IN...
SO YOU'RE SAYING THAT THEY CAME INTO THE FOYER WHILE SHE WAS HERE, RIGHT?
UM... NO, IT MIGHT HAVE BEEN OVER HERE... AN' I THINK THERE WERE *TWO* DRAWERS OPEN...
HEY, PROTO, DO I HEAR WHAT I THINK I'M HEARING?
YEAH... THE PLACE WAS APPARENTLY ALREADY CLEANED UP...
LISTEN, LADY... YOU AWARE WHAT YOU DID MAKES YOU AN ACCOMPLICE TO A *CRIME*!?
W-WHAT'RE YOU TALKING ABOUT?! I'M *SUPPOSED* TO CLEAN THE PLACE UP. THAT'S MY *JOB!*

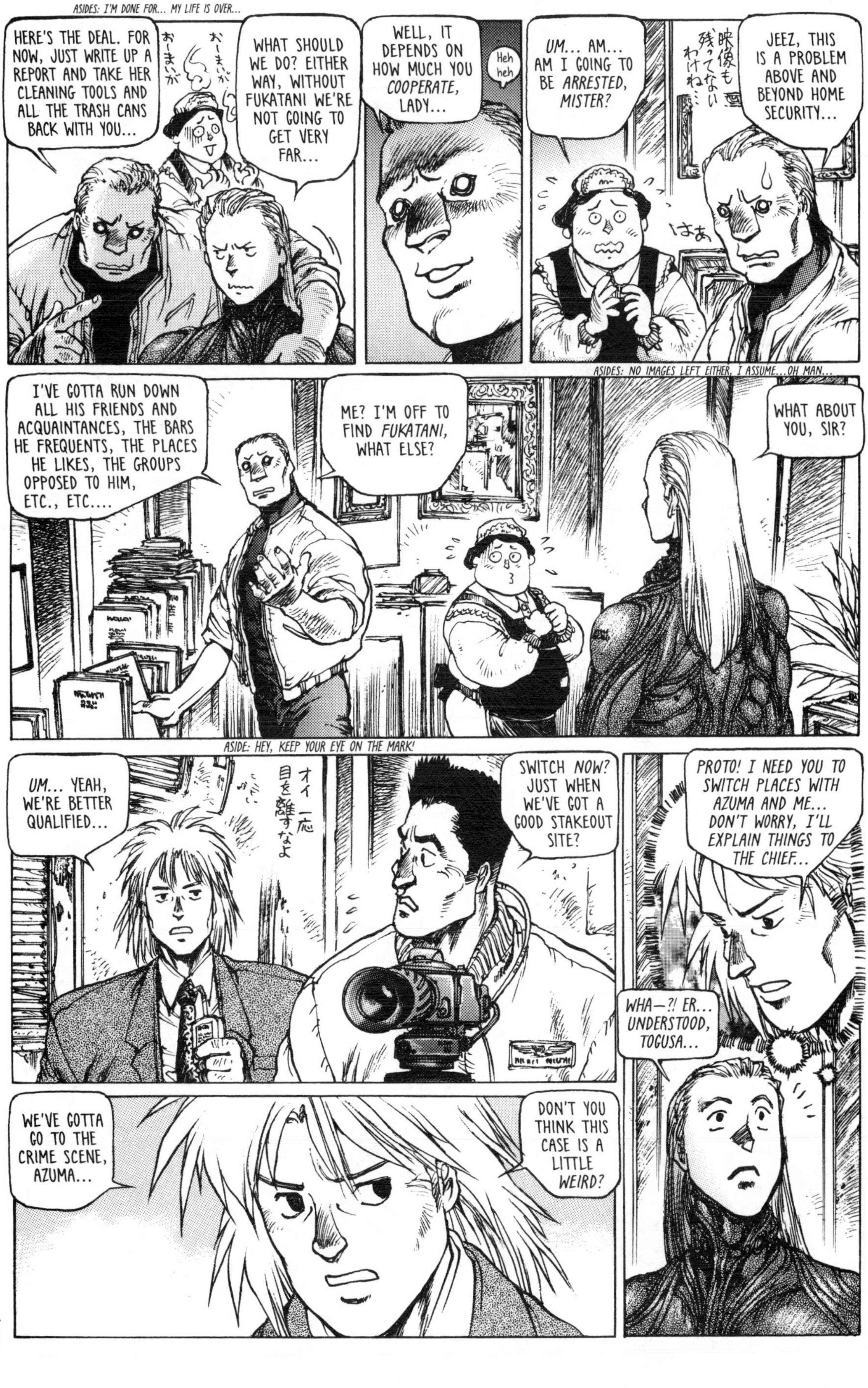
ASIDES: I'M DONE FOR... MY LIFE IS OVER...
JEEZ, THIS IS A PROBLEM ABOVE AND BEYOND HOME SECURITY...
映像も残ってないわけね…
はぁ
UM... AM... AM I GOING TO BE *ARRESTED*, *MISTER*?
Heh heh
WELL, IT DEPENDS ON HOW MUCH YOU *COOPERATE*, LADY...
WHAT SHOULD WE DO? EITHER WAY, WITHOUT FUKATANI WE'RE NOT GOING TO GET VERY FAR...
おーまいが おーまいが
HERE'S THE DEAL. FOR NOW, JUST WRITE UP A REPORT AND TAKE HER CLEANING TOOLS AND ALL THE TRASH CANS BACK WITH YOU...
ASIDES: NO IMAGES LEFT EITHER, I ASSUME...OH MAN...
WHAT ABOUT YOU, SIR?
ME? I'M OFF TO FIND *FUKATANI*, WHAT ELSE?
I'VE GOTTA RUN DOWN ALL HIS FRIENDS AND ACQUAINTANCES, THE BARS HE FREQUENTS, THE PLACES HE LIKES, THE GROUPS OPPOSED TO HIM, ETC., ETC....
ASIDE: HEY, KEEP YOUR EYE ON THE MARK!
PROTO! I NEED YOU TO SWITCH PLACES WITH AZUMA AND ME... DON'T WORRY, I'LL EXPLAIN THINGS TO THE CHIEF...
WHA—?! ER... UNDERSTOOD, TOGUSA...
SWITCH *NOW*? JUST WHEN WE'VE GOT A GOOD STAKEOUT SITE?
オイ一応目を離すなよ
UM... YEAH, WE'RE BETTER QUALIFIED...
DON'T YOU THINK THIS CASE IS A LITTLE *WEIRD*?
WE'VE GOTTA GO TO THE CRIME SCENE, AZUMA...

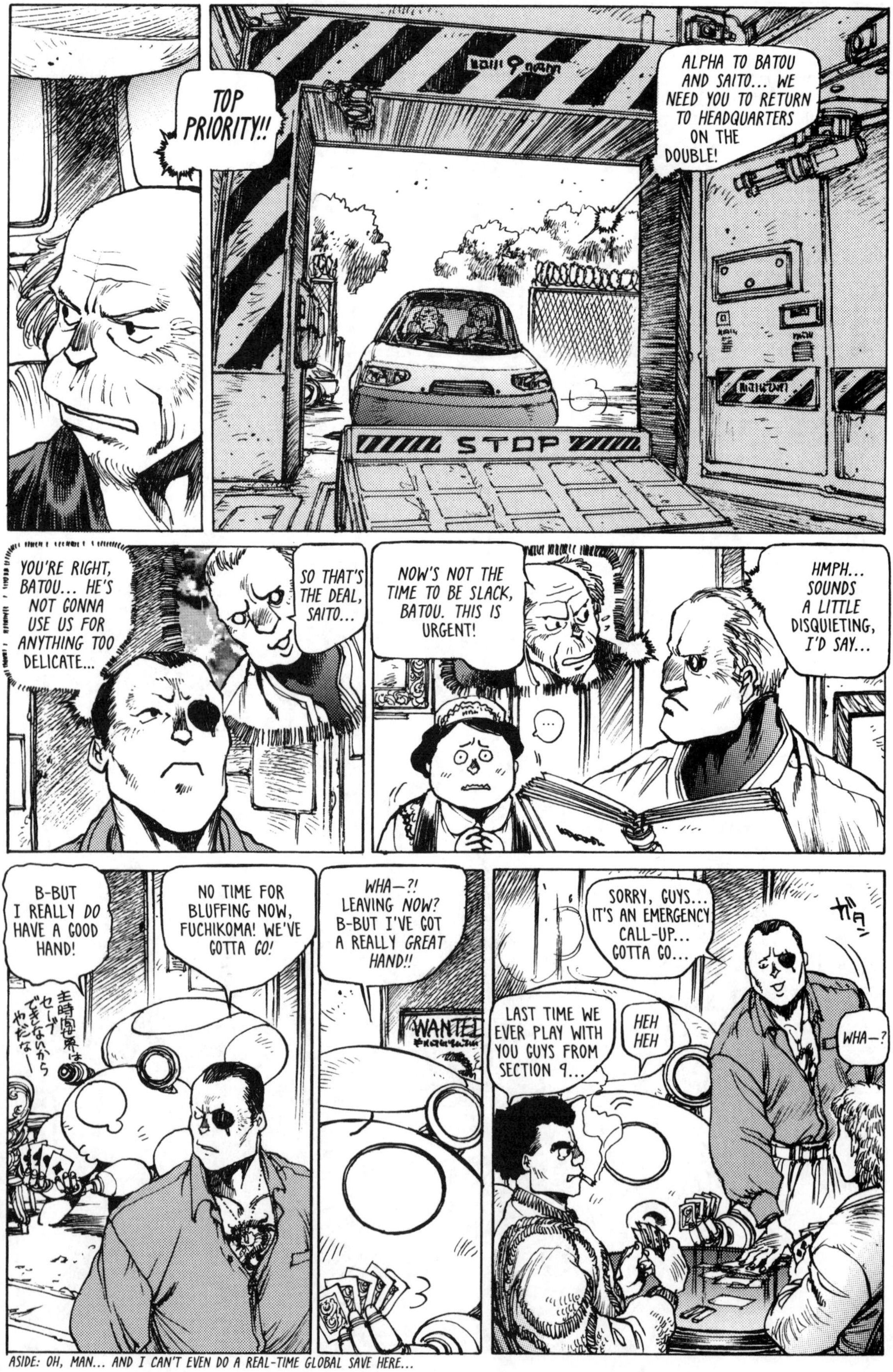
ALPHA TO BATOU AND SAITO... WE NEED YOU TO RETURN TO HEADQUARTERS ON THE DOUBLE!
TOP PRIORITY!!
HMPH... SOUNDS A LITTLE DISQUIETING, I'D SAY...
NOW'S NOT THE TIME TO BE SLACK, BATOU. THIS IS URGENT!
...
SO THAT'S THE DEAL, SAITO...
YOU'RE RIGHT, BATOU... HE'S NOT GONNA USE US FOR ANYTHING TOO DELICATE...
ガタ
SORRY, GUYS... IT'S AN EMERGENCY CALL-UP... GOTTA GO...
WHA—?
HEH HEH
LAST TIME WE EVER PLAY WITH YOU GUYS FROM SECTION 9...
WHA—?! LEAVING *NOW*? B-BUT I'VE GOT A REALLY *GREAT* HAND!!
WANTED
NO TIME FOR BLUFFING NOW, FUCHIKOMA! WE'VE GOTTA *GO*!
B-BUT I REALLY *DO* HAVE A GOOD HAND!
主時間世界はセーブできないからやだなー

ASIDE: OH, MAN... AND I CAN'T EVEN DO A REAL-TIME GLOBAL SAVE HERE...

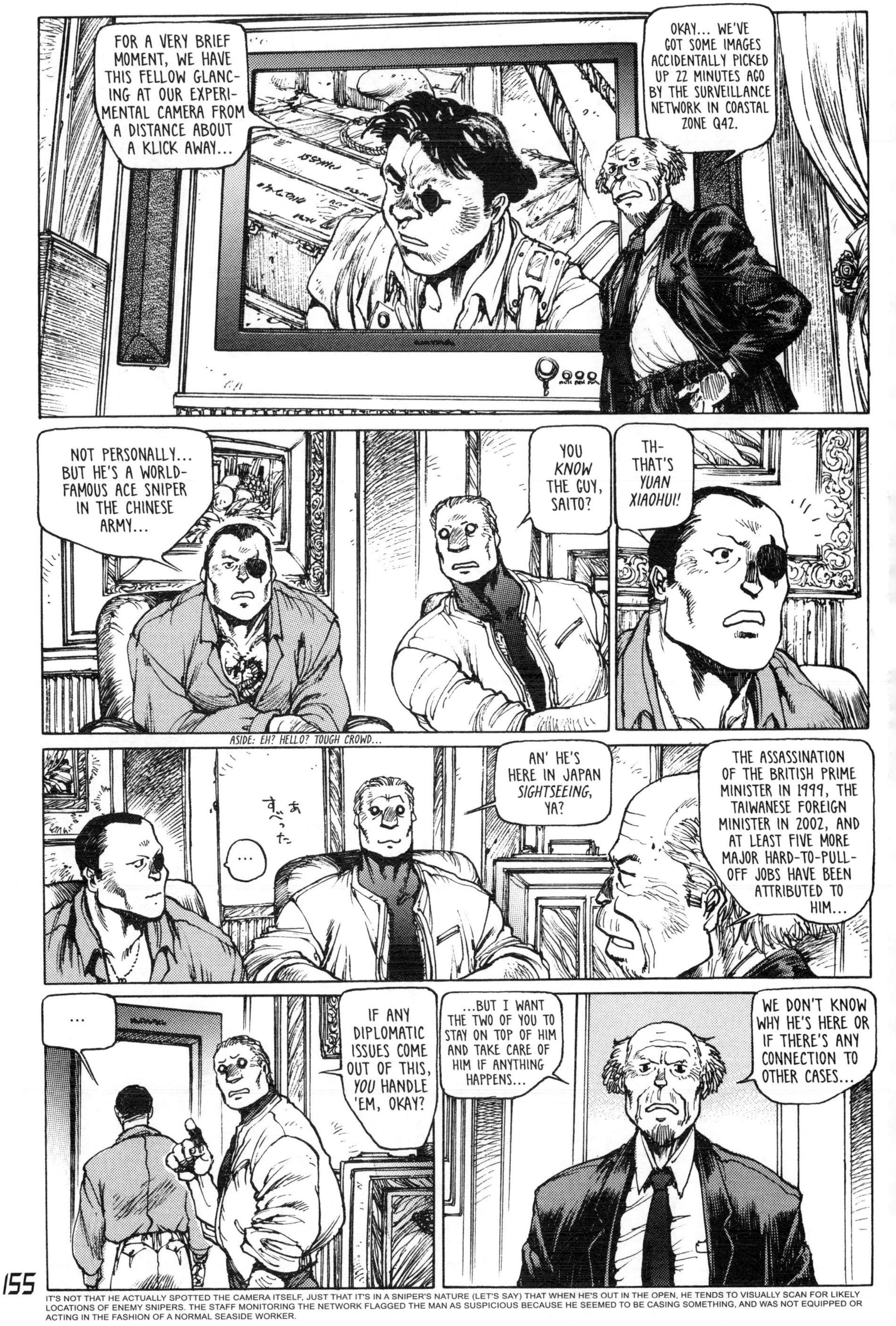
OKAY... WE'VE GOT SOME IMAGES ACCIDENTALLY PICKED UP 22 MINUTES AGO BY THE SURVEILLANCE NETWORK IN COASTAL ZONE Q42.
FOR A VERY BRIEF MOMENT, WE HAVE THIS FELLOW GLANCING AT OUR EXPERIMENTAL CAMERA FROM A DISTANCE ABOUT A KLICK AWAY...
TH-THAT'S *YUAN XIAOHUI!*
YOU *KNOW* THE GUY, SAITO?
NOT PERSONALLY... BUT HE'S A WORLD-FAMOUS ACE SNIPER IN THE CHINESE ARMY...
ASIDE: EH? HELLO? TOUGH CROWD...
THE ASSASSINATION OF THE BRITISH PRIME MINISTER IN 1999, THE TAIWANESE FOREIGN MINISTER IN 2002, AND AT LEAST FIVE MORE MAJOR HARD-TO-PULL-OFF JOBS HAVE BEEN ATTRIBUTED TO HIM...
AN' HE'S HERE IN JAPAN *SIGHTSEEING*, YA?
あ すべった
...
WE DON'T KNOW WHY HE'S HERE OR IF THERE'S ANY CONNECTION TO OTHER CASES...
...BUT I WANT THE TWO OF YOU TO STAY ON TOP OF HIM AND TAKE CARE OF HIM IF ANYTHING HAPPENS...
IF ANY DIPLOMATIC ISSUES COME OUT OF THIS, *YOU* HANDLE 'EM, OKAY?
...

IT'S NOT THAT HE ACTUALLY SPOTTED THE CAMERA ITSELF, JUST THAT IT'S IN A SNIPER'S NATURE (LET'S SAY) THAT WHEN HE'S OUT IN THE OPEN, HE TENDS TO VISUALLY SCAN FOR LIKELY LOCATIONS OF ENEMY SNIPERS. THE STAFF MONITORING THE NETWORK FLAGGED THE MAN AS SUSPICIOUS BECAUSE HE SEEMED TO BE CASING SOMETHING, AND WAS NOT EQUIPPED OR ACTING IN THE FASHION OF A NORMAL SEASIDE WORKER.

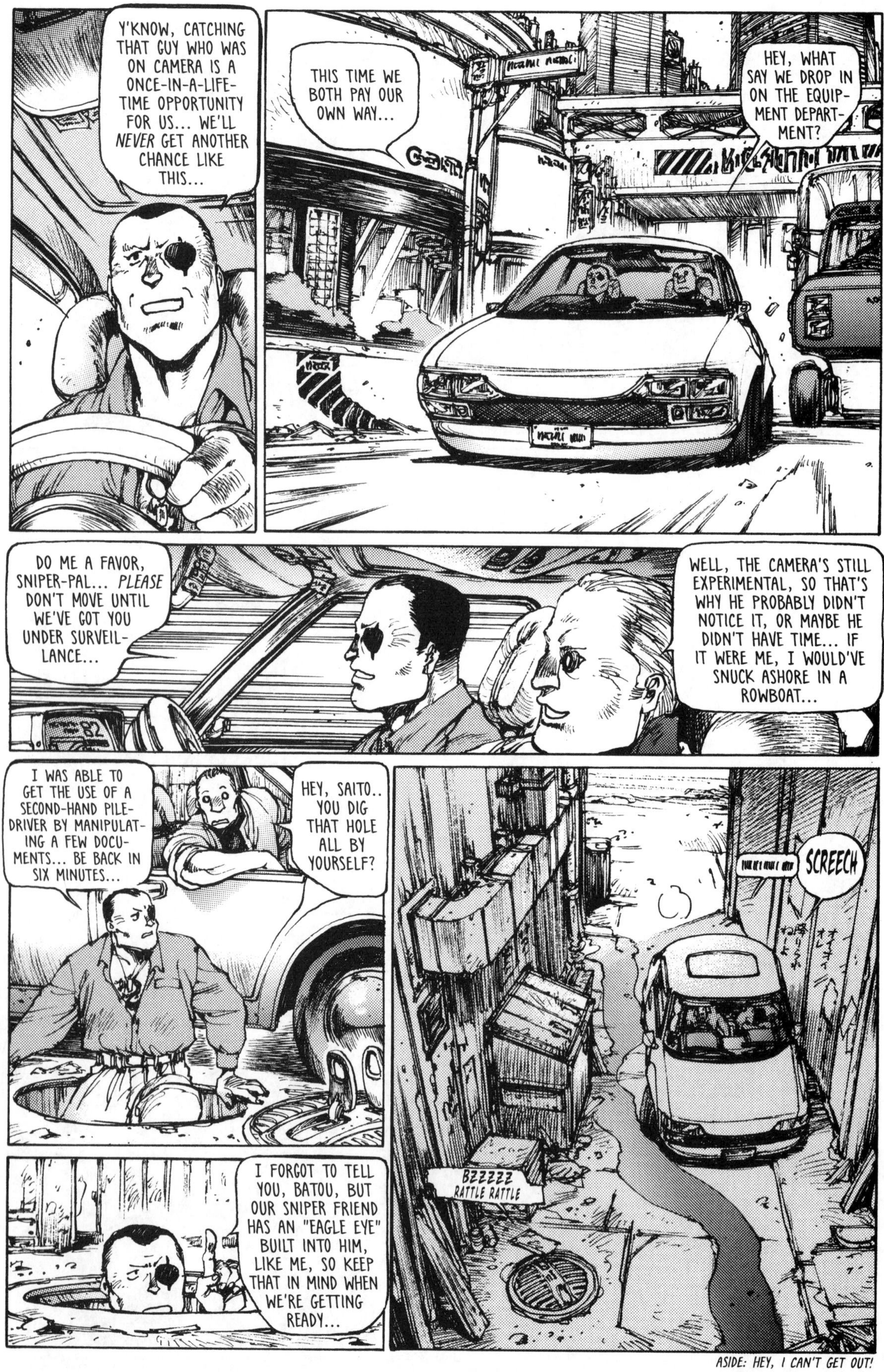
HEY, WHAT SAY WE DROP IN ON THE EQUIPMENT DEPARTMENT?
THIS TIME WE BOTH PAY OUR OWN WAY...
Y'KNOW, CATCHING THAT GUY WHO WAS ON CAMERA IS A ONCE-IN-A-LIFETIME OPPORTUNITY FOR US... WE'LL *NEVER* GET ANOTHER CHANCE LIKE THIS...
WELL, THE CAMERA'S STILL EXPERIMENTAL, SO THAT'S WHY HE PROBABLY DIDN'T NOTICE IT, OR MAYBE HE DIDN'T HAVE TIME... IF IT WERE ME, I WOULD'VE SNUCK ASHORE IN A ROWBOAT...
DO ME A FAVOR, SNIPER-PAL... *PLEASE* DON'T MOVE UNTIL WE'VE GOT YOU UNDER SURVEILLANCE...
SCREECH
BZZZZZ
RATTLE RATTLE
HEY, SAITO.. YOU DIG THAT HOLE ALL BY YOURSELF?
I WAS ABLE TO GET THE USE OF A SECOND-HAND PILE-DRIVER BY MANIPULATING A FEW DOCUMENTS... BE BACK IN SIX MINUTES...
I FORGOT TO TELL YOU, BATOU, BUT OUR SNIPER FRIEND HAS AN "EAGLE EYE" BUILT INTO HIM, LIKE ME, SO KEEP THAT IN MIND WHEN WE'RE GETTING READY...

ASIDE: HEY, I CAN'T GET OUT!

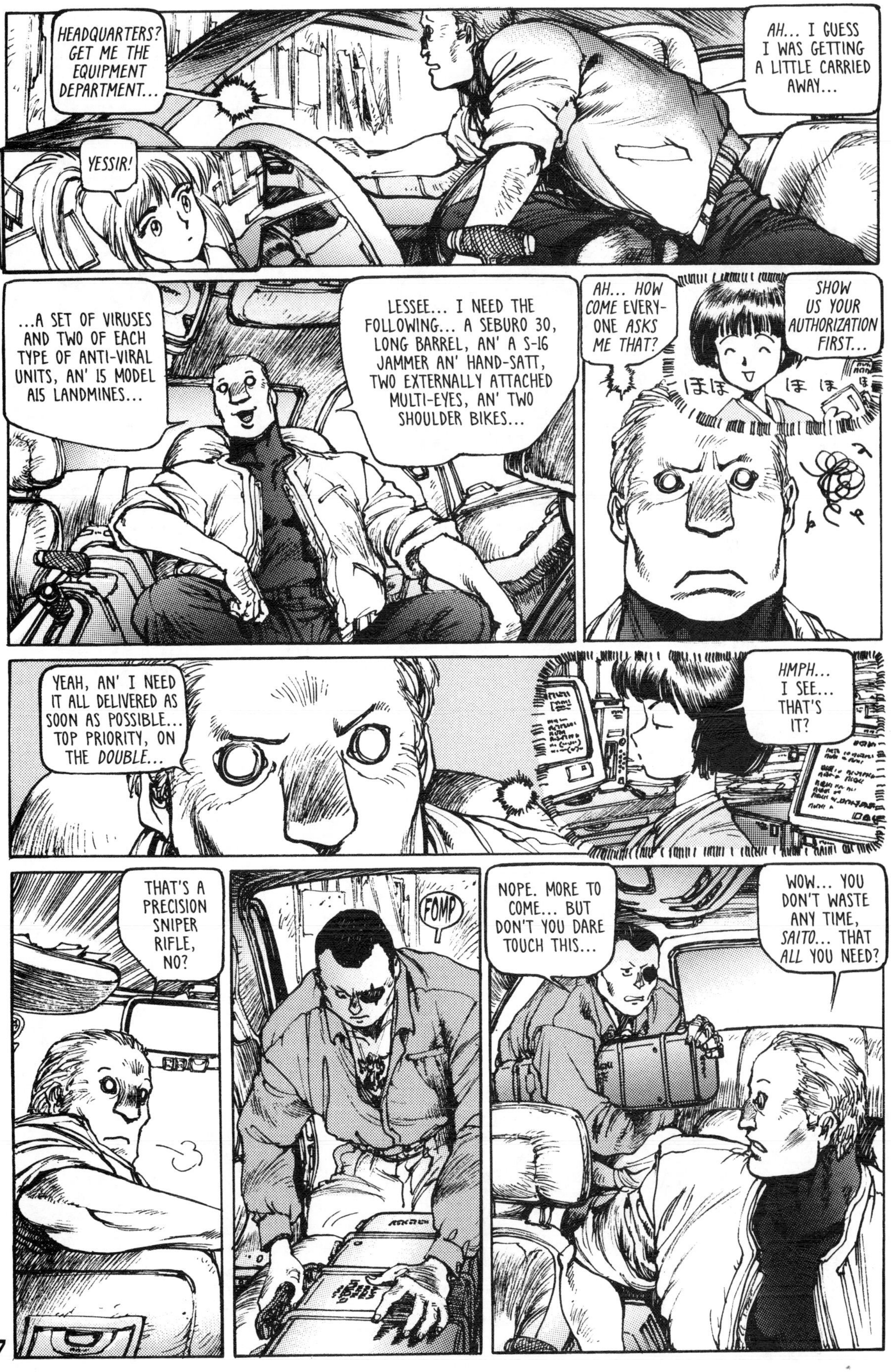
AH... I GUESS I WAS GETTING A LITTLE CARRIED AWAY...
HEADQUARTERS? GET ME THE EQUIPMENT DEPARTMENT...
YESSIR!
SHOW US YOUR AUTHORIZATION FIRST...
ほほ
ほほほ
AH... HOW COME EVERY-ONE ASKS ME THAT?
LESSEE... I NEED THE FOLLOWING... A SEBURO 30, LONG BARREL, AN' A S-16 JAMMER AN' HAND-SATT, TWO EXTERNALLY ATTACHED MULTI-EYES, AN' TWO SHOULDER BIKES...
...A SET OF VIRUSES AND TWO OF EACH TYPE OF ANTI-VIRAL UNITS, AN' 15 MODEL A15 LANDMINES...
HMPH... I SEE... THAT'S IT?
YEAH, AN' I NEED IT ALL DELIVERED AS SOON AS POSSIBLE... TOP PRIORITY, ON THE *DOUBLE*...
WOW... YOU DON'T WASTE ANY TIME, *SAITO*... THAT *ALL* YOU NEED?
NOPE. MORE TO COME... BUT DON'T YOU DARE TOUCH THIS...
FOMP
THAT'S A PRECISION SNIPER RIFLE, NO?

ASIDE: HEY... THIS COAT SMELLS LIKE A DOCTOR'S!!

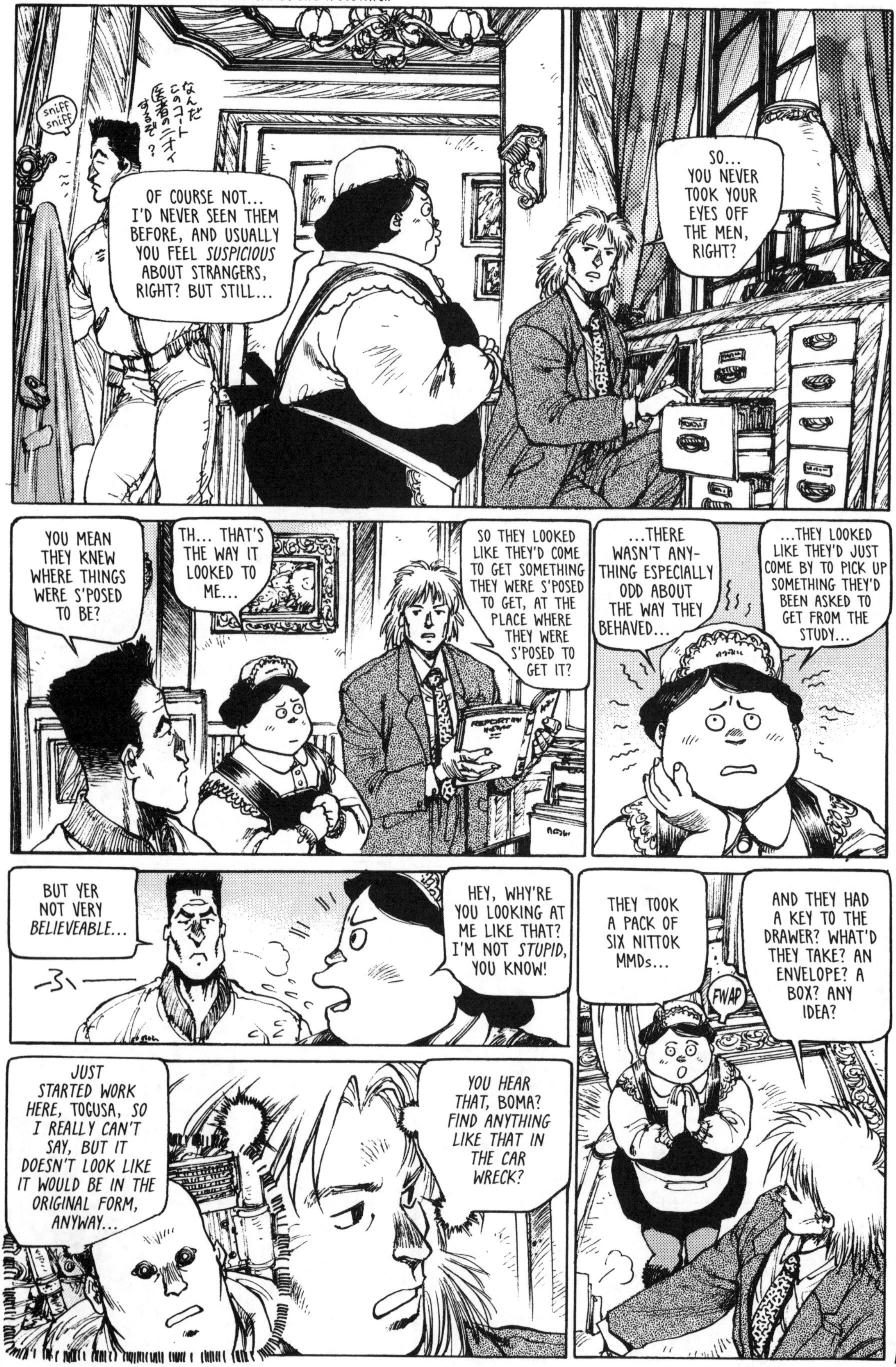

SO... YOU NEVER TOOK YOUR EYES OFF THE MEN, RIGHT?
OF COURSE NOT... I'D NEVER SEEN THEM BEFORE, AND USUALLY YOU FEEL *SUSPICIOUS* ABOUT STRANGERS, RIGHT? BUT STILL...
なんだこのコート医者のニオイするぞ？
sniff sniff
...THEY LOOKED LIKE THEY'D JUST COME BY TO PICK UP SOMETHING THEY'D BEEN ASKED TO GET FROM THE STUDY...
...THERE WASN'T ANYTHING ESPECIALLY ODD ABOUT THE WAY THEY BEHAVED...
SO THEY LOOKED LIKE THEY'D COME TO GET SOMETHING THEY WERE S'POSED TO GET, AT THE PLACE WHERE THEY WERE S'POSED TO GET IT?
TH... THAT'S THE WAY IT LOOKED TO ME...
YOU MEAN THEY KNEW WHERE THINGS WERE S'POSED TO BE?
AND THEY HAD A KEY TO THE DRAWER? WHAT'D THEY TAKE? AN ENVELOPE? A BOX? ANY IDEA?
THEY TOOK A PACK OF SIX NITTOK MMDs...
FWAP
HEY, WHY'RE YOU LOOKING AT ME LIKE THAT? I'M NOT *STUPID*, YOU KNOW!
BUT YER NOT VERY *BELIEVEABLE*...
ふー
YOU HEAR THAT, BOMA? FIND ANYTHING LIKE THAT IN THE CAR WRECK?
JUST STARTED WORK HERE, TOGUSA, SO I REALLY CAN'T SAY, BUT IT DOESN'T LOOK LIKE IT WOULD BE IN THE ORIGINAL FORM, ANYWAY...

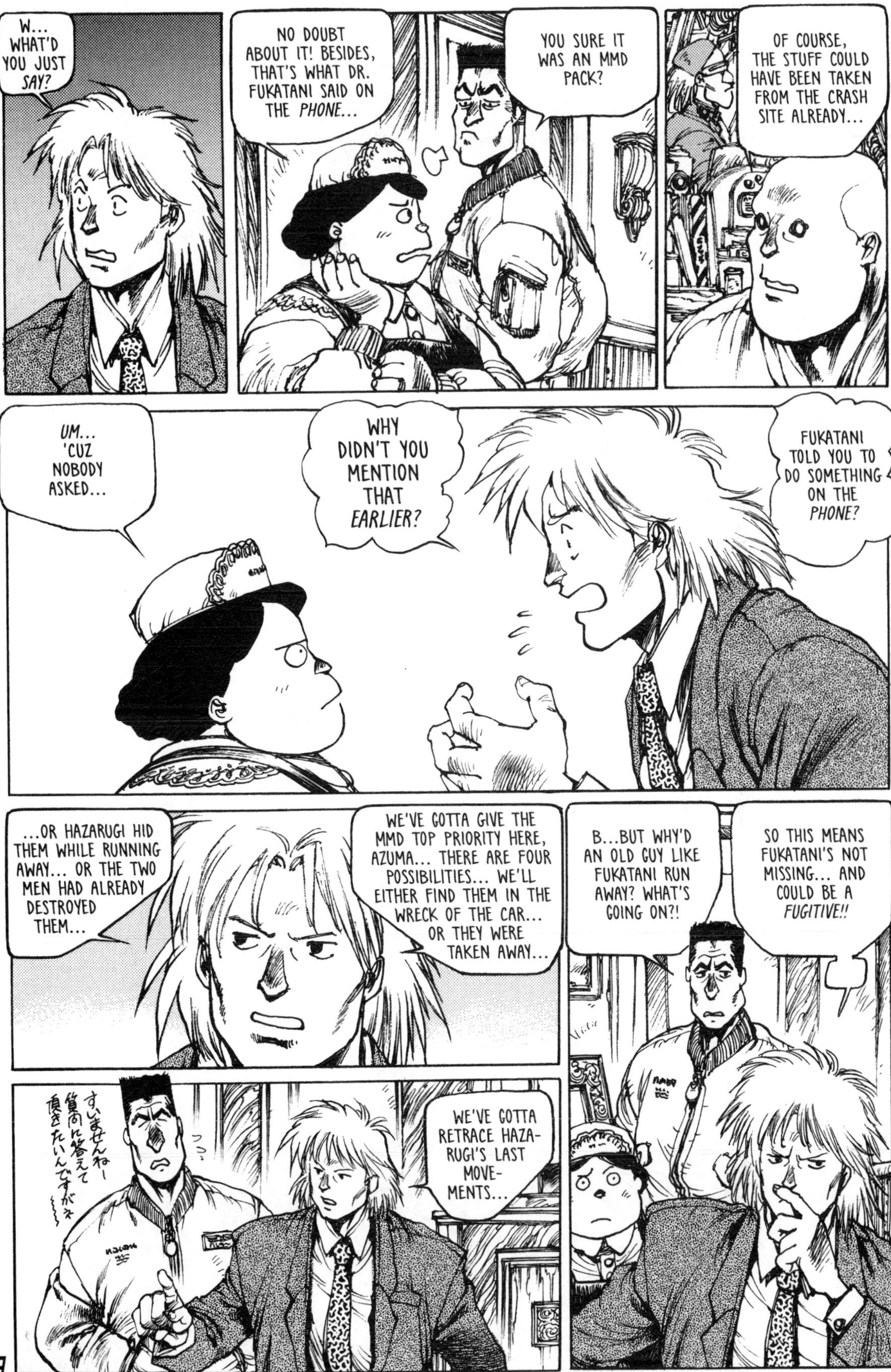
OF COURSE, THE STUFF COULD HAVE BEEN TAKEN FROM THE CRASH SITE ALREADY...
YOU SURE IT WAS AN MMD PACK?
NO DOUBT ABOUT IT! BESIDES, THAT'S WHAT DR. FUKATANI SAID ON THE *PHONE*...
W... WHAT'D YOU JUST *SAY*?
FUKATANI TOLD YOU TO DO SOMETHING ON THE *PHONE?*
WHY DIDN'T YOU MENTION THAT *EARLIER?*
UM... 'CUZ NOBODY ASKED...
SO THIS MEANS FUKATANI'S NOT MISSING... AND COULD BE A *FUGITIVE!!*
B...BUT WHY'D AN OLD GUY LIKE FUKATANI RUN AWAY? WHAT'S GOING ON?!
WE'VE GOTTA GIVE THE MMD TOP PRIORITY HERE, AZUMA... THERE ARE FOUR POSSIBILITIES... WE'LL EITHER FIND THEM IN THE WRECK OF THE CAR... OR THEY WERE TAKEN AWAY...
...OR HAZARUGI HID THEM WHILE RUNNING AWAY... OR THE TWO MEN HAD ALREADY DESTROYED THEM...
WE'VE GOTTA RETRACE HAZA-RUGI'S LAST MOVE-MENTS...
すいませんねー質問に答えて頂きたいんですがねぇ～～～

ASIDE: UM, SORRY TA BOTHER YOU, BUT WHAT ABOUT MY QUESTION?

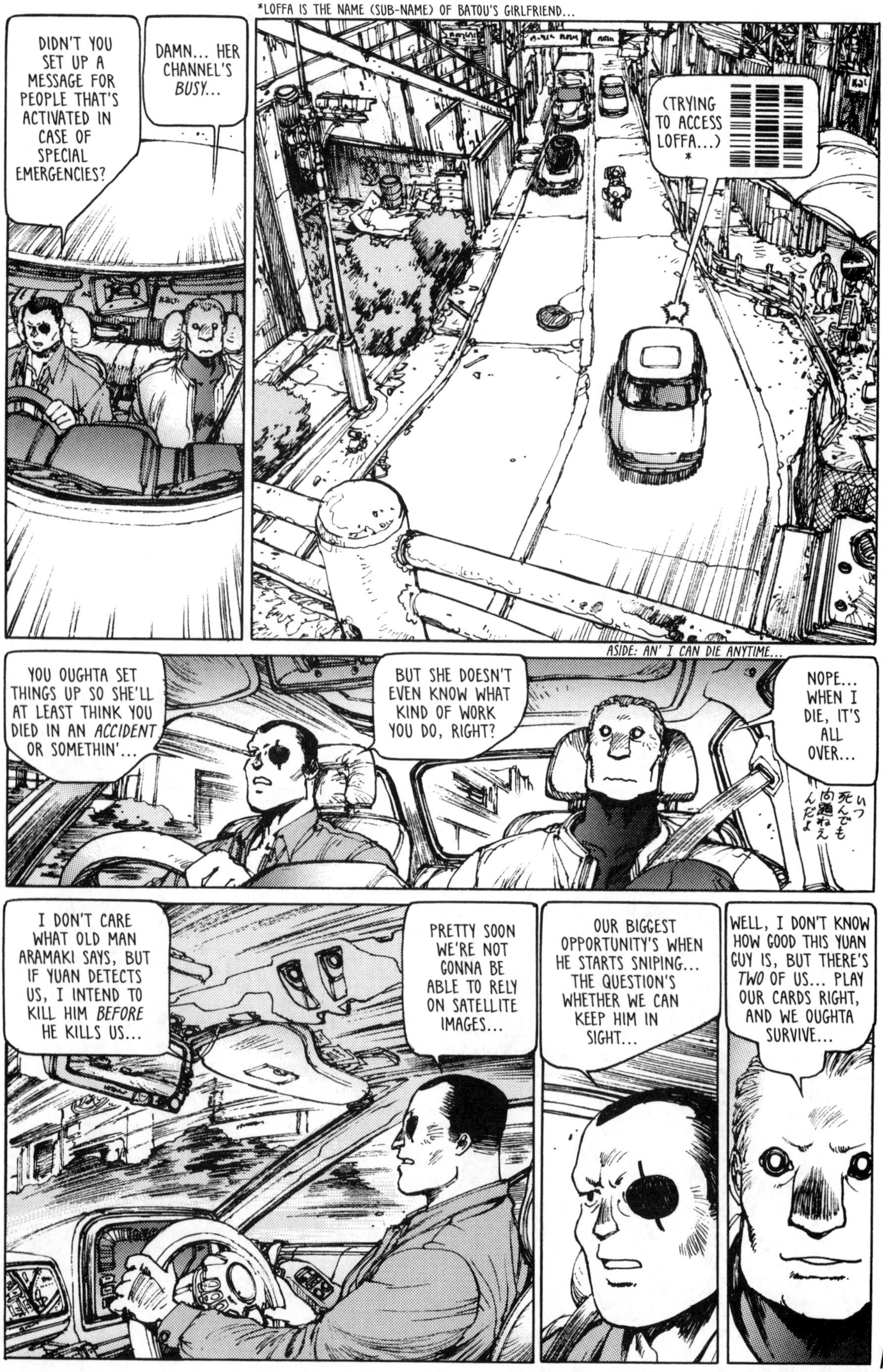
*LOFFA IS THE NAME (SUB-NAME) OF BATOU'S GIRLFRIEND...
(TRYING TO ACCESS LOFFA...) *
DAMN... HER CHANNEL'S *BUSY*...
DIDN'T YOU SET UP A MESSAGE FOR PEOPLE THAT'S ACTIVATED IN CASE OF SPECIAL EMERGENCIES?
ASIDE: AN' I CAN DIE ANYTIME...
NOPE... WHEN I DIE, IT'S ALL OVER...
いつ死んでも問題ねぇんだよ
BUT SHE DOESN'T EVEN KNOW WHAT KIND OF WORK YOU DO, RIGHT?
YOU OUGHTA SET THINGS UP SO SHE'LL AT LEAST THINK YOU DIED IN AN *ACCIDENT* OR SOMETHIN'...
WELL, I DON'T KNOW HOW GOOD THIS YUAN GUY IS, BUT THERE'S *TWO* OF US... PLAY OUR CARDS RIGHT, AND WE OUGHTA SURVIVE...
OUR BIGGEST OPPORTUNITY'S WHEN HE STARTS SNIPING... THE QUESTION'S WHETHER WE CAN KEEP HIM IN SIGHT...
PRETTY SOON WE'RE NOT GONNA BE ABLE TO RELY ON SATELLITE IMAGES...
I DON'T CARE WHAT OLD MAN ARAMAKI SAYS, BUT IF YUAN DETECTS US, I INTEND TO KILL HIM *BEFORE* HE KILLS US...

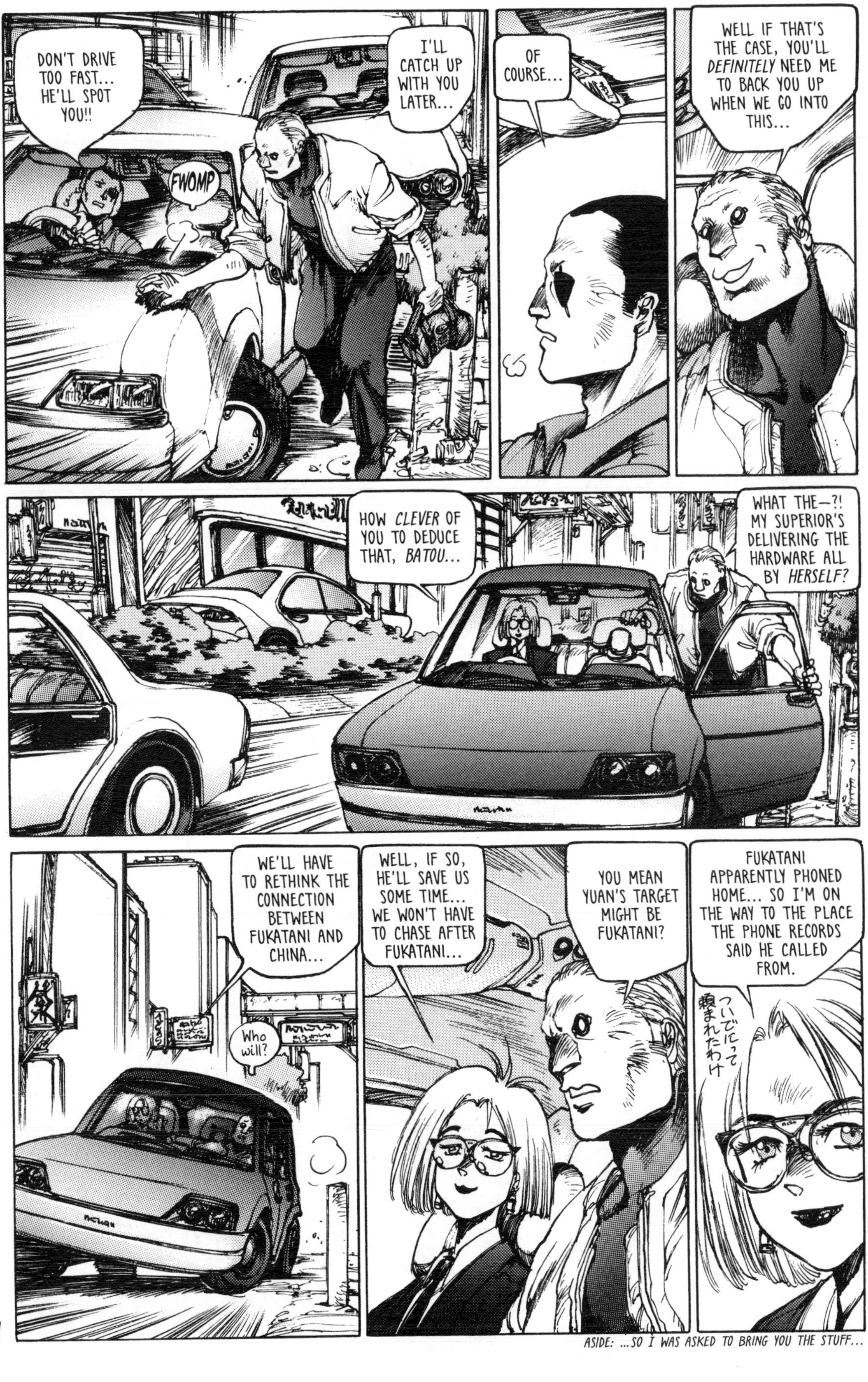
WELL IF THAT'S THE CASE, YOU'LL *DEFINITELY* NEED ME TO BACK YOU UP WHEN WE GO INTO THIS...
OF COURSE...
I'LL CATCH UP WITH YOU LATER...
DON'T DRIVE TOO FAST... HE'LL SPOT YOU!!
FWOMP
WHAT THE—?! MY SUPERIOR'S DELIVERING THE HARDWARE ALL BY *HERSELF?*
HOW *CLEVER* OF YOU TO DEDUCE THAT, *BATOU*...
FUKATANI APPARENTLY PHONED HOME... SO I'M ON THE WAY TO THE PLACE THE PHONE RECORDS SAID HE CALLED FROM.
ついでにって頼まれたわけ
YOU MEAN YUAN'S TARGET MIGHT BE FUKATANI?
WELL, IF SO, HE'LL SAVE US SOME TIME... WE WON'T HAVE TO CHASE AFTER FUKATANI...
WE'LL HAVE TO RETHINK THE CONNECTION BETWEEN FUKATANI AND CHINA...
Who will?

ASIDE: ...SO I WAS ASKED TO BRING YOU THE STUFF...

ASIDE: GOD, I FEEL LIKE SOME KIND OF COP...

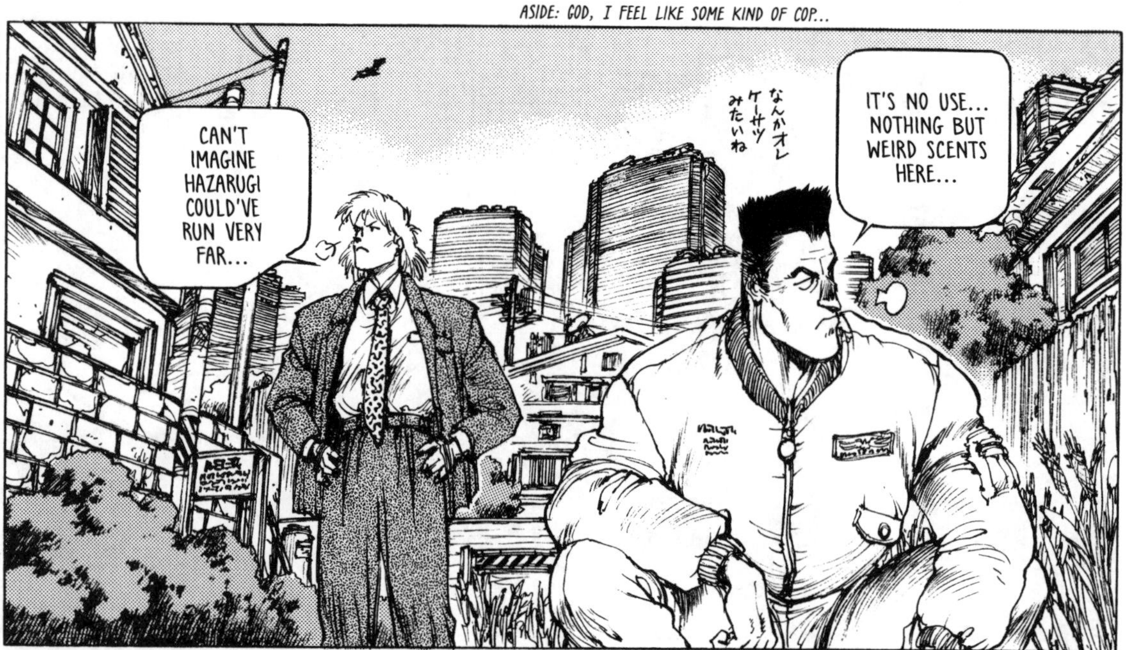
IT'S NO USE... NOTHING BUT WEIRD SCENTS HERE...
なんかオレケーサツみたいね
CAN'T IMAGINE HAZARUGI COULD'VE RUN VERY FAR...

STREETS: NAKASHIMA STREET 2, NAKASHIMA STREET 3

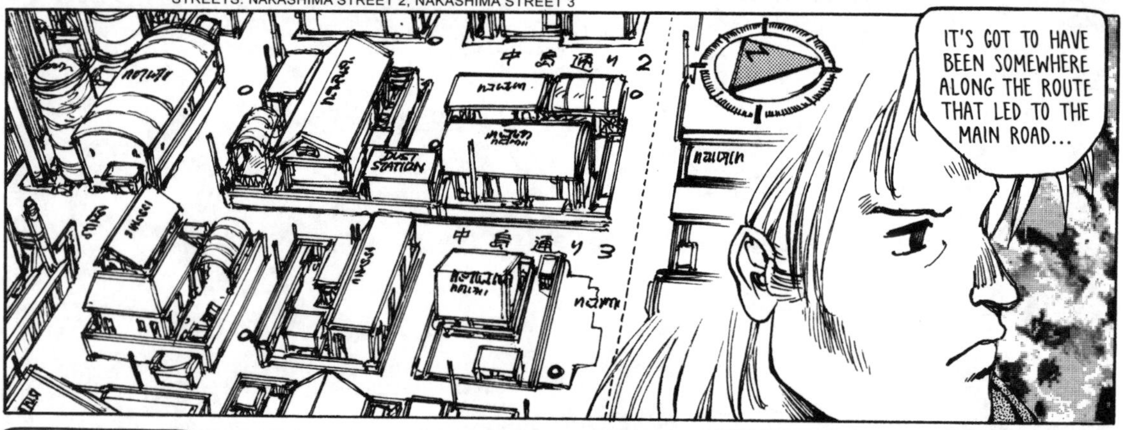
IT'S GOT TO HAVE BEEN SOMEWHERE ALONG THE ROUTE THAT LED TO THE MAIN ROAD...
中島通り2
DUST STATION
中島通り3

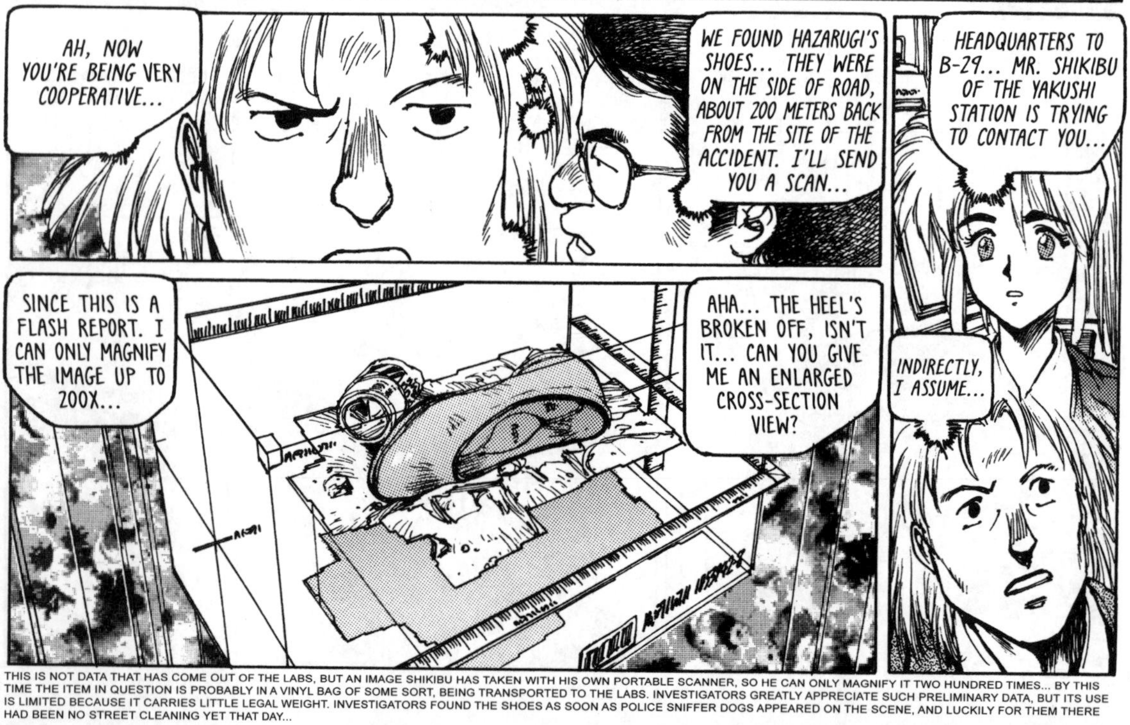
HEADQUARTERS TO B-29... MR. SHIKIBU OF THE YAKUSHI STATION IS TRYING TO CONTACT YOU...
INDIRECTLY, I ASSUME...
WE FOUND HAZARUGI'S SHOES... THEY WERE ON THE SIDE OF ROAD, ABOUT 200 METERS BACK FROM THE SITE OF THE ACCIDENT. I'LL SEND YOU A SCAN...
AH, NOW YOU'RE BEING VERY COOPERATIVE...
AHA... THE HEEL'S BROKEN OFF, ISN'T IT... CAN YOU GIVE ME AN ENLARGED CROSS-SECTION VIEW?
SINCE THIS IS A FLASH REPORT. I CAN ONLY MAGNIFY THE IMAGE UP TO 200X...

THIS IS NOT DATA THAT HAS COME OUT OF THE LABS, BUT AN IMAGE SHIKIBU HAS TAKEN WITH HIS OWN PORTABLE SCANNER, SO HE CAN ONLY MAGNIFY IT TWO HUNDRED TIMES... BY THIS TIME THE ITEM IN QUESTION IS PROBABLY IN A VINYL BAG OF SOME SORT, BEING TRANSPORTED TO THE LABS. INVESTIGATORS GREATLY APPRECIATE SUCH PRELIMINARY DATA, BUT ITS USE IS LIMITED BECAUSE IT CARRIES LITTLE LEGAL WEIGHT. INVESTIGATORS FOUND THE SHOES AS SOON AS POLICE SNIFFER DOGS APPEARED ON THE SCENE, AND LUCKILY FOR THEM THERE HAD BEEN NO STREET CLEANING YET THAT DAY...

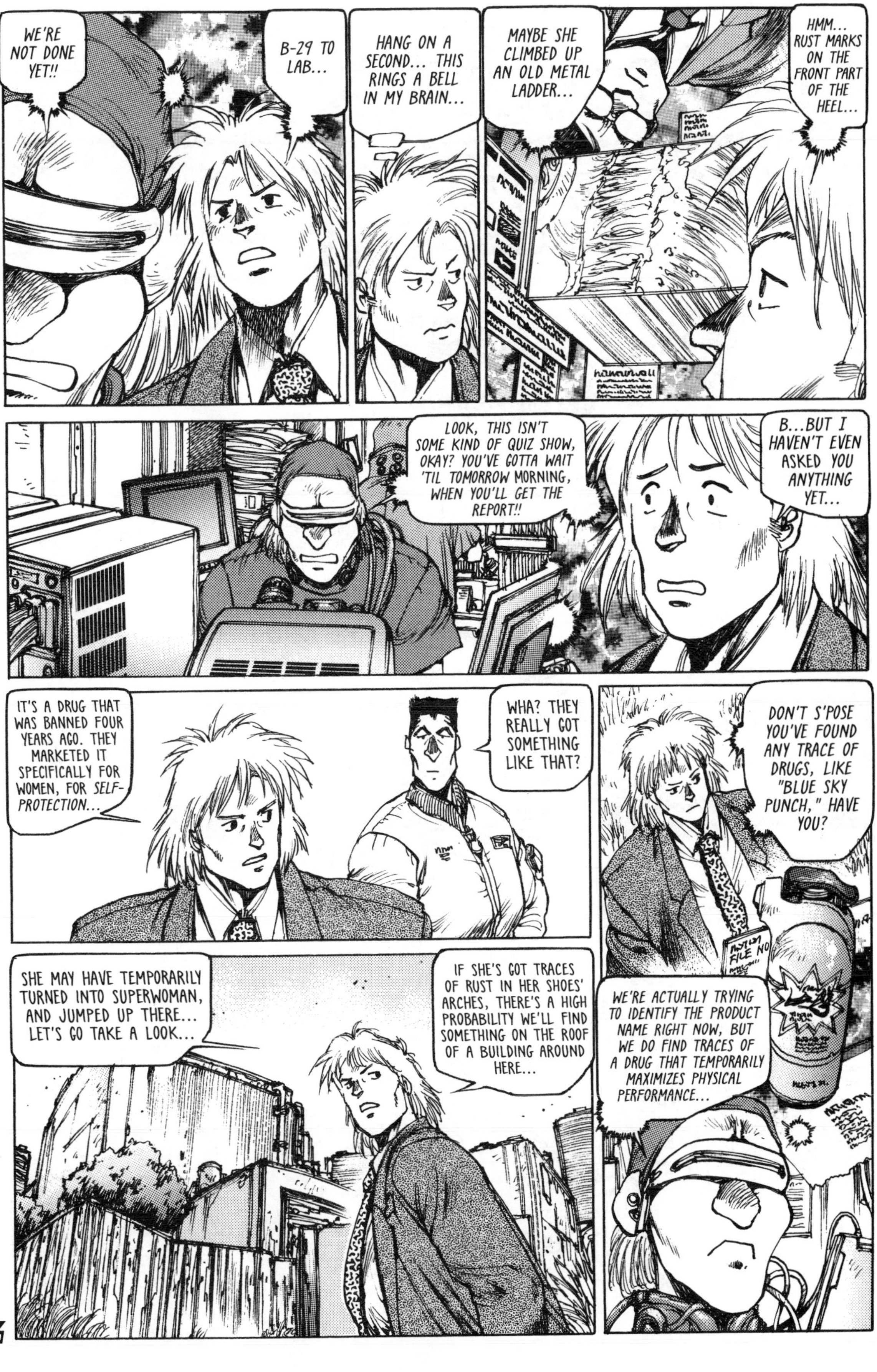
HMM... RUST MARKS ON THE FRONT PART OF THE HEEL...
MAYBE SHE CLIMBED UP AN OLD METAL LADDER...
HANG ON A SECOND... THIS RINGS A BELL IN MY BRAIN...
B-29 TO LAB...
WE'RE NOT DONE YET!!
B...BUT I HAVEN'T EVEN ASKED YOU ANYTHING YET...
LOOK, THIS ISN'T SOME KIND OF QUIZ SHOW, OKAY? YOU'VE GOTTA WAIT 'TIL TOMORROW MORNING, WHEN YOU'LL GET THE REPORT!!
DON'T S'POSE YOU'VE FOUND ANY TRACE OF DRUGS, LIKE "BLUE SKY PUNCH," HAVE YOU?
WE'RE ACTUALLY TRYING TO IDENTIFY THE PRODUCT NAME RIGHT NOW, BUT WE DO FIND TRACES OF A DRUG THAT TEMPORARILY MAXIMIZES PHYSICAL PERFORMANCE...
WHA? THEY REALLY GOT SOMETHING LIKE THAT?
IT'S A DRUG THAT WAS BANNED FOUR YEARS AGO. THEY MARKETED IT SPECIFICALLY FOR WOMEN, FOR SELF-PROTECTION...
IF SHE'S GOT TRACES OF RUST IN HER SHOES' ARCHES, THERE'S A HIGH PROBABILITY WE'LL FIND SOMETHING ON THE ROOF OF A BUILDING AROUND HERE...
SHE MAY HAVE TEMPORARILY TURNED INTO SUPERWOMAN, AND JUMPED UP THERE... LET'S GO TAKE A LOOK...

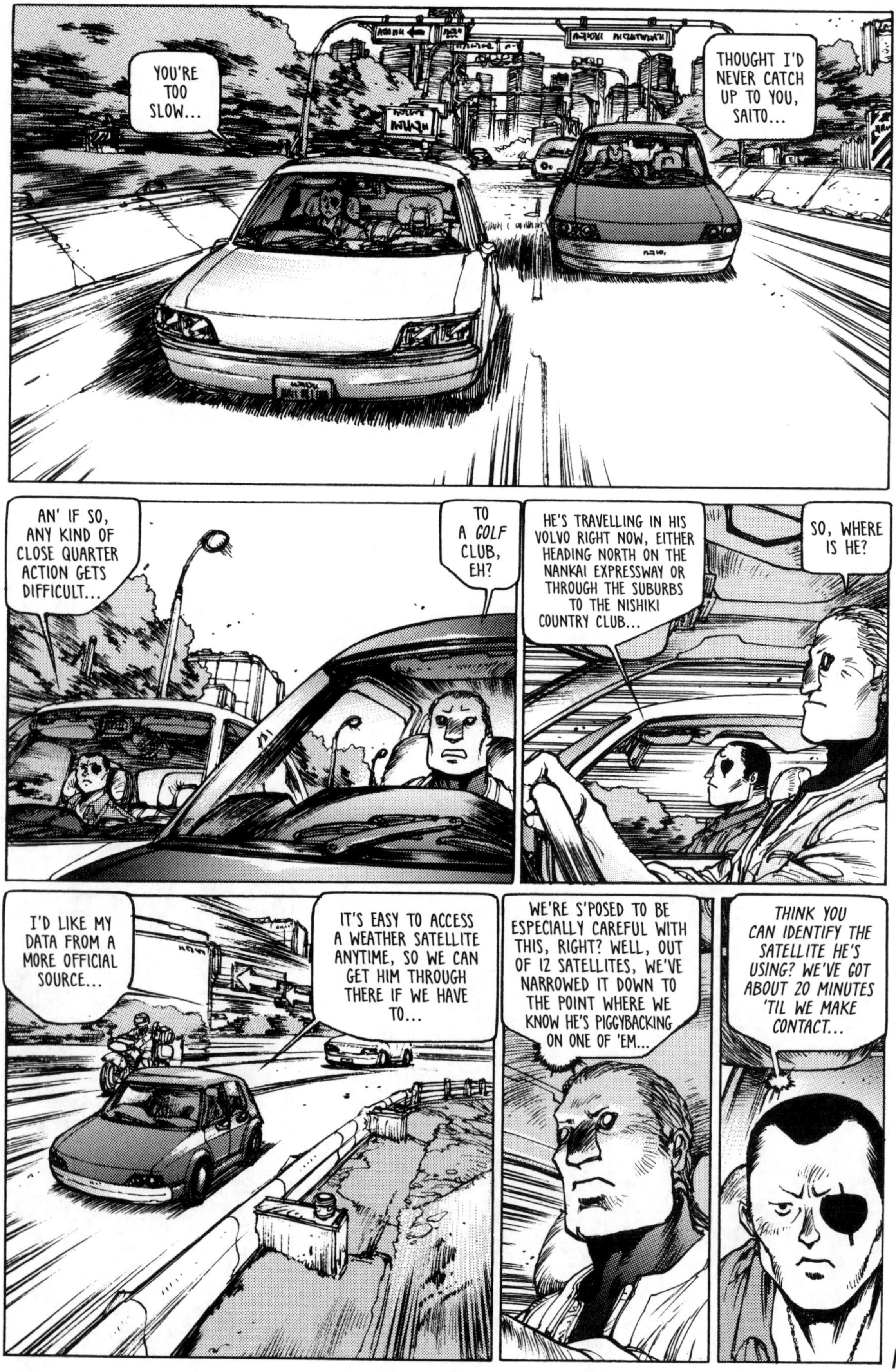
THOUGHT I'D NEVER CATCH UP TO YOU, SAITO...
YOU'RE TOO SLOW...
SO, WHERE IS HE?
HE'S TRAVELLING IN HIS VOLVO RIGHT NOW, EITHER HEADING NORTH ON THE NANKAI EXPRESSWAY OR THROUGH THE SUBURBS TO THE NISHIKI COUNTRY CLUB...
TO A *GOLF* CLUB, EH?
AN' IF SO, ANY KIND OF CLOSE QUARTER ACTION GETS DIFFICULT...
THINK YOU CAN IDENTIFY THE SATELLITE HE'S USING? WE'VE GOT ABOUT 20 MINUTES 'TIL WE MAKE CONTACT...
WE'RE S'POSED TO BE ESPECIALLY CAREFUL WITH THIS, RIGHT? WELL, OUT OF 12 SATELLITES, WE'VE NARROWED IT DOWN TO THE POINT WHERE WE KNOW HE'S PIGGYBACKING ON ONE OF 'EM...
IT'S EASY TO ACCESS A WEATHER SATELLITE ANYTIME, SO WE CAN GET HIM THROUGH THERE IF WE HAVE TO...
I'D LIKE MY DATA FROM A MORE OFFICIAL SOURCE...

ASIDE: DOESN'T LOOK LIKE SHE PUT HER FOOT THROUGH ONE, THOUGH...

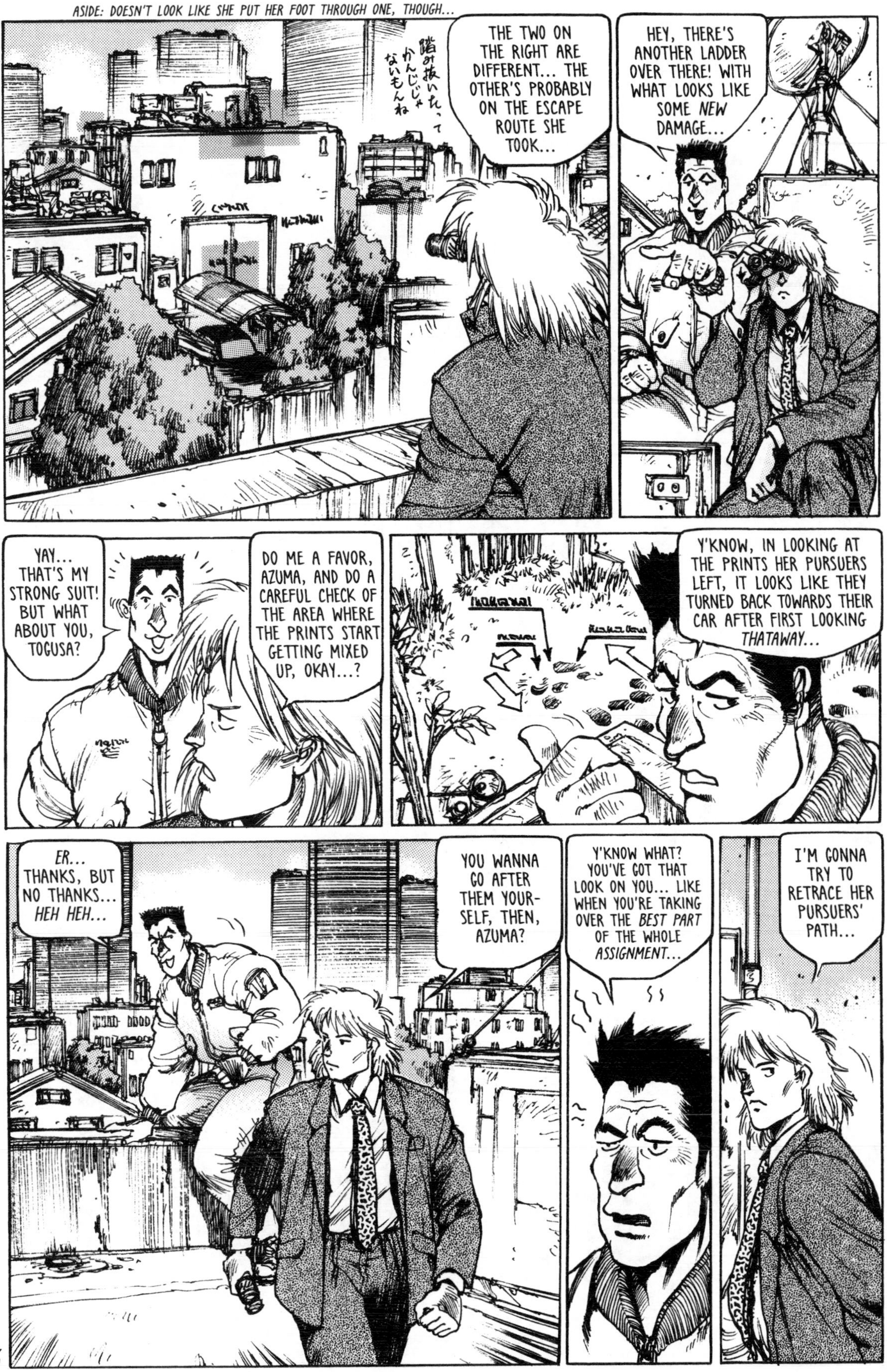
HEY, THERE'S ANOTHER LADDER OVER THERE! WITH WHAT LOOKS LIKE SOME *NEW* DAMAGE...
THE TWO ON THE RIGHT ARE DIFFERENT... THE OTHER'S PROBABLY ON THE ESCAPE ROUTE SHE TOOK...
踏み抜いた、て
かんじじゃ
ないもんね
Y'KNOW, IN LOOKING AT THE PRINTS HER PURSUERS LEFT, IT LOOKS LIKE THEY TURNED BACK TOWARDS THEIR CAR AFTER FIRST LOOKING *THATAWAY*...
DO ME A FAVOR, AZUMA, AND DO A CAREFUL CHECK OF THE AREA WHERE THE PRINTS START GETTING MIXED UP, OKAY...?
YAY... THAT'S MY STRONG SUIT! BUT WHAT ABOUT YOU, TOGUSA?
I'M GONNA TRY TO RETRACE HER PURSUERS' PATH...
Y'KNOW WHAT? YOU'VE GOT THAT LOOK ON YOU... LIKE WHEN YOU'RE TAKING OVER THE *BEST PART* OF THE WHOLE *ASSIGNMENT*...
YOU WANNA GO AFTER THEM YOUR-SELF, THEN, AZUMA?
ER... THANKS, BUT NO THANKS... *HEH HEH...*

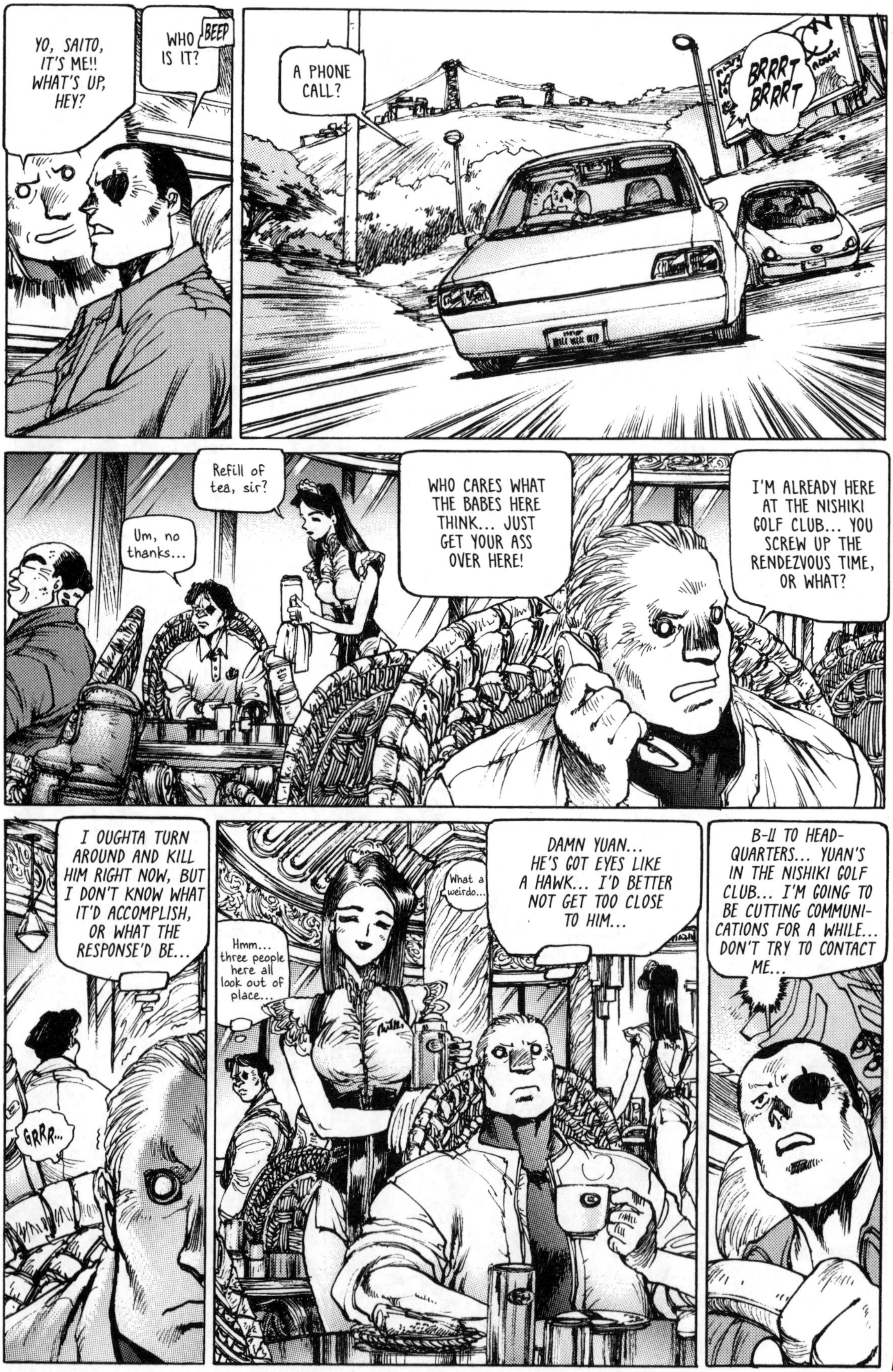
BRRRT BRRRT
A PHONE CALL?
BEEP
WHO IS IT?
YO, SAITO, IT'S ME!! WHAT'S UP, HEY?
I'M ALREADY HERE AT THE NISHIKI GOLF CLUB... YOU SCREW UP THE RENDEZVOUS TIME, OR WHAT?
WHO CARES WHAT THE BABES HERE THINK... JUST GET YOUR ASS OVER HERE!
Refill of tea, sir?
Um, no thanks...
B-11 TO HEAD-QUARTERS... YUAN'S IN THE NISHIKI GOLF CLUB... I'M GOING TO BE CUTTING COMMUNI-CATIONS FOR A WHILE... DON'T TRY TO CONTACT ME...
DAMN YUAN... HE'S GOT EYES LIKE A HAWK... I'D BETTER NOT GET TOO CLOSE TO HIM...
What a weirdo...
Hmm... three people here all look out of place...
I OUGHTA TURN AROUND AND KILL HIM RIGHT NOW, BUT I DON'T KNOW WHAT IT'D ACCOMPLISH, OR WHAT THE RESPONSE'D BE...
GRRR...

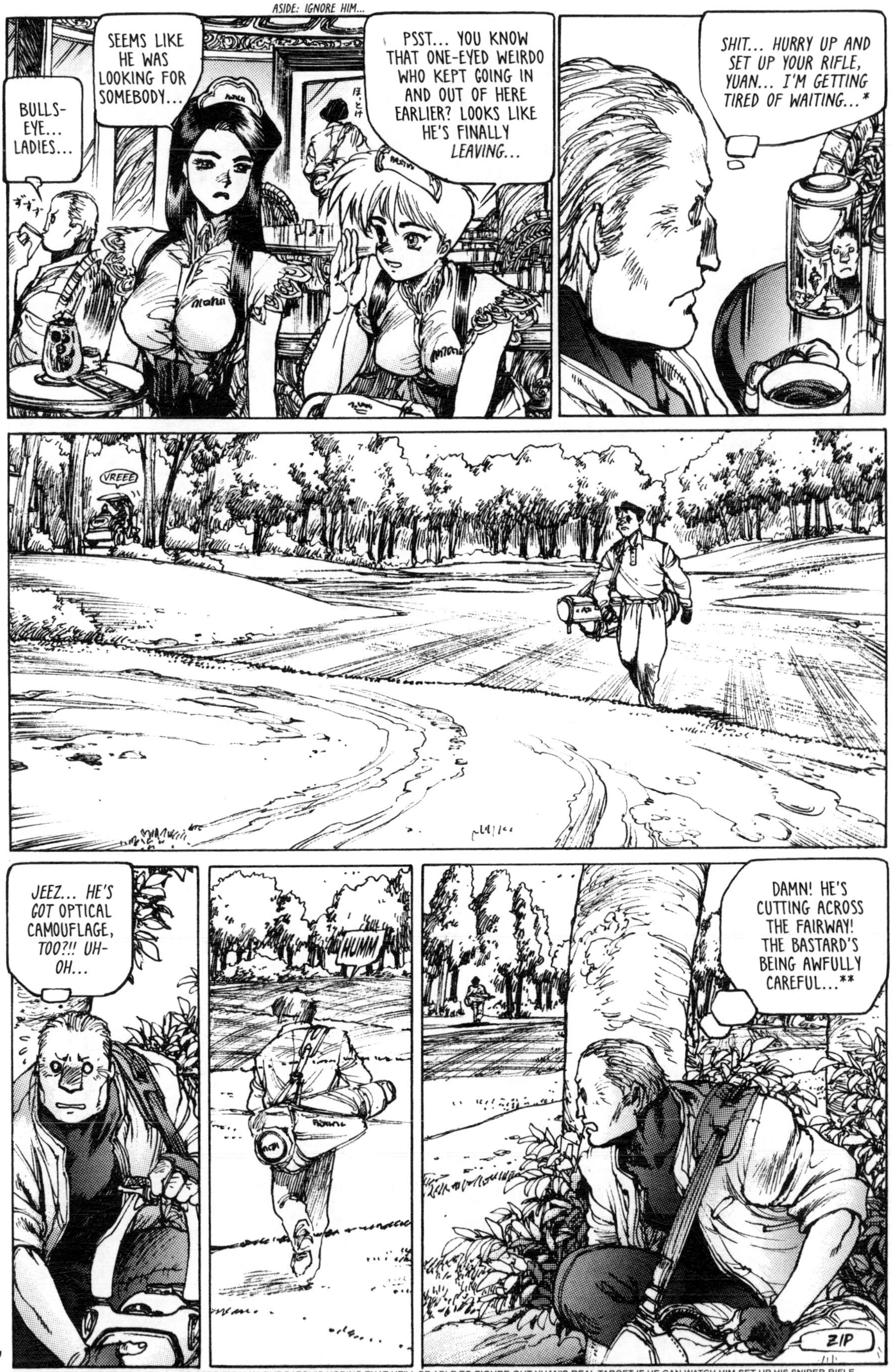
SHIT... HURRY UP AND SET UP YOUR RIFLE, YUAN... I'M GETTING TIRED OF WAITING...*
ASIDE: IGNORE HIM...
PSST... YOU KNOW THAT ONE-EYED WEIRDO WHO KEPT GOING IN AND OUT OF HERE EARLIER? LOOKS LIKE HE'S FINALLY *LEAVING*...
SEEMS LIKE HE WAS LOOKING FOR SOMEBODY...
BULLS-EYE... LADIES...
VREEE
DAMN! HE'S CUTTING ACROSS THE FAIRWAY! THE BASTARD'S BEING AWFULLY CAREFUL...**
ZIP
HUMM
JEEZ... HE'S GOT OPTICAL CAMOUFLAGE, TOO?!! UH-OH...

*THIS HAS NOTHING TO DO WITH SAITO SPECIFICALLY, BUT BATOU'S HOPING THAT HE'LL BE ABLE TO FIGURE OUT YUAN'S REAL TARGET IF HE CAN WATCH HIM SET UP HIS SNIPER RIFLE.
**YUAN LOOKED BACK, RIGHT AFTER CROSSING THE FAIRWAY TO MAKE SURE HE WASN'T BEING TAILED. THAT MEANS BATOU WILL BE FORCED TO GO AROUND THE LONG WAY IF HE WANTS TO CONTINUE TO TAIL YUAN ON THE OTHER SIDE. OR AT LEAST THAT'S WHAT WE'LL ASSUME'S GOING ON HERE...

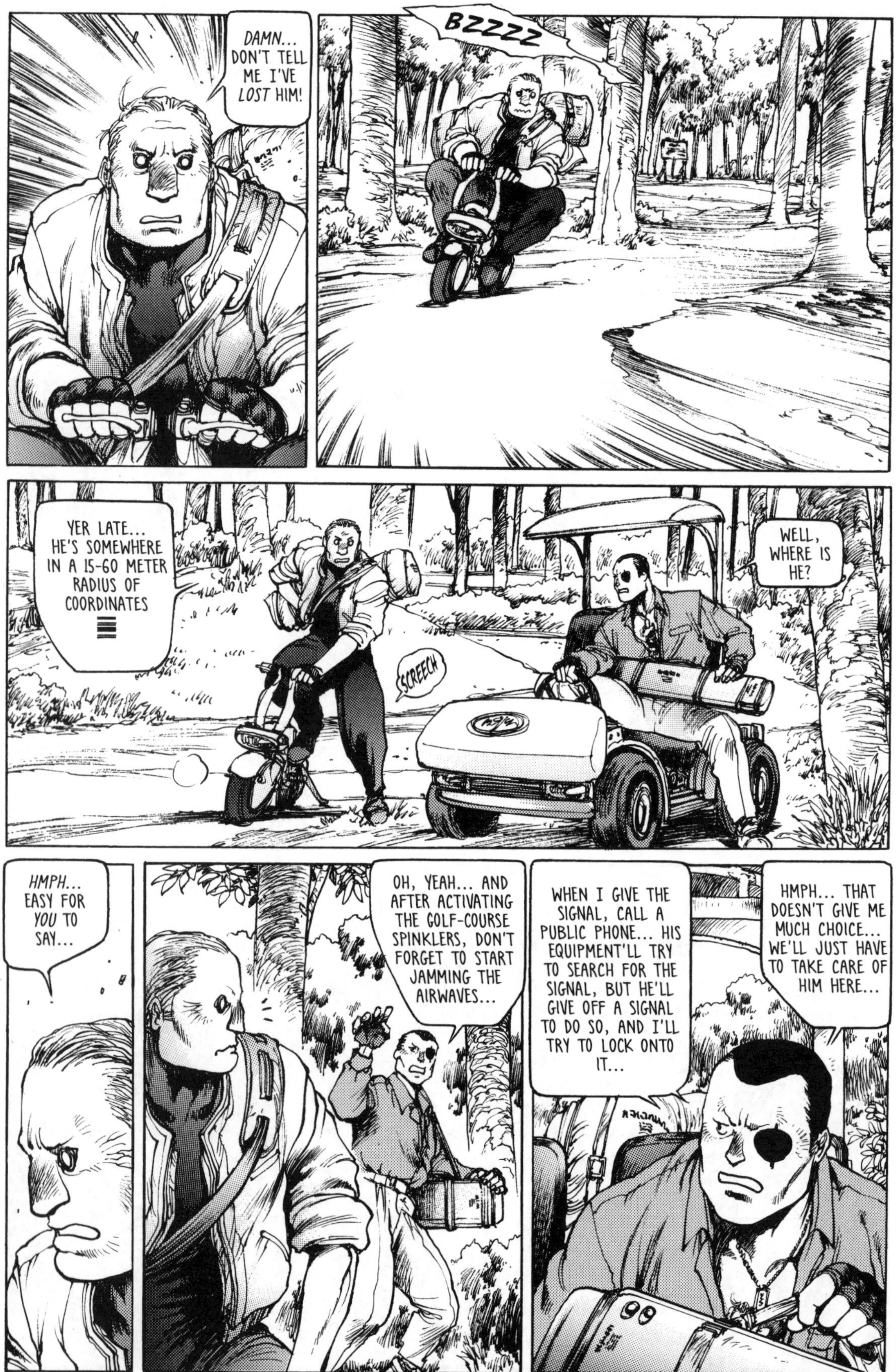
BZZZZ
DAMN... DON'T TELL ME I'VE LOST HIM!
WELL, WHERE IS HE?
YER LATE... HE'S SOMEWHERE IN A 15-60 METER RADIUS OF COORDINATES
SCREECH
HMPH... THAT DOESN'T GIVE ME MUCH CHOICE... WE'LL JUST HAVE TO TAKE CARE OF HIM HERE...
WHEN I GIVE THE SIGNAL, CALL A PUBLIC PHONE... HIS EQUIPMENT'LL TRY TO SEARCH FOR THE SIGNAL, BUT HE'LL GIVE OFF A SIGNAL TO DO SO, AND I'LL TRY TO LOCK ONTO IT...
OH, YEAH... AND AFTER ACTIVATING THE GOLF-COURSE SPINKLERS, DON'T FORGET TO START JAMMING THE AIRWAVES...
HMPH... EASY FOR YOU TO SAY...

BATOU'S SHOULDER BIKE IS ELECTRIC, SO IT'S A LITTLE HEAVY, BUT IT'S QUIET AND HARD TO DETECT. OF COURSE, BATOU'S A CYBORG, SO HE PRESUMABLY COULD JUST RUN AROUND THE COURSE, BUT THE SOUND OF ALL THE WEAPONS JOSTLING AROUND IN HIS BAG MIGHT GIVE AWAY HIS WHEREABOUTS TO YUAN...

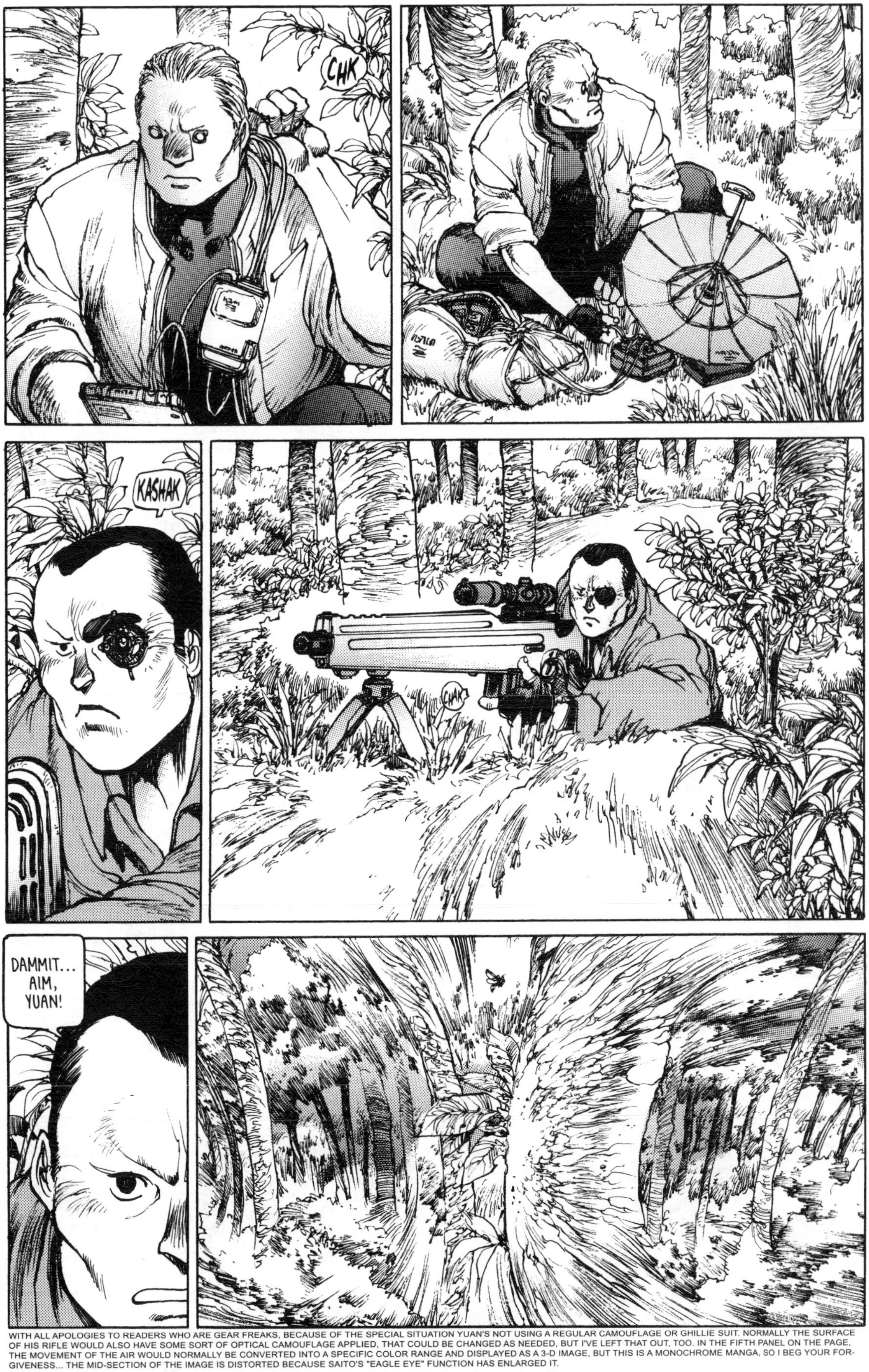
CHK
CHAK
KASHAK
DAMMIT... AIM, YUAN!

WITH ALL APOLOGIES TO READERS WHO ARE GEAR FREAKS, BECAUSE OF THE SPECIAL SITUATION YUAN'S NOT USING A REGULAR CAMOUFLAGE OR GHILLIE SUIT. NORMALLY THE SURFACE OF HIS RIFLE WOULD ALSO HAVE SOME SORT OF OPTICAL CAMOUFLAGE APPLIED, THAT COULD BE CHANGED AS NEEDED, BUT I'VE LEFT THAT OUT, TOO. IN THE FIFTH PANEL ON THE PAGE, THE MOVEMENT OF THE AIR WOULD NORMALLY BE CONVERTED INTO A SPECIFIC COLOR RANGE AND DISPLAYED AS A 3-D IMAGE, BUT THIS IS A MONOCHROME MANGA, SO I BEG YOUR FORGIVENESS... THE MID-SECTION OF THE IMAGE IS DISTORTED BECAUSE SAITO'S "EAGLE EYE" FUNCTION HAS ENLARGED IT.

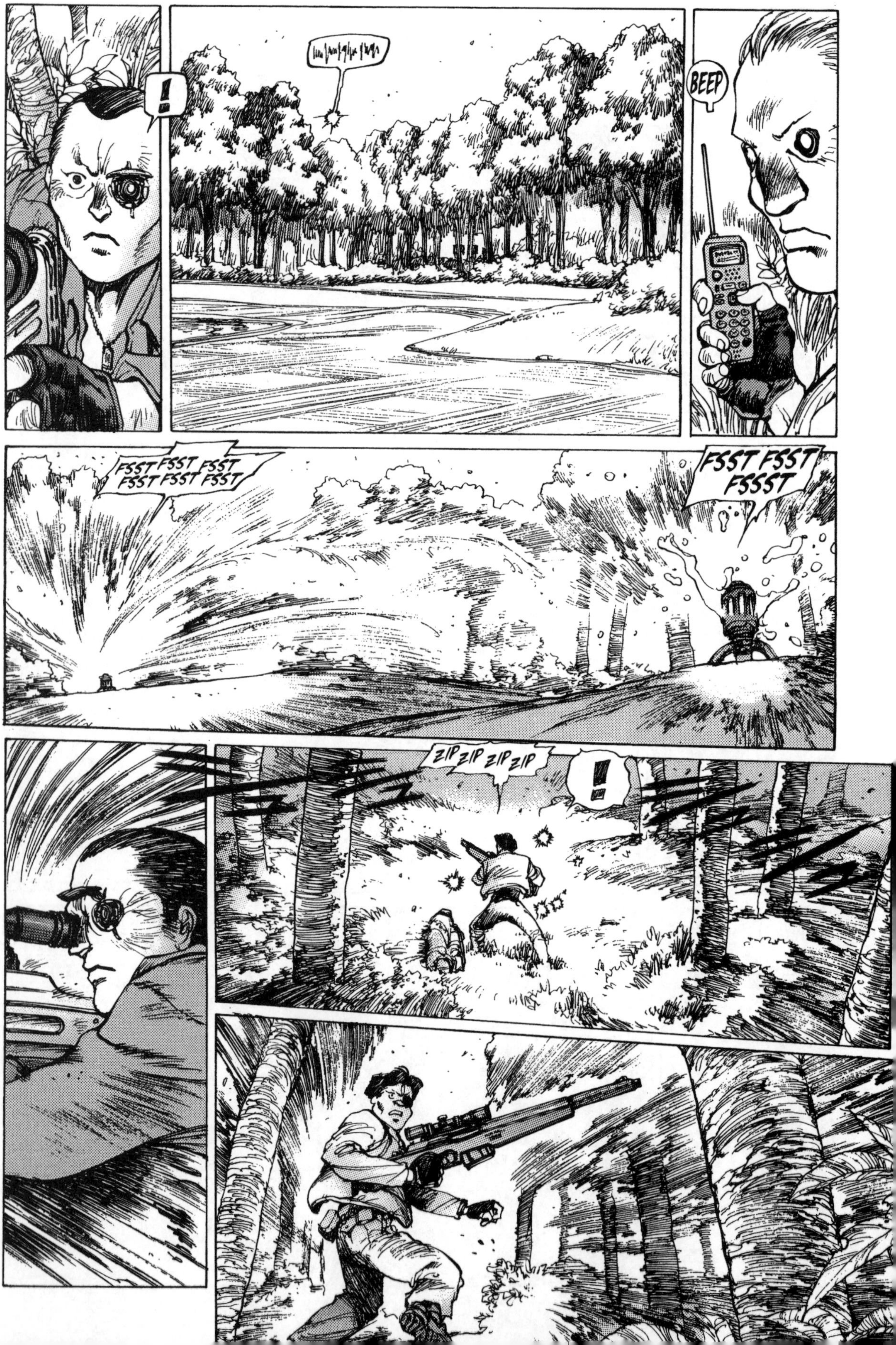
BEEP
!
FSST FSST FSSST
FSST FSST FSST FSST FSST FSST
ZIP ZIP ZIP ZIP
!

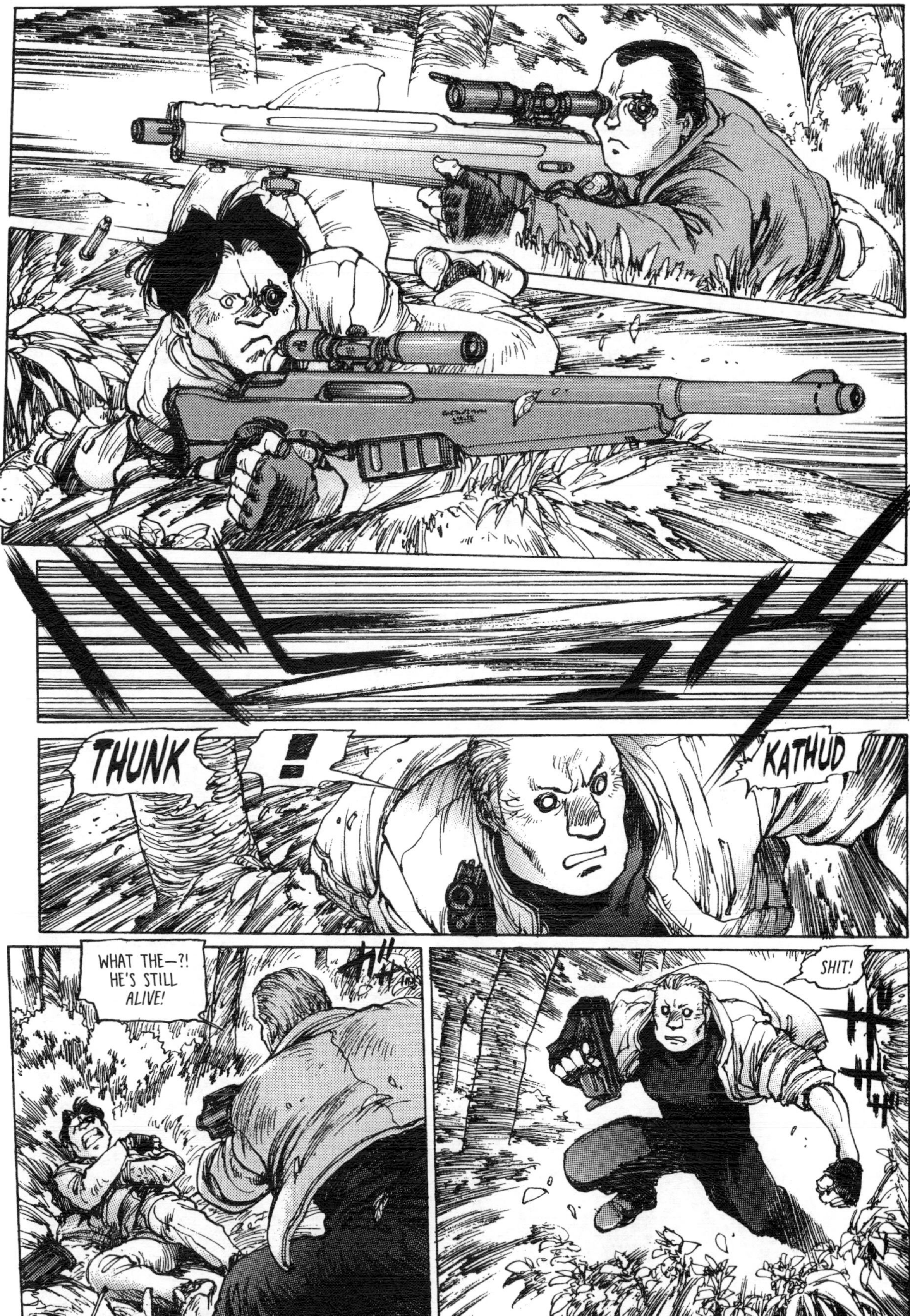
KATHUD
!
THUNK
SHIT!
WHAT THE—?! HE'S STILL ALIVE!

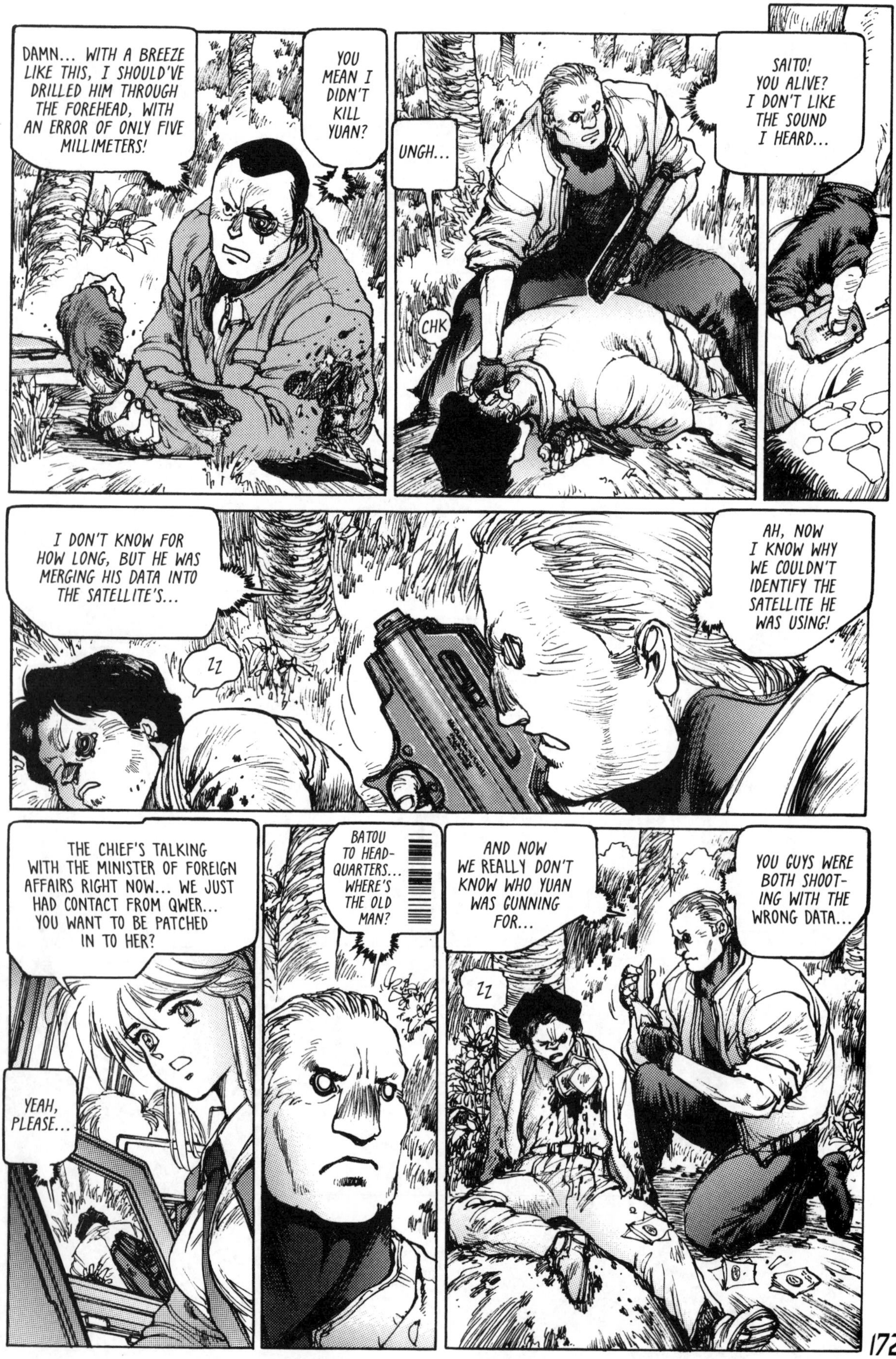
SAITO! YOU ALIVE? I DON'T LIKE THE SOUND I HEARD...
UNGH...
CHK
YOU MEAN I DIDN'T KILL YUAN?
DAMN... WITH A BREEZE LIKE THIS, I SHOULD'VE DRILLED HIM THROUGH THE FOREHEAD, WITH AN ERROR OF ONLY FIVE MILLIMETERS!
AH, NOW I KNOW WHY WE COULDN'T IDENTIFY THE SATELLITE HE WAS USING!
I DON'T KNOW FOR HOW LONG, BUT HE WAS MERGING HIS DATA INTO THE SATELLITE'S...
ZZ
YOU GUYS WERE BOTH SHOOTING WITH THE WRONG DATA...
AND NOW WE REALLY DON'T KNOW WHO YUAN WAS GUNNING FOR...
ZZ
BATOU TO HEADQUARTERS... WHERE'S THE OLD MAN?
THE CHIEF'S TALKING WITH THE MINISTER OF FOREIGN AFFAIRS RIGHT NOW... WE JUST HAD CONTACT FROM QWER... YOU WANT TO BE PATCHED IN TO HER?
YEAH, PLEASE...

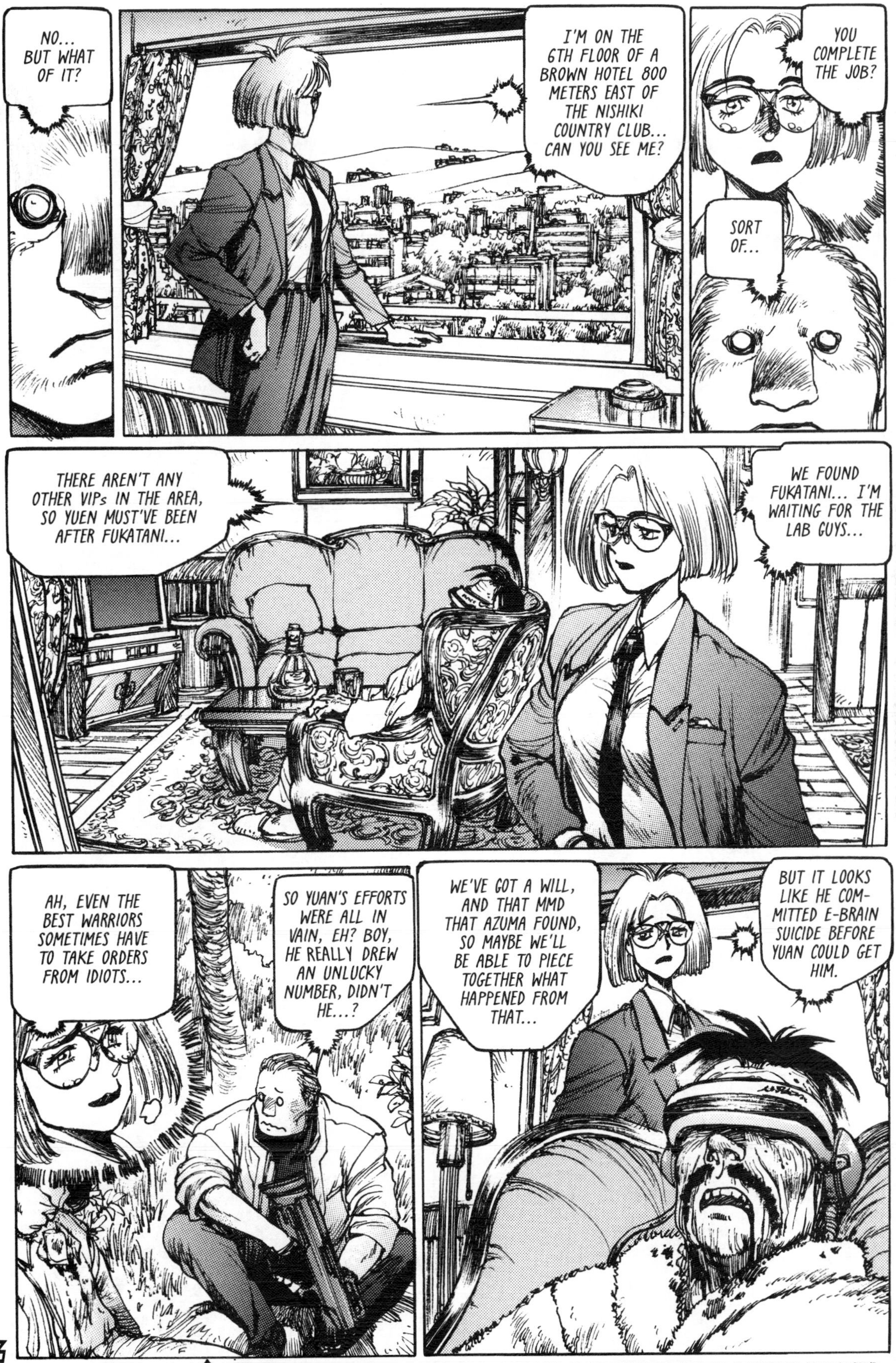
YOU COMPLETE THE JOB?
SORT OF...
I'M ON THE 6TH FLOOR OF A BROWN HOTEL 800 METERS EAST OF THE NISHIKI COUNTRY CLUB... CAN YOU SEE ME?
NO... BUT WHAT OF IT?
WE FOUND FUKATANI... I'M WAITING FOR THE LAB GUYS...
THERE AREN'T ANY OTHER VIPs IN THE AREA, SO YUEN MUST'VE BEEN AFTER FUKATANI...
BUT IT LOOKS LIKE HE COM-MITTED E-BRAIN SUICIDE BEFORE YUAN COULD GET HIM.
WE'VE GOT A WILL, AND THAT MMD THAT AZUMA FOUND, SO MAYBE WE'LL BE ABLE TO PIECE TOGETHER WHAT HAPPENED FROM THAT...
SO YUAN'S EFFORTS WERE ALL IN VAIN, EH? BOY, HE REALLY DREW AN UNLUCKY NUMBER, DIDN'T HE...?
AH, EVEN THE BEST WARRIORS SOMETIMES HAVE TO TAKE ORDERS FROM IDIOTS...

↰ BATOU DOESN'T WANT TO MOVE YUAN AND CAUSE HIM TO BLEED TO DEATH, SO HE'S STANCHED THE WOUND AND IS WAITING FOR HELP TO ARRIVE...

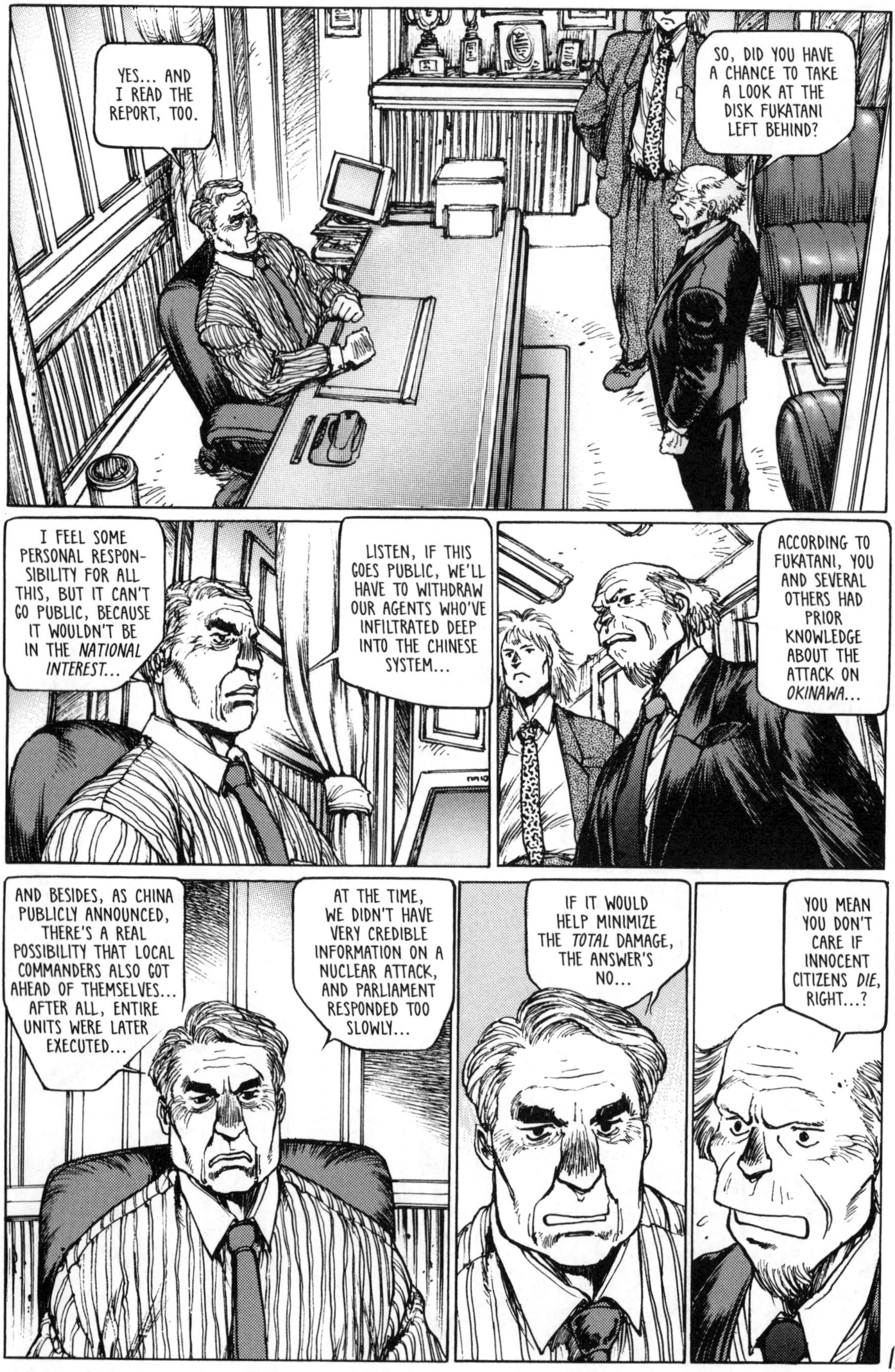
SO, DID YOU HAVE A CHANCE TO TAKE A LOOK AT THE DISK FUKATANI LEFT BEHIND?
YES... AND I READ THE REPORT, TOO.
ACCORDING TO FUKATANI, YOU AND SEVERAL OTHERS HAD PRIOR KNOWLEDGE ABOUT THE ATTACK ON *OKINAWA*...
LISTEN, IF THIS GOES PUBLIC, WE'LL HAVE TO WITHDRAW OUR AGENTS WHO'VE INFILTRATED DEEP INTO THE CHINESE SYSTEM...
I FEEL SOME PERSONAL RESPONSIBILITY FOR ALL THIS, BUT IT CAN'T GO PUBLIC, BECAUSE IT WOULDN'T BE IN THE *NATIONAL INTEREST*...
YOU MEAN YOU DON'T CARE IF INNOCENT CITIZENS *DIE*, RIGHT...?
IF IT WOULD HELP MINIMIZE THE *TOTAL* DAMAGE, THE ANSWER'S NO...
AT THE TIME, WE DIDN'T HAVE VERY CREDIBLE INFORMATION ON A NUCLEAR ATTACK, AND PARLIAMENT RESPONDED TOO SLOWLY...
AND BESIDES, AS CHINA PUBLICLY ANNOUNCED, THERE'S A REAL POSSIBILITY THAT LOCAL COMMANDERS ALSO GOT AHEAD OF THEMSELVES... AFTER ALL, ENTIRE UNITS WERE LATER EXECUTED...

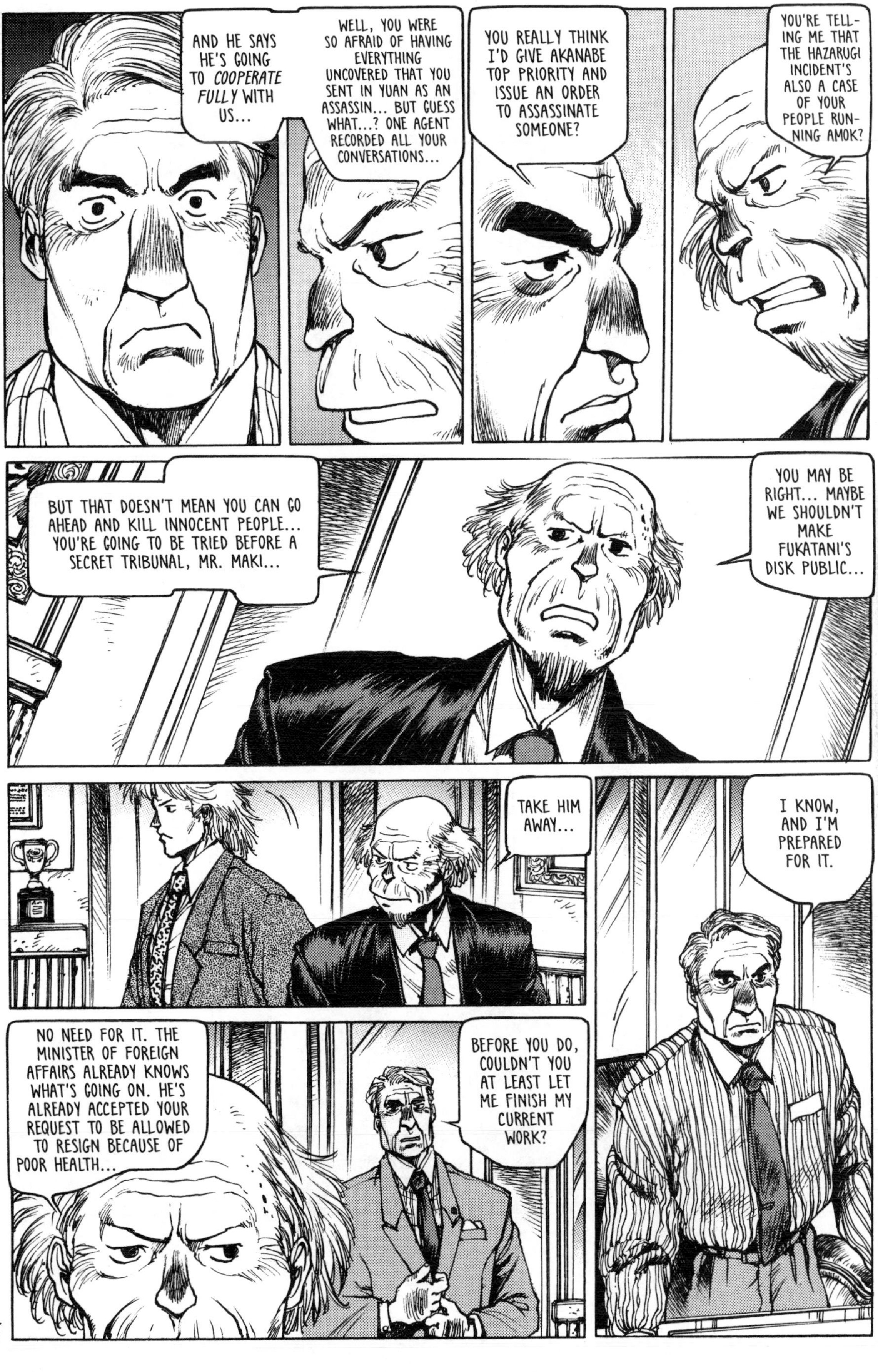
YOU'RE TELLING ME THAT THE HAZARUGI INCIDENT'S ALSO A CASE OF YOUR PEOPLE RUNNING AMOK?
YOU REALLY THINK I'D GIVE AKANABE TOP PRIORITY AND ISSUE AN ORDER TO ASSASSINATE SOMEONE?
WELL, YOU WERE SO AFRAID OF HAVING EVERYTHING UNCOVERED THAT YOU SENT IN YUAN AS AN ASSASSIN... BUT GUESS WHAT...? ONE AGENT RECORDED ALL YOUR CONVERSATIONS...
AND HE SAYS HE'S GOING TO *COOPERATE FULLY* WITH US...
YOU MAY BE RIGHT... MAYBE WE SHOULDN'T MAKE FUKATANI'S DISK PUBLIC...
BUT THAT DOESN'T MEAN YOU CAN GO AHEAD AND KILL INNOCENT PEOPLE... YOU'RE GOING TO BE TRIED BEFORE A SECRET TRIBUNAL, MR. MAKI...
I KNOW, AND I'M PREPARED FOR IT.
TAKE HIM AWAY...
BEFORE YOU DO, COULDN'T YOU AT LEAST LET ME FINISH MY CURRENT WORK?
NO NEED FOR IT. THE MINISTER OF FOREIGN AFFAIRS ALREADY KNOWS WHAT'S GOING ON. HE'S ALREADY ACCEPTED YOUR REQUEST TO BE ALLOWED TO RESIGN BECAUSE OF POOR HEALTH...

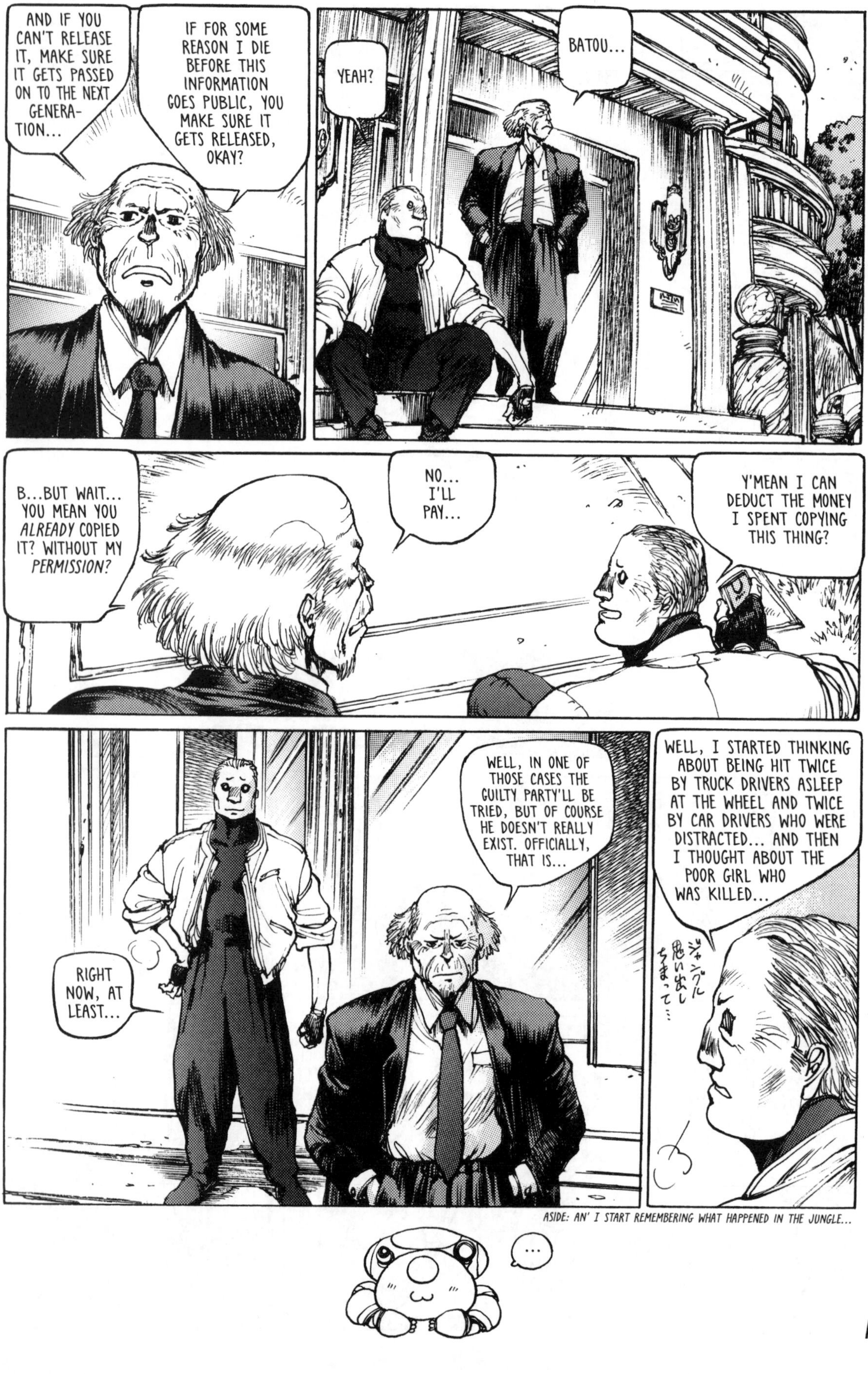
BATOU...
YEAH?
IF FOR SOME REASON I DIE BEFORE THIS INFORMATION GOES PUBLIC, YOU MAKE SURE IT GETS RELEASED, OKAY?
AND IF YOU CAN'T RELEASE IT, MAKE SURE IT GETS PASSED ON TO THE NEXT GENERA-TION...
Y'MEAN I CAN DEDUCT THE MONEY I SPENT COPYING THIS THING?
NO... I'LL PAY...
B...BUT WAIT... YOU MEAN YOU *ALREADY* COPIED IT? WITHOUT MY *PERMISSION?*
WELL, I STARTED THINKING ABOUT BEING HIT TWICE BY TRUCK DRIVERS ASLEEP AT THE WHEEL AND TWICE BY CAR DRIVERS WHO WERE DISTRACTED... AND THEN I THOUGHT ABOUT THE POOR GIRL WHO WAS KILLED...
ジャングル思い出しちまって…
WELL, IN ONE OF THOSE CASES THE GUILTY PARTY'LL BE TRIED, BUT OF COURSE HE DOESN'T REALLY EXIST. OFFICIALLY, THAT IS...
RIGHT NOW, AT LEAST...
ASIDE: AN' I START REMEMBERING WHAT HAPPENED IN THE JUNGLE...
...

THE END

Story Commentary on
GHOST IN THE SHELL 1.5: HUMAN-ERROR PROCESSOR
by Shirow Masamune

Introduction

In the original *Ghost in the Shell*, I had very few opportunities to depict the members of Section 9 going about their daily duties, but in fact I had plot outlines for about 20 different stories. Some of them eventually got drawn and published, but with *Ghost in the Shell 2*, the story shifted to Motoko, effectively shelving the rest of Section 9. I figured that there would eventually be a chance to show that off, or else they would be resigned to the scrap-heap of history—so I feel great gratitude to everyone involved with putting this book out and making it possible to print these leftover stories here. As manga, these stories are kind of all over the place, but I enjoy the atmosphere I created within them.

FAT CAT
Do the decadently wealthy have trouble finding things to spend money on?

Originally published in: *Young Magazine Kaizokuban* October 1991 (Part 1), *Young Magazine Kaizokuban* November 1991 (Part 2)

The title, of course, refers not to a literal overweight feline, but a stereotypical decadent and privileged elite, buying political favors with dirty cash. This actually ties in to *Ghost in the Shell 2*, as a part of the information war of Motoko vs. Motoko. Therefore, it looks a bit flat if taken on its own. It would be a relief if you picked up on that in the scene where the girl rushes out into the road, for example.

Making money is difficult, and spending it properly is even harder. There is lots of information in the world that would be "bad if it were revealed," "preferable if it were not revealed," or "ought not to be revealed." It's hard to define what belongs in those categories, but at any rate, I cannot sign on to the idea that all information should be made public.

Dear readers, please treat risk management seriously with your network machines.

DRIVE SLAVE

No longer a green rookie, Togusa reunites with our leading lady!

Originally published in: *Young Magazine* #26, 1992 (Part 1), *Young Magazine* #27, 1992 (Part 2)

Togusa's built up his own secret armory, and he stars in a fun little opening with Motoko's remote robot. I'm not happy about her expository lines, but what are ya gonna do? I could have depicted Batou being slightly detached from Motoko (if not to the point of being sulky), but that seemed like it might drag on or require further elaboration, so instead I chose to make him exaggeratedly excited, perhaps intentionally so.

Given the setting of the story, there's no reason I had to use a storyline involving manipulating corpses, but I depicted it that way for easier understanding. When they talk about "the dead overflowing the Earth" in Revelations, the natural meaning is that this is from war and starvation. But you could also interpret the "dead" to mean those who have lost their human senses, rationality, or critical thought. All around us, those inhuman beings blinded by greed, superstition, or their own gain are growing.

By the way, in 2003, as of this writing, personal devices using satellite communication are already smaller and lighter than what is depicted in the manga.

MINES OF MIND

Viruses are not the only enemy of an information-based society...

Originally published in: *Young Magazine #49*, 1995 (Part 1), *Young Magazine #50*, 1995 (Part 2)

The story begins with the conversation: "Why can't we meet off-line?" "Why do you want to meet off-line?"

It's a story about a virus that continuously plagues the net, wreaking havoc here and there, but viruses aren't the only things that cause trouble. Old info, bad info, faked info, malicious agitprop and unintentional agitprop (would this be even worse?): all these things are a potential headache.

In a way, these can be even more dangerous than viruses, because they're harder to detect. Let's all be careful out there, people. Always compare against the reality you see with your own eyes.

LOST PAST
What do you need in order to make the wolf work for you...?

Originally published in: *Young Magazine* #33, 1996

The opening contains a wild array of future infrastructure details. There's the scene of an execution via shooting the top of the spinal cord, which would normally be done by firing down at the heart from the hollow above the collarbone—it's the e-brain transformers that prevent that. Then there's the truck driver asleep at the wheel, in a field that seems ripe for automation in the future (Either his e-brain was taken over, or he never got one and just plain fell asleep).

You can't leak information that doesn't exist. And the more you try to hide something, the more likely it will get out. Remember, the "Boy Who Cried Wolf" is necessary for the wolf to function effectively. Let's think very carefully about why the boy's village was still attacked by the wolf, even after he caused a fuss about it. How do we avoid that happening to us?

This is totally unnecessary to add now, but I'll mention that Saito is a precision cyborg enhanced for sniping capability. Therefore, he avoids gunfire and fights that might place extra stress on his body. I could have drawn him long-distance sniping rather than engaging in an ordinary shootout, but the page limitations and scene flow demanded that I scrap that idea.

So both Saito and Yuan come off as second-rate snipers here. There's something about that outcome that just doesn't sit well with me.

Shirow Masamune - July 23rd, 2003

SFX INDEX

10.2	FX:	CHK CHK CHK (chika chika chika: turn signal)
.7	FX:	TMP (ka: stepping down)
.8	FX:	SLAM (bamu!!: slamming door)
12.3	FX:	BEEP BEEP BEEP (pipipi: typing)
13.5	FX:	GACHUNK (gashan: unpacking scooter)
.8	FX:	BZZZZZT (biiii: high-pitched engine)
15.3	FX:	BEEP BEEP BEEP (pi pi pi: phone buttons)
17.1	FX:	BEEP BEEP BEEP (pipipipi: beeping)
18.1	FX:	BOUNCE BOUNCE (waku waku: excitement)
.6	FX:	SCREECH (kiki: tires squealing)
19.7	FX:	VROOOM (vuou: engine roar)
20.1	FX:	KABOOOM (doga: explosion)
.2	FX:	BAVOMP (guwa: blast)
	FX:	BOM BOM (dodododon: series of blasts)
21.3	FX:	SCREECH (kikikyukyu: squealing tires)
.4	FX:	BLAM BLAM BLAM BLAM (vuvuvuvu: gunshots)
.5	FX:	SCREEECH (gyakyagigigi: vehicle scraping)
.6	FX:	SCREECH (kyukyukyukyuo: tires squealing)
	FX:	VROOM (vuo: engine roar)
.8	FX:	BAVOMP (bubo: explosion)
22.1	FX:	TROMP TROMP TROMP (dodododo: running)
.2	FX:	FLICK (poi: tossing)
.5	FX:	SHWIP (za: leap)
.7	FX:	KVAM! (doga: explosion)
23.2	FX:	VWA (wa: leaping around corner)
	FX:	VROOOM (bauuu: bike engine)
.4	FX:	KATHUD (ga: hard crash)
.5	FX:	SCRUNCH (dosha: vehicle crashing)
	FX:	THUNK (go: head impact)
.7	FX:	SCRUNCH (gishi: cracking)
26.2	Aside:	Heh heh...
.5	Aside:	Heh heh.
	FX:	GRRRR (gururuuru: growling)
	FX:	ARF! ARF! (bau bau: barking)
.7	FX:	KABABOOOM (dokkan: explosion)
	FX:	RUMBLE RUMBLE (bara bara: stuff flying apart)
29.2	FX:	WHEEEE (hiiin: whine)
30.3	FX:	FFFFT (suuu: silence)
.5	FX:	SNIP (butsu: cutting)
.6	Box:	Cheap Nails / 200 per case
.8	Box:	Cheap Nails
.10	Aside:	Agh, my neck hurts...
	Aside:	Phew.
31.1	FX:	BEEP BEEP BEEP (pipipi: buttons)
32.6	FX:	Heh heh heh heh heh.
.7	FX:	BEEP (pi!: hanging up phone)
33.1	FX:	SCREECH (kyuki: tire squeal)
37.3	FX:	TAP TAP (ton ton: straightening papers)
38.5	FX:	CH CHAK (kakin gashu: lock opening)
.6	FX:	THUNK (dosa: dropping bag)
39.7	FX:	BZZZZZ (zaaaaa: static)
40.2	FX:	KASHAK (gatan: sudden stand)
.4	FX:	WHOMP (boku: punch)
.5	FX:	GONK (gon: smashing console)
41.1	FX:	SKREEEE (kikikiki: tires squealing)
	FX:	HONNK (papapa: honking)
.6	FX:	SLAM (ban!!: door bursting)
42.1	FX:	PSSSST (shuuuu: hissing)
	FX:	CHK CHK (bachi bashi: popping)
.2	FX:	CHK CHK (bachi bachi: popping)
.3	FX:	CHK CHK (bachi bachi: popping)
46.5	FX:	ROAAR (oooo: engine roar)
47.1	FX:	PUTTER PUTT PUTT (vuu vuu dododo: engine rumble)
.3	FX:	FOMP (bamu: door slam)
.4	FX:	SHWIP (jiii: scanner)
.5	FX:	KAFOMP (bakun: trunk opening)
48.1	FX:	KABOOOM (baga: explosion)
.3	FX:	BZZ BZZ BZZ (bubuvuvuvu: buzzing)
	FX:	GNN (gan: rocks falling)
	FX:	KATHUD (dosa: large debris)
.5	FX:	BZZZ BZZZ (buuuun: wings buzzing)
51.4	FX:	CHAK (cha: door opening)
.6	FX:	WHUMP (bamu: door closing)
.8	FX:	VROM SCRUNCH VROM (pari paki jari jari: tires crackling over debris)
53.1	FX:	KACHANG (gacha: door clicking)
	FX:	BZZT (bun: low hum)
55.1	FX:	SHWOOOSH (shukon: tube ejection)
	FX:	BUZZZ (vuuuu: buzzing)
.3	FX:	CHK CHK CHK CHK (chichichichi: chittering)
.5	FX:	BUZZ BUZZ BUZZZ BUZZ (vuvuvuvuvuvu: buzzing)
56.2	FX:	RUSTLE RUSTLE RUSTLE (gasa basa basa: shuffling)
.3	FX:	PHHHP (basa: yanking bag off)
57.3	Aside:	Heh heh...
.5	Aside:	Ah...
.6	FX:	RATTLE RATTLE CLATTER (gara gara gara: wheels rolling)
.8	FX:	BZZZZ (buun: low hum)
60.1	FX:	TAP TAP TAP (ko ko ko: tapping)
.4	FX:	KAFUMP KAFUMP KAFUMP KAFUMP (dosu dosu dosu: heavy gunfire)
	FX:	SPAT SHOONK (mekyu byu: guts flying)
.5	FX:	KASHONK (gakyun: bullet hitting metal)
.6	FX:	DRIP DROP DRIP DRIP (bota bota bota kyun: dripping)
61.1	FX:	SPAK SPAK SPAK SPAK SPAK (bosu bosu bosu: heavy gunfire)
	FX:	FAK FAK FAK FAK (kakyun kyun baki gakyun hyun: tearing metal)
.3	FX:	VROOM (vuo: engine)
	FX:	VROOM (vuoo: engine)
.4	FX:	SMAK (baki: crunching)
62.1	FX:	BZZZZ (chichichi: skittering)
.2	FX:	BZZZZ BZZZ BZZZ (vuvuvuvuvuvu: buzzing)
.3	FX:	FOMP (bofu: falling back in seat)
.5	FX:	BZZZ BZZZ (buuuun: buzzing)
.6	FX:	KICK (ka: taking step)
63.4	FX:	ZZZIP (hyuu: leaping over)
.5	FX:	THUD (zusha: landing)
.6	FX:	SHAK (sha: undoing hook)
64.6	FX:	THUD (goto: heavy object)
65.4	FX:	BEEP BEEP BEEP BEEP (pi pi pi pi: beeping)
66.1	FX:	BEEP (pi: beeping)
.2	FX:	SHOOMP (zuvuuumu: zooming in)
.3	FX:	SHUNK (kyuuuun: zooming in)
.6	FX:	BEEP BEEP BEEP BEEP (pi pi pi pi: beeping)
67.3	Aside:	Hmph...
68.2	Aside:	Grr...
69.2	FX:	BZZ BZZZ BZZ (buuun: buzzing)
.4	Aside:	Heh Heh...
	Aside:	Yup yup.
.5	FX:	VROOOM (bashuuuu: hydraulic release)
	FX:	RUMBLE RUMBLE RUMBLE RUMBLE (dodododododo: motor running)
	FX:	FSSSHHH (fushu: hydraulic)
	FX:	SQUEE (kiii: brakes)
.6	FX:	VOOSH (zusha: hatch opening)
70.2	FX:	SKREE (gagaga: shoving car)
	FX:	VROOOOM (bouuu: motor)
	FX:	BEEP BEEP BEEP (pi pi pi: backing up alarm)
.4	FX:	KARUMBBLE VOOM VOM VOM (dogagaga: roaring up steps)
.5	FX:	KERAAAASH (gaaaaa: crashing through glass)
	FX:	KAVONK (dogaga: slamming desk)
71.1	FX:	KTUNK (gakon: clunking)
.2	FX:	TUN TUN TUN TUN (do do do: running off)
	FX:	CHAK (jakin: loading gun)
.3	FX:	KAVVVOOOOM (dogagagaga: roaring truck)
	FX:	KRAK SMASH CRACK (baki baki gon: rubble smashing)
	Truck:	Dai Nippon Industries Intron Depot I is delayed to July... Sorry about all the delays, but the colors will be phenomenal! When you see them, sob sob...
.4	FX:	KATHUNK CLATTER (gago godon: cylinders falling)
.5	FX:	RUMBLE CRASH (zugogogogon: distant sounds)
72.3	FX:	KABOOOM (dogagaga: explosions)
.5	FX:	ROAAR (gooooo: rumbling)
.6	FX:	RUMBLE RUMBLE RUMBLE RUMBLE (zugogogogogogo: rumbling)
73.3	FX:	KAVOOOMP (zuvan: collapse)
	FX:	KERASH (gagaga: debris clattering)

	FX:	KRACK (zusha: debris falling)
74.1	FX:	VOMP (vuuuu: automatic fire)
	FX:	GAGAGA GAGGAGA (gagaga: bullets hitting)
.3	FX:	BUDADADADAH (dotatatata: automatic fire)
.4	FX:	SPAK SPAK SPAK BLAM (bashi bashi bashi gakin: heavy shots)
	FX:	ZING ZING ZING (kyun kyun kin: bullet deflections)
	FX:	CLATTER CLATTER (bara bara bara: cartridges flying)
	FX:	BUDDA BUDDA (dotatatata: automatic fire)
.5	FX:	BUDADADADAH (dotatatata: automatic fire)
	FX:	KASHAK (basha: reloading)
75.1	FX:	KRAK (gakyukyun: bullet deflection)
	FX:	KAVOMP (gashi: falling to ground)
.9	FX:	FOMP SPAK SPAK SPAK BLAM (baki byu doshi dokin: gunfire)
76.1	FX:	FSSSSHHH (bushuuuu: sprinkler)
.2	FX:	CREAK CRAK CRAK CLANK (bachi bachi zusha: camo system crackling)
	FX:	SHWWWIPP (gaaaa: door closing)
.3	FX:	KERTHUNK (doka: smashing)
	FX:	THUD THUD (goto gon: rubble falling)
.4	Aside:	Heh heh...
78.1	FX:	BZZZ (vuuuun: low hum)
.2	FX:	BZZZT BZZZT (buuu buuu: low hum)
.6	FX:	FAWOOSH (shukon: shooting grenades)
79.1	FX:	KAVOOOMP (kyubovuwa: explosion)
.2	FX:	KATHUD CRASH (dodogo dodon: crumbling through floor)
.3	FX:	CRUNCH CRACK THUD (zugogogoon: falling through)
	FX:	RUMBLE RUMBLE RUMBLE RUMBLE (dodododo: rumbling)
.4	FX:	FWOOSH (ba: leaping)
80.1	FX:	SHAK (dan: landing)
.2	FX:	RIIP RIPPP RIPP (bikibikibiki buki: arms ripping)
	FX:	CREAK CREAK CREAK (gigigigi: metal creaking)
.3	FX:	FWAK (go: arm blow)
.4	FX:	KERTHUD (dosha: body landing)
.5	FX:	BZZZ BUZZ BUZZ (vuvuvuvun: buzzing)
.6	FX:	BZZZ BZZZ BZZZ (vuuun buuuun: buzzing)
	FX:	CLANK CREAK (zushi zushi: heavy steps)
81.3	FX:	FSSSST (pushu shuuuu: acid dissolving)
.4	FX:	SSSST (uuuu: acid dissolving)
.5	FX:	CLANK CLUNK CLANK CLUNK (goton goton goton goton: heavy steps)
82.1	FX:	SHWIPPP (shururudo: whipping line)
.3	FX:	SHWP (kyu: piercing skin)
.5	FX:	ROAAAAAAR (gooooooo: rushing blood)
	FX:	THMP THMP (dodon dodon: heartbeat)
.6	FX:	THUNK (goto: body thudding)
.7	FX:	ROAAAAR (gooooo: rushing blood)
	FX:	THMP THMP (dodonnn: heartbeat)
83.2	FX:	RUMBLE RUMBLE ROAR (gogogogogo: rumbling)
.3	FX:	WHEEP WHEEP WHEEP (uuuuu: sirens)
.4	FX:	RUMBLE RUMBLE RUMBLE (dodododo: rumbling)
	FX:	WHEEEEP (uuuuu: sirens)
.5	FX:	WHEEEP (uuuu: sirens)
84.1	FX:	VRRP (buru: shiver)
.4	FX:	KACHUNK (bakun: hatch opening)
.5	FX:	RRRR (kyuuu: winding down)
	FX:	CHK CHK CHK CHK (chiri chiri chiri: rattling)
85.2	FX:	WHSHH (vuouuu: car engine)
.3	FX:	KURNK (bekon: giving way)
.5	FX:	FWOMP (ban: cracking open)
86.1	FX:	WHEEEEEP (uuuuu: sirens)
	FX:	RUMBLE RUMBLE ROAR: gogogogo: rumbling)
.3	FX:	VROOOM (vuou: engine roar)
	FX:	SCREECH (kyu: tires)
.4	FX:	RUMBLE RUMBLE RUMBLE RUMBLE (doko-doko-doko: engine rattle)
87.1	FX:	RUMBLE RUMBLE RUMBLE (do do do do: engine idling)
.3	FX:	VRMM VRMM (vun vuou: engine roar)
.5	FX:	VRMM (vun: engine kick)
	FX:	DRRMM (dododo: engine running)
.6	FX:	ROAAAR (oooon: car engine)
88.1	FX:	VROOM VROOM (vuouou: engine rumble)
	FX:	KYU (screech: brakes)
.3	FX:	SLAM (bamu: door slamming)
100.2	FX:	SHAK SHAK SHAK SHAK (dosu dosu dosu dosu: gunshots)
.4	FX:	SMASH (gasha: smashing glass)
.5	FX:	BLAM BLAM (don don: gunshots)
	FX:	SPAK (gasu: bullet strike)
101.1	FX:	CRUNCH (kyu: scraping ground)
.3	FX:	BZZZZZT (vuvuvuvu: buzzing)
.4	FX:	SHWP (gaba: rolling)
.5	FX:	ZUMM (hyuu: swishing)
	FX:	KRAUNCH (dobaki: breaking hull)
102.1	FX:	CRASH (dodovaa: clattering)
.2	FX:	SHWIP (kyu: boot scrape)
.6	FX:	KRUNCH (doka: slam)
.7	FX:	KAROOM (dododon: crashing)
103.1	FX:	SMASH KRAK (pari bashi baki: glass shattering)
.4	FX:	GRSHK (goshu: crunching)
.5	FX:	THUD (bote: flop)
.6	FX:	FSSST (hishu: projectile)
104.1	FX:	BLAM BLAM BLAM (don don don: gunshots)
.2	FX:	FWP FWP (kyun kyun: whipping)
	FX:	KRAK KRAK KRAK (para para: objects falling)
.6	FX:	KABOOOOM (zuzuzuzuzun: explosion)
	FX:	DOOM (don: blast)
105.3	FX:	ZOOOM (biiii: engine)
.4	FX:	CHK CLATTER FMP (goton paki para para: debris falling)
.6	FX:	CHK CRACKLE POP (paki jari mishi: debris falling)
107.1	Aside:	Hmph...
.2	FX:	VROOM (vyuuu: engine)
108.7	FX:	THUD (to: landing)
.8	FX:	FWISH (hyu: spinning)
109.1	FX:	SWOOSH (ba: quick action)
	FX:	FWOMP (gon: kicking can)
.4	FX:	CHAK (kakin: gun)
.7	FX:	SHWIP (shu: returning to normal posture)
117.3	FX:	WSHHH (hyuuu: wind blowing)
	FX:	WEEOOO (pipo pipo: car siren)
	FX:	VRMM (vuou: engine roar)
	FX:	HONK (papapa: car horn)
	FX:	VRMMM (vuouuu: engine roar)
118.1	FX:	WSHHH (hyuu: air rushing)
.7	FX:	BRAT BRAT (papa papa: honking)
	FX:	PUTTER PUTTER (kacha kacha: rattling bike)
	FX:	VROM VROOOM (vyuuu: engine)
120.3	Aside;	Eep!
122.2	Aside:	Hmph...
123.1	FX:	ACK ACK (hogee hogee: gagging)
	FX:	RUSTLE RUSTLE (kara kara: rattling)
	FX:	CHK CHK CHK (chiri chiri chiri: engine rattling)
	FX:	RUMBLE RUMBLE (dodododo: rumbling)
124.2	FX:	FUMP (ban: leaping)
.5	FX:	BAM BAM BAM (gan gan gan: slamming door)
.6	Aside:	Hic.
125.4	Aside:	Ha ha ha.
.6	FX:	KAWUMP (bahyo: ignition)
126.1	FX:	FWOMP (domu: stomp)
.2	FX:	FOOMP (goban: crunch)
130.1	FX:	CRASH (gashaan: glass smashing)
.2	FX:	KAWOMP (bon: explosion)
.3	FX:	RRMMBB (dododo: rumbling)
131.1	FX:	RMMMBBB (dodododo: rumbling)
.2	FX:	FRMP (dodo: swinging)
.3	FX:	THUMP (goton: landing)
	FX:	CHAK (paki: crackling glass)
	FX:	FWMMM (bobobo: flames)
.4	FX:	CHK CHK FLUTTER FLICK (pari pari pari: crackling)
.6	FX:	CHK CHK (pari pari: crackling)
132.1	FX:	VOMP (don: wham)
.2	FX:	KERTHUD (goto: flopping to the ground)
.3	FX:	FWP (hyuu: breeze)
	FX:	CHK CHK CHK (kachi kachi kachi: clicking)
133.3	Aside:	Yup yup.
134.1	FX:	WOPPA WOPPA WOPPA (bara bara bara: helicopter blades)
135.4	FX:	SPLOOSH (gobo: spitting liquid)
138.3	FX:	KRAK (gaku: heel breaking)
139.1	FX:	PANT PANT (ha ha: heavy breathing)
.3	FX:	UNGH (fuu: exhaling)
.4	FX:	CHAK (cha: car door)
.5	FX:	KATHUD (dosa: heavy thud)
.6	FX:	FNNK FNNK (bosu bosu: silenced bullets)
143.6	FX:	DADADADA (ngagagagaa: heavy machinery)
144.2	Aside:	Hmph.
.6	Aside:	Well...
152.2	FX:	SLAM (bamu: door shutting)

154.5	FX:	KTUNK (gatan: scraping chair)
157.2	Aside:	Tee hee hee…
158.5	Aside:	Hmph…
167.2	FX:	SLURP (sususu: drinking liquid)
170.5	FX:	FSST FSSST (shushushushu: sprinklers)
171.3	FX:	KRAK (bahyuu: bullets flying)
.5	FX:	VOOSH (zazaza: rustling)
.6	FX:	SHK (gasa: bushes rustling)

Afterword

As I flip through some of the reference materials here, I'm reminded of just how blessed I am that this story has attracted the assistance of top-notch talent in so many areas: animation, video games, printing, and so on. All of the media projects, from music to video, have been outstanding. This is, of course, thanks to these collaborators' hard effort. For my part, all I'm doing is thanking them and my lucky stars.

With the publication of this book (coming after *Man-Machine Interface*) the manga of *Ghost in the Shell* is hereby concluded. Thank you for reading. You will find that there is no moving, climactic final scene (laughs). This story is structured like a TV show in that it can continue indefinitely as long as there's interest in making it, but I'm calling it quits here. The only *Ghost in the Shell*-related book you might see from me is an art book, if such a project comes about. Hopefully we'll meet again, probably through a different story. Bye for now.

The Ghost in the Shell, Vol. 1.5 Human-Error Processor copyright © 2008 Shirow Masamune
English translation copyright © Kodansha, Ltd.
All rights reserved.

Published in the United States by Kodansha Comics, an imprint of Kodansha USA Publishing, LLC, New York.

Publication rights for this English edition arranged through Kodansha Ltd, Tokyo.

First published in Japan in 2008 by Kodansha Ltd., Tokyo as *Koukaku Kidoutai*, volume 1.5.

ISBN 978-1-63236-422-7
Printed in the United States of America.
www.kodanshacomics.com
9 8 7 6 5 4 3 2 1
Translation and English-language Adaptation: Frederik L. Schodt and Toren Smith
Additional Translation: Stephen Paul
Lettering: Scott O. Brown
Editing: Lauren Scanlan
Editor of the first English version: Chris Warner
Kodansha Comics edition cover design by Phil Balsman